LEARNING FROM SOMALIA

Learning from Somalia

The Lessons of
Armed Humanitarian Intervention

edited by
Walter Clarke and Jeffrey Herbst

WestviewPress
A Division of HarperCollinsPublishers

Written under the auspices of
the Center of International Studies,
Princeton University

Copyright © 1997 by Westview Press, A Division of HarperCollins Publishers, Inc.

Published in 1997 in the United States of America by Westview Press, 5500 Central Avenue, Boulder, Colorado 80301-2877, and in the United Kingdom by Westview Press, 12 Hid's Copse Road, Cumnor Hill, Oxford OX2 9JJ

Library of Congress Cataloging-in-Publication Data
Learning from Somalia : the lessons of armed humanitarian intervention
  / edited by Walter Clarke and Jeffrey Herbst.
    p. cm.
  Includes index.
  ISBN 0-8133-2793-8 (hc).—ISBN 0-8133-2794-6 (pbk.)
  1. Operation Restore Hope, 1992–1993. 2. Somalia—Politics and
government—1960– 3. Peace. 4. Humanitarian assistance.
I. Clarke, Walter S. (Walter Sheldon), 1934– . II. Herbst,
Jeffrey Ira.
DT407.L43 1997
967.7305'3—dc21   96-48453
                                                           CIP

The paper used in this publication meets the requirements of the American National Standard for Permanence of Paper for Printed Library Materials Z39.48-1984

10   9   8   7   6   5   4   3   2   1

Contents

Preface

The U.S.-led intervention in Somalia that began with an airlift of food supplies in August 1992, soon followed by a substantial multinational military intervention in December 1992, was the most significant instance of "peacemaking" by the international community in the post–Cold War era prior to the deployment of the Implementation Force (IFOR) to Bosnia in early 1996. The heady promises of Operation Restore Hope and the subsequent bitter disappointments had a resounding and generally corrosive impact on the development of effective international policies and implementation plans for armed humanitarian intervention.

Although it may be an exaggeration to say that the fates of Kigali, Port au Prince, and Sarajevo were decided in the streets of Mogadishu, it is certainly the case that Somalia has had an unsettling effect on the policies of individual Western governments and the UN as they try to cope with the urgent, complex humanitarian emergencies around the world. However, it is doubtful whether the lessons so quickly promulgated from the Somalia experience were actually correct. Ironically, there were a variety of positive organizational innovations and operational lessons learned during the Somalia exercise that have not received nearly enough attention. Learning from Somalia is therefore critical if the world is to know how to better respond to the rising number of potential tragedies that now threaten humanity.

The chapters presented in this book represent a variety of perspectives and backgrounds, including those of humanitarian practitioners and academic experts on Somalia. The views expressed in this volume are the authors' and do not necessarily reflect those of the organizations or agencies with which they are affiliated. The authors do not agree on every issue. Indeed, we deliberately solicited different viewpoints so that the debate over what happened in Somalia could be as comprehensive as possible. Only through such debate will better policy emerge.

Funding for this project was provided by the Ford Foundation, the Center of International Studies, and the Woodrow Wilson School of Princeton University. At Ford, Dr. Mahnaz Ispahani and her colleagues were exceptionally helpful in guidance and suggestions to make the book as useful as possible. We are also especially grateful to Professor John Waterbury of Princeton for his support for this project from the start.

Ambassador Robert Gosende, who served as special envoy to Somalia in March through October 1993, provided the initial inspiration for this project and helped us at every stage of the process. It was largely due to Bob's efforts that so many critical figures in the Somalia operations were enthusiastic about participating.

We owe special gratitude to Barbara Ellington, our senior editor at Westview Press, for her encouragement and support. No such volume can see the light of day without the assistance of many bright minds, sharp eyes, and precise editorial hands, and we especially thank copy editor Diane Hess and her colleagues at Westview for their patience and support.

Finally, we would like to express our gratitude to the dozens of officials who came to Princeton—often for the first time since they left Somalia—to discuss an experience that was at times both professionally and personally dangerous. Here we must highlight the role of our Somali colleagues who made long and arduous trips to Princeton so that their unique perspective would be understood.

Walter Clarke and Jeffrey Herbst

Acronyms

AID	(U.S.) Agency for International Development
AOR	(UNOSOM II) Area of Responsibility
APC	armored personnel carrier
ASF	(U.S.) Auxiliary Security Force
CARE	(U.S.) Cooperative for Assistance and Relief Everywhere
CDU	Christian Democratic Union
CENTCOM	(U.S.) Central Command, located in Tampa, Florida
CID	Criminal Investigation Division (of the Somali National Police Force)
CINCCENT	(U.S.) Commander in Chief, Central Command
CIVPOL	(UNOSOM II) Civilian Police
CMIO	(UNOSOM II) chief military information officer
CMOC	(UNITAF) Civil Military Operations Center
CRS	Congressional Research Service
DART	(USAID) Disaster Assistance Response Team
DHA	(UN) Department of Humanitarian Affairs
DOD	(U.S.) Department of Defense
DPKO	(UN) Department of Peacekeeping Operations
EC	European Community
ECOMOG	ECOWAS Monitoring Group
ECOWAS	Economic Community of West African States
FAO	(UN) Food and Agricultural Organization
FAST	(U.S. Marine) Fleet Anti-Terrorism Support Team
FFP	Food for Peace
FM	(U.S.) Field Manual
FRUD	Front pour la Restoration de la Démocratie
G-12	Group of 12
HOC	(UN) Humanitarian Operations Center
H.R.	House Resolution
HRO	humanitarian relief organization
HRS	(UNITAF) Humanitarian Relief Sector
ICITAP	(U.S.) International Criminal Investigation and Training Assistance Program
ICRC	International Committee of the Red Cross

IFOR	(NATO) Implementation Force
IFRC	International Federation of the Red Cross
I MEF	First Marine Expeditionary Force, based at Camp Pendleton, California
IO	(U.S. Department of State) Bureau of International Organizations
IRC	International Rescue Committee
JCS	(U.S.) Joint Chiefs of Staff
JTF	(U.S.) Joint Task Force
LPI	(Sweden) Life and Peace Institute
MARFOR	(UNITAF) Marine Force
MEF	(U.S.) Marine Expeditionary Force
MP	military police
MSC	(UN) Military Staff Committee
MSF	Médicins Sans Frontières (Doctors Without Borders)
NCO	noncommissioned officer
NGO	nongovernmental organization
NSC	(U.S.) National Security Council
NSS	(Somalia) National Security Service
OAU	Organization of African Unity
OECD	Organization for Economic Cooperation and Development
OFDA	(U.S.) Office of Foreign Disaster Assistance
OSCE	Organization on Security and Cooperation in Europe
OSD	(U.S.) Office of the Secretary of Defense
PDD	(U.S.) presidential decision directive
PTT	Police Technical Team
PVO	(U.S.) private voluntary organization
QRF	(UNITAF–UNOSOM II) Quick Reaction Force
SDM	Somali Democratic Movement
SNA	(pre–civil war Somalia) Somali National Army; (Post-Barre) Somali National Alliance
SNF	Somali National Front
SOCOM	(U.S.) Special Operations Command, located in Tampa, Florida
SPD	Soziale Partei Demokratishe (Social Democratic Party)
SPM	Somali Patriotic Movement
SPMAGTF	Special Purpose Marine Air Ground Task Force
S.R.	Senate Resolution
SRSG	special representative of the secretary-general
SSDF	Somali Salvation Democratic Front
SSNM	Southern Somali National Movement
SYL	Somali Youth League
TNC	Transitional National Council

UNAMIR	UN Mission in Rwanda
UNCIVPOL	UN Civilian Police
UNDP	UN Development Program
UNDRO	UN Disaster Relief Office
UNHCHR	UN High Commissioner for Human Rights
UNHCR	UN High Commissioner for Refugees
UNICEF	UN International Children's Emergency Fund
UNITAF	Unified Task Force (12/9/92–5/4/93)
UNOMOZ	UN Operation in Mozambique
UNOSOM I	First UN Operation in Somalia (4/92–5/93)
UNOSOM II	Second UN Operation in Somalia (5/4/93–5/24/95)
UNPROFOR	UN Protection Force (former Yugoslavia)
UNSCR	UN Security Council Resolution
UNTAC	UN Transitional Assistance Commission
USAID	U.S. Agency for International Development
USC	United Somali Congress
USIS	U.S. Information Service
USLO	(UNITAF–UNOSOM II) U.S. Liaison Office
WFP	(UN) World Food Program

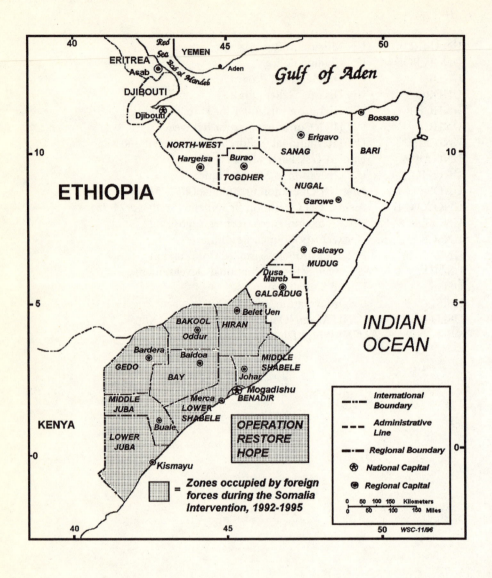

PART 1
Legal Aspects of Intervention

1

Failed Visions and Uncertain Mandates in Somalia

WALTER CLARKE

Conventional foreign policy wisdom tells us that the armed multinational humanitarian intervention in Somalia, which began in December 1992, was a humanitarian success in the short term but became a political and military failure after the operations were turned over to the United Nations in May 1993. Like Vietnam long before it, Somalia has become a "syndrome," held by many to have been a naive attempt to implement benevolent interventionism in a marginal Third World state and doomed to failure. The specter of Somalia has loomed above every world crisis since mid-1993, inhibiting debate and limiting options. In the misery of Bosnia prior to the late 1995 IFOR (Implementation Force [of NATO]) intervention, UN forces under fire or taken prisoner by Serbian forces were expected to turn the other cheek for fear of "crossing the Mogadishu line." This expression was reportedly coined by former UNPROFOR (UN Protection Force [in the former Yugoslavia]) commander Lt. Gen. Sir Michael Rose to describe the supposed need to maintain absolute neutrality in the face of all provocation for fear of becoming unwilling participants in a civil war.[1] With all due respect, General Rose was incorrect in his interpretation of events in Somalia, just as he may have underestimated UN tactical possibilities in Bosnia.

The Flawed Paradigm

Obstinate notions of external force neutrality, coupled with unquestioning respect for state sovereignty where clearly none exists, can effectively negate the potentially beneficial effects of multilateral armed humanitarian intervention. A passive or benign military force in a lawless environment inevitably affects the political dynamic of regions in which it is operating, and the force cannot avoid the political impact of its own presence. A military force committed to the maintenance of abstract political passivity quickly becomes an easy mark for unprincipled local gang leaders and warlords. Inability or unwillingness to discern the essential political dynamics of the country and to effect remedial measures to foster civil society—out of expedience, disinterest, or naive "neutrality"—lie at the root of the world's failure in Somalia.

With the potential for more state breakdowns caused by ethnic and regional stresses, it must be recognized that Cold War etiquette no longer provides the basis for relations with distressed states. Internationally mandated political action, backed by military force, may be the sole formula to halt or blunt chaos and the endless cycle of violence brought on by complex manmade disasters. Doctrine is not needed for a return to trusteeships or "recolonization"; political-military interventions should normally end when political processes are satisfactorily on the mend.

The first step in planning for a humanitarian peace enforcement-operation must be the articulation of an integrated humanitarian-political-military strategy that responds to the immediate humanitarian crisis while outlining a longer-term process designed to resolve the underlying political issues that may have brought on the crisis in the first place. These actions must be consistent with international values and standards of conduct. In failed-state situations, or when the functions of a state are sharply curtailed or neutralized, with accompanying wide-scale human suffering, the world must be prepared to offer political and military assistance in an imaginative, constructive, and decisive manner. Political solutions are complicated, elusive, and usually long term; international intervention ultimately is sustainable only when there is an agreed political end result of the intervention.

The initial intervening force in Somalia avoided the establishment of a political agenda for its actions. It had no definition of what it hoped Somalia would look like at the end of the intervention. Rather than facilitating the work of the follow-on UN political and military force, the initial intervention force maintained, at least at command levels, an adversarial attitude toward the UN force that would relieve the U.S.-led Unified Task Force (UNITAF). Lacking political purpose, UNITAF focused its tactics on force protection rather than the achievement of strategic goals. Much loss of time, money, and domestic U.S. commitment to multilateral action resulted. The collapse of the subsequent UN political and military efforts was probably rendered inevitable by the narrow construction of the UNITAF mandate.

The Dynamics of the Failed State

Although usually considered a nation with a common language and religion and common social traditions, Somalia has a political history determined by its highly segmented clan structures. Composed of six main clan families, Somalia's social structure is subdivided into dozens of subclan groups and hundreds of smaller units. There are many mixed cultural zones within regions, especially in larger cities, and most geographical localities have specific clan identifications; the mixed areas tend to be the most heavily contested zones.[2] With the disappearance of the state after Siad Barre's retreat from Mogadishu in January 1991, power and leadership naturally drifted to local communities and subclan-level leadership. The two Somali militia leaders best known to the world in 1992 represent specific ethnogeographical interest areas: Mohamed Farah Aideed's irregular forces were primarily composed of Hawiye Habr Gedr nomadic groups from the Mudug region north and west of Mogadishu; Ali Mahdi Mohamed, not a military leader, was spokesman for the tradespeople and native Hawiye Abgal, who were the majority population in the pre–civil war Mogadishu (Benadir) region.[3]

The internal population movements, sparked first by the war against Siad Barre and accelerated by the civil war and power struggles that followed, created multiple humanitarian disasters: (1) displaced city dwellers and native rural agriculturalists congregated in the Mogadishu-Baidoa-Bardera "triangle of death"; (2) these unfortunates consequently became hostage to militia leaders who established and maintained control of ports and highways by Habr Gedr militiamen and local surrogates; and (3) refugees and internally displaced persons were blocked by the warlords from returning to their places of residence, which were controlled by victorious nonlocal clan groups. At the time of the initial UNITAF deployment in December 1992, warlords had extended their personal and clan influence into many areas occupied by smaller, weaker, and marginal clan groups. This contentious zone coincided almost precisely with the operational areas of the intervening UNITAF forces, thus setting the stage for confrontations between the warlords and the occupying forces. Reluctant to take on UNITAF, Aideed assembled a force to attack the second United Nations Operation in Somalia (UNOSOM II) just one month after UNITAF's departure.

What the world generally judged was a clash of personalities and ambitions between Hawiye/Abgal leader Ali Mahdi Mohamed and Hawiye Habr Gedr champion Mohamed Farah Aideed was far more complex. Aideed believed that the collapse of the Somali state provided him and his numerous subclan members with the license to extend their influence from their barren, arid central region into Mogadishu and the rich Shabelle and Jubba valleys. Aideed's lust for personal power was not tempered by any squeamishness about human rights or the effects of his operations on the innocent. The group that gathered around Ali Mahdi shared his fear and antipathy toward his country cousins, especially his distrust of the Habr Gedr leader. The Mahdi political faction also tended to attract groups fearing the extension of Habr Gedr hegemony over their houses and property in the hinterlands.

Aideed's force included more aggressive, better-armed but essentially undisciplined militia.[4] His force played a significant but not solo role in the final months of the successful struggle against Siad Barre. Aideed opposed UN intervention because he feared that it would ratify Ali Mahdi's questionable election as president in a UN-supported conference in Djibouti in mid-1991. The fighting between these two groups between November 1991 and March 1992 caused 30,000–50,000 noncombatant deaths and nearly completed the destruction of the city.

Contrary to conventional belief in late 1992, Aideed's Habr Gedr political base was far from secure. In haste to convert his military force into a political party, Aideed established the Somali National Alliance (SNA) only in October 1992. The post–UNOSOM II split between Aideed and his erstwhile deputy and financier, Osman Hassan Ali 'Ato, demonstrates the intrinsic cleavage between expansionist and pragmatic elements within the Habr Gedr.[5] At the time of the initial UNITAF deployment, these internal stresses may have been less clear than they are today, but without political guidelines and objectives, neither UNITAF nor UNOSOM had the option to exploit these vulnerabilities in the interest of the broader Somali community.

The Failure of Diplomacy and Mediation

However one views military intervention, conventional diplomacy and mediation remain the first line of attack in response to likely failed-state situations. During the December 1990–January 1991 battles in and around Mogadishu, which led to the shattering of the central government and the departure of dictator Siad Barre, nearly all foreign diplomatic officials and international agency representatives departed the capital and the country. Apart from the journalists,[6] Somalia's agonies in the following twelve months were witnessed only by representatives of the Médicins Sans Frontières (MSF) and a handful of courageous nongovernmental organizations (NGOs). The UN was conspicuous by its absence. It was only in his final four days as secretary-general that Javier Pérez de Cuéllar informed the Security Council (December 27, 1991) that he proposed to send Undersecretary for Political Affairs James O.C. Jonah to Somalia to explore the opportunities for a cease-fire.[7]

As the first secretary-general inaugurated in the post–Cold War period, Boutros Boutros-Ghali strongly believed that the United Nations emerged as the "central instrument for the prevention and resolution of conflicts and the preservation of peace." Somalia was the first opportunity for the United Nations, liberated from its Cold War constraints, and its new leader to act aggressively to restore order to a troubled community.[8]

In the new secretary-general's first report to the Security Council on Somalia,[9] doctrinal and procedural difficulties that were to plague the UN operation right to the end were already apparent: (1) Credentials issues – Who represents which group? The United Nations, contrary to usual diplomatic conventions but following standard peacekeeping practice, made no judgments other than to accept the invariably overblown claims of the individual warlords. (2) Venue issues – None of the militias wanted to meet in Somalia. To do so would give a symbolic advantage to one group or another. The preferred sites were Addis Ababa, Nairobi, and Asmara.[10] There was no serious consideration of any political track other than accommodation.

The significance of the Jonah visit was not lost on Aideed. To develop tactics to thwart the new UN interest in Somalia, Aideed called a meeting of his coalition at a settlement in the Shabelle valley. Attending were Aideed for the United Somali Congress (USC), Ahmed Omar Jess for the Somali Patriotic Movement (SPM), Mohamed Nur Aliyow for the Somali Democratic Movement (SDM), and Abdi Warsame Isaw for the Southern Somali National Movement (SSNM). This meeting of the "hard core" members of Aideed's group was to decide strategies and to demonstrate solidarity in the face of the UN-sponsored cease-fire talks that were soon to begin in Mogadishu.[11] This meeting established a pattern of opposition to external intervention that Aideed maintained until his death by a stray bullet in Mogadishu in August 1996.

Following the signature of a cease-fire agreement on March 3, 1992, that satisfied the desires of both sides to maintain an armed status quo, the secretary-general requested Mohamed Sahnoun to undertake a fact-finding mission to Somalia. The highly skilled and reputed Algerian career diplomat knew the Horn of Africa well; he had served as deputy director of the Organization of African Unity (OAU) in Addis Ababa for several years. He visited Mogadishu and found that most of the city's inhabitants had fled into the surrounding countryside, where they lived in the most pitiful conditions. Soon appointed special representative of the secretary-general (SRSG) to Somalia, the Algerian career diplomat brought great sensitivity to the job, and he was the first major foreign actor to attempt to reassemble Somalia. He believed that Somalia's problems could be resolved through effective diplomacy. His book describes his efforts to rebuild confidence in legitimate political processes by contacting the warlords, intellectuals, and elders—a broad swathe of Somali society.[12] Sahnoun made no secret of his belief that "if the international community had intervened earlier and more effectively in Somalia, much of the catastrophe that has unfolded could have been avoided."[13] But just as Ambassador Sahnoun believed that the UN had been too late in bringing to bear its political and humanitarian resources in Somalia, it was also too late to rely on traditional diplomacy and accommodation to solve the crisis.

In the same United Nations Security Council Resolution (UNSCR) that spelled out Sahnoun's formal mission to Somalia (UNSCR 751, April 24, 1992), the first UNOSOM was established, and a force of fifty UN technical observers to monitor the cease-fire in Mogadishu was authorized. Sahnoun secured grudging acceptance by Aideed to UNOSOM's military expansion. Ambassador Sahnoun's diplomatic efforts to obtain Aideed's agreement to the deployment of uniformed UN observers in mid-1992 quickly dissolved when it became known that the same UN-chartered aircraft used for transporting UN officials around the country was found to have accepted a side contract from Ali Mahdi to transport new Somali shilling notes for distribution in his area of influence. Aideed seized this incident as a pretext to "suspend" the arrival of the final forty-six UN military observers.

By mid-1992, Somalia appeared ready again to explode all over the landscape. Troubles erupted in the Northeast with Islamic zealots, there was growing repression in the South as local peoples resisted their new overlords, and Mogadishu was still a tinderbox. Security Council Resolution 767 (July 27, 1992) further raised the UN silhouette in Somalia. An additional 450, now-military, forces were deployed. A national conference was also envisaged. A decentralized zonal approach for the UN intervention in Somalia was mandated. Accommodation mixed with persuasion remained the underlying philosophy of the UN operation. Aideed's rejections of UN initiatives were vociferous, and he demonstrated his power by blockading several hundred Pakistani peacekeepers within the premises of the airport, where they would not be relieved until the arrival of UNITAF in December.

By mid-1992, thanks to a media aroused by angry humanitarian groups that pointed to the starvation in central Somalia, the drastic humanitarian problems of Somalia were well known. General Aideed's continued truculence called for more resolute action. After Aideed's initial refusal to accept UNSCR 767, the world should have been aware that a more forceful UN mandate would be needed. The UN Security Council passed Resolution 775 on August 28, authorizing an additional 3,000 armed troops to protect food aid convoys, without previously informing Sahnoun. Aideed was livid; with the expectation that his military strength would bring him the presidency of Somalia, Aideed was the warlord most affected by any external intervention.

If political doctrine on international humanitarian intervention had been available at the time, it would probably have indicated that mid-1992 was the proper time to introduce a substantial military force. Many more lives would have been saved, and opposition to effective international political action would have been weaker. In the absence of a doctrinal basis for Sahnoun's operation, his disagreements with the UN Headquarters staff and subsequent dismissal by the secretary-general in October 1992 were probably inevitable. Sahnoun's efforts were not diminished by his summary dismissal; the irony is that by mid-1992, diplomatic efforts to resolve the Somalia problem were already too late.

UNITAF, UNOSOM II, and the Failure of U.S. Resolve

The humanitarian disaster in Somalia was on all the television screens in the United States by August 1992. A sense of urgency about Somalia within the U.S. Congress and public significantly raised the pressures on the U.S. administration. Using the awesome logistical resources under its command, the U.S. military established an emergency airlift from Mombasa, Kenya. In the six months of the military and civilian flights by the U.S. Air Force and the State Department Office of Foreign Disaster Assistance out of Mombasa, nearly 45,000 metric tons of food were delivered to Somalia and northern Kenya. But few people were satisfied with the airlift. It is an expensive way to deliver bulk food and medicine.[14] Without some military support on the ground, the unarmed U.S. transports were vulnerable to ground fire. It would be necessary to break the warlord blockade closing the surface flow of relief supplies to the interior.

U.S. voters appeared to have forgotten the euphoria of the military victories in the Gulf War when they entered the ballot booths in early November 1992. In an effort to leave office on a high note, President Bush finally decided that something had to be done about the humanitarian disaster in Somalia. In the limited space of this chapter, I cannot recount the background to the "Thanksgiving decision" to intervene in Somalia, which is described very well elsewhere.[15] However, to appreciate the special shape of the U.S. intervention in Somalia, one must realize the extent to which the Somalia humanitarian enterprise was developed as a purely military operation.[16] After the interagency process in Washington reviewed three force recommendations made by the Pentagon, the president approved the strongest option, which called for a two-division joint task force to be deployed to open the Mogadishu warehouses and the highways into the Somali interior for food shipments. Operation Restore Hope's political guidance, coordinated with the appropriate agencies and approved by the president, was duly forwarded to Central Command (CENTCOM) headquarters in Tampa, whose theater includes the Horn of Africa.

As the document was translated into military tasking orders for the joint task force, CENTCOM carefully removed the critical civil affairs and military police training components from the package.[17] This was unusual; civil affairs officers are specialists in foreign cultures and are used for liaison with local communities. The U.S. military deployed approximately 1,000 civil affairs officers to Panama in December 1989 and about 300 to northern Iraq after the Gulf War. Under UNITAF, the numbers ranged from 7 to 30. Although they were deployed to Somalia, UNITAF decided not to use the army military police (MP) units that were part of the original staffing plan for Restore Hope. The restoration of the Somali National Police Force was a very high political priority, but instead of using the MPs to help retrain the Somali police, UNITAF turned this matter over to the warlords for action, with predictable results.[18]

CENTCOM changes to the agreed political guidance, however unusual such changes may have been, were based on several apparent concerns: (1) The original concept of the operation was that it would be over within weeks ("out by inauguration day"). CENTCOM wished to ensure that no encumbering activities developed during the operation to prolong its stay. (2) The U.S. Marine Corps is an expeditionary force that specializes in short-term, high-intensity combat operations. It is not trained or equipped for longer-term occupation-type operations. (3) CENTCOM wished to ensure that no encumbering requirements would be placed on the mission by the United Nations or other agencies of the U.S. government. In a virtually unprecedented development for the United Nations, the first drafts of UN Security Council Resolution 794 (December 3, 1992), which authorized UNITAF, and later Security Council Resolution 814 (March 26, 1993), authorizing the expanded mission of UNOSOM II, were written in the Pentagon.[19] There were several modifications during the Security Council debates on these resolutions, but the essential substance of the resolutions was designed to satisfy the concerns of CENTCOM.

The U.S. military opposed disarmament during the debate between Secretary-General Boutros-Ghali and the White House in December 1992 because it pictured an effort to root out arms on an impossible house-to-house search basis. In a pro-active political reconciliation program, other incentives would have been devised for the *mooryaan* to lay down their weapons.[20] What was clearly lacking was a coherent overall humanitarian-political-military game plan to provide the parameters for a more powerful UN mandate to establish a secure environment. As such, the UNITAF deployment provided the force necessary to impress the warlords, but it lacked the political objectives to cause them to back down.

The Inapplicability of Traditional Peacekeeping Doctrine in Troubled States

The nonexistence of the state or situations in which the normal functioning of the state is impaired through civil war or other human-created disaster change the relationship between the intervening force and the community it is empowered to assist. There being no legally sanctioned authorities or state structures to provide legitimate consent, the actions of the international force are governed exclusively by the United Nations, normally authorized by a resolution under Chapter VII of the UN Charter. This can give the intervening force the power to compel compliance to Security Council resolutions. In Somalia, both UNITAF and the UNOSOM II force that followed it were authorized under a Chapter VII mandate. The administration of George Bush, which wrote both the UNITAF and UNOSOM II mandates, chose to restrict the rules of engagement of the U.S. expeditionary force to little more than those that would apply in a Chapter VI situation. This decision had a profound influence on the logical development of Operation Restore Hope, with repercussions that fostered the political and military confrontations that plagued the UN successor force.

Analysis of the various Security Council resolutions and periodic secretary-general reports on the situation in Somalia to the Security Council demonstrate that traditional peacekeeping doctrine had little utility in securing the cooperation of Somalis and was probably counterproductive. In the "failed state" environment of Somalia, the UN embarked for the first time in its history on a peace-enforcement situation in which there were no legitimate authorities to provide consent. Experience was not a good guide, and there was an almost irresistible impulse on the part of UN personnel and foreign civilian and military authorities to confer legitimacy on one or more participants in the ongoing Somali political crisis. The UN pursuit of impartiality among the various factions led to a kind of "collective legitimacy" consecrated by the various Addis Ababa and Nairobi conferences. The political results were negative and, because of the exclusive nature of the results, distorted political rehabilitation. The warlords successfully played to the desire of UNITAF to have the least amount of trouble before getting out.[21] International organizations and nongovernmental agencies remained subject to the predatory activities of warlords holding their own communities hostage.[22]

A number of respected authorities and observers object to the use of the word "warlord" on the ground that it attaches a pejorative characterization to leaders who are indisputably part of the political environment.[23] It was my impression in Somalia that most "warlords" were rather proud of the title because it implied strength and leadership. For the purposes of this chapter, a warlord is a leader of a local or regional military organization or militia that operates independently of sanctioned national authority and projects its political influence primarily through armed force. By this definition, the leaders of all of the various armed clan elements that formed in Somalia before and after the fall of Siad Barre are warlords, including the leaders of the defeated Siad forces.

In terms of relations between intervening forces and warlords, it seems contrary to accepted international humanitarian values and U.S. basic beliefs to cede authority to one or another warlord simply because that person has more men, more guns, or a more effective media apparatus. Yet as I will discuss further on, the international community treated certain warlords as though they were legitimate political authorities when it was patently clear that they were not. It was perfectly understandable that Special Presidential Envoy Robert Oakley, named in late November 1992 by President Bush, would wish to arrange a peaceful military entry in early December. It is less understandable that these early gestures were permitted to develop into a one-sided relationship favorable only to a communal leader whose crimes against his own people were well known.[24]

Before I review potential peace-enforcement doctrine, it may be useful to look first at the areas of distortion created in the Somalia intervention by adherence, more or less, to traditional peacekeeping techniques. These techniques favor unscrupulous leaders who are prepared to throw their countries into chaos in order to profit personally and in the name of their ethnic group from the virtual impunity that follows the collapse of public order.

Gaining legitimacy from the intervening force. In a failed-state environment, by definition, no local leader can claim authority on the basis of legitimate selection by the broader national community. An intervening peace enforcement entity, however, brings with it a mantle of legitimacy accorded by its Security Council mandate. No matter how circumspectly it may interact with local militia leaders, the intervening force leadership will find itself under pressure to confer some kind of legitimacy by words, symbols, or deeds on warlords. In peace enforcement, a military commander must be as resourceful in political and media tactics as he is on the traditional battlefield. If the intervening foreign commander permits himself to be drawn into protocol charades with local potentates, he will quickly lose moral authority and credibility.[25]

Maintenance of local power bases. Local leaders will attempt to derive whatever advantages they can from proximity to the intervening authority. Dependence on Mogadishu for logistical support led the United States and the UN into a pattern of frequent meetings with Aideed. He used these meetings to convince his own sometimes skeptical clan supporters and clan allies that he was duly sanctioned as the next leader of Somalia. If a warlord can control, or better yet divert, the distribution of humanitarian food and medicines to his own partisans at the expense of the general community, he gains power and resources that can be used immediately against his enemies and ultimately the intervening force. One should never assume that warlords share an interest in a return to stability and law and order. Ali Mahdi generally supported the intervention force because he thought it would at least maintain the status quo in the face of Aideed's growing force. Aideed and his small coalition would have accepted a return to stability only if it meant that their enemies had been thoroughly neutralized with themselves securely in control.

Neutralization of enemies.   Warlords naturally prefer to have the intervening forces fight their battles for them whenever possible.[26] If a local warlord perceives he is losing authority over conquered territories, he will insist that the intervening force provide assistance either to retain the status quo or to return to an earlier situation more favorable to the warlord. When Omar Jess's forces were driven out of Kismayu in March 1993, the Aideed coalition not only blamed UNITAF but demanded that UNITAF drive the offending force out of the city. In a stateless situation, every use of force by the intervening powers is guaranteed to favor one side or another. In cases that clearly require the use of force, such as the need to deliver a riposte to the ambushers of the Pakistanis on June 5, 1993, the intervening force must ensure that it is not being lured into combat for reasons other than for self-defense or to accomplish the broader political goals of the operation.

Enhanced credibility through special relationships.   High-level exchanges with senior officials and officers in the intervening force were used by warlords in Somalia to demonstrate their credibility through the media. The most effective Somali warlord in exploiting such opportunities was Mohamed Farah Aideed, who always had a cameraman ready to record the visits to his office of senior U.S. and UN officials. The nearly daily calls on Aideed by diplomats on Oakley's team and often slavish kowtowing by local UN figures and international visitors to Aideed was baffling to most Somalis.

Continued free hand in areas of influence.   In Somalia, the UNITAF-UNOSOM zones of operation fell astride the most hotly contested areas of the country. This directly affected the internal lines of communication of clan militia leader Mohamed Farah Aideed in late 1992 at a time that he believed he was consolidating his faction's power over a number of weaker clans in the South. Aideed's petty harassment of UNITAF activities was a prelude to later full-scale attacks on UNOSOM.

International standing and recognition.   This warlord goal was amply met by the UN decision to support conferences restricted to a few factions in the elegant hotels and conference sites in Addis Ababa and Nairobi. The ability to stage-manage the visits of international personalities is also a favored technique for warlords. Access to the international media is also an advantage more easily met in the relative luxury of neighboring capitals. Part of the importance of being able to demonstrate international standing is to show your clan supporters that their investment in maintaining you and your force is reaping desired political dividends.

Some pressure to accommodate warlords is generated by the entirely legitimate concerns of all military commanders to protect their forces, particularly in the opening phase of a deployment. The Somalia experience demonstrated that warlords were initially prudent in the face of UNITAF's overwhelming force. This respect rapidly dissipated when it was seen that UNITAF would not intervene in Somali-on-Somali violence. When UNITAF took steps to support the establishment of the local police force, it was the UN's turn to abstain from decisive action.[27] Later tragedies might have been avoided if UNITAF had been authorized to use its overwhelming advantages in military force, command and control, logistics, and communications to support a political agenda. This would have required political tactics to undercut the power of the warlords in favor of normal Somalis who were striving against mighty odds and a lot of firepower to reinstate local authorities, create self-help groups, open schools, reopen farms and shops, and restore community services.

Intervention Doctrine

The simple dynamics in Somalia in 1992 point to a political solution built around loose federal structures.[28] This was the objective of U.S. and UN planning for the March 1993 Addis Ababa national reconciliation conference. This idea was such an anathema to the warlords' club that they effectively hijacked the conference from the UN. Lacking a clear political vision of the necessary political process, the UN later improvised a process to establish local and regional councils. Working within a tight calendar and eager to show political progress, the leaders in this process succeeded only in creating new cleavages at the local level. What was needed was a national conference that would have permitted everyone, including the warlords, an opportunity to play a role in the system.

The poverty of existing protocols and the inability to develop new doctrine for application to failed states are manifest in each of the seventeen operational Security Council resolutions developed for the combined humanitarian and political crisis in Somalia, 1992–1994.[29] An arms embargo was proclaimed in UNSCR 746 (January 23, 1992), but it was unenforceable. As noted previously, Aideed openly defied UNSCR 751 (April 24, 1992) and UNSCR 775 (August 28, 1992), which established and expanded the UN observer force. Empty resolutions create disdain. In formulating effective international-intervention doctrine, policymakers should address the following points:

Formal intervention doctrine must accommodate the requirements of "hard" cases. In territories where there is no state, as in Somalia, or where there is disputed, ineffective, or unclear sovereignty, as in Afghanistan, Bosnia, and Liberia, responsible countries of the world must be prepared first to offer their good offices to mediate political solutions and provide resources to facilitate the return to order. If, in time, these peaceful efforts are unavailing and it is perceived that substantial portions of the populations of the afflicted territories are suffering from unacceptable inhumanities, common morality then requires that responsible states, preferably in coalition, mount a coordinated political-military intervention to create the conditions that may lead to the restoration of civil order. Intervening forces must have the mandate to take those measures necessary to promote public safety, including the use of force against recalcitrant members of the society. Whenever possible, the local police and justice system should be restored early in the engagement.

It is important to keep in mind that military intervention is not necessary or desirable in every complex humanitarian emergency. Just doing it correctly once or twice might serve to create a new body of credible doctrine that would provide warnings to potential warlords and examples for leaders in faltering states not to resort to chaos in the pursuit of their ambitions.

The underlying political issues must be addressed. The fundamental issues underlying the Somalia starvation emergency in 1992 were political and not the results of natural disaster. There were elements in Somali culture and tradition—not to mention the availability then of thousands of well-intentioned and hopeful Somalis—that could have been liberated by the international intervention forces to provide the framework for a meaningful political restoration process. Neither the UN nor the U.S. administrations involved recognized the special characteristics of the failed Somali state and therefore failed to develop those measures to facilitate the restoration of Somali civil society. The lack of political vision on the part of the international actors in the Somali drama was in large part willful, in the case of the U.S. government, and international civil servants and the professional peacekeepers were blinded by their traditional political passivity. The international force must make clear that it is not bound by arbitrary decisions of local leaders until some form of legitimacy is developed by the larger community.

Military tactics must support the political agenda. Although the ultimate responsibility for restoration of their state was always the responsibility of the Somali people, in 1992 an outside military force was almost certainly necessary to act as catalyst to neutralize the hold of warlords on local communities in order to permit the traditional problem-solving mechanisms of Somali culture to flourish. The *shir,* or *guurti,* as is it is known variously in Somalia, consists of meetings of elders to discuss political or economic matters of particular interest to the community.[30] All members in such convocations are equal, and their decisions are binding on all involved.[31] Such meetings were not theoretical in the Somalia situation in 1992. The principles of the *shir* were later employed with relative success at the Borama conference in "Somaliland" in March–May 1993, in Kismayu throughout most of 1993, and at the Benadir conference process in Mogadishu, which began in 1994 and was still viable in the early months of 1995.[32]

Political conciliation techniques must spring from the society under stress. Had there been a political strategy involved in the UNITAF operation, the planners would have focused on Somali cultural traditions and political techniques to facilitate reopening civil society. Fundamental to all such plans is the need to establish a political dynamic that seizes political initiative from warlords and other miscreants and places it under the control of positive elements of society. In Somalia, there were four significant groups that would have cooperated in such an endeavor: (1) Somali women who, overwhelmingly and courageously, demonstrated by their actions their commitment to peace and a return to civil society; (2) traditional elders and other local leaders who resented the actions of the warlords and would have provided the basis for restoration of local government legitimacy; (3) downtrodden agriculturalists and other southern minorities who saw no difference between the stranglehold of Siad's army and secret police on their communities and the warlords; and (4) tradesmen, intellectuals, and other urban elites who wanted the nomadic militiamen and *mooryaan,* the heavily armed teenagers who formed the base of General Aideed's forces in 1993, out of their homes and business sites. Just as humanitarian policy must focus on the victims of chaos, so must international political doctrine be just and favor political victims rather than their oppressors.

The agreed political objectives should broaden the political base. Under UN leadership, the people of Somalia should have been invited to choose their representatives to be sent to a national conference within the country. The favored conference sites, Addis Ababa and Nairobi, were expensive and favored deals between warlords and their henchmen. For many reasons, it would have been necessary to hold such a conference outside any of Somalia's major cities. In early 1993, most major Somali cities and towns were incapable of supporting a large meeting. The intervening force would have been obliged to create a conference village. If such a conference had been held in Somalia, participation would have been greater and the deliberations could have been observed by a larger number of citizens. A national *shir* would have been expensive, but even if it lasted a year, it would have cost the UN forces a lot less than sponsoring an armed conflict.

The military force should be ready to protect the political process. For obvious psychological and political reasons, a Somali reconciliation conference should have been held in a geographically neutral zone, that is, a site in which the ethnic group did not have a champion vying for national power. This was one of the factors that led the minority Gadaboursi people in Somaliland to call a "national conference" in their hometown of Borama.[33] Not a serious contender in Somaliland politics, the Gadaboursi provided a safe and effective place for a "national" meeting. In parallel fashion, the primarily agricultural Ranhanweyn people of Baidoa would have also been good hosts for a national conference. Baidoa had been one of the sites of greatest human suffering in the starvation crisis of 1991–1992. Symbolically, the intervening force could have focused the aspiring political leadership of a new Somali state on the humanitarian issues of the civil war by establishing, maintaining, and protecting a national conference tent village on the outskirts of Baidoa. Some military means would also be required to ensure safe passage for delegates to a national conference in order to avoid efforts by certain groups to prevent attendance by opponents. Warlords, naturally, would also be welcome to take part in the national conference. No arms would be permitted in the national conference village, and it would be necessary to set up some kind of internal police to ensure that "accidents" did not take place.

By following these strategies, the intervening force could have facilitated reconciliation and taken the initiative away from the troublemakers. It is important to remember that in 1992–1993 in Somalia, no warlord could have maintained power without powerful support from his own ethnic group. A conference in Somalia outside the main Hawiye cultural zone would have pressured Aideed to join internationally sanctioned moves toward a return to civil society. The true center of gravity in Somalia was the nexus of warlord-ethnic group ties.

Lessons for the Future

Many U.S. political figures look at the world's experience in Somalia and decide that the United States should not be involved in peace enforcement. It is hard, expensive, and dangerous. The public is ambiguous: It generally supports UN efforts but is reluctant to place U.S. military forces in harm's way. U.S. military leadership fears that peacekeeping does not fit the missions for which U.S. forces have been trained.

In my view, peace operations require the highest level of political-military skills. No one should suggest that the U.S. soldier or marine lacks resourcefulness or courage. Since the original Somalia deployment, the U.S. military has taken great strides to understand and prepare for peacemaking operations. The idea that some military objectives can be achieved through nonmilitary means in a peace-enforcement operation is a notion that is gaining greater respect within the U.S. military. The special skills and equipment of U.S. forces are particularly adaptable to peace-enforcement operations, and they can be expected to respond to the most difficult situations that draw the attention of the U.S. public.

Effective application of integrated military and political policies in the multi-lateral arena is one of the most important tasks now challenging policymakers around the world. The world cannot back away from the moral challenges inherent in ministering to the distressed, defeating chaos, and facilitating the restoration of states. There is a peculiar irony in the fact that many of the top policy architects of the Cold War era now appear agape and witless in the face of these new political-military challenges. Convincing evidence of the passing of the Cold War strategic mentality can be found in recent comments of no less a student of strategy and definer of U.S. national interests than former secretary of state Henry Kissinger. In a 1995 interview while in India, Kissinger noted that he opposed sending U.S. peacekeepers to Somalia, believing that diplomatic rather than military pressure should be brought to bear to work for peace. Kissinger observed, modestly, that "once upon a time, we had all the answers to world problems—today we don't. . . . In 1962, I lauded India's role as a non-aligned nation—today, we prefer to be non-aligned ourselves."[34]

As a responsible leading member of the world community, the United States cannot remain neutral before disorder and suffering. Even as an isolationist surge laps at the foot of Capitol Hill, most opinion polls show that the U.S. public supports continued U.S. engagement in peacekeeping activities. If the U.S. role is properly articulated by national leaders, the public is willing to pay the price of global leadership. The U.S. public intuitively appreciates that the ability to project power for humanitarian purposes over long distances is the singular mark of a world power. The experience of Operation Restore Hope in Somalia, no matter how painful the memories of the loss of U.S. service personnel, can be positive if the proper lessons are drawn from it.

Notes

1. John Darnton, "U.N. Buildup in Bosnia Eyes 'Mogadishu Line,'" *New York Times,* June 7, 1995, p. A18.

2. See the collection of essays by Ioan M. Lewis, *Blood and Bone: The Call of Kinship in Somali Society* (Lawrenceville, NJ: Red Sea Press, 1994).

3. For a stimulating examination of Somalia immediately before the fall of Siad Barre, see Anna Simons, *Networks of Dissolution: Somalia Undone* (Boulder: Westview Press, 1995).

4. See "Somalia: A Fight to the Death? Leaving Civilians at the Mercy of Terror and Starvation," *Africa Watch* 4(2), February 13, 1992, p. 10.

5. For an excellent summary of developments after the departure of UNOSOM II in March 1995, see Ken Menkhaus and John Prendergast, "Governance and Economic Survival in Post Intervention Somalia," *CSIS Africa Notes* no. 172, May 1995.

6. Of particular note is the series of excellent articles by the *New York Times*'s Jane Perlez, who served as the newspaper's correspondent in central and eastern Africa during all of 1991–1992.

7. UN Department of Public Information, *The United Nations and the Situation in Somalia* (New York: UN, March 1994), p. 1.

8. See Boutros Boutros-Ghali, *An Agenda for Peace* (New York: UN, June 1992).

9. Boutros Boutros-Ghali, *Report of the Secretary-General on the Situation in Somalia* (S/23693) (New York: UN, March 11, 1992).

10. Boutros-Ghali, *Report of the Secretary-General on the Situation in Somalia* (S/23693), p. 12.

11. "USC, SDM, SPM, SSNM Issue Communiqué," Radio Mogadishu in Somali 1700 GMT, February 29, 1992, FBIS-AF–92–041 (March 2, 1992), pp. 6–7.

12. Mohamed Sahnoun, *Somalia: The Missed Opportunities* (Washington, DC: U.S. Institute of Peace, 1994), p. 15.

13. Sahnoun, *Somalia,* p. xiii.

14. John G. Sommer, *Hope Restored? Humanitarian Aid in Somalia 1990–1994* (Washington, DC: Refugee Policy Group, Center for Policy Analysis and Research on Refugee Issues, November 1994), pp. 22–23.

15. Ibid., pp. 29–33.

16. A well-placed contact in the Pentagon told me in early 1994 that the essential understanding between the Pentagon and the National Security Council in November 1992 was that the military would begrudgingly accept the Somalia mission "so long as the State Department and the United Nations kept out of the way."

17. This information comes from several military participants in the planning phases of Operation Restore Hope.

18. See Martin Ganzglass's Chapter 2 in this volume.

19. At the Princeton conference, a senior UN official described UNSCR 814 as "the mother of all resolutions." The UN remains nettled by the fact that it is blamed for introducing "nation building" into Operation Restore Hope; the original authors of the resolution belong to the "member-state" that most criticizes the action.

When I admonished a senior official about the negative ramifications of UNSCR 814 on U.S. multilateral policy, he remonstrated that when it was originally drafted in the Pentagon, "well, no one expected the UN to be able to do it!"

20. At one point, a Somali women's group proposed an effort to entice the rootless teenage *mooryaan* fighters off the streets by offering to exchange their weapons for an opportunity to attend school to learn a trade. Initial planning efforts were discussed, but events soon intervened to frustrate another potentially useful Somali initiative.

21. See Ken Menkhaus, "Getting Out vs. Getting Through: US and U.N. Policies in Somalia," *Middle East Policy* 3(2–3), March-April/May-June 1994, pp. 146–162.

22. This is the idea behind the title of the recent book by Mariam Arif Gassem, *Hostages: The People Who Kidnapped Themselves* (Nairobi: Central Graphics, 1994). Gassem is a lawyer, accountant, and banker and a native Mogadishan. Her book describes the civil war and its effects on her family and the people of Mogadishu.

23. See Alex Shoumatoff, "The US, the U.N. and Aidid: The 'Warlord' Speaks," *Nation*, April 4, 1994, pp. 442–450.

24. See "Somalia Beyond the Warlords: The Need for a Verdict on Human Rights Abuses," *Africa Watch* 5(2), March 7, 1993), p. 29. It was clear from the information contained in this report and many others that Aideed and several of his allies had dubious human rights records.

25. Many serious authorities continue to confuse "impartiality" and "neutrality," which are not synonymous. Laws must be applied *impartially*; but one is not *neutral* in the face of lawbreakers. For more on this ambiguity, see the otherwise excellent recent doctrinal publication, U.S. Army Headquarters, *FM* [Field Manual] *100–23: Peace Operations* (Washington, DC: December 1994), 123 pp.

26. The publicly declared decision of Ambassador Robert Oakley to shun General Mohamed Said Hersi "Morgan" because of the latter's leadership role in the destruction, at great cost in civilian lives, of Hargeisa in 1988 removed any pretense of impartiality in dealing with Somali warlords. When Morgan regained control of Kismayu in March 1993, UNITAF was nonetheless accused by Aideed of partiality in its dealings with his opponents.

27. See Philip Johnston, *Somalia Diary: The President of CARE Tells One Country's Story of Hope* (Atlanta: Longstreet Press, 1994), pp. 97–101. The police initiative foundered on the grounds that the UN had never financed a police force. Aideed and Ali Mahdi quickly volunteered to set up their own police forces, which they did with the help of Robert Oakley and UNITAF resources. These policemen were highly selective in applying local laws.

28. The generally muddled agreements made by the warlords during and after the March 1993 Somali reconciliation conference in Addis Ababa included a mandate to establish local and district councils. Unfortunately, this was accomplished through the imposition of such councils by itinerant UNOSOM officials. This was probably better than nothing, but the process would have been more credible if there had been time to let the local communities make their own selections.

29. See the appendix to this book for a list of UN Security Council resolutions on Somalia.

30. Problem solving at the national level in a segmentary lineage society is a difficult, though not impossible, matter. It is a subject well studied in anthropological literature on Somalia. See the excellent review article by Erika Pozzo, "Customary Law of Somalis and Other African Peoples," in Hussein M. Adam and Charles L. Geshekter, eds., *Proceedings of the First International Congress of Somali Studies* (Atlanta: Scholars Press, 1992), pp. 277–288.

31. Margaret Castango, *Historical Dictionary of Somalia* (Metuchen, NJ: Scarecrow Press, 1975), p. 142.

32. See Menkhaus and Prendergast, "Governance and Economic Survival in Post Intervention Somalia." Also see Menkhaus's Chapter 3 in this volume.

33. The Somaliland National Conference was held in Borama from February through April 1993 and led to the election of Mohamed Egal as president of the aspiring new state.

34. Reuter, New Delhi, March 22, 1995.

2

The Restoration of the Somali Justice System

MARTIN R. GANZGLASS

Operation Restore Hope covered 40 percent of Somalia. It was limited to the central and southern regions, and neither UNITAF nor UNOSOM, with some almost irrelevant exceptions, established a presence in the northwestern or northeastern areas of the country. However, the operation had an impact on all of Somalia, and its effects countrywide are the focus of this chapter.

International efforts to restore the Somali justice system contained fundamental flaws in operational planning and implementation.[1] Perhaps reflecting its obsessive fixation on Mogadishu, UNITAF failed to capitalize on the successful Australian program to rebuild the Somali police and judiciary in Baidoa and the Bay region.[2]

U.S. planning for Operation Restore Hope did not follow successful lessons from the Gulf War, after which civil affairs units in Kuwait helped rebuild the police and judiciary.[3] UNITAF was crippled by a narrow definition of its mission and its undue haste to hand over responsibilities to the UN. UNOSOM was institutionally incapable of acting quickly and decisively to adopt a plan to restore the Somali justice system within the operational zone, let alone in the Northwest and Northeast, where such programs had significant possibilities of success.

The Police and Judiciary After the Overthrow of Siad Barre

After January 1991, Somalia descended into anarchy and disintegrated into clan-dominated areas. In this patchwork of tribal fiefdoms, some areas fared better than others. What follows is a description of the efforts and failures in trying to restore the Somali justice system in a country in name only, and among a people whose common language, religion, and culture no longer bound them together as a nation.

Before January 1991, the Somali National Police Force numbered approximately 15,000 nationwide. It was divided into eighteen regional divisions with approximately ninety police stations located in the districts and over 100 police posts in smaller towns. Nearly 6,000 were Darawishta, a highly mobile, heavily armed force designed to separate warring clans and stop tribal warfare.[4] With the outbreak of full-scale civil war in Mogadishu and the South in January-February 1991, many police returned to their clan areas to avoid being slaughtered. This had the unintended result of creating de facto regional police forces.[5] These forces, particularly in the Northeast, carried out routine police duties. However, they were poorly equipped and in dire need of transport and communications equipment.[6]

The police had remained substantially uncorrupted by Siad Barre, but the same could not be said for the judiciary. Prior to 1969, Somalia had a three-tiered independent judiciary, applying a uniform penal code and code of criminal procedure. By 1987, the Supreme Court existed in name only; the president of the court, appointed by Siad Barre, was deemed corrupt if not incompetent; and the two courts of appeal were no longer functioning. Judges were poorly paid and generally compelled to render decisions based on political considerations.[7] Following the overthrow of Siad Barre, the judges, like the police, also sought protection among their clans from the ravages of civil war. In some areas, again where the population was relatively homogenous, the judges were in a position to dispense justice acceptable to the community.[8]

Efforts to Rebuild the Somali Justice System Under UNOSOM II and UNITAF

The First Phase: Ambassador Sahnoun

Security Council Resolution 733 focused UN attention on Somalia and created UNOSOM I. In April 1992, Mohamed Sahnoun was named the special representative of the secretary-general (SRSG). He traveled extensively and met Somalis from all factions. At a meeting in Bosasso with the Somali Salvation Democratic Front (SSDF) chair, General Mohamed Abshir Musa, the UN was urged to assist the regional police force.[9]

In Mogadishu, Sahnoun met with General Ahmed Jama, the last commandant of the Somali National Police Force, who advocated broad disarmament of the factions. The police would be used to maintain law and order in those sectors of the city where they were accepted by the population.[10]

In the Northwest, the Council of Elders of Somaliland asked General Jama Mohamed Ghalib, also a former Somali National Police commandant, to address the problem of rebuilding the police. He proposed a decentralized police instead of deploying UN troops in the Northwest. Before these proposals could be presented to UN headquarters, Ambassador Sahnoun resigned. This created "a serious vacuum of even limited normal contacts between the UN and Somaliland."[11] On October 12, 1992, Ambassador Sahnoun, addressing the UN Somali donors' conference in Geneva, stated:

We ... decided to establish a small security force of Somalis to assist United Nations forces at the airport, seaport and the distribution centers, starting with Mogadishu where the United Nations troops have already arrived. It is only an arrangement of this nature that can assure safety for relief workers and protection for humanitarian supplies. This could ultimately form the nucleus of a Somali police countrywide. These proposed Somali guards would require uniforms, transport and communications equipment. It is an area where we need urgently the support and assistance of governments.[12]

Sahnoun failed to capitalize on what all reports confirmed: The Somali police were well-trained, disciplined, and generally nontribal. The nucleus for a Somali police already existed, acceptable to Somalis in regions where they were stationed. A senior member of the SSDF Council observed that had Ambassador Sahnoun made an offer to train and equip regional police in the Northeast, it would have been accepted immediately.[13] Nothing came of Sahnoun's call for assistance. Unfortunately, this was not the last time an "urgent" request for assistance to train and equip the police was ignored by donor nations.

Ambassador Kittani and the Drysdale Report

In October 1992, Ambassador Ismat Kittani was named as SRSG to replace Sahnoun. In November 1992, John Drysdale, a consultant to UNOSOM I, prepared a confidential report for Kittani concerning the "establishment of a nucleus of Police Forces throughout Somalia." Drysdale noted that "without government revenue there is no security. Where there is no security it is difficult to generate revenue. The circle has to be broken if the country is to get on its feet again." He proposed supporting and paying a nontribal Somali police force as part of an overall plan with "provisions to ensure that the continuity of the force is assured." Somalis would accept the deployment of foreign troops if they left behind an "enduring asset" such as a trained police force. "There is considerable urgency behind any such decision [recruitment and training of the Somali police] because, if only for financial reasons, the tenure of foreign troop deployment will be limited. Unless the police recruitment and training were instituted on the arrival of foreign troops the latter might have departed before recruitment and training got underway. This would not contribute to good public relations with the UN."[14]

Drysdale's comments were deeply prophetic in light of the subsequent failure of UNITAF and UNOSOM to "urgently" rebuild the police and the ultimate UNOSOM pullout with no durable police organization left behind.

Operation Restore Hope: A Flaw in the Initial Planning

On December 9, 1992, the first contingent of U.S. Marines arrived in Mogadishu. President Bush initially promised that U.S. troops would be home by Inauguration Day. The mission, pursuant to Security Council Resolution 794 (December 3, 1992) was to use "all necessary means to establish as soon as possible a secure environment for humanitarian relief operations in Somalia." The original operational plans for Restore Hope included the activation of eight to ten U.S. Army Reserve Civil Affairs units. These units would have assisted in restoration of governmental functions, particularly the police and judiciary. The decision not to activate these units was made by the Joint Chiefs of Staff (JCS). The JCS apparently opposed activating reserve units because Operation Restore Hope was scheduled to take only six weeks and its purpose was to feed starving Somalis, not rebuild institutions. The State Department was either unable or unwilling to push the National Security Council to reverse JCS.[15]

The two active companies of the 96th Civil Affairs Battalion that were sent provided support to military units with respect to related civilian issues, such as coordinating food convoys and forming refugee camps. They set up the Civil Military Operations Center (CMOC) in Mogadishu. Arguably, their role was in keeping with the "six-week humanitarian nature" of the operation and did not threaten to become "mission creep" by rebuilding institutions.

It soon became apparent that Operation Restore Hope was not a six-week endeavor. Ronald M. Smith, chief of the Civil Affairs Task Force for Kuwait, consisting of U.S. Army reservists from civil affairs units, noted in early January that "it is imperative that Somali police be put on the streets as soon as possible so that American combat forces can concentrate on the security missions" and not end up killing Somalis. In Kuwait, Smith and his staff had been responsible for advising "the Kuwaiti government on the restoration of the legal and judicial systems, and police services." In sixty-five days, they successfully assisted the Kuwaitis in reopening the courts and putting a "minimal police force back on the streets." In Smith's opinion, 200 civil affairs reservists could in ninety days assist in restoring public order "if proper logistic support is provided and follow-up civilian police trainers are prepared to continue training at the end of the 90 days."[16]

Security Council Resolution 814, adopted on March 23, 1993, also written by the United States, set the date of May 4, 1993, for the transfer from UNITAF to UNOSOM II. In March, when joint planning between UNITAF and UNOSOM began, the United States should have reevaluated its decision not to provide reserve civil affairs units to UNITAF or planned to provide such resources to UNOSOM.

Civil affairs reserve units may not have been activated because of the rivalry between the reservists and the only active-duty civil affairs unit in the army, the 96th Civil Affairs Battalion (Airborne), Fort Bragg, North Carolina. According to Lt. Colonel Andrew Natsios, then an assistant operations office in the reserve 352nd Civil Affairs Command, "There's always been interservice/interbranch rivalry in the military, and there always will be. There's nothing wrong with it so long as it doesn't get in the way of combat effectiveness."[17]

Unfortunately, in Somalia, the failure to implement a civil affairs program using reservists capable of rebuilding the police ultimately led to the insertion of U.S. combat forces in the hunt for General Aideed after a warrant had been issued for his arrest. A retrained Somali police force would have been much better suited for what was essentially a police function in the back streets of Mogadishu.

The Mogadishu Police Committee:
Institution Building as Humanitarian Relief

In early December 1992, General Ahmed Jama, who knew U.S. Special Envoy Robert Oakley from his tour as U.S. ambassador in Somalia, met with Oakley, U.S. Army Lt. Colonel Steven Spataro (UNITAF provost marshal) and Colonels Mentemeyer and Hagee, UNITAF liaison officers. The general proposed that as an initial step, the police be reestablished in every area under UNITAF control. He suggested that the police be immediately encouraged to perform their duties in those areas where public support for them already existed. Oakley proposed to start organizing the police by district, followed by regions, leaving open the issue of combining regional commands into a national force. The immediate problem was Mogadishu, divided by the "green line" into two war zones. General Ahmed Jama's advice to Oakley was to force Aideed and Ali Mahdi to disarm together. In his view, "the better people were silenced by the gun." After disarmament "people would come out and compete with the warlords." The police themselves were separated by the green line and unable to function freely throughout the city.[18]

Accordingly, Ahmed Jama proposed the establishment of a police committee in Mogadishu. Each faction would nominate policemen to the committee. In his view, as the police officers had worked together in the Somali National Police Force, they would do so again provided there was no political interference from either factional leader. Aideed, to his credit, nominated five former police officers to represent his group. Ali Mahdi however, nominated only one police officer. The other four were either from Siad Barre's despised National Security Service (NSS) or were army officers. This structure was not challenged by Oakley, UNITAF, or Aideed, perhaps in the interest of getting the committee off the ground.[19]

In January 1993, the three UNITAF colonels, presumably with Oakley's approval, offered Ahmed Jama the command of the Mogadishu police force. He declined "because this was not a national Police Force. It was for Mogadishu only and it was dominated by people from the Aideed and Ali Mahdi factions."[20] The Police Committee met in the Conoco compound in Oakley's office. On January 25, 1993, the Subcommittee for Reorganizing the Mogadishu Police agreed to appoint eleven officers for district stations in Mogadishu. The criteria for selecting police included service in the Somali National Police Force for two years prior to January 6, 1991, some degree of literacy, and no prior tangible offense against the Somali people.[21]

One initial problem in reorganizing the police was the poor condition of personnel records at national police headquarters in Mogadishu. Policemen, under the auspices of the Police Committee, had to piece together torn and scattered personnel files. Another problem was pay. Initially, relief organizations contributed food to UNITAF, which was used in lieu of salaries to pay the police. Subsequently, limited funds became available from UNOSOM I operational monies to pay for equipment, uniforms, and salaries.[22] By March 1993 there was a 3,000-man police force in Mogadishu (an additional 2,000 in the rest of the UNITAF zone), security had noticeably improved, and the police were arresting criminals for the first time in nearly two years.[23] However, they had served without pay since February and were not finally paid until April. After May, they were paid from UNOSOM II funds. There was no budget, no planning, and no way of "even getting the Police paper."[24]

No thought was given to expanding the concept of the Police Committee to the rest of the country. Once the Police Committee in Mogadishu had the authority, under UNITAF, to review personnel records and pass on applications from the regions for admission into the police, the committee should have been expanded to include police from those regions.[25] If participation on the committee from the regions had been limited to former Somali National Police officers, this would have enhanced practical cooperation, since, as Ahmed Jama observed, these were officers who had worked together in the past.

Despite the policy that Operation Restore Hope was only for humanitarian relief, there was general recognition that rebuilding the police was necessary for the restoration of law and order. The establishment of the Police Committee was a limited effort to get around the implications of a purely humanitarian relief policy to deal with practical issues of lawlessness in the zone of operations.

UNITAF Creeps into the Judicial Field

With the police in Mogadishu beginning to function and prisoners being held in the Mogadishu prison, UNITAF recognized that there was a need to get the courts functioning. Initial meetings with former judges and lawyers took place in January. According to Colonel Frederick M. Lorenz, staff judge advocate, UNITAF, U.S. military lawyers had been meeting "only with Somali lawyers aligned with warlord General Aideed, and the US was subject to criticism for ignoring other factions."[26] A meeting was called for all Somali jurists on March 3, 1993, with UNITAF providing armed escort and transportation from Ali Mahdi's sector to the meeting in Aideed's area. Forty-three jurists attended. The U.S. Information Service (USIS) officer hosting the meeting was questioned by members of the Ali Mahdi–Aideed joint political committee about the reasons for calling the jurists together. In their view, the Peace Subcommittee had already created the interim police force and set forth the guidelines for a court system, a legal code, and rehiring of judges. Therefore, U.S. Liaison Office (USLO) efforts were viewed as an attempt to create a competing organization. The USIS response was "USIS and UNITAF—setting the stage for UNOSOM II—simply wanted to bring together a broad group of Somali jurists." Despite a request by USLO for attendance by a representative from the UNOSOM I political office, no UNOSOM official attended. USLO noted, "The absence of a UNOSOM representative may make it more difficult to hand off the catalyst role for the legal group to UNOSOM II."[27]

The UN Police Technical Team: A Nationwide Study

In January 1993, the UN sent the three-man Police Technical Team (PTT) to examine the Auxiliary Security Force (ASF) to determine whether a national police force could be established. In addition, the team was to explore what could be done to rebuild the judicial system and whether a civilian police component of UNOSOM was desirable. The PTT met with three former Somali National Police commandants, the Police Committee, and UN officials. The PTT reached three fundamental conclusions.[28] First, a Somali national police force should be established at its pre–civil war level of approximately 18,000–20,000 men. This force would be monitored and assisted by a 500-person UNCIVPOL (UN Civilian Police) contingent. This was considered "a matter of the highest priority for Somalia" in order to "encourage and assist the economic reconstruction [of Somalia] by creating and maintaining a countrywide secure environment." The new force would be built around former policemen and extended to the Northwest. A special force would be established within the police to cope with security matters that spilled over regional borders. This recommendation was apparently in response to the point made by General Ahmed Jama that the Darawishta had be to reactivated to deal with organized roving bandit groups.

The PTT report included manpower estimates for the police and organization charts for the UNCIVPOL units. Its recommendations concluded with the call for the nomination and dispatch to Somalia of the "appropriate UN CIVPOL staff and expert committees [for technical assistance and training] as soon as possible." On March 3, the UN secretary-general submitted a report as required by Security Council Resolution 794, referring to the PTT team.[29] Under the heading "Establishment of a Somali Police Force," the secretary-general restated his view: "I consider the establishment of a Somali police force as a crucial step in the efforts of UNITAF and UNOSOM to create a secure environment in Somalia." He referred to the expert team he had sent to Somalia to work with his special representative to "prepare a plan for the establishment of a neutral police force in Somalia . . . outline appropriate training . . . and to study integrating some of [the auxiliary force] into a new civilian police force."

No subsequent action was taken by the secretary-general on the PTT recommendations. No UNCIVPOL team was dispatched to Somalia. Instead, the U.S. government sent its own police team to Somalia.

Enter the U.S. Department of Justice:
The ICITAP Mission (Mogadishu Only)

In early March, Patrick H. Lang and Donald G. Havekost of the U.S. Department of Justice's International Criminal Investigation and Training Assistance Program (ICITAP) arrived in Mogadishu. Their mission was to evaluate the ASF established by UNITAF.[30] At the time of the mission, they noted that the ASF "is derived completely from elements of [the] former National Police Force." It numbered approximately 4,000 and "appears to generally retain the favorable reputation reportedly enjoyed by the former National Police." In their opinion, the ASF represented "a usable foundation . . . to address the short term requirements for Somalis to . . . participate in the process of meeting public order and safety requirements."[31]

However, the ICITAP report cautioned that any effort to rebuild the police, using the ASF as a base, required substantial funding, and there could not be "any expectation that in Somalia's current dangerous environment an under-prepared, under-resourced police organization of any kind can successfully meet the full range of Somalia's public order and safety requirements." Lang and Havekost proposed a "notional budget" of $12,659,600 for a six-month start-up program for 5,000 police in Mogadishu.[32]

The Australians in the Bay Region: The Right Approach

When the Australians arrived in Baidoa in early January, they found a fairly homogenous and indigenous Ranhanweyn people terrorized by armed Habr Gedr outsiders of Aideed's faction. The NGOs in Baidoa were paying subclan leaders extortion of between $2,000 and $6,000 per flight of relief supplies and had been compelled to hire Habr Gedr "security guards" for protection. There was a strong criminal element engaged in "entrepreneurial banditry."[33]

The Australians, like other UNITAF forces, had broad policy guidelines, including authorization within precise rules of engagement, to confront any armed threat to the principal mission of promoting a secure environment for humanitarian relief. However, the Australians, unlike the Americans, arrived with a civil affairs plan. "That was the heart of our relationship with the community and our mission . . . because having a functioning police and judiciary eased the security burden on us. . . . Having a secure law and order environment encourages renewal of economic activity."[34]

Initially, the Australians set up an auxiliary police force in Baidoa, using former members of the Somali National Police Force whose names were vetted through the Police Committee in Mogadishu. The elders proposed a police commander for Baidoa acceptable to the community at large, who was first investigated by the Australians. The Australians also set up a criminal investigation unit consisting of former Criminal Investigation Division members of the Somali National Police Force. Ultimately, there were twenty former CID officers as part of the new police force. In the opinion of the Australians, their criminal intelligence was "100% reliable" and they were exceptionally effective.

Equipment for the police came from UNITAF in coordination with Lt. Colonel Spataro. UNITAF provided typewriters, stationery, VHF radios, uniforms, batons, and whistles.[35] The Australians armed the police in accordance with the UNITAF guideline of up to 25 percent of the force; arranged for a police-training program, initially using a former instructor from the Police Academy; and obtained two barely serviceable trucks as transport. Once the police were established in Baidoa, the Australians set up police units throughout the Bay region.[36] Former judges and court workers who had survived the civil war in the Bay region were selected with the approval of the community. Initially, seven judges were nominated in Baidoa, which had both a district and a regional court. They heard civil and criminal cases and organized lectures for the police on the Somali penal code. In early

March, after meeting with the elders and determining that the penal code was acceptable to the community, the Australians implemented the code as the criminal law of the region. Pay for the police was initially under a food-for-work scheme, with the International Rescue Committee (IRC) providing the food. Later the police in Bay were paid by UNITAF. The Australians, unable to persuade UNITAF or UNOSOM to pay the judges, simply submitted their names as policemen.[37]

The Australians rebuilt the police station, the court, and a small prison, all part of the same compound. "That area quickly became a . . . town center. People would gather in the mornings in the courtyard in the police station and it became a center of communal activity. . . . It . . . was quite clear to us that it . . . had been adopted by the community as a dispute resolution center." At the end of the Australian unit's tour of duty, the Bay region was "completely secure" with approximately 260 Somali police and a functioning court system, and the community had confidence in the system of law and order. However, Bay still had to rely on either UNITAF or UNOSOM to prevent factional militias from moving back into the region. There was nothing magical about the Australians' performance. They had a full civil affairs program and they implemented it.[38] UNITAF did not and had to improvise. To the extent that U.S. forces, particularly the marines, assisted in rebuilding the police, they considered these activities as "mission creep."[39]

Meanwhile, in the Rest of the Country . . .

In the non-UNITAF part of Somalia, efforts to rebuild the Somali justice system, although supported by the communities, were severely hampered by lack of resources. When the PTT mission visited the Northwest, the "militias which are estimated to be almost 5,000 by the security committee of Hargeisa" were completely out of control. The auxiliary police force numbered only 340 and consisted of both former members of the Somali National Police Force and recruits from the army and militia.[40] The security committee wanted a strong police force to demobilize and disarm the militias, but it was reluctant to accept UNOSOM supervision. It was, however, willing to accept a small group of Criminal Investigation Division (CID) advisers. With respect to restoring the judicial system, the Northwest's leaders regarded even the Somali penal code of 1962 as tainted by the Siad Barre regime. Therefore, they preferred the Indian penal code, which the British imposed as the colonial power.[41]

By April 1993 there were an additional seventy police in Borama with no more than the original 340 in Hargeisa. However, there was now agreement to accept the same criteria for recruiting and training police and establishing a rapid mobile deployment force.[42] In the Northeast, a 700-man police force existed as of April 1993. About 70 percent were former members of the Somali National Police Force. There were police stations in the thirteen districts of the three regions composing the Northeast, as well as 100 Darawishta split between Garoe and Galkayo.[43] The police had four vehicles to cover the entire territory and lacked any functioning communications equipment. Police in Bosasso were paid from port revenues. Police in the rest of the Northeast were unpaid. Written proposals for assistance in training and equipping the police were made to Ambassador Oakley by the SSDF when he visited Bosasso. These proposals were tied to the Addis Ababa accords, reached by all factions in Somalia, to disarm and simultaneously move toward establishing a police force to maintain security.[44]

Up to April 1993, judges had been administering customary or Islamic law in criminal cases. This meant, as a practical matter, that those convicted of serious crimes were either executed or blood money was paid. The SSDF leadership was prepared for UNOSOM to declare which laws would apply and to follow uniform criteria established by UNOSOM for the selection of police and judges.[45]

Another Consultant: Another Report

In April 1993, I was hired to make yet a third study how to rebuild the Somali police and judiciary. My principal recommendations were that UNOSOM should give the utmost priority to establishing

- a functioning 10,000 man Somali police force, based on regions, by October 30, 1993;
- a functioning court system of district and regional courts by the same date, operating under the 1962 Somali penal code and the 1963 Somali code of criminal procedure, and;
- police-court-prison complexes in each district, along the lines of the Australian model. The 10,000 man force would include 2,000 Darawishta for deployment against organized bandit units operating across regional borders.

I further suggested that UNOSOM had to act quickly. It should give priority to those regions where UNOSOM was likely to succeed in a short time. These were Bay, which had benefited from the Australian initiative; the Northeast, which was relatively stable; and Gedo, where there was also relative peace but danger of resumption of "entrepreneurial banditry" due to a long-exposed border.[46]

UNOSOM II: "Our Ticket Out"

At the handoff of the Somali baton by UNITAF to UNOSOM on May 4, 1993, Admiral Howe, the SRSG, declared in the absence of any Somali transitional government that the 1962 Somali penal code would be the law enforced by UNOSOM II. Admiral Howe was empowered by Security Council Resolution 814 (March 26, 1993). He was to assist in "the re-establishment of national and regional institutions and civil administration in the entire country; . . . in the re-establishment of Somali police, as appropriate at the local, regional or national level [and] in the restoration and maintenance of peace, stability and law and order." A detailed plan and budget for the reestablishment of the police, judicial, and prison systems was prepared by Ann Wright, chief of UNOSOM II's Justice Division. The total projected cost for reconstituting the Somali justice system was $45 million for one year. It was deemed cost effective because it would reduce UNOSOM's military presence in Somalia.[47]

Approximately $42 million was budgeted for rebuilding the police force on a nationwide basis. The program contemplated the establishment and financing of a 10,000-man police force for one year by October 1993. It included a Mobile Quick Reaction Force in each region, totaling 2,000 men, to be created "on a priority basis." It called for the renovation of seventy basic police stations throughout the country and provision of "modest" transportation and communications equipment. Operational control of the police was to be under UNOSOM Forces Command sector military commanders until a UNOSOM civilian police (CIVPOL) force of 152 assumed control. Operational control over the police would be relinquished by UNOSOM "as soon as Somali governmental authority is ready to take over responsibility and authority from UNOSOM."[48] The criteria initially established by the Mogadishu Police Committee for recruitment into the ASF were adopted by UNOSOM II. The overall goal was to have an 18,000-person police force in operation by March 1995.

The plan for reconstituting the judiciary was equally ambitious. The court structure was modeled on the 1962 Somali three-tiered judicial system. Initially, there were to be twenty-one district courts, regional courts in seven regions, and two courts of appeal, one in Hargeisa and the other in Mogadishu. A modest program was also proposed for rebuilding the prisons and recruiting former members of the Custodial Corps. By October 31, 1993, two prisons were to be rehabilitated, one in Mogadishu and the other in Hargeisa, employing approximately 500 prison guards. Prisons were to be reestablished in Bosasso and Kismayu by March 31, 1994. The UNOSOM Justice Program and budget were approved in concept by Kofi Annan, head of the UN Department of Peace Keeping Operations (DPKO) at a meeting held in Mogadishu on May 16, 1993.[49] Following that meeting, Admiral Howe and his staff assumed that DPKO in New York was in the process of implementing the staffing and funding for the Justice Program as approved by Annan. However, without informing Admiral Howe, Annan decided to hold off requesting donor countries to contribute police instructors, equipment, and funding. Annan's rationale was that UNOSOM had to wait, pursuant to Security Council Resolution 814, until the Somalis set up the local, district, and regional councils that would have supervisory authority over the police and judiciary.[50]

Annan's decision, which was not required by Resolution 814, was strategically flawed and fatal to the Justice Program. First, Resolution 814 did not specify that UNOSOM should first assist in forming regional councils prior to reconstituting the police and justice systems. If anything, the resolution emphasized the urgency in reestablishing the police. Admiral Howe, as SRSG, was directed "with assistance, as appropriate, from all relevant United Nations entities, offices and specialized agencies [which would include DPKO] . . . to assist in the re-establishment of [the] Somali police." It was the admiral's decision how and when to proceed. The Security Council's intent to give priority to reestablishing the Somali police is evident from paragraph 18, directing the secretary-general to keep the Security Council "fully informed on action taken to implement the present resolution, in particular to submit as soon as possible a report to the Council containing recommendations for establishment of Somali police forces and thereafter to report no later than every ninety days on the progress achieved in accomplishing the objectives set out in the present resolution."[51]

The need to rebuild the police and restore a system of justice was clear. In the words of Admiral Howe, it was "our ticket out of Somalia."[52] For UNOSOM II to succeed, it had to rebuild and leave behind a force capable of preventing Somalia from descending again into the chaos of civil war. The Australians in Bay and the French in Hoddur had already demonstrated broad Somali support from all sectors of the public in their zones for rebuilding the police and reopening the courts. In addition to UNOSOM regional representatives' daily reports, there were enough missions and consultants' reports to confirm the Australian and French experience. Similarly, the same daily reports, studies, and analyses confirmed that in the Northeast, the SSDF represented the people of the region.[53] The Council of Elders, held in Borama, was in favor of UNOSOM II assistance for reestablishing a judicial system. Annan, despite this wealth of information, including field reports by UNOSOM representatives, apparently could not accept that Somalis supported the restoration of the embryonic police and court systems already in place.

One month later, following the attack on the Pakistani troops on June 5 in Mogadishu, the "war with Aideed" began. Not only did this concentrate UNOSOM's attention even further on Mogadishu, it effectively ended any efforts to establish councils in the capitol. However, it was still possible in June to bypass Mogadishu and focus on progress being made in the other regions. Admiral Howe attempted to do just that, apparently still unaware that DPKO was not working to fill the Justice Program's requests for personnel and funding. Howe prepared Annex 1 to the secretary-general's report dated August 17, 1993, updating the facts for the changed security situation in Mogadishu but maintaining all of the elements of the May Justice Program and the $45 million budget.[54] That report stated as fact what Annan knew and refused to act upon: Security had improved in the Northeast, where the SSDF "exert[ed] administrative control over the region"; in the Northwest, where the "successful conclusion of the four-month Borama conference" had resulted in agreement to disarm and demobilize the clan-based militias"; and in the Bay and Gedo regions. After discussing the need for disarmament, the report states: "The restoration of law and order, peace and stability in Somalia requires not only the strengthening of the police forces but also a legal system that provides the basis and framework for police activities. This should include the basic laws that the police will have to enforce, a judicial system to adjudicate the cases of those arrested by the police and a penal system that can detain and punish offenders."

In his annex report, Admiral Howe proposed a 10,000-person police force by December 1994, still in advance of the "currently projected time for completion of the UNOSOM mandate" by March 1995. In addition, he proposed that by March 1995, it would be desirable to reach the pre–civil war level of 18,000 and suggested that this could be accomplished if "two additional training academies are made available through international donor programmes." The annex retained the ambitious timetable for establishing the three-tier court system by October 31, 1993.

In discussing the financial aspects of the justice program, Admiral Howe anticipated that the UNOSOM CIVPOL staff would cost approximately $10.308 million per year and would be "funded under the peace-keeping budget." Unknown to Admiral Howe, DPKO had not even sent out the hiring notices for the UNCIVPOL positions. Pursuant to Security Council Resolution 794, voluntary contributions in cash or equipment by donor nations were to cover the costs of the Justice Program. If there was a shortfall between the amounts pledged and "the costs of the re-establishment of the Somali justice system," Admiral Howe stated that he would "not hesitate to recommend alternative financing arrangements to meet the shortfall."

At the time of the report, in August 1993, the shortfall between the $45 million needed and the amounts in the pipeline was $45 million. DPKO had simply not made any requests to any prospective donor nations for funding, staffing, or equipment for the police, judiciary, or Custodial Corps.

Funding for the Justice System:
Contingency Funds Versus Member Nation Donations

From the beginning of the UN presence in Somalia, member nations were requested to provide donations for rebuilding the police. Security Council Resolution 794, adopted on December 3, 1992, called upon member nations to make "additional [contributions] in cash or in kind" to support the UNOSOM operation in Somalia. The resolution further authorized the secretary-general to establish a fund for this purpose. The Security Council never authorized expenditures of Security Council funds for rebuilding the police. Any effort to restore the justice system was thus dependent upon both the goodwill of member nations and the speed with which they acted.

The use of UNOSOM I and II operational funds for police and judicial functions was haphazard and unbudgeted. UNOSOM could not sustain a program to rebuild the Somali justice system. The UN consistently took the position that it could not fund rebuilding the police and judiciary from the DPKO operating budget because these were inherently humanitarian or developmental activities. Therefore, they had to be funded by donations from member states or by either Humanitarian Affairs or the United Nations Development Program (UNDP).

In January 1993, DPKO agreed that as a onetime payment, the UN Operations Division would pay $2 million to purchase uniforms, food, and some equipment for the police. The rationale was that the police were providing security for the distribution of humanitarian relief by engaging in traffic and crowd control.[55]

As of May 1993, UNOSOM assumed the responsibility of paying salaries to the approximately 3,000 police in Mogadishu and 2,000 in southern Somalia. Some UNOSOM sector commanders provided no assistance to the police. In General Ahmed Jama's view, "There was not solid support by UNOSOM, and the Police were at the mercy of the warlords and factional militias."[56]

The UNOSOM provost marshal handled all requests for service support for the police, such as station construction, uniforms, communication, and transport, as well as police vetting. Equipment and training had been promised by a few member nations, notably Italy and Egypt; other countries that had agreed to contribute did not. One official of the Justice Division noted, "At this point, a lot of talk, but little action."[57]

On October 3, 1993, U.S. Rangers suffered eighteen dead and seventy-eight wounded in a battle as part of the hunt for Aideed.[58] The United States announced that it would withdraw from Somalia by March 31, 1994. Ironically, at this time, belated U.S. support for the Justice Program became a face-saving way out of Somalia. At a December 1993 conference of donor nations in Addis Ababa, the United States agreed to contribute $12 million for police training, $6 million to the judiciary, and about $25 million in U.S. Department of Defense (DOD) excess equipment, mainly vehicles. The DPKO conference chair indicated that DPKO had still not issued hiring notices for the vast majority of the CIVPOL positions. Ten other countries made belated commitments of funds, equipment, training, or personnel at that conference.[59]

These contributions were too little and too late. The Justice Program proposed by UNOSOM in May 1993 and approved in principal by DPKO was dead by December. It was another casualty of the focus on Mogadishu and the war with Aideed. But it was killed at birth by DPKO and the failure to staff CIVPOL and immediately seek funding from member nations. UNOSOM's "ticket out" was never even purchased.

Enter ICITAP: Too Little Too Late

The United States funded an ICITAP program to train the police. ICITAP sent instructors to Somalia in early March 1994. The first phase, budgeted for $7 million, was a 120-day "tactical effort" concentrating on "training and equipping the former SNPF police within Mogadishu, refurbishing police stations and delivering needed equipment to police in Mogadishu and outlying districts."[60] The second phase, to develop the police capability throughout Somalia, never began. ICITAP's program was based on the assumption that "the Mogadishu effort [would] not be initiated until sufficient stability is attained" in Mogadishu and that the entire two-year program required "a stable civil structure during the term of the program."

ICITAP established a provisional police-training center at the UN compound in Mogadishu, which was within Aideed's zone. It is highly likely that only police from Aideed's faction attended the training sessions. A police station commander course was presented in both Baidoa and Mogadishu. A regional training center and vehicle repair depot was developed in Baidoa with assistance from the Indian brigade's engineering troops. ICITAP's report concluded with the statement that the future of the project was "dependent upon Somalia's security situation . . . in the coming months."[61] ICITAP left by mid-June 1994.

Conclusions and Lessons Learned

There were several major mistakes in the overall implementation of Operation Restore Hope by UNITAF and UNOSOM that made the task of restoring the justice system in Somalia more difficult but not impossible. First and foremost was the failure to disarm the factions of all weapons.[62] In early 1993 this would have meant enforcing the disarmament the Somalis had accepted in the March 1993 Addis Ababa accords. One knowledgeable Somali, before the beginning of Operation Restore Hope, urged UNITAF to disarm the factions or not come to Somalia at all.[63]

Second was the initial failure to extend UNITAF's writ nationwide. This mistake in turn led to ignoring those areas of relative stability such as the Northeast, which were ready to cooperate and where immediate progress could have been made on restoring the police and judiciary. The lack of at least some presence in the rest of Somalia caused UNITAF to miss the opportunity of building on stable areas and working around pockets of instability.

The concentration of UNOSOM in and the resulting obsession with Mogadishu caused neglect of other more secure regions, such as Bay and Gedo, within the operation's own limited zone. Instead of isolating Mogadishu because of its special security problems, UNOSOM let events in Mogadishu dictate its agenda for the entire zone. The focus on Mogadishu also led to overemphasis on the two factions in the capitol and misperceptions of those factions' strengths relative to others throughout the rest of Somalia. Despite these mistakes, the Justice Program could have succeeded. The fact that it did not is due to other lessons to be learned from Operation Restore Hope.

In combined operations involving the United Nations, U.S. forces must include adequate civil affairs units from the beginning. The question is not, as some have posed, whether the United States was in Somalia solely to "establish a secure environment for humanitarian relief" or to engage in nation building. The mission was defined by the fact that the United States acted in concert with other nations pursuant to Security Council Resolution 794. The mission was to complete Operation Restore Hope and then transfer authority to UNOSOM. What did we need to do to end the mission?

When the United States is part of an operation that will terminate with a transfer to the UN, it is in U.S. parochial interest to make sure that this occurs successfully. Jump-starting the restoration of the Somali justice system with an adequate civil affairs program would have ensured a smoother transition to UNOSOM II.

There would have been police and judges in place on a regional basis throughout the UNITAF zone of operations, as in the Bay region under the Australian program. The Australian success undercuts the argument that because the U.S. presence was short term, restoring the police and judiciary could not have been accomplished. The Australian and U.S. presences were coterminous from December 1992 to May 1993.

A civil affairs program would also have helped to ensure the success of the UN operation. No one disputes that rebuilding the police and judiciary would have provided stability and encouraged economic activity. These functions should have been carried out by reserve civil affairs units of the U.S. Army attached to UNITAF. Ideally, civil affairs units would have functioned in the Northeast as well, supporting an already well organized but poorly equipped police force. Admittedly, the problems with the Northwest were more difficult due to its declaration of independence. However, there was acceptance of the need for uniform police recruitment criteria and training.

The importance of reserve civil affairs units attached to U.S. forces in combined operations taken pursuant to UN authorization has been proven not only by subsequent events in Haiti but by prior actions in Kuwait. The United States simply ignored what it had learned in Kuwait and eliminated civil affairs from Operation Restore Hope. Perhaps the United States was the victim of its own propaganda that the operation was about humanitarian relief and feeding starving Somali children. Perhaps the civil affairs component was omitted because of obsessive fear of "mission creep" or interservice rivalry between the marines and the army or competition between the active army civil affairs unit and civil affairs reserve units. Whatever the reason in Somalia, in Haiti the United States reverted to the immediate and effective use of civil affairs units. In addition to civil affairs troops, more than 800 police advisers were sent to Haiti. Shortly after the initial landing, the United States began a police recruitment and training program.[64]

Somalia was an aberration between the lessons learned in Kuwait and implemented in Haiti. One of the consequences of this aberration was the failure to have a trained, functioning Somali police force in place in October 1993. Instead, U.S. Rangers were used to perform the essential police function of attempting to capture General Aideed pursuant to a warrant issued for his arrest. The Rangers' casualties and lack of success can, in large part, be traced back to the decision to eliminate reserve civil affairs units from the operation.

There must be either adequate UN funding for restoring a justice system or the donor nations must be committed in advance to supply funding, personnel, and equipment. When the operation began, there were no funds for either equipping or paying police. The efforts to pay police salaries and obtain uniforms and equipment, using UNOSOM I and II operational funds, were hand-to-mouth at best. In May 1993 a tentative program for restoring the Somali justice system was approved with a budget of $45 million. The Security Council had not authorized the use of UN contingency funds for that program and was dependent upon donations by member nations. Without funds or commitments, there simply was no way to implement the justice program in May 1993.

The United States did not make any commitment until December 1993, when the security situation had markedly deteriorated, eighteen U.S. Rangers had lost their lives, and the United States had announced that it intended to withdraw by March 1994. At that point it was probably impossible to obtain significant donations from member nations to restore the justice system. With the announced U.S. departure, there was less interest on the part of other nations to assist. There were real concerns for the safety of foreign police trainers in Mogadishu. As usual, the more secure areas of the country were ignored. Member nations have to either build up a UN contingency fund for such operations or be prepared to commit the necessary funding, equipment, and personnel before the operation begins. The lack of funding and commitments undermined the Justice Program from the beginning, creating a haphazard method of payment of police salaries. There was constant scrounging for basic materials such as paper, files, and typewriters. Ideally, the Justice Program should have been implemented in May when it was proposed. Instead, almost half a year was lost before the United States funded the ICITAP program and other nations made limited commitments.

In the long run, if the United States is going to put together a coalition, initiate an operation pursuant to Security Council resolutions, and then transfer authority to the UN, it must be prepared to allocate the resources necessary to make the operation a success. Haiti is an example where the civil affairs units began the work, civilian police trainers continued it, and the United States withdrew, leaving the UN to finish up. In Haiti, the United States paid for most of the police training with Canadians and French contributing to the effort. There were no questions of UN contingency funds or lack of member nation donations, as in Somalia. Commitments appear to have been obtained in advance from other nations so that assistance in rebuilding the police could begin immediately.[65]

There must be clearly defined, enforceable lines of authority within the UN operation. UNOSOM's effort to restore the Somali justice system never got off the ground because DPKO made a decision not to proceed with the program. The SRSG, who had clear authority to act pursuant to Security Council Resolution 814, was not informed of this decision and, worse, assumed that DPKO was proceeding with the UNCIVPOL hiring and seeking member nation assistance of material, funding, and personnel. The unilateral, secret decision by DPKO effectively derailed the justice program, which the SRSG had determined essential as UNOSOM's "ticket out."

In the future, Security Council resolutions or directives from the secretary-general should make clear that the SRSG has ultimate authority for UN actions in operations. He or she should be answerable only to the secretary-general, and all UN department heads should be responsible to the SRSG for their activities in the country of operation.

In situations of anarchy, the UN should promptly reestablish a rule of law. When Operation Restore Hope began, there was no national government and no legal system. The Australians, by February 1993, were applying the penal code and criminal procedure code in the Bay region. UNITAF did not apply the same laws anywhere in the zone of the operation. UNOSOM declared the penal code to be in effect in early May. Both UNITAF and UNOSOM seemed to be squeamish about imposing a law upon Somalia. For there to be a rule of law in the absence of a government, there is no other choice.

Epilogue

At the time of this writing, three leaders have declared themselves president of all or part of the country. There is a split in United Somali Congress (USC) leadership that has led to bitter fighting in Mogadishu. There is increased clan fighting in the Northwest and banditry elsewhere. A system of justice can be restored only by outside forces or after a political solution is achieved by the Somalis themselves. Both possibilities seem remote. The withdrawal of UNOSOM forces restored the natural balance of power among the factions. Perhaps this is a necessary first step in allowing the Somalis to sort out their own political relationships.

One Somali friend asked what the United States accomplished for the $2 billion it spent in Somalia. Many Somalis were saved from starvation and some lessons were learned. On balance, those were pretty expensive lessons.[66]

Notes

1. See Refugee Policy Group, *Hope Restored? Humanitarian Aid in Somalia, 1990–1994* (Washington, DC: Refugee Policy Group, 1994), p. 33; S. L. Arnold and David T. Stahl, "A Power Projection Army in Operations Other Than War," *Parameters* 13(4), Winter 1993–1994, p. 6.

2. See Martin Ganzglass, "Evaluation of the Jucicial, Legal and Penal Systems of Somalia," USAID report, Mogadishu, April 22, 1993. A similar successful French effort in Hoddur was also ignored.

3. Marine units in Bardera and Mogadishu made gestures toward restoring police, but these isolated activities were not employed in other areas under U.S. control.

4. General Ahmed Jama Musse, interview with the author, Washington, DC, January 17, 1995. At the end of the Siad Barre regime, the Darawishta were not being used, since the government itself was fostering clan warfare.

5. Somali police policy had been never to send a police commander to his home area prior to retirement. See also Refugee Policy Group, *Hope Restored?* p. 10. Some members of the police, despite great risks, decided to remain in Mogadishu to do what they could to restore law and order. Also see Jan Westcott, "The Somali Saga: A Personal Account, 1990–1993," in Refugee Policy Group, *Hope Restored?* pp. 13, 23.

6. General Abdullahi Ali Holif, interview with the author, Washington, DC, January 25, 1996.

7. Ahmed Jama interview, January 17, 1995. Judges' salaries were kept to levels roughly equivalent to that of a police sergeant (2,000 Somali shillings a month).

8. Maj. Michael Kelly (Australian Department of Defense, Directorate of Legal Services), interview with the author, Washington, DC, January 19, 1995.

9. Holif interview, January 25, 1996; and Westcott, "The Somali Saga," p. 37. The SSDF signed an agreement with Sahnoun to disarm in return for assistance to rehabilitate the police, judiciary, and the prisons.

10. Ahmed Jama interview, January 17, 1995.

11. General Jama Mohamed Ghalib, "Statement to the Elders," undated, provided the author by Ghalib in Borama, April 1993.

12. Mohamed Sahnoun, *Somalia: The Missed Opportunities* (Washington, DC: U.S. Institute of Peace, 1994), p. 29; Wescott, "The Somali Saga," pp. 37–38.

13. Holif interview, January 25, 1996. The SSDF made such a request to SRSG Kittani when he visited the Northeast, without response. Ironically, at the October 1992 Geneva donors' conference, Sahnoun lauded the Northeast's stability, saying that this area was deserving of special attention "aiming at a comprehensive recovery programme." Sahnoun, *Somalia*, p. 36.

14. John Drysdale, "Establishment of a Nucleus of Police Forces Throughout Somalia," November 18, 1992. Drysdale states that normal police procedures were largely abandoned during the twenty years of Siad Barre's misrule, implying that the police were no longer suited for reactivation. This implication is belied by the interest of the SSDF and the decision of the Northwest Council of Elders to ask General Jama Mohamed Ghalib to advise them. Drysdale was also disproved when many former police, unarmed and without clan protection, later emerged and attempted to restore order during the UNITAF period.

15. Ann Wright, letter to the author from Bishkek,, January 18, 1995. A U.S. Foreign Service Officer, Wright served as chief of UNOSOM's Justice Division from May to August 1993. Prior to that, she served on the department's Somalia Task Force with liaison responsibilities with the UN and UNITAF on police and justice issues.

16. See Ronald Smith, "Restoring Civil Order in Somalia," *Washington Post*, January 3, 1993.

17. "Guard and Reserve: All Dressed Up, Hard to Find Anywhere to Go," *Army Times*, June 14, 1993, p. 30. Of the 25,640 UNOSOM troops deployed in September 1993, 2,900 were U.S. logistical forces under UN command. An additional 14,000 U.S. troops under U.S. command were serving in or near Somalia in support of UNOSOM II. In retrospect, an additional 200 U.S. Army Reserve Civil Affairs specialists, if available from March to May 1993, might have had a far greater impact on the success of the operation than the combat forces under U.S. command.

18. Ahmed Jama interview, January 17, 1995.

19. The appointments made by Aideed and Ali Mahdi were political, in the longer-term interest of gaining control of the Mogadishu Police Committee.

20. Ahmed Jama Musse, interview with the author, January 25, 1995.

21. Ibid. Somalia previously maintained a uniformed prison custodial corps. Some veteran prison guards resurfaced to man the prisons, but UNITAF was unable to finance salaries, uniforms, or prison rehabilitation.

22. Major Mark Inch, telephone interview with the author, February 13, 1995; and LTC Stephen Spataro, telephone interview with the author, February 24, 1995. These operational expenditures were expected to come from member nations' donations.

23. Frederick Lorenz, "Will the Rule of Law Replace the Law of the Gun?" *Washington State Bar News*, February 1994, p. 18. Other reports indicate 4,000 police total.

24. Inch interview, February 13, 1995. Prior to Inch's arrival, Spataro provided planning for a 5,000-man force to UNOSOM and Colonel Mentmeyer. A UNITAF manual on procedures for obtaining police equipment was not used by UNOSOM II. Following the June 1993 ambush of Pakistani peacekeepers, the UNOSOM logistical director moved to Nairobi, and the supply of police equipment became seriously disrupted.

25. Ahmed Jama interview, January 17, 1995. Police officials and political leaders in the Bay and Northeast regions complained to me that only the two Mogadishu factions were passing on the names they submitted and said the committee ought to be expanded or not have the authority to review names from their areas. See Ganzglass, "Evaluation of the Judicial, Legal and Penal Systems of Somalia."

26. Lorenz, "Will the Rule of Law Replace the Law of the Gun?" p. 19.

27. U.S. Liaison Office (USLO) for UNITAF–UNOSOM II, unclassified cable to the State Department, March 3, 1993.

28. Police Technical Team, "Reconstitution of a National Police of Somalia," report submitted to the UN, February 22, 1993.

29. Boutros Boutros-Ghali, *Report of the Secretary-General on the Situation in Somalia* (S/25354) (New York: March 3, 1993), paras. 46–49.

30. Havecost is a former Peace Corps volunteer, having served as a science teacher at Afgoi in 1964–1966.

Several former Peace Corps volunteers, some with excellent Somali language skills, returned to Somalia during Operation Restore Hope and UNOSOM II. Their participation was due more to their own initiative than an organized effort by the U.S. government to locate and utilize them. Another former Somali volunteer, Charles R. Baquet III, was fortuitously serving as U.S. ambassador to Djibouti and was heavily engaged in meeting with leaders from the Northwest and Northeast.

31. "Evaluation of the ASF Somalia," ICITAP report, March 5–10, 1993, p. 2; Refugee Policy Group, *Hope Restored?* pp. 34–35, refers to the same force as "unarmed and with uncertain loyalties," a comment attributed to Ambassador David Shinn, then in charge of Somali affairs in the Department of State. There is nothing in the ICITAP report or my experience to justify that assertion. It seems particularly inappropriate in view of the fact that former Somali National Police officers were serving, unarmed and without equipment, according to the ICITAP report, "in spite of the inherent dangers and the obvious hardships." See also Keith B. Richburg, "Somali Police Force Back on the Beat," *Washington Post,* May 17, 1993.

32. Lang and Havecost also met with the Jurists Committee in Mogadishu, which urged that the courts and the prisons be included in the rehabilitation plans.

33. The guards, authorized to carry weapons, were guards during the day and part of organized bandit groups at night, sometimes attacking the very compounds they were hired to protect. Kelly interview, January 19, 1995.

34. Kelly interview, January 19, 1995.

35. In addition, members of CID who were primarily plainclothes policemen were authorized to carry pistols. Patrick Vercammen, UNOSOM representative, Baidoa, April 10, 1993.

36. Building up the police throughout the region reduced the security burden of the Australian troops. Ultimately, there were functioning stations in Dinsor, Qansardheere, Buurhakaaba, Ufurow, Berdaale, Awdinle, and Gut Guduud North. Ibid.

37. According to Major Kelly (interview, January 19, 1995), the judges agreed, at a meeting on March 6, 1993, to apply the 1962 Somali penal code. No other UNITAF unit applied

the penal code, and UNOSOM did not adopt it until May 4, 1993, when it assumed responsibility from UNITAF.

38. Kelly interview, January 19, 1995. Kelly favored the reestablishment of the highly mobile Darawishta within the police, under UNOSOM control, to deal with cross-regional banditry.

39. It is possible that the marines have an institutional bias against civil affairs. The marines have no civil affairs units on active duty. Nevertheless, I observed instances of individual marine units assisting the police, in effect adopting police and using them to assist in liaison with Somali communities. For example, in Bardera, the marines obtained uniforms, berets, whistles, and lanyards for the police and engaged in joint patrols. However, there was no effort to rebuild the police station, which in April 1993 was leased to an NGO with the rent reportedly being paid to the elders.

40. PTT report, pp. 20, 26.

41. This was confirmed to me in interviews with General Jama Mohamed Ghalib at the Borama conference in April 1993. Although the penal code was in fact being applied, along with the Sudanese code of criminal procedure, the Borama conference had recently approved the adoption of all laws in effect in British Somaliland prior to July 1, 1960.

42. Ganzglass, "Evaluation of the Judicial, Legal and Penal Systems of Somalia," pp. 22–23, 25–26. General Jama Mohamed Ghalib cautioned me at the Borama conference that the name "Darawishta" would not be acceptable in the Somaliland Republic. Apparently in deference to these sensitivities, the UNOSOM Justice Program proposed the establishment of a "mobile quick reaction force."

43. Ibid., pp. 25–26.

44. Holif interview, January 25, 1996. When Oakley came to Bosasso, General Mohamed Abshir Musa, on behalf of the SSDF, told him that SSDF forces were ready to disarm in accordance with the Addis Ababa accords of March 1993. Heavy weapons were in fact placed in agreed upon containment areas in Galkayo, Gardo, Bosasso, and Garoe. Oakley told Abshir, "We have the power and the will to disarm you." This seems to contradict the ambassador's other public and better known statement: "We can't even disarm New York or Washington; how can we disarm Mogadishu?" In perspective, see Refugee Policy Group, *Hope Restored?* p. 43, quoting Kofi Annan after the U.S. Ranger casualties on October 3, that the United States had become the weakest link in peacekeeping in Somalia.

45. Holif interview, January 25, 1996.

46. Ganzglass, "Evaluation of the Judicial, Legal and Penal Systems of Somalia," pp. 1, 29–31.

47. UNOSOM accepted the UNITAF legal operations program on April 23, 1993. According to Inch (interview, February 13, 1995), some UNOSOM military commanders had never accepted control of the police in their areas. The UNOSOM Justice Program made an exception for the Northwest, accepting the decision of the Borama conference to readopt the Indian penal code and criminal procedure code in effect in British Somaliland prior to independence.

48. *UNOSOM Justice Programs,* n.p., n.d. In the May version of *Justice Programs,* provided the author by Ann Wright, operational control over the police was to be relinquished by UNOSOM "whenever a civilian government structure (national or regional) is ready to assume responsibility/authority from UNOSOM for the forces." The willingness to turn over control to regional governments was deleted and the more ambiguous phrase, "Somali governmental authority," was adopted.

49. This meeting was directed by SRSG Howe and included Elizabeth Lindenmayer, special assistant for Somalia; the undersecretary for peacekeeping operations, Kofi Annan; Howe's staff; and other representatives of UNITAF legal operations, which were winding down.

50. The substance of the meeting was provided the author in the Wright letter, January 18, 1995.

51. UN Security Council Resolution (UNSCR) 814. No such requirement existed with respect to the establishment of regional and district councils.

52. Refugee Policy Group, *Hope Restored?* p. 47.

53. Holif interview, January 25, 1996.

54. Boutros-Ghali, *Report of the Secretary-General on the Situation in Somalia* (S/26317), annex 1.

55. According to Ann Wright, when the UNDP head visited Mogadishu in mid-January 1993 and saw the positive influence of Somali police on the streets, he made a public announcement that UNDP would also provide $2 million for their support. These funds were never forthcoming. The UNDP representative in Mogadishu took the position that although his superior had promised the money, UNDP Mogadishu had never been authorized to disburse the funds.

56. Ahmed Jama interview, January 17, 1995. Police were paid regularly on a two-month schedule from April to September 1993. Inch interview, February 13, 1995.

57. Major Mark Inch, deputy force provost marshal, UNOSOM II Force Command, "Somali Police Program Briefing Notes," November 2, 1993.

58. See Rick Atkinson, "The Raid That Went Wrong," *Washington Post,* January 30, 1994; and "Night of a Thousand Casualties," *Washington Post,* January 3, 1994.

59. As the situation in Mogadishu worsened, the full $12 million was not spent. Many of the vehicles off-loaded in Mogadishu were reclaimed for fear they would be taken from the police and reappear on the nightly news as "technicals."

60. International Criminal Investigative Training Assistance Program (ICITAP), "Somalia Concept Paper," draft, October 29, 1993.

61. ICITAP, *1994 Third Quarterly Report,* n.p., n.d.

62. There was confusion between disarming warlords of "technicals" and artillery and ammunition, and the problem of disarming individual Somalis of their AK-47s. There was the preposterous situation of an open-air arms market in Mogadishu during UNITAF, with armed NGO guards moonlighting as bandits at night, while UNITAF struggled in vain to find money for batons, berets, and whistles for the police.

63. Jane Perlez, "Expectations in Somalia," *New York Times,* December 3, 1992; Raymond Baner, "The Dilemma of Disarmament," *Time,* December 26, 1992.

64. Tod Robinson, "Building a Trusted Police Force in Haiti Challenges US Trainers," *Washington Post,* November 2, 1994.

65. See "Timid Globalism: The US Is Taking a Tentative Approach to Rebuilding Haiti," *Wall Street Journal,* February 23, 1995.

66. Total U.S. government expenditures between April 1992 and July 1994 were $2.2 billion, with $1.5 billion attributable to DOD. See Refugee Policy Group, *Hope Restored?* C–5.

3

International Peacebuilding and the Dynamics of Local and National Reconciliation in Somalia

Ken Menkhaus

> The warlords are now peacelords.
>
> —*Ambassador Lansane Kouyate, acting special representative of the secretary-general to Somalia, June 1994*

When Operation Restore Hope was launched in Somalia in December 1992, the Bush administration took pains to portray the intervention as a "strictly humanitarian" mission, limited in both scope and duration. But all understood that a lasting solution to the crisis in Somalia would have to go beyond the provision of emergency relief and address the daunting tasks of national reconciliation and the resuscitation of governance in Somalia. These challenges of "nation building" in a failed state were left to the UN Operation in Somalia (UNOSOM), which replaced the U.S.-led UNITAF mission in May 1993.

Formally, the mandate for fostering national reconciliation in Somalia was given to UNOSOM in UN Security Council Resolution 814 (1993), which authorized UNOSOM under Chapter VII of the UN Charter "to assist the people of Somalia to promote and advance political reconciliation, through broad participation by all sectors of Somali society, and the reestablishment of national and regional institutions and civil administration in the entire country [and] to create

---

This is a slightly revised version of the author's article that appeared in *International Peacekeeping* 3(1), Spring 1996.

conditions under which Somali civil society may have a role, at every level, in the process of political reconciliation."[1]

This mandate placed UNOSOM at the forefront of most reconciliation work in Somalia, although peacebuilding efforts there were frequently crowded with outside political players. U.S. officials played assertive roles both within and outside UNOSOM, advocating approaches to reconciliation that they felt were most appropriate but that were often contradictory. Also, both before and during the intervention, states with regional or historical interests in Somalia, including Egypt, Italy, Ethiopia, and Eritrea, attempted to broker peace accords among the Somalis. Additionally, various international nongovernmental organizations (NGOs) supported numerous local-level peace initiatives. The Somalis independently sponsored a number of local and national peace conferences reflecting their own political agendas.

Collectively, this cacophony of peacebuilding yielded, from 1991 into early 1995, no fewer than seventeen national-level and twenty local-level reconciliation initiatives, many sponsored by UNOSOM. Some of the regionally based efforts produced lasting peace accords, but none of the national-level peace initiatives, despite considerable international funding and pressure, yielded constructive results. A frustrated UN Security Council, under pressure from the United States, opted to terminate UNOSOM by March 1995, leaving Somalia still divided by dozens of clan and factional conflicts and without a national government.

Conventional analyses of this failure to achieve national reconciliation in Somalia tend to lay the blame on personalities and flawed policies both within the UN and U.S. administrations and within the Somali body politic. Many of these critiques are reviewed further on. This chapter's analysis, however, highlights the structural impediments to reconciliation in the collapsed Somali state. Without embracing the fatalistic notion that the Somali conflict simply wasn't "ripe" for resolution and without excusing either mediocre UN efforts or myopic Somali leadership, I argue that from the outset, the Somali crisis presented domestic protagonists and international peacemakers with unique political dilemmas within a menu of very unpalatable options, all of which posed a high probability of failure. There were, in short, no easy and obvious reconciliation strategies.

The most daunting challenges to peacebuilding in Somalia included the following.

- A crisis of legitimate authority existed in Somalia. The shattered society and collapsed state engendered a shortage of legitimate and authoritative political representatives able to broker and enforce peace accords at the national level.
- In the absence of legitimate authority, Somali political figures perceived internationally sponsored peace conferences as tools for enhancing their status rather than peacemaking opportunities;
- Powerful vested interests in continued instability, conflict, and anarchy undermined reconciliation efforts and threatened "peace constituencies."

• Somali political culture—in which conflict management is an ongoing process of consultations, assemblies, and negotiations rather than a discrete event—was incompatible with internationally sponsored, rigidly structured reconciliation initiatives.
• Traditional conflict management mechanisms and practices proved to be effective only at the local and regional levels.
• The tendency for grassroots approaches to peacebuilding to yield new coalitions at a third party's expense frustrated national reconciliation.
• The UN's twin roles of peace enforcer (a role that calls for *impartiality*) and mediator-facilitator in national reconciliation (a role that demands *neutrality*) were incompatible.
• Efforts aimed at reviving local and regional governments—another UNOSOM mandate—tended to exacerbate rather than reduce communal strife.
• Economic scarcity in war-torn Somalia made conflicts over the shrunken "national pie" more likely.

These structural impediments to peace are not unique to Somalia but are symptomatic of other "complex emergencies" in Rwanda, Bosnia, Afghanistan, Liberia, and elsewhere. In situations of partial or total collapse of the state and of law and order, disintegration of fundamental social norms and patterns of authority, rise of a heavily militarized and predatory economy of plunder, massive population displacement, and communal hostilities stoked by years of atrocities and even genocide, peacebuilders work in nightmarish conditions. Groups and individuals who foster reconciliation in such cases have few road maps to guide them. The Somali experience thus may yield valuable lessons for reconciliation initiatives in other complex emergencies.

A Typology of Reconciliation Efforts in Somalia, 1991–1995

The road from the first, hopeful days of Operation Restore Hope in December 1992 to UNOSOM's harried evacuation from Somalia in March 1995 is littered with the carcasses of failed peace conferences. A number of noteworthy local-level peace efforts bore fruit. Of the rest, some held promise but were undermined by spoilers or overtaken by events; others were fatally flawed and doomed from the start.

These reconciliation efforts had four key features:

1. *The level of the agenda.* National-level initiatives attempted to lay the groundwork for a comprehensive peace and supposedly represented the entire nation. Subnational or local initiatives typically dealt with more narrow conflicts and involved representatives without national aspirations from the affected areas.

2. *The nature of political representation.* Faction-based conferences drew on the fifteen recognized Somali factions for legitimate representatives of the Somali

people; in this type of conference other social leaders were either not present or held observer status. Community-based or grassroots meetings drew on traditional leadership, typically including clan elders, intellectuals, professionals, clerics, businesspeople, women's group leaders, and local NGO leadership. If present, factions played muted roles in these proceedings.

Whereas this dichotomy between factional and grassroots representation is recognized by Somalis and foreigners alike, care must be taken not to reify these social categories. In reality, elders and factional politicians and militia leaders enjoyed complex relationships, at times competing for authority but at other times cooperating. Likewise, individuals often wore more than one hat, alternately assuming roles of factional representative and traditional elder or intellectual.

3. *Sponsorship.* Sponsorship typically provided some or all of the necessary financial support for the meeting, public relations assistance, and logistical support (transportation, communications, accommodation). Additionally, sponsors could at times go beyond the role of facilitator and provide good offices to the parties in conflict or, in rare instances, assume the role of mediator. Sponsorship was important not only in practical terms; it played a vital role in lending or depriving meetings of national and international legitimacy. Most of the conferences under review were sponsored by UNOSOM; several were hosted by regional states or by a combination of local interests and international NGOs.

4. *Format of the meetings.* Most of the initiatives assessed here were formal conferences, marked by an admixture of traditional Somali and international diplomatic procedures, with formal agendas and high-profile proceedings and personalities. These were usually held in hotels and often in regional capitals outside Somalia. Traditional assemblies (*shir*), by contrast, featured customary Somali negotiating procedures, usually featured elders as negotiators, and were held near the conflicts, ensuring close contact with the affected constituencies. Other types of peacebuilding formats—consultations, "two-track" diplomacy, and peace workshops—were sponsored by international NGOs or diplomatic delegations from interested states and concentrated on provision of "good offices," informal problem-solving approaches, training in conflict management, or the strengthening and encouragement of peace constituencies in zones of conflict. In practice, eight types of peace initiatives were most prevalent in Somalia:

National-level, factionally based, UNOSOM-sponsored peace conferences. These were widely publicized and ultimately were the least successful reconciliation efforts. The Addis Ababa Conference on National Reconciliation of March 1993 was held under the glare of international media attention. UNOSOM brought together delegates representing the fifteen recognized factions[2] to negotiate an accord that committed them to the cessation of hostilities, complete and rapid disarmament of militias, peaceful restoration of stolen property, and the establishment of a process by which a transitional national council (TNC) would be established to serve as the repository of Somali sovereignty until national elections were held.

Problems abounded even before the conference began. In the January 1993 preparatory meeting in Addis Ababa, General Aideed insisted that only delegations that had played active military roles in deposing Siad Barre's regime could participate, a criterion that ensured that only a handful of militia leaders—including Aideed—would have control of the proceedings. Somali representation selected by UNOSOM was sharply disputed from all quarters. Many Somalis and international observers criticized the UN for selecting "warlords" as the centerpiece of reconciliation, arguing instead that the peace process could be achieved only through community-based delegations.[3] UNOSOM's mandate called specifically for a process of reconciliation "through broad participation by all sectors of Somali society." Ultimately, several hundred Somali community leaders attended as observers.[4] This made neither community leaders nor factions happy but served to persuade the factions to agree to a transitional national council that was formed via a bottom-up approach: District councils were created "through election or through consensus-based selection in accordance with Somali traditions."[5] However, the factions subsequently reversed this provision in a secret meeting, agreeing on an "appendix" that arrogated to the factions the right to select regional council representatives.[6] This action did not bode well for either the accountability or the legitimacy of the factions to the Somali people. Following the Addis Ababa meeting, it immediately became apparent that the factions had no intention of abiding by the accords signed in Addis Ababa.[7]

In the aftermath of the armed conflict with the Somali National Alliance (SNA) militia in late 1993 and 1994, UNOSOM pursued national reconciliation efforts with great urgency as its mission became recognized as a UN disaster. One UN initiative followed another: the "Addis informals," political talks on the heels of the Fourth Humanitarian Conference (December 1993); the "Nairobi Informals," originally a meeting on the Kismayu conflict that evolved into a meeting of national reconciliation (March 1994); preparatory meetings for a national reconciliation conference in Mogadishu, often-postponed and eventually forgotten (April–September 1994); and a series of efforts to transform a proposed "all-Hawiye" conference into a national reconciliation deal between Aideed and Ali Mahdi (July–September 1994). All were nonstarters. By mid-1994, UNOSOM efforts were actually focused on brokering an arrangement in which a coalition, centered around General Aideed, would actually declare a transitional national authority *in the absence of national reconciliation*. Had such an incautious move been made, it would have almost certainly triggered armed reactions by clans left out of those discussions.

The benefits of UNOSOM efforts accrued only to the factions; they found the meetings profitable, often claiming (and receiving) hundreds of thousands of UN dollars in "conference expenses." With so much money to be made from staging peace conferences, peacebuilding soon degenerated into a cynical cottage industry dominated by entrepreneurial Somali politicians. Factional leaders were quick to appreciate, and exploit, the fact that UNOSOM needed Somali national reconciliation far more than they did. A discouraged U.S. official complained in

September 1994, after yet another pledge by Somali factions to convene a national reconciliation conference, that "financing a conference in Somalia is shorthand for giving cash to people. It's an obscene expenditure of money for no results."[8] But a senior UN official justified the expenses: "You have to follow every avenue to achieve peace. If it means spending half or a quarter of the $2.5 million a day [UNOSOM's daily operating costs] on peace talks, you're ahead of the game."[9]

National-level, factionally based, state-sponsored peace initiatives.   States in the Horn of Africa made efforts to broker national peace talks among the Somalis. In May and July 1991, two conferences in Djibouti (known now as Djibouti I and Djibouti II) were sponsored by the Hassan Gouled government and backed by Egypt, Italy, and Saudi Arabia. They fell victim to the same disputes over representation and leadership that were later to plague the UN. General Aideed derided the Djibouti process as little more than a "Manifesto Group" meeting and rejected Ali Mahdi's interpretation of the Djibouti II accord as acknowledgment of his claim to the position of interim president. As a result, the Djibouti II conference, which could have set the stage for the re-creation of a state authority and spared the country two years of war and famine, was stillborn.[10]

Throughout the UNOSOM operation, separate U.S. and Italian diplomatic initiatives sought to broker a peace between the SNA and the Group of 12 (G-12), with only cosmetic results. Ambassador Robert Oakley wrested a declaration of peace (the "seven-point agreement") between Ali Mahdi and Aideed in the first weeks of Operation Restore Hope. Their public embrace, however, did little to alter political realities in Mogadishu.[11]

Ethiopia and Eritrea attempted to broker a peace among the Somalis in the aftermath of the cease-fire between UNOSOM and the SNA in fall and winter 1993. Ethiopia was especially active in what came to be known as the Addis Informals of December 1993, a set of political consultations by the Somali factions in rump meetings following a UNOSOM-sponsored humanitarian conference. Ethiopia was encouraged to assume the lead role in mediating the Somali dispute by the United States, which was espousing a policy of "African solutions to African problems" as a fig leaf to cover its speedy withdrawal from the Somali quagmire. But Ethiopian president Meles Zenawi and his aides quickly took pro-Aideed positions, which poisoned their relations with the Group of 12 and undermined hopes that Ethiopia might play a constructive and neutral role as mediator of the Somali dispute.

The Ethiopian misstep followed a frustrating pattern for states that hoped to play a role in facilitating or mediating a Somali reconciliation; in each instance, real or perceived political preferences on the part of these outside states rendered them suspect in the eyes of some or all of the Somali players. In some cases their interests were overt—Egypt, for instance, was known to be sympathetic to Ali Mahdi and the G-12 and went so far as to sponsor a G-12 peace conference in Cairo in January 1994. Though a number of states continue to offer to facilitate Somali reconciliation—Ethiopia, for instance, sent a peace delegation throughout

Somalia in March 1995—state-sponsored reconciliation efforts have yet to yield fruitful results.

National-level, factionally based, locally sponsored peace conferences. Most of the Somali-sponsored peace initiatives between 1991 and 1995 were subnational in scope, typically cease-fire agreements between two rival clans or factions. At least one major local effort produced an agreement with national implications. In fall 1994, General Aideed and the SNA promised a disillusioned international community that it would produce national reconciliation and a new government in Somalia. To that end, he hosted a "conference of national reconciliation" in Mogadishu. In reality, the meeting forged only an accord within the narrow constituencies of the Somali National Alliance to declare unilaterally an interim national government. Had the conference been successful, it would undoubtedly have promoted less, rather than more, national reconciliation, as sizable Somali communities left out of the negotiations would have immediately reacted against the SNA. As it happened, however, Aideed miscalculated his ability to forge an agreement within his own alliance over the distribution of positions in the proposed government. After several weeks of discord and frustration, his reconciliation meeting broke up empty handed.

Revealingly, the effort left Aideed far weaker politically than when he started. His inability to deliver agreement even within his own alliance exposed the sharp limits on his authority within the SNA and encouraged key political figures within his faction and clan to attempt to wrest control of the political process away from him and pursue their own political initiatives (mainly joint control of the seaport and airport) with Abgal leadership in the so-called Mogadishu Peace Committee. Aideed discovered what the UN had already learned—that the cost of failure in high-profile national reconciliation initiatives is substantial.

National-level, community-based, NGO-sponsored consultations and workshops. Most NGO-sponsored peace advocacy work in Somalia has focused on local conflicts rather than national reconciliation. However, some of the peacebuilding workshops and consultative conferences convened by the Swedish Life and Peace Institute (LPI) and the Mennonite Central Committee have attempted to promote peacebuilding networks nationally. The most publicized effort of this kind was the LPI-sponsored Seychelles consultations of October 1992, which brought together leaders from Somali civil society—heads of local NGOs and women's groups, intellectuals, and professionals—to discuss with UN representatives the most appropriate approach to reconciliation in Somalia. The meeting was intended to provide the UN with advice from respected Somali civic leaders but also was designed to promote informal dialogue across clan and factional lines and underscore international support to the Somali "peace constituency." Notably, key militia leaders such as General Aideed sharply rejected the conference and threatened clan members who wished to attend.

In principle, informal peace advocacy meetings such as this one (sometimes termed "two-track diplomacy") should have catalyzed social pressure on the faction and militia leaders to commit to a peace process. However, Somali peace constituencies never found their collective voice to mobilize their communities against recalcitrant militia and faction leaders. This was due in part to risk-averse behavior—once it was clear that UNITAF forces had no intention of disarming militias, Somali community leaders understood that they placed themselves at great risk for speaking out against the militias. But it is also worth emphasizing that this type of peacebuilding work is long term in nature; the strengthening of grassroots peace constituencies takes time and is intended to reap benefits well into the future. It is thus far too early to tell if the networks and training programs developed by these local and international peace advocates will bear fruit.

Subnational, community-based, NGO- and locally sponsored peace conferences. In 1991, prior to the international intervention in southern Somalia, a series of traditional assemblies between clan elders in the Northwest (or Somaliland) was held to resolve a number of simmering clan conflicts. The first meetings were highly localized; gradually, the assemblies expanded to include regional-level interclan reconciliation. This process culminated in the Borama "national" conference from February to May 1993, where elders from all the clans in the northwestern region agreed to a national peace charter for secessionist Somaliland. Later that year, another clan-based conflict was resolved in the Northwest, in the Sanaag conference. It too involved a series of grassroots assemblies over the course of a year, which culminated in a regional peace accord. Notably, these peace conferences received only modest external support, mostly from international development or peace advocacy NGOs.

These two traditional peace processes in the Northwest clearly constituted the most successful peace processes in Somalia, achieving regionwide reconciliation and producing broadly accepted local administration in Somaliland.[12] This success attracted considerable attention from international observers who wondered why this indigenous peace process appeared to yield far more positive results than the southern peace conferences sponsored by UNOSOM.[13] Various observers conclude that peacebuilding in Somalia must be rooted in the customary conflict-management practices of traditional elders, who have long played the lead role in reconciliation and negotiation, a natural bottom-up approach. UNOSOM's formal, rushed, faction-centered peace conferences in luxury hotels abroad were seen as the antithesis of appropriate peacebuilding in Somalia.

Lessons learned from the Northwest were probably not fully exportable to the much more troubled and disrupted southern Somalia. There, traditional elders faced heavily militarized gangs of youth answering to no one, militia leaders who rejected their authority, and whole zones of territory occupied by new clans. In the South, traditional mechanisms of conflict management were by no means extinct; but they operated in an environment transformed by violence, and their effectiveness was therefore limited.

The most dramatic illustration of this point occurred in the ill-fated "Waamo" peace initiative in Kismayu in February 1994. There, a group of leading elders of the Harti and Absame clans, supported by moderate intellectuals, began a series of meetings to reach a full peace between them in defiance of the militia leaders of their respective clans. On the eve of a planned peace declaration, a militia leader from the Absame clan ordered his "technicals" (battle vehicles with mounted guns) into the city to provoke a conflict. He succeeded, and in the armed hostilities that followed, the Absame clan was completely driven out of the city, the two communities polarized, and the moderates among the elders and intellectuals discredited within their own clans. It proved easy for spoilers within the militias to undermine a traditional peace assembly—and the authority of the elders—when they concluded that such an assembly threatened their own power base.

Subnational, community-based, UNOSOM-sponsored peace conferences. By late May 1993, UNOSOM officials concluded that national reconciliation in Somalia could be secured only if a number of dangerous regional conflicts were defused before they exploded and jeopardized national reconciliation. There were several major fault lines where significant clan and factional interests collided— Mogadishu (intra-Hawiye), Galkayo region (Habr Gedr–Mijerteen), the Lower Shabelle region (Habr Gedr–Hawadle–Biimaal), and the towns of Bardera (Marehan–Ranhanweyn), and Kismayu (Harti–Absame). At the same time, UN and U.S. officials increasingly looked to clan elders and other notables to promote broader reconciliation. From late May 1993 through February 1994, UNOSOM sponsored a number of local-level, community-based reconciliation conferences—including peace conferences on "Jubbaland" (Harti–Absame–Marehan, June-August 1993), Afmadow (Mohamed Zubeir–Bartirre, October 1993), Hirab (Habr Gedr–Abgal, January 1994) and Bardera (Marehan–Ranhanweyn–Aulihan, December–March 1994). These initiatives did not exclude continued dialogue with the factions; indeed, in certain negotiations, factional participation was significant. Several, including the Afmadow accord and the Bardera reconciliation conference, yielded durable and relatively satisfactory peace agreements.

One of the most politically important of these peace efforts was the Jubbaland peace accord. It was the first attempt by UNOSOM to resolve a regional conflict and the first to embrace clan elders rather than faction leaders as the centerpiece of peacebuilding. It also attempted to resolve the single most volatile regional conflict in the country—namely, ongoing armed conflict over control of the Lower Jubba valley and the prized port city of Kismayu.

The conflict had two distinct levels. On the one hand, it was based on a deep-seated clan dispute over regional hegemony between the more urban Harti, who historically dominated the city of Kismayu and its immediate hinterland, and the Ogadeni, a large clan dominating the pastoral range throughout the trans-Jubba region and northeastern Kenya. The actual hostilities were being played out between two faction-based militias, the Somali Patriotic Movement (SPM; led by General Morgan, drawing on Harti and Marehan support) and the Somali

Patriotic Movement–Somali National Alliance (SPM-SNA; led by Col. Omar Jess, drawing on Ogadeni support). Significantly, nearly all of the top militia and political figures in both factions were outsiders to the region.

UNOSOM's decision to work with a combination of clan elders, politicians, and intellectuals from the two clans rather than with the two factions was made by default, not by design. On the SPM-SNA side, Colonel Jess rejected the proposal for a conference and tried to prevent "his" Ogadeni elders from participating; in a very significant move, the Ogadeni elders openly broke with Jess and the SPM-SNA at considerable personal risk in order to proceed with peace talks they deemed to be in the long-term interest of the clan.[14] UNOSOM had little to do with this internal Ogadeni political struggle. On the SPM side, UNOSOM had no choice but to insist that General Morgan not participate directly in the talks; he had already been banned by UNOSOM from the vicinity of Kismayu. His pariah status in Somali politics, moreover, forced UNOSOM to keep him at arm's length. In reality, however, Morgan's SPM faction was able to exert considerable indirect influence on the peace conference.

The Jubbaland accord was reached in August 1993 after over two months of meetings and a full-scale communal conference attended by 154 delegates and 30 observers. Procedurally, the conference was far superior to anything UNOSOM had sponsored in the past. For one thing, it was held in Kismayu, allowing delegates to meet daily with their constituencies. This simple but critical provision was pivotal in legitimizing the proceedings in the eyes of the community, enabling local people to play the nightly role of "ratifier" to the negotiating teams. UNOSOM also provided elders with occasional helicopter transport to consult with key groups and leaders in the hinterland. The conference reflected a creative hybrid of the best of formal, structured proceedings and traditional Somali assemblies. UNOSOM officials in Kismayu had the conference break up each morning into four separate functional committees to hammer out details of specific provisions but meet each afternoon in open plenary session. As a result, intellectuals and politicians negotiated specifics in committee, but elders controlled the overall direction of the negotiations in the plenary sessions. Because the conference was kept simple and low budget, there was little financial pressure on UNOSOM to press for a rapid conclusion; thus the zone director in Kismayu allowed the proceedings to continue for as long as was necessary (over two months), giving the delegates the necessary time to reach an accord.[15] Finally, the formal peace talks were accompanied by a number of informal, social meetings designed to bring the communities directly back in communication again. Elders held "peace feasts" with one another, and women's groups and intellectuals crossed conflict boundaries to meet and reconcile. This two-track diplomacy was occasionally facilitated by UNOSOM but was always initiated by the communities themselves and helped reestablish old affiliations between clans and place social pressure on political elements that distrusted the peace process.

Substantively, the Jubbaland accord had mixed results. It reopened Kismayu City to the displaced Ogadeni and temporarily reduced tensions between the two clans. But it was never fully implemented, and eventually violent conflict exploded between the two clans in February 1994 (described previously). It can be seen now that neither militia intended to abide by the accord, and the elders were unable to force either to adhere to its provisions. On the Ogadeni side, the Jess militia, which had rejected the conference outright, prevented the reopening of the Jubba valley. As for Morgan, he made no move to demobilize his forces and blocked UNOSOM efforts to integrate the local police force with Ogadenis. These issues became festering grievances on both sides and ultimately undermined a promising accord.[16]

The Jubbaland accord had other shortcomings. For one thing, minority clans in the Kismayu area felt inadequately represented and protested at UNOSOM's seeming legitimization of Harti, Absame, and Marehan domination. The Ranhanweyn were especially aggrieved over the unfortunate choice of the word "Jubbaland" by the conference delegates, which suggested that the accord's jurisdiction reached into Ranhanweyn lands in the Middle Jubba and Gedo regions. In addition, the accord was seen by the entire Hawiye clan as the germ of a pan-Darod alliance that would develop at their expense. Thus what appeared to UNOSOM to be a positive building block for national reconciliation was perceived by a key Somali clan as a hostile new coalition formed with UN assistance.[17]

The Hawiye leadership also rejected the composition of the Jubbaland conference, contending that the Hawiye have an important demographic presence in the area and therefore are central players in any peace treaty reached on Kismayu. Indeed, Hawiye in both Aideed and Ali Mahdi camps argued forcefully that the Hawiye are the majority clan in the Lower Jubba. This claim, although exaggerated (there are only pockets of Gaaljaal and Sheekal indigenous to the Kismayu region), is firmly believed by most Hawiye in Mogadishu. The enormous disparities in each Somali clan's perceptions of its relative demographic and political weight in the country make compromise in peace accords difficult.

Subnational, factionally based, locally sponsored peace conferences. In May 1993, General Aideed proposed that UNOSOM sponsor a regional peace conference on Mudug, ostensibly to put an end to conflict between the Habr Gedr and the Mijerteen clans in Galkayo. Initially UNOSOM was enthusiastic; however, it soon discerned that Aideed planned to use the proposed Mudug conference to drive a wedge between the Somali Salvation Democratic Front (SSDF) (Mijerteen) leadership of Gen. Abshir Musa (chair of the SSDF and a principal political rival of Aideed's) and Col. Abdullahi Yusuf (head of the SSDF militia).[18] Aideed's machinations were his business, but not something that UNOSOM could or would underwrite.[19] When Aideed declared that he alone would serve as chair, UNOSOM balked and withdrew its support. An angry Aideed accused the UN of "interference in Somali internal affairs" and convened the Mudug conference on his own.[20] The "Mudug accord" was signed on June 4, one day before SNA ambushed Pakistani UNOSOM forces in Mogadishu. It established a tentative understanding between Col. Abdullahi Yusuf and Aideed that fell short of an open alliance but that strengthened the position of both leaders.

More important, the accord produced a lasting cease-fire between the Habr Gedr and Mijerteen in Galkayo. This beneficial effect was due less to the goodwill of the two militia leaders than to local businessmen and pastoralists who, according to some reports, were desperate to revive commercial activities in Galkayo and end a conflict that had disrupted trade.[21] Despite the positive impact of the Mudug accord on the Galkayo area, the accord also increased intra-Mijerteen tensions considerably, thus displacing the conflict rather than resolving it. It has been due to considerable effort on the part of Mijerteen elders that the dispute between Col. Abdullahi Yusuf and Gen. Abshir Musa, which the Mudug accord exacerbated, has not broken out into armed conflict.

Subnational, factionally based, UNOSOM-sponsored peace conferences.   By 1994, UNOSOM's quest for reconciliation was growing desperate. During December 1993 Ambassador Lansana Kouyate assumed more direct control over UNOSOM's diplomatic course of action,[22] and reconciliation strategy narrowed with the aim of brokering a deal between the most powerful militias in the country. Over time, this strategy more or less explicitly embraced the notion that any reconciliation process would place Aideed and the SNA at the center of an interim government.

It was with this streamlined vision of Somali politics that UNOSOM approached the renewed outbreak of hostilities between the Absame and Harti clans in Kismayu in February 1994. To resolve the conflict, UNOSOM sought to secure a direct accord between General Morgan, who was the most powerful militia figure in Kismayu, and General Aideed's SNA. UNOSOM leadership hoped that such an accord would help seal a broad alliance between three of the nation's most visible militia leaders—Morgan in the South, Aideed in Mogadishu and the central region, and Abdullahi Yusuf in central-northeast Somalia.

This attempt to parlay a regional clan conflict into a national accord reflected a disturbing unfamiliarity with the Kismayu conflict. It eventually led to the signing of yet another peace declaration by the Somali factions in Nairobi in May 1994, prompting UN Special Representative Kouyate to make the ill-fated proclamation, "The warlords are now peacelords." That accord, pledging its signatories to convene a full national reconciliation conference, was never fulfilled. The regional peace conference it generated in Kismayu between Morgan's SPM and the SNA (represented by Osman 'Ato) completely excluded the main party to the Kismayu conflict, the Absame clan, which refused to recognize either the legitimacy of Habr Gedr representation or the subordinate position UNOSOM offered it in the proceedings. Finally, the Kismayu Peace Conference was entirely irrelevant to the fundamental conflict in the region; inasmuch as it was proclaimed as a solution to the Kismayu conflict, it came dangerously close to false advertising. Relations between the SNA and Morgan, meanwhile, never improved significantly. By summer 1994, any opportunity to publicize a successful "peace accord" in Somalia was seized upon by the UN to justify renewal of its troubled mandate.

The question that this long and diverse list of peace conferences immediately raises is whether there was any effort made to integrate them into a coherent reconciliation strategy or whether they were merely ad hoc and uncoordinated initiatives. UNOSOM attempted to portray its simultaneous pursuit of regional and national accords, and its work with both faction leaders and civil leaders, as coherent two-track diplomacy. The United States, for its part, described its policy as "constructive ambiguity."[23] In truth, very little thought was given to how these different peace initiatives related to one another. The plethora of peace conferences held through 1993 and 1994 reflected reactive, crisis-driven, and ad hoc policymaking.

Conventional Critiques of the Reconciliation Process in Somalia

From the outset of Operation Restore Hope, there was no shortage of criticism—both local and international—of the reconciliation processes attempted in Somalia. Over the course of 1993, as UN failures mounted, these critiques grew louder and more caustic. Collectively, however, they often contradicted rather than reinforced one another. The most prevalent of these critiques include the following:

The UN lacked an adequate understanding of the nature of Somali political culture and hence worked against rather than with indigenous practices of conflict management. This criticism was voiced especially by academic area specialists on Somalia.[24] Specifically, they argued that the UN tended to look to factions to promote reconciliation, ignoring the fact that clan elders customarily play a critical role in reconciling conflicts. The UN seemed unable to grasp that the traditional Somali reconciliation process can take a long time—weeks and even months—and is more of an ongoing process of consultations than a discrete event. Instead, the UN insisted on very hasty peace conferences, more concerned with its own timetables in New York than with Somali political realities.

The only exception to this critique was the diplomatic work done in 1992 by the first UNOSOM special representative, Ambassador Mohamed Sahnoun, prior to the intervention. He was widely credited by international observers and Somalis alike for possessing a deep understanding of the Somali situation and for pursuing a broad-based, patient diplomatic effort to encourage intrafactional dialogue and protect international relief efforts from banditry during the worst part of the famine in mid-1992. His public criticism of UN inaction in Somalia led to his forced resignation in October 1992 and elevated his status among critics of the UN still further.[25] But whereas Sahnoun's respect for Somali political culture is incontestable, it is less clear that a diplomatic strategy that worked with rather than against lengthy Somali practices of negotiation and consultation was appropriate in the context of the urgent humanitarian crisis of 1992, when thousands of famine victims were dying each week.

The focus on militia leaders rather than legitimate community leaders in the search for peace was misguided. Many international and Somali observers, led by peace activists and academic specialists, forcefully argued for centering a peace process on a bottom-up approach, citing the success of the grassroots, traditional assemblies in Somaliland in forging durable peace accords there.[26] "Warlords" whose power base rested on fear, conflict, and an economy of plunder had no interest in peace, these critics reasoned, and so could hardly be relied upon as architects of national reconciliation. UNOSOM's initial decision to place factions at the centerpiece of national reconciliation in the Addis Ababa talks was met with widespread criticism and disappointment.[27] These observers also voiced repeated concern that UNOSOM's highly centralized operation focused far too much importance on Mogadishu rather than the countryside and poured millions of dollars into the coffers of the urban factions, rendering them stronger than before the intervention.[28]

Two distinct strands of thought emerged from this perspective. One concluded that the "warlords," having demonstrated a clear intent to disrupt reconciliation, should be explicitly marginalized; some human rights advocates even called for their arrest for crimes against humanity, as the primary culprits in provoking a famine that killed over 200,000 people. As with other peace operations, however, calls for the marginalization or arrest of militia leaders for war crimes carried a real risk of provoking armed confrontation and polarizing rather than reconciling parties to the conflict and so was not taken up by the UN.

Others called only for UNOSOM to "create a level political playing field" so that militia leaders, like other political aspirants, had to demonstrate possession of a bona fide constituency in order to participate in Somali political life. This, in fact, was what U.S. and UN officials attempted to do in the aftermath of the Addis Ababa conference in March 1993 in an effort to correct what was seen as a pro-Aideed policy tilt on the part of Robert Oakley. But the policy faced two problems. First, it was perceived as an anti-Aideed maneuver that raised tensions with the SNA. Second, officials were well aware that a truly level political playing field would likely work against the interests of several militia leaders, all of whom could be expected to violently disrupt the mission as soon as they discerned that it was eroding their power base.

UN attempts to marginalize militia leaders, particularly Aideed, were politically naive and explosive, violated the UN's stated neutrality, led to the armed confrontation in June 1993, and set back reconciliation efforts. UNOSOM also felt the heat of critics who charged that its efforts to foster grass-roots representation, especially through the nascent district councils formed in the countryside throughout 1993, were to blame for inflaming tensions with militia leaders.[29] These critics alleged that efforts to cultivate grassroots representation in Somalia represented the worst sort of nation-building naïveté and ignored the cold political reality that those who possessed the guns in Somalia possessed political preeminence. Some mistakenly argued that Somalia had no tradition of representative democracy and accused UNOSOM of attempting to impose Western notions on the Somalis.[30] Reconciliation, these critics insisted, had to focus on coaxing the armed militias into an accord, not ignoring them.

In addition, some observers of Somali affairs argued that clan loyalty to "warlords" like Aideed and Morgan was far stronger than internal divisions between civil and militia leadership. Thus, efforts to arrest or marginalize warlords failed to account for the deep-rooted notion of collective responsibility in Somali political culture and were doomed to fail. Actions taken against a clan's militia leader were seen by Somalis not as justice done to an errant individual but as a hostile action against the entire clan. This point is noteworthy—corporate responsibility is indeed enshrined in Somali customary law and is the basis for payments of blood compensation, or *diya*, in Somalia. The extent to which members of the Habr Gedr clan rallied around General Aideed during the armed conflict with UNOSOM in summer 1993 took UN officials by surprise and can be in part attributed to the dynamic of corporate responsibility in Somalia. Yet, like other elements of political culture, this is a complex phenomenon, and there were many instances of clansmen turning against militiamen, who in their view dragged them into unwanted conflicts.

UNOSOM's vacillation between a grassroots approach and the faction-based accords undermined the reconciliation effort.   Analysts Terrence Lyons and Ahmed Samatar recently proposed this nuanced critique of UNOSOM's reconciliation initiatives. In its attempts to identify which social forces it could work with toward national reconciliation, UNOSOM faced unavoidable choices; it could work with civil society leadership (a bottom-up approach) or factional and militia leaders (a top-down approach), but not both. A clear and firm choice of either of these courses of action, suggest Samatar and Lyons, might have delivered peace. But UNOSOM's equivocation between the two was a recipe for confusion, conflict, and stalemate.[31]

The entire effort to enforce peace on Somalia was inappropriate and doomed to fail. There were several quite different variations on this theme. One view, a conservative "realist" perspective on conflict and war, contended that the imposition of a peace process on belligerents who had chosen against seeking a negotiated settlement was a dangerous illusion. Richard Betts argued that UN peace operations assume "that outsiders' good offices can pull the scales from the eyes of fighting factions, make them realize that resorting to violence was a blunder, and substitute peaceful negotiation for force. But wars," he asserts, "are rarely accidents." [32]

Other commentators drew on often sweeping generalizations about the bellicose nature of the Somali people to make essentially the same claim: There was nothing the international community could do to assist a nation determined to commit "national suicide." U.S. Ambassador to Kenya Smith Hempstone was an outspoken advocate of this view, describing the Somalis in a widely publicized cable to Washington as "natural born guerrilla fighters." A related view, quite popular among international diplomats in Somalia, held that the Somali conflict was simply not ripe for resolution—the Somalis, it was said, just hadn't grown adequately weary of war yet and perhaps needed a decade or two, like the fighters in Angola and Mozambique, before they were ready to sit at the negotiating table in good faith.

Some leftist and pacifist groups shared Betts's criticism of the use of the military to impose a peace on Somalia but arrived at the same conclusion via quite different logic. Rakiya Omaar and Alex de Waal were vocal critics, espousing the view that a large-scale military intervention would exacerbate rather than facilitate reconciliation.[33] This set of critics often voiced support for the patient, consensus-oriented diplomatic efforts of the preintervention UNOSOM representative, Ambassador Mohamed Sahnoun, as an alternative to military intervention and as the only viable international role to promote Somali reconciliation.

Structural Impediments to Reconciliation

Despite the policy errors, misdirected approaches, and uninspired leadership outlined previously, reconciliation initiatives in Somalia ultimately foundered on the shoals of much greater obstacles.

First, in the absence of either a Somali state authority or clearly recognizable social and political leadership, reconciliation efforts were chronically weakened by disputes over legitimate and effective authority. Who had the right to represent whom in Somali peace talks? With few exceptions (notably, the traditional assemblies in northwestern Somalia), nearly every national and regional peace initiative faced this question. In the context of a collapsed state, and the tremendous social disruption born of protracted banditry, warfare, and displacement in southern Somalia, it was never apparent to Somali and foreigner alike who possessed the legitimacy to represent Somalis at the negotiating table and who possessed the authority to enforce an accord. This seemingly irreconcilable issue, which caused so much political turmoil within Somali politics, was central to nearly every failed peace conference.

This problem spilled over into the clan composition of conferences as well. In many respects, the preparatory committee work to determine the numbers of delegates per clan, and which clans were to be involved and which were not, was more important to Somalis than the actual outcome of the conference, since that preliminary work established the most critical issue—the relative importance of clans to one another. This might not have been so problematic had the Somali clans shared a rough agreement about their relative size, power, and territorial rights; but they did not. Each clan possesses a vastly inflated view of its domain and numbers and hence its rightful share of political representation.

Representation at regional peace conferences became the lightning rod for these disputes, as it forced Somalis to agree on fixed numbers of representatives per clan and in the process made them quantify their relative importance. Thus, although the *outcome* of these accords—reconciliation—was usually a positive-sum game for the participants, the *process* of pursuing reconciliation often degenerated into zero-sum politics. Astonishingly, top UNOSOM officials seemed unable to appreciate this fact even after long and bitter experience. The last UN special representative, Ambassador Victor Gbeho, dismissed it as a mere bureaucratic snag. "What is dividing them is participation criteria, which is a procedural problem . . . which in most conferences is dealt with by a credentials committee," he opined in November 1994, referring to the eight-month impasse in convening national reconciliation talks.[34] It was remarks like this that led so many to conclude that UNOSOM officials simply didn't understand Somalia.

Second, in the context of disputed leadership, Somali political figures frequently viewed peace conferences more as vehicles for enhancing their own status within their clans than for advancing the cause of peace. Whereas the international community viewed the Somali conflict as primarily interfactional and interclan, in reality nearly all of the political energies expended by Somali political players were devoted to internal struggles for power within their own communities. Aideed, Morgan, Ali Mahdi, and others all had to cope with elders, rival political figures, disgruntled subclans, clerics, intellectuals, and ambitious militia leaders laying claim to authority over some or all of the clan's political dealings. All of these political players thus viewed peace initiatives—especially well-funded, high-visibility, internationally sponsored peace conferences—as an excellent tool for elevating their own status within the clan. This was one important reason disputes over participation in the conferences were so ferocious. And as a result, UNOSOM found that delegates often had very different agendas as they gathered in session—some were interested in peace, but others were entirely focused on their own internal political struggles and would use the conference, and the UN, at every opportunity to that end.

Third, the peace process in Somalia was under constant threat from a sizable "conflict constituency" that had vested interests in continued instability. These interests included, and continue to include, those who profit from an economy of plunder, Mafia-like extortion rackets, and various other unlawful economic dealings; militia leaders whose power base rests on conquest and fear, not on popular referendum and peace; the *mooryaan*, young armed men whose status and wealth would be dramatically reduced in a civil society under rule of law; and entire clans that have benefited from occupation of new and valuable real estate in Mogadishu and the river valleys and that would stand to lose considerably in a peace that might involve the return of stolen property. It was not difficult for this loose coalition to mobilize against reconciliation efforts it viewed as counter to its interests. Ironically, in a number of cases, reconciliation efforts actually united rival militia leaders temporarily in common cause to disrupt reconciliation meetings and intimidate Somali peacemakers.

The international community thus had an unpalatable choice: Either it could work to marginalize the conflict constituency, with the very real risk of protracted armed conflict, or it could attempt to transform the interests of those communities, to give them a stake in peaceful reconciliation. This latter option would have required a great deal of economic development funding, which UNOSOM did not have, to provide market incentives to lure merchants into a peace constituency and job training to give young militiamen alternatives to banditry and war.

Fourth, in the collapsed Somali state, it was never apparent that either a top-down or a bottom-up approach to national reconciliation was viable; both seemed flawed in practice. The national-level conferences simply failed to translate into meaningful changes on the ground and quickly were seen as a waste of time, money, and UN credibility. But the alternative, building a national-level peace by starting at the local level, could exhibit its own pathologies as a strategy and had to be embraced with care. In particular, international facilitators had to cope with the fact that local-level peace accords sometimes translated into new coalitions at a third party's expense, which actually raised tension at the regional or national level even as it reduced tension locally. Unfortunately, it was difficult to discern in advance when a local peace conference would serve as a legitimate building block for a broader peace and when it was a war party in disguise.

Fifth, UNOSOM found its role as a facilitator-mediator in Somali national reconciliation incompatible with its mandated role of peace enforcement. For peace enforcement, the UN had to be *impartial*—that is, it had to enforce certain rules of the game on all parties concerned. That role can include, if violations are serious, military measures. As long as the peace-enforcement operation imposes the same penalties on everyone for security infractions, it maintains its impartiality. But having once embarked on enforcement measures against a serious violation (Aideed's attack on UNOSOM forces in June 1993), the UN cannot simultaneously play the role of a *neutral* mediator in national reconciliation. This is precisely the impasse that UNOSOM met in summer 1993 as it was drawn into a protracted conflict with the SNA. In future peace enforcement operations, serious consideration needs to be given to this structural impediment to the UN's own mediating role.

Sixth, UNOSOM's efforts to revive Somali state structures, one of its mandates from the Security Council, worked at cross purposes with its reconciliation efforts, often fueling conflict instead of reducing it. The dynamic was immediately apparent on the ground. Different clans were often able to coexist in relative peace in a single location. However, if asked to form a local governmental structure with a fixed number of seats, they often fell into heated disputes, sometimes ending in casualties and dramatically worsening local security. The fixed number of seats in local councils forced each clan to quantify its relative importance at the district and regional level, a zero-sum game that even in the best of times could provoke disputes. In the midst of massive population displacement and militia occupation of vast stretches of land in southern Somalia, it was almost certain to do so. The unpleasant reality UNOSOM confronted was that the formation of government is inevitably conflict producing. It lacked a careful and credible process to reassure constituents and keep conflicts manageable.

Finally, the dramatically reduced pool of economic resources in a country that was desperately poor even before the civil war heightened conflicts over what was left of the "national pie." In the past, the strong centrifugal forces pulling at

Somalia's seams were held in check by generous levels of government patronage, courtesy of high levels of Cold War–driven military and economic foreign aid.[35] Disgruntled clans and recalcitrant public figures could be assuaged with a position in a lucrative government post or a foreign aid project. That level of foreign aid is gone forever; at the same time, local resources have been decimated by the war. Reconciliation, which nearly always entails an accord over how communities share economic resources fairly, is much more difficult as a result.

Conclusion

Taken collectively, of the seventeen national-level and twenty subnational Somali peace conferences from 1991 to 1995, the only examples of successful reconciliation occurred at the local and regional level. Somalis have well-established social mechanisms for managing interclan conflict at the local and regional level, traditional practices that were resilient enough to step into the vacuum created by the collapsed Somali state. When those grassroots institutions were recognized and assisted rather than marginalized, they were at least sometimes able to overcome deep-seated clan hostilities and forge durable local reconciliation.

The partial success of subnational peace processes reflects the fact that politics in contemporary Somalia has become intensely localized. What matters in the lives of ordinary Somalis is peace and stability in their immediate region, not deals cut in distant Mogadishu; communities are more likely to mobilize to support local reconciliation because they see tangible results from those efforts.

Local-level peace processes fare poorly in regions that have experienced conquest and occupation by new clans. In regions such as the Lower Shabelle and Lower Jubba valleys, local elders find themselves negotiating not with comparable representatives with whom they share long common experience and social contracts but with young, armed militiamen whose interests and actions place them outside the pale of Somali customary law. Although there are indications that even in these zones of territorial conquest new clans are reaching accommodations with existing communities, the process of reconciliation there is far slower.

If it is true that at least some local-level peace initiatives bore fruit, it is also the case that their success remained strictly a local affair. This disappointed some UN officials and others who hoped that local reconciliation would culminate in a national accord "from the bottom up." In hindsight, it is clear that this was no shortcoming on the part of local-level reconciliation efforts. Instead, it is yet another indicator of the powerful economic and social forces in contemporary Somalia mitigating against any central or centralizing political arrangement. Indeed, all indications are that "Somalia" may be heading toward a future as a fluid set of polities that collectively add up to something less than a conventional state.[36] If so, the entire effort to craft national-level peace accords, whether from the bottom up or the top down, was destined to fall victim to Somalia's centrifugal politics.

Notes

1. The Chapter VII "peace enforcement" mandate was first issued in Security Council Resolution 794 (1992).

2. At the outset of the intervention, UNOSOM was inundated with announcements of the formation of new factions, each representing subclans seeking a place at the negotiating table. To cope with this chaotic political development, UNOSOM's director of political affairs established a cutoff date after which no new factions would be recognized. Unfortunately, this deprived several bona fide political movements, such as the Ranhanweyn-based Bonka group, from gaining a seat in national conferences and legitimized several factions that were virtual fictions.

3. This complaint was first voiced in December 1992, when the UN sponsored the Informal Preparatory Meeting for National Reconciliation in Addis Ababa, which was exclusively faction-based. In the process, UNOSOM established a precedent that crystallized the factions as the centerpiece of national reconciliation.

4. This group was already in Addis Ababa, invited by donor agencies and international NGOs to attend the Third Coordination Meeting on Humanitarian Assistance for Somalia in mid-March.

5. "Addis Ababa Agreement of the First Session of the Conference of National Reconciliation in Somalia," Section 4, no. 4, March 27, 1993.

6. UNOSOM chose to view the March 27 accord as binding and the appendix as invalid (at least until March 1994, when, in an attempt to bargain for factional cooperation in national reconciliation, it acquiesced to factional "review" of district councils).

7. For an assessment of the Addis Ababa conferences, see Walter Clarke, "Testing the World's Resolve in Somalia," *Parameters* 23(4), Winter 1993–1994, pp. 42–58.

8. Quoted in Donatella Lorch, "Despite Chaos in Mogadishu, UN Hopes New Talks Will Bring Peace," *New York Times,* September 22, 1994, p. A10.

9. Ibid.

10. For somewhat distinct accounts of the Djibouti process (the latter being a very pro-Aideed interpretation) see Patrick Gilkes, *The Price of Peace: Somalia and the United Nations 1991–1994* (London: Save the Children Fund-UK, September 1994), pp. 32–35; and John Drysdale, *Whatever Happened to Somalia?* (London: Haan, 1994), pp. 29–38.

11. For extensive treatment of Oakley's diplomatic experiences, see John L. Hirsch and Robert B. Oakley, *Somalia and Operation Restore Hope* (Washington, DC: U.S. Institute of Peace Press, 1995).

12. Tensions have worsened in the Northwest since fall 1994, in part due to UNOSOM meddling in internal Somaliland affairs by providing financial support to a political figure, Abdirahman "Tuur," who rejects northern secession. Repeated outbreaks of clan conflict in the Northwest since 1994 suggest that the peace accords reached in 1992–1993 are not holding.

13. See especially Ahmed Yusuf Farah (with I. M. Lewis), *Somalia: The Roots of Reconciliation: A Survey of Grassroots Peace Conferences in North West Somalia/Somaliland* (London: ActionAid, 1993); Mark Bradbury, "The Somali Conflict: Prospects for Peace," Oxfam research paper no. 9, London, October 1993; Somali Development and Relief Agency and Mennonite Central Committee, "Proceedings of the Erigavo Peace Conference, Sanag Region, Somalia," Djibouti, May 1994; and Rakiya Omaar, "Somaliland: One Thorn Bush at a Time," *Current History,* May 1994, pp. 232–236.

14. The Ogadeni clan, it should be noted, had been driven out of Kismayu by the SPM in late February and was living in displaced persons camps up the Jubba valley in very harsh conditions. Unquestionably, community pressure to reach an agreement so that the Ogadeni could return to their homes in Kismayu was a major factor in the elders' decision to pursue a peace despite SNA threats.

15. In fact, the local UNOSOM office was given almost no financial support from headquarters for the conference. Much of the food, blankets, water, and other support for the conference was provided by UN agencies, NGOs, and the Belgian peacekeeping force operating in Kismayu. The talks were a happy (but rare) example of cooperative partnership between these international players in support of local reconciliation.

16. For fuller assessments of the Jubbaland peace accord, see John Prendergast, "The Gun Talks Louder Than the Voice: Somalia's Continuing Cycles of Violence," Center of Concern discussion paper, Washington, DC, July 1994, pp. 22–24; Bradbury, "The Somali Conflict"; and Ken Menkhaus, *Peacebuilding in Collapsed States: Dynamics of Local-Level Peacebuilding in Somalia* (forthcoming).

17. This same problem plagued the Hirab peace conference in March 1994, in which Abgal and Habr Gedr clans were brought together, raising deep misgivings among other Hawiye clans–especially the Hawadle and Murosade–that they were being marginalized in Mogadishu affairs. Tensions resulting from the Hirab initiative may in fact have helped spawn subsequent armed conflict between the Hawadle and Habr Gedr (March-August 1994) and between the Murosade and Abgal (September 1994 to 1996).

18. Later the UN learned that Aideed was also hoping that a peace in Mudug would free up SNA technicals and other military hardware for relocation to Mogadishu in anticipation of hostilities with UNOSOM.

19. Some within UNOSOM and the U.S. mission demonstrated a marked preference toward Abshir Musa as a national statesman and viewed the Aideed effort to weaken his political base with particular misgivings as a result.

20. For a short account of the politics of the Mudug conference, see Clarke, "Testing the World's Resolve in Somalia."

21. Michael Maren, "Leave Somalia Now," *New York Times,* July 6, 1994, p. A19.

22. The SRSG's Admiral Jonathan Howe had become too closely identified with the UN's aggressive hunt for Aideed and was recalled to New York to placate Aideed so that he would acquiesce to a role for UNOSOM in facilitating Somali reconciliation.

23. Thomas Friedman, "Dealing with Somalia: Vagueness as a Virtue," *New York Times,* October 15, 1993.

24. The most concise and penetrating of these critiques is I. M. Lewis, "Misunderstanding Somalia," *Anthropology Today* 9(4), August 1993.

25. Sahnoun provides his own account in *Somalia: The Missed Opportunities* (Washington, DC: U.S. Institute of Peace, 1994).

26. A group of academic specialists on Somalia, convened by the Life and Peace Institute, formed the Somalia Reference Group for the UN; it argued from the outset for a peace process based on Somali civil society, highlighting the role of elders in reconciliation. Likewise, the Somali intellectuals convened in October 1992 at the Seychelles consultations with the UN made a strong case for supporting civil society as the linchpin of peacebuilding in Somalia. For examples of this view, see Lewis, "Misunderstanding Somalia," and Africa Watch, "Somalia Faces the Future: Human Rights in a Fragmented Society" (New York: Africa Watch, April 1995).

27. See Jennifer Parmalee, "Waltzing with Warlords," *Washington Post,* June 23, 1993, pp. C1, C2. The article provides an excellent analysis of the UN's problems coping with the recalcitrant militia leaders.

28. See, for instance, "The Intervention in Somalia: What Should Have Happened. An Interview with John Paul Lederach," *Middle East Report,* March-April 1993, pp. 38–42.

29. Former special envoy to Somalia Robert Oakley went so far as to accuse the UNOSOM strategy as "tantamount to re-establishing some kind of trusteeship or colony." Quoted in *Somalia News Update,* December 18, 1993. Oakley presents a more nuanced critique of UNOSOM's relations to the militia leaders in Hirsch and Oakley, *Somalia and Operation Restore Hope,* pp. 156–158.

30. In fact, Somalia's traditional political heritage is a far richer direct democracy—a "pastoral democracy" in which all adult males had the right to participate in clan assemblies—than those in most Western states. How much of this political culture has survived twenty years of dictatorship and four years of anarchy is open to question.

31. Terrence Lyons and Ahmed Samatar, *Somalia: State Collapse, Multilateral Intervention, and Strategies for Political Reconstruction* (Washington, DC: Brookings Institution, 1995), appendix A.

32. Richard Betts, "The Delusion of Impartial Intervention," *Foreign Affairs* 73(6), November-December 1994, pp. 21–22. See also William Murchison, "Vietnam Then and Somalia Now," *Washington Times,* October 12, 1993; and Robert Novak, "Nation-Building, Anyone?" *Washington Post,* October 14, 1993.

33. Rakiya Omaar and Alex de Waal, "Somalia, Operation Restore Hope: A Preliminary Assessment," *African Rights,* May 1993. Omaar and de Waal, whose views were prominent in the media, actually shifted positions on intervention in Somalia, originally advocating limited intervention in mid–1992 but then rejecting the actual intervention in late 1992 on the grounds that it was too massive and too late.

34. Aden Ali, "UN Envoy Says 'Little Bridge' Divides Somalis," Reuters, November 8, 1994.

35. Government coercion and repression, it should be added, were also part of the mix that temporarily held communal grievances in check but that eventually fueled them.

36. Evidence for this thesis is presented in Ken Menkhaus and John Prendergast, "Governance and Economic Survival in Post-Intervention Somalia," *CSIS Africa Notes* no. 172, May 1995.

PART 2
Economic Aspects of Intervention

4

Somali Land Resource Issues in Historical Perspective

Lee V. Cassanelli

One of the driving forces behind the civil war in southern Somalia was the competition for access to natural resources—notably productive farmland, dry-season pastures, and fuelwood reserves—in the Shabelle and Jubba River valleys and adjacent interriver regions. Initially, this dimension of the conflict received scant attention; most of the news coverage and commentary on Somalia in the two years after the fall of Siad Barre in 1991 focused on the struggles between factional militias for power and for geopolitical advantage in the key cities of Mogadishu and Kismayu. The emphasis was on clan recriminations, warlord rivalries, and the seemingly universal looting of property and productive assets by gangs of armed youths.

As the war continued into 1993, observers began to take note of what seemed to be a much more systematic takeover of valuable farmland by the dominant warlords and their supporters. The territorial map of Somali clans was being redrawn as armed Hawiye and Darod factions moved in and established de facto authority over "minority" communities and farming districts where previously they had enjoyed scant presence or influence. This war for land has only begun to inform analyses of the Somali conflict,[1] and as a result its impact on the success or failure of Operation Restore Hope has yet to be appraised. That the contending factions might have had long-term strategic objectives in the resource-rich areas of southern Somalia does not appear to have figured significantly in the planning or deployment of international peacekeepers. Nonetheless, an appreciation of the land resource issues at stake in the civil war seems absolutely critical not only for understanding Somali militia movements during the course of the war but also for assessing the likelihood of renewed conflict in the postintervention era.

In this chapter I argue that the transfer of southern land resources from local clans to other, favored ones was on the agenda of Somalia's national leaders at least from the early 1970s but that this agenda was obscured for outsiders by international preoccupation with a succession of other, more visible conflicts: the Ogaden War in 1977–1978, the Barre government's efforts to quell opposition movements in the Northeast and North in the 1980s, and, after Barre's ouster in 1991, the Hawiye factional struggle for control of the capital city of Mogadishu. The land war accelerated after 1991 with the expulsion from most of the Shabelle valley and Bay region of Darod clansmen and their replacement by well-armed militias of other clans (predominantly Hawiye) who claimed to have "liberated" the land from the former dictator.

The long and still active history of this war for land may well undermine any agreements reached in coming years regarding power sharing at the national or regional levels. For purposes of this volume, it is also important to ask whether a greater awareness in 1992–1993 of the "land resource" aspect of the civil war could have affected U.S. and UN decisions about where to deploy peacekeepers, when and where to begin efforts to establish local police forces, and how best to have reduced refugee flows from the country's most productive agricultural districts. I offer some speculations on these matters in the concluding section.

Evidence for a Land Resource War

One is hard pressed to find in the thousands of pages of coverage of the war in Somalia any analysis of underlying patterns in the deployment of Somali militias in the rural areas apart from their obvious attempts to drive rival forces out of these areas. As the warlords attempted to mobilize urban and rural backers along lines of clan solidarity, it was easy for observers to confuse the form the conflict took—clan against clan—with its motives and objectives.

However, evidence for these objectives is certainly there in the record of recurrent militia movements into settled farming communities such as Afgoye, Bur Hakaba, Shalambood, Jilib, and Jamame. Even after UNITAF forces had helped stabilize a general territorial equilibrium among the major players early in 1993, the Shabelle and Jubba valleys continued to be zones of instability. This was not simply because they served as strategic corridors to the contested ports of Mogadishu and Kismayu; the fertile valleys were targets for occupation in their own right. In the early months of the civil war, the riverine farming districts provided the mobile armed gangs with food and with materiel (pumps, plumbing, tools) that could be plundered and sold as scrap for hard currency. However, after the first cohort of victorious fighters had been rewarded with the expropriated urban properties of Darod clansmen fleeing Mogadishu, Hawiye military leaders needed to continue to recruit new supporters; only the prospect of expansion into new territory could satisfy this dynamic.

In retrospect, it is easy to see the factional battles for Merka and Brava and for Jilib and Jamame (not to mention Kismayu and Bardera) as part of a cumulative effort by armed clans to consolidate their hold over districts that had proven commercially viable in the past and might be expected to be in the future. The early

1995 "banana wars" in the Merka-Shalambood area reveal how quickly those who gained control of the productive plantation zones and their adjacent ports could reestablish (and compete over) the banana export business, even in the absence of a functioning central government. We now see why the recurrent battles in 1993–1994 for control of Merka amongst local Biimaal clansmen, the Southern Somali National Movement, and the various components of the Somali National Alliance were so important to the contending parties—or at least to their leaders, who must have anticipated the future value of a revived export economy.

Despite their considerable successes, what UNITAF and UNOSOM II were not able to do was curtail the steady penetration of armed militia influence into the local economies of the southern fishing and farming communities, the majority of them "minorities."[2] Despite occasional charges that the militias had as their goal the forcible expulsion of these minorities—a form of "clan cleansing"[3]—the occupying forces more typically sought to intimidate and co-opt the local leadership. The short-term objectives were to appropriate portions of the harvest (a form of agricultural tribute), to skim off any NGO aid directed toward the local population, and to pressure local elders into offering public support and legitimation to the occupiers. These techniques of forced compliance took on added significance when UNOSOM began to establish district councils with the aim of identifying "representatives" of local interests.

In the longer run, the infiltration of outside clans raised the possibility that entire sets of rights in local resources might ultimately be transferred to the newcomers. There is, for example, evidence from the Bay region that armed outsiders sought to marry into locally established lineages.[4] Intermarriages between formerly belligerent clans can in some instances contribute to local reconciliation processes, as was seen in the northern Somaliland peace negotiations. But in the context of clan expansion, as is occurring in the South, such marriages can ultimately lead to the loss of local control over inheritance rights and resource allocation. The occupying clans appear to be positioning themselves to have a say should land claims ever become an issue in a reconstructed Somali state.

If outside analysts failed to notice the systematic expansion of armed clan militias into districts where they previously enjoyed no rights, Somalis themselves were quite aware of these underlying trends. Two respected Somali scholars have argued that "the Somali conflict has been and is a conflict between the southern agropastoral groups and the northern nomadic groups. More specifically, it has been a conflict between Darod and Hawiye for the control and domination of the interriverine region." They further argue that the Barre regime's decision after 1969 to administratively subdivide the interriverine area into several new regions was intended "to create regions for favored clans [and] was merely a pretext for division and re-appropriation of the farming lands of the interriverine region by more nomadic groups of the country."[5] Currently "the struggle continues to replace Darod hegemony with a Habargidir one."[6]

However much this may sound to outsiders like Somali clan paranoia, it is central to Somalis' analyses of their situation and shapes both their perceptions of and prescriptions for collective action. I have heard no more succinct (and accurate) analysis of the late Mohamed Farah Aideed's military strategy than the one proposed to me by a Benadiri refugee in April 1994: "General Aidid has been stalemated in Mogadishu by the Abgal, in Bardera by the Marehan, in Baidoa by the reinvigorated Ranhanweyn, and in Kismayu by the Harti. All he has left to try and dominate is the Shabelle valley and its unarmed minorities."[7]

There were, to be sure, foreign observers who pointed to the vulnerability of the country's "minority" riverine farmers and to the systematic efforts by militias to appropriate their land. As early as July 1991, Ken Menkhaus called attention to the special plight of Somalia's Bantu farmers;[8] and African Rights issued a working paper in October 1993 that argued that land resources lay at the heart of the bloody factional confrontations along the Jubba and Shabelle.[9] But such appeals do not seem to have visibly influenced U.S. or UN policy. One can only speculate on the reasons: Somalia's riverine farmers were minor players in the political negotiations aimed at national reconciliation. They had few arms at their disposal and hence no real leverage on the negotiating front. Abandoning them and their land resources to the more powerful factions seemed a small price to pay if such concessions could bring the major warlords to the peace table. It was really a question of political priorities with potential national-level reconciliation taking precedence over issues of local economic justice and (I would argue) longer-term economic viability.

Origins of the New "War for Land"

One of the singular features of the Somali case is that those clans which traditionally occupied the country's richest agricultural districts have enjoyed only a marginal role in the country's national politics over the course of the twentieth century. Consisting predominantly of minority communities[10] of heterogeneous origins that speak a variety of distinctive dialects, Somalia's southern farmers had been targets for labor conscription in colonial times and victims of social discrimination by the country's pastoral majority. Their exclusion from any significant role in Somalia's public sector was sealed after 1955 when the Italian Trusteeship Administration abandoned its support of the southern regional political parties in favor of rapprochement with the Somali Youth League (SYL). The SYL had its strongest support among Darod, Hawiye, and Isaaq clans, and it was these groups who came to dominate the national army, police force, and civil service as Somalia moved toward independence in 1960.

The interest of Somalia's new political elites in appropriating rural assets for their own use had precedents in the 1950s and 1960s,[11] but national competition for the resources of the southern riverine areas began in earnest in the early 1970s. Land and water rights, always objects of contestation at the local level, now became embedded in state policies and programs. This phenomenon appeared to coincide with the accession to power of Mohamed Siad Barre in 1969, but his takeover was not, in my view, the cause of this new national agenda. Rather, what transformed the struggle for land resources from a local to a national one was the convergence of several trends that initially had little to do with the 1969 military coup. However, once these trends became apparent, Barre's regime was well positioned to exploit the possibilities and to use land as a tool for building domestic political support. The patterns established during the Barre years continued when the civil war erupted in 1991.[12]

The first trend to affect the distribution of land rights in the South was the planned resettlement of nomads that followed the severe drought of 1974–1975 and the Ogaden War of 1977–1978. In each case, several hundred thousand displaced Somalis from resource-poor regions were resettled in relief camps or planned villages. This required the appropriation by the state of substantial tracts of productive land in Middle Shabelle (Jalalaqsi), Lower Shabelle (Kurtun Waareey and Sablaale), Middle Jubba (Dujuma), and several districts in Hiran and Gedo. Although many of the displaced nomads eventually left the resettlement sites to return to their home districts or to seek employment in the Persian Gulf, the land remained in state hands. Many men who left their wives and children in the new southern settlements later returned to reassert their claims to the land there. Some of the earliest cases of land disputes between local residents and "outsiders" resulted from these refugee-resettlement schemes.[13]

A second key trend and one that continued to inform the behavior of the major players in the post-Barre era was the rise in agricultural land values. Whereas the process was somewhat belated in the Somali case (farmland had been the object of political contestation in most African countries since the 1950s), a series of events in the 1980s—high inflation rates that encouraged investment in durable assets, a decline in the overseas markets for Somali livestock, the return of Somali laborers from the oil fields of the Middle East with capital to invest, the abolition of price controls on grains, and the growing demand for fruits and vegetables in Somalia's burgeoning urban centers—prompted an unprecedented land rush in Somalia. When plans for building a large dam on the Jubba River above Bardera were disclosed, there was a flood of land speculation.[14]

The 1970s and 1980s also witnessed an accelerated process of class formation in Somalia, fueled by the influx of new wealth in the form of foreign refugee and development aid, overseas remittances from the Gulf, livestock export earnings, and Cold War military and economic subsidies. Although Somalia has relatively few multimillionaires, its class structure definitely became more pronounced in these decades. One indicator of favored status—apart from the ability to build a villa in the capital and to educate one's children overseas—was title to a piece of fertile riverine land, which provided rental income, collateral for bank loans, and a source of speculation. Those Somalis who got rich quick during the Barre years set an example for all future power seekers. The current array of "warlords" is striving to reproduce for its own kin and clientele the kind of lifestyle—including absentee ownership of expropriated land—that enabled Siad Barre to make his supporters a privileged class in a country where neither traditional wealth nor noble ancestry guaranteed prosperity over the long haul.

Perhaps because Siad Barre could never effectively capture the wealth generated by Isaaq and Mijerteen livestock exporters and *qat*[15] importers—since this wealth was largely monopolized within the overseas trading networks of these diasporic clans—his government concentrated increasingly on controlling the fixed assets of land and water *within* the country. The Land Registration Act of 1975, ostensibly a "modernizing" tool, played a key role in this strategy. It made all collective land the property of the state and facilitated titled access to those who supported the regime. State courts were given the authority to adjudicate inheritance claims, and favored clans were armed to enable them to seize land from rival clans—the Ogaden occupation of Isaaq lands in the North being the most obvious example. Finally, the Jubba Valley Ministry was created to plan and promote the building of a large hydroelectric and water storage dam above Bardera, which although promising to supply the capital with a cheap source of energy also gave Barre's Marehan kinsmen in Gedo a potential bonanza of irrigated farmland and grazing reserves.

Barre's aims may have been first and foremost to win political allies; but the cumulative effect of these policies was to bring resources previously in the hands of local communities under the control of the national leadership, where they could be parceled out to relatives and potential allies. That he did this parceling out along lines of kinship gave precedence to clan-based analyses of Somalia's crisis; but in fact, it was the control of new resources that underpinned the system of favoritism and rewards. Valuable farmland was high on the list of these new resources, and much of the best land was transferred through title registration to those around the president. The vast numbers of weapons in the government's arsenal eventually were turned on domestic foes, thus further militarizing the process of resource control. It was only to be expected that the regime's opponents, once victorious, would replace his force with their own.

The final trend that contributed to the intensification of the land war was urbanization. The phenomenal growth of Mogadishu from a city of 50,000 in 1960 to one of over a million by the mid-1980s was the most dramatic manifestation of this process, which also included the sedentarization of tens of thousands of nomads in refugee camps and agropastoral settlements. Such rapid urbanization was accompanied, as elsewhere in Africa, by increased demands for meat and vegetables and for fuelwood for cooking. The need for charcoal presented another challenge to traditional resource-management systems; resettled refugees and government agents began to lay claim to communal wood reserves in the Bay region and along the Jubba and Shabelle.[16] State farms, which officially were established for the production of rice and sugar for the nation, became (in a way that should now seem familiar) the private preserves of regime allies.

The outbreak of civil war following the overthrow of the dictator did, to be sure, display elements of clan vendetta as old scores were settled and members of clans privileged by the expelled regime were systematically hunted down. But below the surface of militia mobilization was a struggle by the new "warlords" to seize landed resources in an economy where most other avenues of accumulation had been shut off. Along with the extortion of food relief, the plundering and sale of movable assets, and the protection racket, Somalia's wartime political economy included the imposition by armed militias of predatory regimes in the main farming districts of the country. The war for land had entered a new phase, one that continues in the post-UNOSOM era.

Lessons for History, Lessons of History

What are the implications of this analysis for the conduct of Operation Restore Hope?

One is that U.S.-UN preoccupation with the struggles for turf in Mogadishu and Kismayu obscured the many smaller battles for control of land in the countryside—notably along the Shabelle and Jubba valleys and on the peripheries of the Bay region. The displacement of thousands of riverine farmers to relief centers in Mogadishu and Kenya should have clued observers to the seriousness of the rural disruption caused by the disparities of power between the mobile militias and the unarmed farming communities of the interior. A longer-term war was being fought beyond the sight of international monitors.

It also seems clear that UN attempts to establish representative councils in the riverine areas concentrated on mediating among the various armed factions that were present in these districts, usually to the neglect of the interests of local minorities. Adjudication of land claims was not on UNOSOM's agenda, and for good reason. As Menkhaus's chapter shows, efforts to sort out Somali claims to political representation at the district level required a knowledge of local history and politics that was beyond the expertise of most outsiders. To have included questions of land allocation or compensation in the negotiations would have almost certainly scuttled the entire project. As it was, Somali participants recognized that political legitimation as district representatives was the first step to advancing claims to local resources. The long-term stakes were high; dealing with tenure issues required a vision and commitment that went beyond the goal of filling seats on a district council.

Because indigenous farmers, ousted members of the old regime who had obtained written titles, and the new militia "liberators" all had an interest in the outcome, UNOSOM's only recourse would have been to establish a mechanism whereby the multiplicity of claims to productive assets could have been heard before an impartial body—a land claims tribunal, perhaps, as the first step toward the creation of a postwar land claims court. Early attention to the tenure security issue in these contested rural districts could have provided UNOSOM with a clear objective around which to justify its presence and to mobilize its energies. Legal procedures backed by an international military presence might have stemmed the forcible takeover of land and commercial property by armed outsiders.[17]

There is no underestimating the difficulties that such a strategy would have entailed under the conditions of near anarchy that prevailed in 1993–1994. Deployment of peacekeepers to other agricultural areas (as was done in Bay and Bakool) might have significantly reduced the displacement of local farmers and facilitated a more rapid recovery of the agricultural sector; but wider dispersal of peace-keeping forces would have exposed them (at least initially) to greater risks and probably would have posed a logistical nightmare. Defending Digil, Ranhanweyn, and Bantu lands from the predatory militias might also have raised the cost and reduced the incentive for young Somali recruits initially drawn by the prospects of easy territorial aggrandizement; but it would ultimately have entailed the arming for self-defense of protected "minority" communities and thereby probably hindered longer-term goals of reconciliation in the country.

Whether the deployment of UN forces to prevent land grabbing could have been justified under the terms of the "enforcement" provisions of the initial mandate to protect relief operations is another question. It is possible that such deployment could have been justified under the provisions of Resolution 814 (March 26, 1993), whatever one thinks about the wisdom of that resolution, which called for the "expansion and maintenance of a secure environment throughout Somalia." However possible or desirable such actions might have been, they presume an understanding of the underlying dynamics of the civil war in the South that, as seems clear, was simply not available or not sufficiently acknowledged at the outset of the international mission. The result was the continuation of this war behind the war throughout the UNITAF and UNOSOM periods.

In retrospect, there is probably little that Operation Restore Hope, given its limited mandate and time frame, could have done to halt the land grab in southern Somalia. The harsh reality in the Somali case is that the process of land expropriation by the powerful at the expense of the less powerful had been going on well before the collapse of the Barre regime. Local lineages and communities along the Shabelle and Jubba Rivers had already begun to lose their role as the primary repositories of land rights. The anarchy of the post-Barre period only accelerated the occupation of southern farmlands by clans (Habr Gedr, Hawadle, and Ogaden) that were expanding well beyond their previous home territories. For a historian, it appears as a familiar process, one that had in fact been occurring in Somalia for centuries. In the sixteenth century, Abgal pastoralists (whose descendants now inhabit northern Mogadishu) drove the Ajuran out of that city's hinterland and toward the Jubba; in the nineteenth century, Ogaden refugees from Ethiopia crossed the Bay region and occupied portions of the Lower Jubba, displacing the previous Oromo residents. The process of "pastoral" expansion is a deeply rooted pattern in Somali history, and in one respect the events of the recent war are only the latest manifestation of this territorial imperative.

History also shows that, over time, the "invaders" tend to settle down and establish relations with the existing inhabitants—sometimes as their dependents, sometimes as allies, sometimes as overlords. In Somalia's current situation, expanding Hawiye militias have tended to seek alliances in the Ranhanweyn-dominated Bay region and to assert hegemony over the local communities of the Lower Shabelle and Jubba regions. In both instances, they have sought to gain access to local resources and, in doing so, will probably eventually acquire an interest in protecting rather than pillaging them. In the course of infiltrating these areas, the "invaders" have used a combination of armed force, marriage alliances, and promises of security and stability to assert their presence; the indigenous inhabitants have in many instances become clients of the new overlords either as tenant farmers or as reluctant business or marriage partners. This may not be an outcome that justice and humanitarian sentiment would prefer; but if history is any guide, it does represent an established "Somali solution" to the struggle for land.

To avoid such a solution, international peacekeepers in Somalia (or in any other collapsed state) would have had to make a priority of protecting the vulnerable, nonbelligerent parties in the conflict—which in the Somali case happened to be the most productive segments of society. However, crisis intervention in conditions of civil war make it extremely unlikely that nonbelligerents can expect anything more than a cessation of overt conflict through brokerage with the belligerents. Peacekeeping operations—at least as currently conceived—must invariably put their resources into dealing with those who are most capable of and prone to disturbing the peace—that is, those with weapons. In the Somali case, it was unfortunate but perhaps inevitable that in attempting to bring the warlords together for national-level negotiations, the United States and the UN also effectively legitimated their authority and gave them added leverage in their local wars for land. Until peacekeeping mandates include a component that commits military and legal resources to the protection of land and other productive assets, the most we can expect is a superficial peace.

Notes

1. See, for example, African Rights, "Land Tenure, the Creation of Famine, and Prospects for Peace in Somalia," discussion paper no. 1, London, October 1993; John Prendergast, *The Bones of Our Children Are Not Yet Buried* (Washington, DC: Center of Concern, January 1994), esp. pp. 5–12; Catherine Besteman and Lee Cassanelli, eds., *The Struggle for Land in Southern Somalia: The War Behind the War* (Boulder: Westview Press, 1996). For a parallel analysis of the resource issues behind the recruitment of clan militias in the pastoral regions of northern and central Somalia and around Afmadow, see African Rights, *Grass and the Roots of Peace: Pastoral Resources. Conflict and Conflict Resolution in Somalia and Somaliland* (London: African Rights, April 1994).

2. The situation of Somalia's minorities during the war, and the reasons for their particular vulnerability, are discussed in Bernhard Helander, "Vulnerable Minorities in Somalia and Somaliland," *Indigenous Affairs* (Copenhagen) no. 2, 1995, pp 21–23.

3. Claims of genocide and "clan cleansing" are discussed by Prendergast in *The Bones of Our Children*, pp. 7–8. See also Mohamed H. Mukhtar and Abdi M. Kusow, "The Bottom-Up Approach in Reconciliation in the Inter-River Regions of Somalia," unpublished visiting mission report for the Peace Institute of Scandinavia, August 18–September 23, 1993. Refugees from the town of Brava whom I interviewed in Mombasa in November 1993 were convinced that the recurrent rapes, house searches, and beatings visited on their community by occupying militias were aimed at shaming uncooperative family heads to the point that they would choose to abandon the town to the newcomers.

4. Mukhtar and Kusow, "The Bottom-Up Approach," p. 18.

5. My understanding is that Gedo, for example, was designated as a region to be controlled administratively by the Marehan, the Middle Jubba by the Ogaden, the Lower Jubba by the Mijerteen, and so on.

6. Mukhtar and Kusow, "The Bottom-Up Approach," pp. 5–6, 11.

7. General Aideed's claims to these riverine districts, advanced at the Addis Ababa conferences in 1993, seem to have been based primarily on his militias' success in ousting the Darod forces previously in control—that is, his legitimacy derived from effective armed occupation. Some Habr Gedr nomads were resettled at Sablaale on the Lower Shabelle following the 1974–1975 drought, but this seems a rather tenuous basis on which to assert rights to sovereignty in the area. Whereas it is true that most Hawiye were excluded from the southern land rush during the Barre years, and a few individual families have marriage ties to local residents, claims by Habr Gedr and other Hawiye clans to collective land rights in Bay, Lower Shabelle, and Lower Jubba have little historical foundation.

8. Kenneth Menkhaus, "Report on an Emergency Needs Assessment of the Lower Jubba Region (Kismayu, Jamaame, and Jilib Districts), Somalia," submitted to World Concern, July 1991.

9. African Rights, "Land Tenure."

10. As currently used by both Somalis and foreigners, the term "minorities" refers to any clans or communities in the country that do not belong genealogically to one of the four major "noble" clan families of Darod, Hawiye, Isaaq, or Dir. Although some of the minority clans are in fact small, the agro-pastoral Ranhanweyn centered on the Bay region consist of some three dozen clans and number over a million—hardly a numerical minority. In fact, collectively the so-called minorities probably make up over one-third of the total Somali population, but until the civil war they had no sense of political solidarity or common "minority" consciousness.

11. Investments by urban elites in cement water reservoirs, enclosed fodder reserves, and uncleared riverine land marked the earliest signs of privatization of rural productive assets. Some well-connected politicians bought banana plantations from departing Italians after independence.

12. The following argument is presented in greater detail in Lee Cassanelli, "Explaining the Somali Crisis," in Besteman and Cassanelli, *The Struggle for Land in Somalia*, ch. 2.

13. See, for example, Allen Hoben, "Resource Tenure Issues in Somalia," prepared for USAID, Boston University African Studies Center, 1985, esp. pp. 32–39.

14. See Besteman and Cassanelli, *The Struggle for Land in Somalia*.

15. *Qat* is grown in the highland regions of Yemen and northeastern Africa. Its leaves are chewed as a stimulant by large numbers of Somalis.

16. Examples of pressures on local controllers of wood reserves can be found in Gill Shepherd, "The Reality of the Commons: Answering Hardin from Somalia," Social Forestry Network paper, Overseas Development Institute, London, May 1988; and Thomas Zitelman, "'We Have Nobody in the Agencies!' Somali and Oromo Responses to Relief Aid in Refugee Camps (Hiraan Region/Somali Democratic Republic)," *Sozialanthropologische Arbeitspapiere* (Berlin) no. 17, 1989, esp. pp. 17–19.

17. Colonel Michael Kelly, who was part of the Australian UNOSOM contingent in Somalia, is preparing a research thesis based on his unit's experience in Baidoa, where attempts by a segment of the Habr Gedr clan to take over local businesses were exposed through court hearings and the perpetrators expelled from the region through the cooperation of local authorities and international peacekeepers.

5

Humanitarian Relief Intervention in Somalia: The Economics of Chaos

ANDREW S. NATSIOS

Doctrines develop in foreign affairs as a response to challenges. The doctrine of humanitarian interventionism has developed as one response to the rising tide of ethnic and religious conflict spreading through much of Africa, the Arab world, the Balkans, and the former Soviet states. Of all the humanitarian interventions undertaken since the end of the Cold War, Somalia was one of the most visible, expensive, and debated. A good deal of the Clinton Administration's reluctant response to complex emergencies generally has issued from its unhappy experience with Somalia. Measured by the number of lives lost in a relatively small geographic area in a relatively short period of time, Somalia was the worst humanitarian tragedy since the Ethiopia famine of 1984–1985. In fact, the Center for Disease Control reported that in the greater Baidoa area, the death rates were proportionally the highest in recorded famine history.[1] Somalia has engaged the attention of the senior foreign policy leadership of the U.S. government through two presidencies.

I will argue in this chapter that, judged by the more limited objectives set forth by the U.S. Agency for International Development (USAID) and by President Bush in his television address announcing the Somalia intervention in early December 1992, the effort was a success. These limited objectives included restoring enough order that the relief operation could be conducted without large loss of relief commodities through theft and the restoration of food security so that people could supply their own needs. The difficulty is that other actors involved in the undertaking, UN Secretary-General Boutros-Ghali among others, had other objectives that were much more elusive and much more difficult to measure, such as disarmament, restoration of the Somali state, political reconciliation, and formation of a coalition government. Doctrines are beginning to form around our perceived experience in Kurdistan, Somalia, Bosnia, and a dozen and a half other complex humanitarian emergencies now raging over three continents. These unstudied perceptions may well be inaccurate, and we may be in danger of learning the wrong lessons, as Jim Kunder, the former director of the Office of Foreign Disaster Assistance (OFDA), has suggested.

Unlike in the Kurdish and Bosnia emergencies, the U.S. role in Somalia was based entirely on humanitarian rather than geopolitical objectives. Studying it allows us to subtract the geopolitical and geostrategic calculation from the analysis. During one of the deputies' committee meetings on Somalia, the vice-chair of the Joint Chiefs of Staff, Admiral David Jeremiah, remarked that there was nothing of geopolitical value in Somalia that should engage U.S. interest and that the intervention therefore had only one motivation—humanitarian.[2] A week following the ground intervention, President Bush told Phil Johnston (president of CARE and then acting as the director of humanitarian relief operations for the UN in Somalia) in a conversation in the Oval Office that the last time he had seen Johnston was in Sudan during the Sahelian famine of the mid–1980s at a feeding center for severely malnourished children.[3] Bush, clearly troubled by his memory of that feeding center, drew a direct parallel between that famine and Somalia, a parallel that spoke much about his motivation for sending in U.S. troops. In President Bush's address to the country announcing the Somalia intervention, he reasserted this motive for the effort.

This chapter addresses one of the central questions raised by the Somalia and by other humanitarian interventions: What was the adverse or salutary affect of the humanitarian relief effort on the political and military situations? One study of the Somalia intervention concluded that the conflicting objectives of humanitarian relief, political reconciliation, and military security caused the discontinuities in the international response that led to the killing of Pakistani and then American soldiers in summer and fall 1993.[4] These killings, President Clinton's decision to withdraw U.S. troops, and the subsequent withdrawal of all UN peacekeeping troops in March 1995 have labeled the Somalia intervention as a failure. Were there relief interventions that improved the security or political situations that done earlier or more comprehensively might have changed the tragic course of events in Somalia for the better?

Causes of the Humanitarian Crisis

Two circumstances led to the Somalia famine of 1992, one apparent and the other less so. The inability of any single Somali clan or alliance of clans to form a government following the ouster of Siad Barre as dictator of the country plunged the country into a convulsive civil war centered in Mogadishu. Civil war might be too formal a term for what approached anarchy; the anti-Barre alliance quickly fell apart and the southern part of the country descended into warlordism that was loosely affiliated with clans and their respective political parties. U.S.-supported efforts to form a provisional government failed twice because General Aideed, a major figure in the fight to oust Barre and a man who believed he was entitled to be named the new president, refused to support the reconciliation effort. He instead launched a protracted battle against the choice of most of the clan leaders to head the provisional government—a businessman from North Mogadishu, Ali Mahdi. Perhaps 20,000–30,000 people died in these confrontations, most in Mogadishu, where the conflict was centered. The deaths as a result of the conflict probably would have ended there had not a serious drought occurred at the same time in the southern part of Somalia beginning in late 1991: Many who died in the drought could have been saved if the chaos had not made it impossible to deliver relief food. This same drought devastated southern Ethiopia and northern Kenya, but there were few deaths there because relief efforts succeeded in getting food to the vulnerable without incident. Civil war and drought in Africa inevitably produce starvation because access problems impede relief efforts.

Hardest hit by these two deadly circumstances was the area between the Jubba River and the Shabelle River further north. This interriverine area contains the country's richest agricultural land and serves as its breadbasket. The area is inhabited by the Bantu and Benadir people, who are outside the clan structure, and by the Ranhanweyn clan; these ethnic groups had the misfortune of being the weakest from a military perspective. They died in the famine in numbers grossly disproportionate to their share of the Somali population, a consequence of this military weakness. In Somali culture, nomadic herders take a dismissive view of sedentary agriculture, believing that farmers do not possess the noble fighting character of pastoralists. Ranhanweyn and Bantu farmers were caught in the clan feud between the Darod and the Hawiye, who traditionally controlled the area to the north, west, and south of this interriverine region. Barre's retreating troops targeted the Ranhanweyn for massacre. These warring clans took, then lost and took again this farming area from each other. Each time the area changed hands the supplies of food dwindled. The Ranhanweyn clan and Bantu farmers hid food stores to keep people alive during the drought; they were discovered and raided by the occupying conquerors with disastrous results. The atrocities against these militarily weak interriverine people by more powerful clans were just as widespread and brutal as those against the Bosnian Muslims.

Armatya Sen's groundbreaking research on famines suggests that they are caused by the disparity between food prices, which rise rapidly during a drought, particularly when aggravated by civil war, and family income, which declines precipitously as traditional coping mechanisms are exhausted during food-insecure periods. Families typically sell off household goods to purchase more food after they have consumed their reserves from the previous harvest. They then sell their animals, after which males migrate to find work in urban areas. Remaining family members will migrate when all other coping mechanisms fail. Food prices in Somalia had risen between 800 and 1,200 percent in some cities during the latter stages of the drought in spring and summer 1992.[5]

Perhaps 80 percent of Somali households' income came from their animal herds, which accounted for 74 percent of Somali export earnings prior to the collapse of government.[6] As a result of the collapse of the Barre regime, the price obtained for animals exported to Saudi Arabia and Yemen fell by as much as 50 percent because there was no government to inspect the animals and certify their health. This dramatic decline in household income for herders seriously exacerbated the food insecurity caused by the civil war and the drought. The fall in animal prices combined with the drought in the South, which drove up cereal prices, led to a dramatic increase in food insecurity over a very short period of time.

The U.S. Government Response

Given the controversy surrounding the U.S. military intervention in Somalia in December 1992, it would be instructive to provide an account of the humanitarian relief program that preceded it. Without this perspective on the alternative courses of action considered, the steps previously taken, and the successes and failures of each humanitarian initiative, the atmosphere surrounding the decisionmaking process is obscured.

The Office of Foreign Disaster Assistance (OFDA), part of USAID, is charged under federal law with leading U.S. government responses to natural and man-made disasters outside the United States. From the beginning of the emergency, OFDA actively supported relief interventions in Somalia with support from the State Department's Africa Bureau. Within one month of Siad Barre's overthrow on January 27, 1991, OFDA had appointed a relief coordinator based out of Nairobi to manage its program of assistance. Two months later, on March 25, Assistant Secretary of State Herman Cohen made a formal declaration that a disaster existed. This declaration formally activated the OFDA response mechanism under USAID procedure. The early period of the relief program centered around providing assistance to civilian casualties of the war or people displaced by its violence. Mass starvation was neither an immediate problem nor one that anyone at this point anticipated. OFDA relief interventions were made through a half-dozen nongovernmental organizations (NGOs) and the International Committee of the Red Cross (ICRC), then operating in the country. By January 1991 the UN had withdrawn from the country because of security concerns.

The intensity of the fighting in Somalia swelled the population of internally displaced and refugee populations attempting to escape the violence. When people left their homes, they became much more vulnerable: They congregated in squalid refugee camps where poor sanitary conditions encouraged epidemics, unaccompanied women were subject to violence, and traditional ties to family and friends in the village were broken in the chaos, eliminating the most important coping mechanism of all. The people in these camps for displaced persons regularly came under the control of the local warlord, who would recruit young men in the camps for his armies, an attractive alternative to the terrible conditions and hopelessness of the camps. It was in this context that death rates began to accelerate. Southern Somalia was already traumatized by the civil war, and when in fall 1991 a severe drought struck the region, people simply could not cope with multiple disasters simultaneously and starvation occurred on a massive scale.

The OFDA and Food for Peace (FFP) interventions through NGOs and the ICRC were not of sufficient size to stop these ever expanding death rates; a two-pronged strategy was developed to respond to the growing crisis in August and September 1991. First, OFDA offered to second one of its senior officers, Joe Gettier, to the UN Disaster Relief Office (UNDRO) to coordinate relief efforts on the ground in Somalia. OFDA made this offer because the UN argued that the security situation was too dangerous to put a UN official in Mogadishu. Although the UNDRO leadership was enthusiastic about his secondment, the UN Security Office in New York vetoed it with the argument that it was paying too much insurance for employees killed in conflicts in other areas of the world. Gettier never went.

Second, OFDA requested that the U.S. embassy in Geneva petition the ICRC general-secretary to expand ICRC's relief interventions in Somalia dramatically in order to make up for the UN's absence. General Cornelio Samaruga, the head of ICRC, agreed to this expanded effort contingent on funding, which the United States pledged to provide. The State Department requested that donor governments support the ICRC effort, and the other Western democracies responded generously. Somalia became the ICRC's largest relief effort since World War II, dwarfing all other NGO efforts combined in Somalia and consuming nearly 50 percent of the ICRC worldwide budget.

In January 1992 at a humanitarian conference convened in Addis Ababa to address the spreading crisis of drought, civil war, and epidemics in the Horn of Africa, senior USAID and State Department officials met as a group with representatives of all of the political factions in the Somalia conflict. The officials gave them a blunt warning: Working in Somalia for the international humanitarian organizations was becoming progressively untenable because of the mindless violence, attacks on the relief effort, and methodical destruction of the remaining infrastructure in the country. The three U.S. government officials explained that unless the Somali factions began to cooperate on facilitating instead of impeding the relief effort, limited U.S. government relief resources would be diverted elsewhere—specifically to the looming southern African drought, the Sudanese and Angolan civil wars, and the food security crisis threatening the former Soviet Union.[7] Though the Somalis pledged their cooperation, neither they nor most of the factions they represented were in enough control of events to change their course.

In April 1992, the UN Security Council considered resolutions that would place a force of peacekeeping troops in Somalia to protect the humanitarian relief agencies. A contentious debate within the Bush administration took place with USAID, the State Department's Refugee Office, and the Africa Bureau of State on one side and the Bureau of International Organizations (IO) on the other. IO argued that Somalia was not a central strategic interest of the United States and that the UN was already overextended in peacekeeping operations and unable to handle any further pressure. USAID, the Refugee Program Office of State, and the Africa Bureau of State argued that an immediate and robust UN intervention was essential if the rising death rate was to be arrested and a full-scale famine prevented. In the end the United States supported a modest, and finally ineffective, proposal to send 500 UN peacekeeping soldiers to Somalia—soldiers who had already been volunteered by the Pakistani government—and the secretary-general appointed Mohamed Sahnoun, an Algerian diplomat and former ambassador to the United States, to be his special representative in Somalia.

A Center for Disease Control study of the famine from a public health perspective suggests there were three successive waves of starvation when the death rates climbed, plummeted, and then climbed again. The last two of these periods were the most extreme in January 1992 and September 1992.[8] In July 1992, the director of OFDA, Jim Kunder, and a team of technical personnel accompanied Senator Nancy Kassebaum (R–Kans.) on a visit to southern Somalia. They returned to Washington, D.C., with a troubling report of the deteriorating security situation and rising death rates. At the same time, a now famous cable arrived at the White House as part of the president's daily foreign affairs briefing book from the U.S. ambassador to Kenya, Smith Hempstone. Hempstone titled the communication "A Day in Hell." In it he described horrific conditions in a Somali refugee camp in Kenya, a description that stunned President Bush. He wrote comments on the cable, demanded more information, and wanted a report on what was being done about the situation.

A policy review began as a result of the two reports—from OFDA and the Kenya embassy—along with media coverage that led in August to President Bush announcing a more aggressive strategy for addressing the growing crisis. This included the appointment of a special coordinator of Somali relief within the U.S. government, plans for an international donor conference to increase resources flowing to Somalia, an additional pledge of 145,000 metric tons of food aid by the U.S. (the United States had already delivered 88,000 metric tons), the dispatch of the OFDA Disaster Assistance Response Team (DART) to the region, and a U.S. military airlift of relief food to urban areas in the southern part of the country.

The Unintended Consequences of the Relief Effort

The OFDA field reports of the food and security situations in Somalia in summer 1992 presented a more complex situation than may have been readily apparent. These analyses aggregated the views of NGO staff in the field; the OFDA team led by Kate Farnsworth, an experienced and widely respected OFDA expert on African emergencies; and Fred Cuny, a much published author on disaster response and an admired field manager who had been hired to provide consulting services to the OFDA team. Food had become the medium of exchange and a principal source of wealth in Somalia. Because food was so scarce—as a result of both drought and civil conflict—its absolute value had risen to an extraordinarily high level. This factor combined with collapse of the economy causing mass unemployment and a dramatic drop in family income increased its relative value. Thus food imported through the relief effort became an enormously attractive objective of plunder by merchants, by common working people without a source of income, by organized gangs of young men, and by militia leaders in need of the wealth represented by food aid, which they would use to purchase more weapons and to ensure the loyalty of their followers.[9]

Some observers saw the diversion of food by the warlords and gangs of looters as an accountability problem, but it was much more than that. Although this was a proper cause for concern, it was the least important of all of the reasons for focusing on the diversion problem, as the OFDA field reporters were to show. The diversion of relief assistance was in fact exacerbating the violence and reinforcing the power of the warlords, who were destroying southern Somalia.

Cuny observed that food markets in several cities were receiving most of their food for sale from looted stocks. Merchants would actually request the local militia or bands of thieves to steal more food as their stocks diminished each day. The relief effort was the cheapest and nearest source of the commodity. The market demand was driving some of the looting, though it was difficult to quantify its proportionate effect on the disorder. In more stable social orders the merchant class supports law, order, and stability because they are essential to commercial exchange. The precise reverse of this inherent disposition toward order was operative in Somalia: Markets were distorted by the unnatural increase in food value, the interruption of transport lines, and the collapse of law and order. Merchants needed food, and the relief effort was the most efficient source of it.[10]

OFDA staff noticed that merchants' food was seldom looted. There were three reasons for this. First, Somali merchants were part of the clan system. This system included a still sporadically functional legal tradition in which a merchant from one clan aggrieved by the theft of animals or commodities by someone from another clan could seek restitution from the clan elders of the thief. This traditional mechanism served to settle disputes before they deteriorated into clan blood feuds that might last years. Clan elders who had to pay money to the aggrieved merchant could discipline the men responsible for the theft, acting as a constraint on illicit behavior. Second, the Somali merchants hired unemployed police to patrol the marketplaces to prevent petty theft. These police, whom one could see walking the marketplace even during the worst days of the chaos, were the remnants of the old Somali police force, one of the most disciplined and best trained in Africa. Even in the days of the worst abuses by the Barre regime, the police held the respect of the Somali population. Finally, when merchants moved commodities purchased abroad by convoys over long distances, they hired small private armies to protect their investments from those thieves who had separated themselves from the discipline of the clan elder structure. Tampering with a Somali merchant's wealth was a dangerous undertaking under any circumstances. This informal system of private law and order was maintained in most markets during the worst of the chaos and protected the investments of the merchant class.

While visiting several cities in Somalia in late August and again in September 1992, I noticed that food prices were quite unstable, varying widely from day to day, and discovered that they dropped on days when airlifted relief food arrived at the local airport and increased on succeeding days. Stolen relief food was a notably unreliable and unstable source of supply for the merchants; there was never enough, and the price varied according to how much was stolen. In some cities, merchants in business partnership with powerful local warlords manipulated food prices using large stocks of hoarded food. Rumors circulating among NGO workers had it that the most powerful warlords were hoarding tens of thousands of tons of food stocks stolen from the relief effort. These rumors took on greater credence when the U.S. military airlift was announced on BBC. Overnight, food prices dropped fairly dramatically in the cities these warlords controlled. Merchants dumped hoarded food onto the marketplace, fearing their investment would lose value as soon as the airlift was in full swing. Within a short time after the U.S. military airlift was fully operational, food prices dropped in most cities because of the release of these hoarded reserves. [11] The airlift did not, in fact, increase the aggregate amount of relief food in the country; it merely replaced an airlift being run by the ICRC and the World Food Program (WFP). (The military flights, limited by military procedure and security requirements, did not carry the tonnage that the private flights did, and so although the number of planes in use increased, the tonnage moved did not.)[12]

Young men with guns were the principal source of most of the violence in Somalia; they had no jobs and could find cheap weapons in local markets. The Marxist Ethiopian regime had maintained the second largest military force in sub-Saharan Africa until its defeat by the Eritrean and Tigrayan rebel movements in spring 1991. When this massive force collapsed, Ethiopian merchants purchased the huge remaining arsenals, both ammunition and weapons, and began selling them to the Somali warlords, moving shipments easily across the unpatrolled border between the two countries. Most NGOs, indeed the U.S. government, never realized how massive and organized this arms trading would become during the course of the chaos. All the elements were there for major weapons and ammunition trafficking: demand created by the warlords for their private armies and by NGOs for their guard forces, supply from the Ethiopian merchants, cash generated by the large-scale looting of food stocks and infrastructure, and protection rackets run by the warlords.[13]

The best way to make up for the absence of a job was a weapon, a traditional symbol of manhood in nomadic culture and now a source of income as well. The relief agencies—the UN, the ICRC, and the NGOs—increased the market for weapons and ammunition because they hired large armies to protect their convoys and distribution sites. The ICRC was reported to have 15,000 to 20,000 armed guards on its staff at the height of the anarchy. This exaggerated demand drew ever more weapons and ammunition from other areas of the Horn of Africa into Somalia. The economics of the weapons trade that made Somalia an armed camp has not been widely studied and yet had a profound effect on the security situation. It is indeed ironic that the very humanitarian organizations demanding so vocally that U.S. and later UN peacekeeping forces disarm Somalia inadvertently fueled a good deal of the Somali appetite for weapons both by hiring guards and by agreeing to the warlords' diversion of food resources in order to gain their protection and purchase more weapons.

These conditions created the chaotic situation that the relief agencies faced as events unfolded. With no formal court system or police force, relief agencies had no way of protecting themselves from abuse: Unrestrained looting of convoys and warehouses, kidnapping of NGO staff for ransom, demands for higher wages by Somali staff who used their weapons as negotiating tools against their NGO and ICRC employers, checkpoints on every road where protection money was demanded, and warlord demands for a share of the food stocks going into their areas all contributed to the problem. NGOs were simply not prepared for the extortion, looting, and protection rackets they faced at every turn. These private NGO armies created a demand for weapons and ammunition, driving their price up higher than they would have been if only the civil conflict were affecting weapons prices. These higher prices in turn attracted more weapons from across the Ethiopian border. The NGOs created a premium for armed men who did little all day but hold their weapons and who received high wages when there was generally massive unemployment.

The drought, the chaos and violence, and the relief effort forced large numbers of farmers into urban areas and refugee camps in Kenya for protection and food. Thus farmers were not in their villages to plant the next crop even if the rains were good. A significant portion of the sedentary agriculturists were either displaced persons or refugees: Entire villages across the Lower Shabelle region were uninhabited. One study suggests that 50 percent of those who died in the famine were displaced people and the other 50 percent were people who did not migrate but died in their home villages.

Pouring more food into this unnatural and corrupted economic system would do more harm than good without a dramatic change in the security situation. It would reinforce the power of the warlords by giving them more wealth with which to keep their followers loyal, purchase more weapons, and capture the loyalty of other unallied clans. Said Samatar, a noted Somali scholar, regularly observed in his television appearances in the United States that the young men who were drawn into the warlord militias were living better than they had ever lived before, given that many of them had been nomadic herders in the bush. This dramatic improvement in lifestyle would have been nearly impossible to maintain if there were peace and stability. Stealing had become a way of life; an entire economic system was built around it. The system would continue to reward antisocial behavior by young men with guns and continue to corrupt both the militias and the merchant class, the latter of which could have been a force for order and the restoration of some political authority. It was dangerous for relief agencies to rely for their own protection on such an unstable security system of undisciplined private armies.

The clan elders held in their traditional authority a means for restoring some measure of normalcy to Somalia, authority that was not dependent on violence for the settlement of disputes. But the corrupted system just described diminished at every turn the authority of clan elders. In Belet Weyn in August 1992, a group of a dozen clan elders told me of a group of teenagers who had been raiding villages in the area and had come to their city to wreak havoc. The most revered and respected elders of the subclan from which the boys came were dispatched by the city to stop the boys from entering. In the ensuing debate between the elders and the boys, one of the thirteen-year-olds went up to one of the old men, put a gun to his head, and shot him to death. The community was so outraged that a mob took the boys and dragged them into a house and placed them under arrest. The elders were clearly terrified that this scene would become more and more common as their society deteriorated further into chaos. They were afraid to exercise their traditional authority for fear of their lives.

The chaos and the relief effort together conspired to create a set of pernicious incentives that simultaneously corrupted the natural instinct of the merchant class for some modicum of law and order and reinforced the power of the most irresponsible elements of Somali society, the warlords. [14] Mohamed Sahnoun told me that he was not always certain whether the warlords he was negotiating with were in control of the militias they led or prisoners of them, given the lack of militia discipline and training. The tenuousness of the warlords' grasp on power put a premium on providing their militias with booty to keep their loyalty. And feeding the militias was not enough; the warlords were pressed to maintain their militias in the lifestyle to which they had become accustomed.

The acceleration of these destructive forces undermined at every turn the natural stabilizing forces in Somali society—the clan elders. Never as powerful in the South as in the northern part of the country, the clan elder system restrained much of the more atomistic and contentious aspects of the Somali national character. Demoralized by the violence, eclipsed in authority by the warlords, separated from the communities they led by massive population displacement, and deliberately subverted by the Barre government over a period of years, what was left of the clan elder class tried with modest success in certain areas to tie the fragmented social order back together.[15]

Although it would be unfair and inaccurate to suggest that the relief effort alone was responsible for the creation of these pernicious incentives, it is the case that the relief agencies had been drawn into this social pathology themselves, accidentally reinforcing its most destructive characteristics and undermining the few stabilizing forces at work in the society. Absent the intervention of an outside security force, some programmatic measures needed to be taken to change the dynamic operating in Somali society.

New Approaches to the Somalia Crisis

The OFDA strategy, designed to influence decisively the course of events in southern Somalia, set five critical objectives:

- Stop the starvation by flooding the country with food in order to drive down and then stabilize food prices to the level prior to the drought. The regular NGO and ICRC distributions of relief food to the most vulnerable people would continue, but a portion of the food was to be monetized, the term used in the relief and development discipline to describe the planned sale of food aid in commercial markets.

• Increase the security of the relief effort by encouraging more soup-kitchen feeding and by replacing rice, a highly valued commodity, with a much less valued food such as sorghum.

• Discourage the exodus of Somalis from their villages and encourage the resettlement and repatriation of displaced and refugee populations so that the restoration of the animal herds and rehabilitation of farms could begin as soon as possible, both essential tasks if food security for the country was to be permanently restored. In Somalia, food security was tied to animal herds more than to sedentary agriculture, except in the interriverine area, since the society at its economic heart remains nomadic.

• Create mass employment programs at a modest wage to get young men off the street, get the economy moving again, and begin the rehabilitation of the ruined infrastructure of the country. The local currency generated from the food monetization would be used to pay for these mass employment programs. The decisions on how the currency was to be spent in each area were to be made by the clan elders, a mechanism for strengthening their position in Somali society. In the most stable areas in the South, clan disputes were settled by negotiation rather than by violence; these areas would be targeted to receive this rehabilitation assistance as a reward for responsible behavior.

• Decentralize the relief effort to the smaller cities and villages. The effort had for too long been concentrated heavily in Mogadishu and thus had tended to increase the importance of the two most powerful and destructive warlords—Aideed and Ali Mahdi.

The first objective—flooding the country with food—was designed to have a salutary affect on both the security situation and the rates of severe malnutrition. Since food had become a medium of exchange, devaluing it would theoretically diminish the incentive for looting. Unlike money, which is easy to store and exchange in a purely physical sense, food is bulky and therefore difficult to keep, particularly if its value drops significantly. The nongovernmental organization CARE reported a fascinating experience along the Jubba River where one of its food convoys had been attacked by a band of thieves. Upon seeing that the convoy was carrying sorghum—the least valued grain, eaten primarily by poor people—the thieves left the trucks and grain in disgust without stealing anything. Based on this and similar anecdotal information, the OFDA strategy was to flood the country with maize, bulgur wheat, and sorghum in place of rice as the principal cereal import for the relief effort.

A plan was designed to sell these cereals as well as pulses and cooking oil to Somali merchants in northern Somali ports, in Kenya, and in Djibouti and let them be responsible for the security of their own investment as it made its way to market. More important, the share of the relief food for warlords and their militias and for organized bands of brigands would decline, though probably not be eliminated, thus diminishing their resources for clan warfare. As the price of food declined, nutritional conditions would improve because people would be able to buy much more food with their limited incomes. Instead of receiving free food, people would have to pay for their own food with money from the economic activity stimulated by the monetization and mass employment programs, thus reducing the effect of the dependency syndrome. Finally, the monetization strategy forced onto the markets all the hoarded food held by the organized criminal elements and the warlords. This approach to relief put into practice the research of Armatya Sen on the true cause of famine: the disparity between family income and food prices.

At the same time that these monetization plans were under consideration, the ICRC was methodically expanding its vast network of open-air soup kitchens; by November 1992, 980 of these kitchens were feeding 1.17 million people a day.[16] By using a decentralized approach, the ICRC was able to feed smaller groups of people once or twice a day. Food was transported in small quantities so as not to draw attention to it and cooked immediately, cooked food being unmarketable by the thieves or warlords. The ICRC soup kitchens provided a measure of self-selection of the recipients being served: The clan elders and more prosperous members of the community found standing in lines for hours a humiliating experience and did not want to be seen taking charity. Many asked for separate private facilities in which to be served.

Although this ingenious ICRC tactic partially addressed the security issue, perhaps the single most serious challenge for humanitarian agencies, it had pernicious side effects. The soup kitchens did much damage to the agricultural economy, acting as magnets that drew people away from their farms and villages to displaced persons' camps. These people weren't able to plant their crops, tend their animal herds, or run their small businesses. Many of the kitchens were located in areas held by General Aideed because that is where the affected populations were. Thus the soup kitchens delivered hundreds of thousands of Somalis into General Aideed's political influence, providing a source of recruits for his militias and denying them to his rival warlords. This disastrous consequence of the soup kitchens was exacerbated by the manner in which the U.S. troops entered Somalia—Mogadishu first and then gradually the other cities; they established little presence in the rural areas. Large population movements took place toward each successive area the U.S. military controlled. According to Fred Cuny's reports, there was a 25 percent increase in the number of soup kitchens in the immediate aftermath of the military intervention, at a time when dependence on the kitchens should have been diminishing. This insidious effect began subsiding in the spring 1993 as the ICRC began reducing its use of soup kitchens: Between January and June 1993 ICRC food distributions through all mechanisms declined from 17,000 metric tons a month to 3,000. Finally, the soup kitchens had the catastrophic health consequences that result when large groups of people are crowded into small areas. Although the social, economic, and political disruption caused by the soup kitchens was relatively short lived, it nevertheless postponed the return to normalcy of Somali society by strengthening Aideed's hand and increasing the number of displaced persons. Given all these unfortunate consequences of the soup kitchens, however, it must be remembered that they did save perhaps a million lives, a not insignificant accomplishment in chaotic circumstances.

During this same period NGOs began moving food distributions and health services to the remote villages, thus slowing the disastrous migration of people from their home villages to the cities and camps for displaced persons. Had there been more security in the rural areas, this decentralization of the relief effort could have started earlier and covered a much wider area. Seed and tools programs were initiated in the sedentary agricultural areas to ensure the availability of inputs needed to plant the next crop. Using grant money from OFDA and local currency generated by the monetization scheme, some NGOs designed innovative public employment programs. Save the Children (U.S. office) employed 12,000 farmers at modest wages to reconstruct the massive irrigation ditches in the Lower Shabelle valley that had fallen into disrepair during the preceding three years. In fact, the project was so successful that the irrigation ditches were extended beyond their former limits, increasing agricultural yields in those areas. The farmers working on the project were able to feed their families with their wages while they worked on the irrigation system, planted the next crop, and cultivated their fields until the harvest in August of 1993.

The strategy with the greatest potential remained monetization; however its execution was quite another matter. In my capacity of assistant administrator of the Bureau of Humanitarian Assistance in USAID during all of 1992, I seriously underestimated the barriers to the fast implementation of this strategy.

Barriers to Innovation

Although OFDA's objectives were widely publicized among the actors—U.S. military, State Department, NGOs, UN agencies, and ICRC—the monetization innovation was generally misunderstood given that on its face it was counterintuitive. The notion that humanitarian organizations would sell food in a famine mystified some and appalled others. State Department diplomats initially opposed the monetization scheme, then offered support after it was explained and reexplained. OFDA received calls from some members of Congress who found the idea very troubling. The media raised similar objections, though after repetition of the concept, several opinion columns, and television interviews by OFDA senior officers, the controversy surrounding the concept dissipated.

At the donor pledging conference called for by President Bush and held in Geneva, Switzerland, I explained the concept to the assembly, and Ambassador Sahnoun, the senior UN official in Somalia, gave it his hearty endorsement. At a fall 1992 meeting of the World Food Program governing board, I again explained the concept and proposed that WFP policy be changed to encourage the use of monetization as a famine-response intervention. Although most of the large food NGOs and the WFP had used monetization previously in development projects, this was their first attempt in a complex emergency, and the purposes in this case were very different than in the past. The senior NGO and UN executives understood the concept quickly; however, their field staffs split over it. The UN field staff of the World Food Program and the UN Development Program initially resisted the concept: They opposed the scheme because they thought it abusive to sell food to starving people (which of course was not what the plan proposed to do) and they were uncomfortable with the practical mechanisms for carrying it out. Because of these misgivings, they slowed the implementation in its formative early months. Later the WFP staff accepted the idea and aggressively facilitated the program. CARE and the International Rescue Committee (IRC) endorsed the notion. The IRC showed the greatest energy early in the effort in implementing its program along the Kenyan border, which included the monetization of veterinary medication for animal herds. CARE attempted to carry out a test sale of food in the stable northeastern region of the country using available European Community (EC) food. This scheme failed when a gang of looters stole all the food before it was sold.

Initially, CARE and the IRC had difficulties expanding the program in the South because there were simply not enough Somali vendors willing to make large purchases (there were many interested in small purchases), which were needed to affect market prices and produce enough currency to begin using it for rehabilitation projects. Thus the timing of the monetization scheme became skewed. The novelty of it and its potential consequences politically (for the warlords), managerially (for the NGOs and WFP), and securitywise (for the merchants) were beginning to be calculated by all of the actors.[17]

The ICRC, the major food distribution agency in Somalia, supported the monetization scheme, but it stubbornly resisted the substitution of bulgur wheat, sorghum, and maize for rice, arguing that rice was more nutritionally balanced and more acceptable to Somali tastes. When USAID pressed the ICRC too strongly to make the change, the ICRC went to the European Community for food aid.

UNICEF reported the second week in September that one of its medical doctors was murdered in the northeast part of the country. The staff believed that Somali merchants disgruntled by the monetization project, which they believed was designed to drive market prices for food down, were to blame. The program would, of course, profoundly affect their profits for existing stocks of food and profit margins of future trading. Later investigation cast serious doubt on the accuracy of this story, but the very existence of the rumors was troubling. The merchants and the OFDA staff I spoke with indicated enthusiasm for the project, but some merchants were concerned that moving from rice to sorghum might put them at risk of being killed by warlords angered by the prospect of their principal source of wealth being diminished in value. Although they were willing to take this risk, they were nevertheless more concerned with their own personal security rather than with the country as a whole, a barrier we at USAID had not originally contemplated.[18]

Food prices did begin to drop significantly by late October, more because of the increased distribution of relief food and the dumping of looted food onto the markets than from monetization. It was at this point that the law of unanticipated consequences became operative. In a dramatic turn of events, Fred Cuny reported in late October that the reduction in the value of food had an effect exactly the opposite of what we had intended. Instead of reducing the level of violence, the drop in food prices increased it: Warlords and thieves alike stole a greater volume of food to make up for its diminished value. One goal had been achieved—flooding the country with food to reduce the rates of severe malnutrition. Perhaps the two objectives of decreasing violence and increasing nutrition were mutually exclusive in the absence of a disciplined security force.

The monetization scheme did expand sufficiently by early 1993 to affect market prices and to produce enough currency to fund significant rehabilitation and reconstruction projects. Some warlords with substantial hoarded stocks that would have been devalued by the monetization effort may have had a vested interest in seeing to it that the monetization program did not work, a factor that should not be discounted in future monetization schemes in complex emergencies. This expansion in the scheme, however, occurred after the introduction of 27,000 U.S. troops, which profoundly changed the dynamic at work in Somalia. We have no way of knowing whether monetization alone would have transformed the merchant class into advocates of stability and order, since military intervention took place before monetization had proceeded to such a degree that it could affect merchant behavior. It is theoretically possible that if enough food had been forced onto the market earlier and its price depressed enough, it would not have had sufficient value to appeal to gangs of looters. However, such a collapse in food prices would likely have had a disastrous disincentive effect on the next crop, and the lower the prices, the less likely merchants would have been to participate in the monetization program in the first place. And ultimately, changing the market dynamic was insufficient to improve the security situation; the intervention of an outside military force was also needed.

Attempts to provide security so that displaced and refugee populations could return to their homes ran up against one immovable impediment. U.S. military commanders became increasingly, some would say exclusively, focused on the security of U.S. forces and refused to consider creating secure corridors for travelers, particularly refugees in Kenya. They repeatedly opposed OFDA requests to move their forces into the countryside in the Lower Shabelle valley. Repatriation of Somali refugees in Kenya would have required the military to expand operations into the area between the Jubba River and the Kenyan border, which some reports indicated held some risk. This the U.S. military steadfastly refused to do, arguing that it amounted to mission creep, the two words most feared among U.S. commanders. Some people who did try to return through this corridor without security were killed, robbed, or beaten by the gangs of thieves in the area, word of which instantly got back to the remaining population in the Kenyan refugee camp. Absent security, people were more reluctant to leave their camps. Over time, people did go home, but clearly their return would have proceeded much faster if security had been provided.

Military reluctance to define its narrow mandate constructively may have prolonged rather than diminished the time its services were required. In future complex emergencies, mission statements and operational plans should be directed toward measurable relief indicators such as morbidity and mortality rates, agricultural harvest cycles, and repatriation and resettlement of refugees and displaced persons.

Although security did not improve for many NGOs after the military intervention, this lack of improvement was to a great degree a function of their own inability to change their working arrangements and lifestyles. The military considered providing them with security details on the condition that they would consolidate the over 500 NGO facilities in Mogadishu alone into a much more manageable number and live in compact facilities with more rigorous security procedures. NGO autonomy made this difficult—NGOs refused to agree to the consolidation, and the military in turn refused to provide protection.

The military intervention allowed the monetization scheme to proceed with much greater dispatch and efficacy: Transport routes were much safer; brokers could be dispensed with, reducing the merchants' overhead; and wholesale food could be sold closer to markets. The U.S. military intervention did provide security for food warehouses and distribution centers, food convoys by relief agencies, and port and airport facilities, ending protection rackets and massive food diversions. The private armies of guards were no longer as necessary and many were laid off by the relief agencies. This ended perhaps the most pernicious element of the relief effort: the strengthening of the power of the warlords through the diversion of food and relief equipment. Aideed's income was substantially reduced and thus so was his political power. This warlord's income was to rise again when the UN infrastructure was set up in Mogadishu, which was controlled by his subclan. Aideed and his allies took a generous share of the UN contracts for commodities, Somali workers, and home rentals.

Perhaps the most instructive recent trend in Somalia has been the precipitous decline in the power of General Aideed now that the UN has completely withdrawn from Mogadishu and food shipments have declined as the agricultural system has recovered—events that are not unrelated. A committee of Somali businessmen from various clans are having some success in taking back the port and airport facilities in Mogadishu from warlord militias to bring some discipline and order to the transport infrastructure so critical to their commercial transactions. The merchant class is reasserting itself as an independent force in Somali society.

Conclusion

Innovation is difficult during crisis, particularly when time is a critical factor. The weight of research and analysis strongly supports the proposition that stabilizing markets and prices ought to be a central objective of relief efforts in a food security crisis, but convincing all of the actors at the field and central headquarters levels that the proposition should be transformed into a programmatic initiative proved frustrating and time consuming. The humanitarian relief structure for dealing with complex humanitarian emergencies is enormously complex—including NGOs, ICRC, UN agencies, donor government aid agencies, and now military peacekeeping forces—and the actors have conflicting mandates and interests and report to different headquarters. Getting agreement on a single strategy for dealing with a crisis is difficult, particularly in a short period of time. The market interventions attempted by USAID during summer and fall 1992, however appropriate and innovative, fell victim to this complexity. The fact is that the existing structure of relief response—NGOs, the UN, and ICRC—is a blunt instrument for carrying out any coherent strategy that might change the course of events for the better. Organizational autonomy and complexity are enemies of speed and strategic coherence. This reality profoundly affected the capacity of the U.S. government to implement any nonmilitary strategy for dealing with the Somalia crisis.

The absence of a general agreed upon strategy for relief efforts in complex humanitarian emergencies effectively hands control over events to chance or to the combatants who have a strategy for using the wealth represented by the relief agencies for their own military and political objectives.

Markets, including weapons markets, and the pricing of food affect not only food security but military security, the balance of power among political factions, the way in which merchants behave, and the respective authority of armed and unarmed elites within the clans themselves. The more chaotic the security situation and the more traumatized the social order, the more likely this axiom of complex emergencies will be operative. In Somalia, the more the mediating and value-forming social and religious institutions were damaged—and they received the brunt of the institutional damage—the more military force and economics determined people's behavior. Neither diplomats, military officers, nor humanitarian relief agencies have shown any particular skill in understanding the economics of chaos and the role they as organizations play, deliberately or accidentally, in making matters more chaotic with their unstudied relief interventions. Simply providing life-saving interventions—food, water, sanitation, medical care, and shelter—is no longer enough in the relief discipline, particularly during conflicts.

This analysis suggests a painful proposition: The more sides in a conflict, the more uncontrollable and undisciplined the actors in a conflict, the more dangerous humanitarian interventions may be absent an outside military force to protect the relief agencies. It may be that in the future, humanitarian relief agencies should consider not intervening in a conflict without military security to protect them unless the sides to the conflict exercise enough control over their own forces to ensure that relief can be provided to noncombatants without furthering the combatants' ends. Saving lives over the short term may increase deaths over the longer term and increase the damage to civil society.

If anything, the Somalia intervention has taught us that restoration of the state is a difficult task, requiring a much longer time period than the local restoration of law and order and the rehabilitation of the agricultural economy. Political settlements have not taken place in most of the other complex emergencies of the past six or seven years. Those that have were the result of one side or the other winning militarily (Eritrea and Ethiopia) or of four or five years of negotiation after a decade or more of civil war in which the contestants became completely exhausted (Cambodia, Mozambique, and Angola). If we are to insist on political settlements in each complex emergency before we withdraw peacekeeping troops, we should prepare for lengthy stays—which we cannot sustain militarily, politically, or financially. A much more feasible strategy would be to delink military and humanitarian objectives, both of which can be achieved within a year or two in most emergencies, from political objectives, which require much longer periods of time to accomplish. Under this approach, military intervention would serve humanitarian objectives only and have no political goals.

The reality is that complex humanitarian emergencies vary so much that no one strategy will work in each case: Each humanitarian effort must have its own plan that is carefully fashioned according to the unique circumstances of the emergency. In some instances where the humanitarian crisis is entirely political (Sudan, Bosnia, and Rwanda) and will not end until there is a political settlement, delinking would be inadvisable, but in some instances the humanitarian and military efforts can be separated from the political and still make sense. Countries can survive and even prosper without national government.

In the end the Somalia intervention did restore food security to much of the South: Crop production has returned to prechaos levels; in fact, sorghum production was 10 percent higher in 1994 and 1995 than in the late 1980s before the conflict. A million people do remain partially dependent on food aid distributed by relief agencies, mostly in the large cities, which will have trouble sustaining such large populations until economic activity has created more urban jobs. Although 465,000 Somali refugees remain in neighboring countries and another 300,000 remain internally displaced, these figures are down from the nearly 2 million people who were driven from their homes at the height of the crisis.[19] Morbidity and mortality rates have returned to normal levels. Public schools have opened sporadically across southern Somalia with the support of elders, women's groups, and NGOs. The opening of schools, if it had been accomplished more broadly in the large cities, might well have measurably affected both the security situation and urban economies. The merchant class has begun to reassert itself and civil society is reconstituting itself at the local level.

One report has it that the Ranhanweyn elders, using the proceeds from a particularly bountiful crop in August 1994, have purchased weapons and organized a 2,000-man militia to protect their relatively defenseless farms in the interriverine area. This balance of militia power might provide sufficient protection for this militarily weaker clan to avoid the atrocities and starvation it experienced in 1992.

In the end Somalis can survive without government, but they cannot survive without food, water, and shelter. Civil society has begun to repair itself, and the social order has been gradually sewn back together by the Somali people themselves.

The Somalia intervention did meet limited rehabilitative objectives without a political settlement or the establishment of a national government, which may take many years to accomplish. Though it remains to be seen how the health and food security of Somalia will fare now that UN peacekeeping forces have fully withdrawn, I suspect the Somalis will cope without a central government for some time to come and that the starvation of 1991–1992 will not recur.

Notes

1. Center for Disease Control, "Morbidity and Mortality Weekly Report 41" no. 49, December 11, 1992, pp. 913–917.

2. I attended most of the deputies' meetings of the National Security Council during the Somalia crisis.

3. I attended this meeting between Philip Johnston and President Bush in the Oval Office on December 12, 1992.

4. See Refugee Policy Group study on Somalia, *Lives Lost, Lives Saved* (Washington, DC: Refugee Policy Group, November 1994).

5. These data come from my informal market surveys in southern Somali cities during two field trips at the end of August and September 1992. See Andrew Natsios, "Feeding Somalia," *Christian Science Monitor*, September 11, 1992, p. 18.

6. Fred Cuny (Intertect Corporation), letter to the author, March 14, 1995.

7. Princeton Lyman, director of the Refugee Program Office in the State Department; Jim Kunder, USAID-OFDA director; and I were the three U.S. officials who met with these Somali representatives.

8. See Refugee Policy Group, *Lives Lost, Lives Saved,* p. 12.

9. Upon the arrival of the OFDA field team in late August 1992, daily situation reports were sent back to Washington, D.C., that aggregated data from other NGOs, the ICRC, UN officials, and their own observations. See Jan Wescott, *The Somalia Saga: A Personal Account 1990–93* (Washington, DC: Refugee Policy Group, November 1994), p. 30.

10. Fred Cuny, telephone conversations with the author, October and November 1992.

11. Natsios, "Feeding Somalia," p. 18.

12. USAID was unable to get DOD to waive its airlift standard operating procedure to increase the volume of food being moved.

13. See Cuny, letter to the author, March 14, 1995.

14. During the civil war in Sri Lanka between the Tamils and Sinhalese, merchants who had been encouraging widespread theft of food as a source for their markets became advocates of peace, putting heavy pressure on political leaders after a monetization program was begun to sell food to the merchants on a more regular and legitimate basis.

15. Said Samatar, the Somali scholar, in his book *Nation in Search of a State* (Boulder: Westview Press, 1987), argues persuasively that the clan elder system was a major stabilizing force in Somali society and publicly advocated throughout the Somali crisis that it be strengthened.

16. See ICRC, report for November 1992 on Somalia Kitchen Program. Geoff Loane, project direction.

17. See Refugee Policy Group, *Hope Restored? Humanitarian Aid in Somalia 1990–1994* (Washington, DC: Refugee Policy Group, November 1994), p. 99.

18. Fred Cuny, memo to the author, September 12, 1992, p. 4.

19. See OFDA situation reports for August 1992 and December 1994.

PART 3
Military Aspects of Intervention

6

The Relationship Between the Military and Humanitarian Organizations in Operation Restore Hope

KEVIN M. KENNEDY

The principal reason for launching Operation Restore Hope in December 1992 was to relieve the suffering and starvation of the Somali people. To achieve this objective, the Unified Task Force (UNITAF) intervention force was required to work closely with the humanitarian organizations carrying out relief activities in Somalia.[1] The purpose of this chapter is to describe how the relationship between the military forces and the humanitarian community evolved, the problems encountered, and the lessons learned by the participants and to suggest how future such operations can benefit from the Restore Hope experience.

This chapter focuses on the relationship between the military and the humanitarian organizations during the period of the initial intervention by the U.S.-led Unified Task Force, which extended from December 9, 1992, to May 4, 1993, when the transition to United Nations Operation in Somalia (UNOSOM II) occurred. Although the experiences of UNOSOM II with humanitarian organizations are also worthy of analysis, the focus of the UNITAF mission on humanitarian support as well as the relative stability of the UNITAF period compared to UNOSOM II (where military activities obscured humanitarian efforts) render the UNITAF mandate an optimum period to examine military-humanitarian relationships.[2]

The UNITAF Mission

When the First Marine Expeditionary Force (I MEF) at Camp Pendleton, California, received deployment orders to Somalia in late November 1992, little

---

This chapter is written from the vantage point of my service as the director of the UNITAF Civil Military Operations Center for the entire UNITAF intervention. The opinions expressed reflect my experiences and observations and are solely my responsibility.

was known about the situation in Somalia and what the forces would encounter upon arrival. There had been no official U.S. presence in Somalia since the fall of the Siad Barre government in January 1991. U.S. intelligence networks had been dismantled and were just being reestablished. The principal sources of information were media reports and the limited experience of U.S. forces (many from I MEF) participating in Operation Provide Relief, the Somalia airlift that had begun the previous August. Although this experience was helpful, the airlift had delivered to only a few key locations in central and southern Somalia (Baidoa, Bardera, Belet Weyn, and Hoddur) where time on the ground was kept to a minimum for security and efficiency reasons. The airlift had not operated regularly into either Mogadishu or Kismayu, and Americans had had only a temporary presence in Mogadishu airport during the introduction of UNOSOM I troops in September and October 1992. It was well understood that lack of security prevented food deliveries, but the full dimensions of the problem were not known.

During the planning phase for the deployment, there was no contact at the operational level (I MEF) with representatives of the humanitarian organizations working in Somalia. What parties the MEF would be working with, their expectations, and the scope of their requirements were largely unknown to the military forces charged with carrying out the humanitarian intervention.

In this context, I MEF (then called Joint Task Force Somalia and subsequently Unified Task Force Somalia) developed its mission statement based on guidance received from the National Command Authorities and U.S. Central Command. The mission had four principal elements:[3]

• Secure Mogadishu port and airfield.
• Secure lines of communication to the interior.
• Provide security escorts for relief supply convoys and relief organization operations.
• Assist the United Nations nongovernmental organizations in providing humanitarian relief under UN auspices.

The I MEF commander, Lt. Gen. Robert B. Johnston, further elaborated on the missions of UNITAF. He emphasized the creation of a secure environment within which UN and NGO humanitarian organizations could operate. Opening the ports and airfields and securing the routes to the interior as well as distribution sites would improve security and end the famine. Creating this environment would permit transition to a UN force, which was the end goal of the operation.

For planning purposes, it was assumed that arrangements similar to Operation Provide Relief would be established to identify humanitarian organization requirements. During Provide Relief, members of the Office of Foreign Disaster Assistance (OFDA), Disaster Assistance Response Team (DART), were collocated with the headquarters of the Joint Task Force. Requests for airlift support and food and other logistical requests were transmitted directly to the DART team either from humanitarian organization representatives in Kenya or else directly from field sites in Somalia. The DART would validate the requests and pass them to the U.S. Joint Task Force (JTF) for execution. This system had worked well in the context of the airlift operation, and it was hoped it could do the same on the ground in Somalia.

During preparations at Camp Pendleton, Brigadier General Anthony C. Zinni, the newly assigned J-3 (Operations) for UNITAF, directed that a Civil Military Operations Center (CMOC) be formed from J-3 personnel and newly arriving elements of Company C of the 96th Civil Affairs Battalion (Airborne) from Fort Bragg, North Carolina, which were joining UNITAF for the operation. The CMOC would coordinate military support for humanitarian operations.

Briefings on the humanitarian situation in Somalia were held at Camp Pendleton for key commanders and staffs. In addition to identifying what was known about major relief players in Somalia (based on the Provide Relief experience), these briefings provided guidance on the operating styles of the humanitarian relief organizations and potential problems. These briefings noted the decentralized and independent nature of humanitarian organizations, the need for proactive efforts to overcome any antimilitary sentiments, and the necessity of considering the needs of the humanitarian community before satisfying military requirements if the right atmosphere and working relationships were to be established.[4]

Deployment and Establishment of Coordination Mechanisms

The lead elements of the UNITAF command element arrived in Mogadishu on December 10 after a twenty-two-hour flight from Marine Corps Air Station, El Toro, California, with only a brief stop for final consultations at U.S. Central Command at MacDill Air Force Base, Tampa, Florida. Once in Mogadishu, the command element linked up with the Special Purpose Marine Air Ground Task Force (SPMAGTF), which had come ashore the previous day. The following day, December 11, a UNITAF representative (Colonel Kevin M. Kennedy, USMC) arrived at the headquarters of UNOSOM I in south Mogadishu where he met with DART representatives (led by Bill Garvelink) to begin putting in place the necessary coordination and liaison arrangements with the humanitarian organizations.

In mid-December 1992, the humanitarian community in Mogadishu consisted of twenty-one international NGOs, six UN agencies, the ICRC, and the IFRC. The ICRC and a handful of NGOs had remained in Somalia throughout the civil war and ensuing conflicts; many of these organizations had only recently arrived or reestablished operations in Somalia. These organizations not only conducted relief operations in the greater Mogadishu area but also functioned (with a few exceptions) as the country headquarters for their respective operations throughout Somalia. Mogadishu thus represented the nerve center for relief operations and the principal location for coordination between the military and humanitarian organizations.

Within the UNOSOM headquarters was the office of the UN humanitarian coordinator, Philip Johnston, who had initially been posted to Mogadishu in October 1992 as the coordinator of the UN 100 Day Emergency Program.

Johnston had been seconded from his regular assignment as president and chief executive officer of CARE USA. He and a very talented but small team of approximately a half-dozen staff were charged with the enormous task of coordinating relief and assistance efforts throughout Somalia. They had made substantial progress in setting up a coordination structure, but many of their efforts had been frustrated by the insecure conditions prevailing in Somalia and their limited staff resources. Lack of security in Mogadishu, especially in the port, had prevented the import and distribution of food in any significant quantities. Food deliveries to Mogadishu port, difficult under the best of circumstances, had stopped completely on November 14, 1992, when a relief ship had been taken under artillery fire while attempting to enter the port. Since then, the only food arriving in Mogadishu had come by air into Mogadishu airport, which was also insecure due to militia activity. Moreover, without the delivery of food in quantity into Mogadishu, no significant quantities could be forwarded to the interior. The lack of staff also made it very difficult for the humanitarian coordinator's office to respond to the many demands placed upon it in an exceedingly difficult working environment.

Given Lieutenant General Johnston's orders to the CMOC to "Get things going and get it going fast"[5] and the existence of a basic UN humanitarian coordination structure (which fit neatly with the UNITAF mission statement), it was decided to join forces and collocate the UNITAF CMOC with the UN facility. This was not a particularly deliberate decision, but it seemed to be the most convenient place to meet with the humanitarian organizations and support the UN's efforts to coordinate and lead the assistance efforts. There was no additional guidance on command relationships between the CMOC and the UN humanitarian coordinator; the CMOC still reported directly to the UNITAF J-3 (Operations) but also informally "seconded" itself to the United Nations. This rather ambiguous relationship was left deliberately vague and worked for the best interests of all.

OFDA made a similar judgment and assigned personnel to work with the UN humanitarian coordinator on a full-time basis. Initially, Bill Garvelink was the senior representative; his duties were subsequently assumed by Kate Farnsworth, also of OFDA.

The coordination arrangements established at the beginning of UNITAF remained essentially the same throughout the operation and consisted of two structures: the UN Humanitarian Operations Center (HOC) and the UNITAF Civil Military Operations Center (CMOC), which became an integral component of the HOC.

The organization of the HOC is in Appendix B. Johnston led the HOC (as the operations coordinator) with a civilian deputy (Garvelink) and a military deputy (Kennedy). Its components included an information management unit, a regional liaison, CMOC, and a sectoral liaison that worked with the sectoral core groups established by the UN-NGO humanitarian staff. Policy oversight was provided by a standing liaison committee composed of various UN, UNITAF, NGO, and ICRC representatives.

The stated mission of the HOC was "to plan, support, and monitor delivery of humanitarian assistance."[6] Conceptually, the HOC was to

- serve as the focal point for all humanitarian relief organizations;
- increase the efficiency of humanitarian operations through planning and coordination;
- gather and disseminate information among all humanitarian relief organizations; and
- provide the link for the humanitarian community to UNITAF and UNOSOM military forces.

The Mogadishu HOC was linked by radio with UN field representatives at key relief sites throughout central and southern Somalia. In these locations, UNITAF forces worked with UN and NGO representatives to form regional HOCs to perform humanitarian coordination functions. Participating military elements were either U.S. Army Civil Affairs teams supporting U.S. forces or designated humanitarian liaison officers from allied UNITAF contingents. These regional HOC arrangements are depicted in Appendix C. The organization of the CMOC is in Appendix D. Throughout Operation Restore Hope, it remained a small and austere organization for several reasons. It was recognized early on that the sheer size and complexity of the military could easily overwhelm the humanitarian community (at its height, UNITAF had a strength of over 38,000; there were never more than 300 international humanitarian relief workers in the whole of Somalia). Within the confines of the HOC, a large uniformed presence was considered inappropriate, particularly while the military-humanitarian relationship was still developing. UNITAF very much wanted to remain in a support role and let the humanitarian organizations take the lead. Accordingly, the CMOC normally comprised about five U.S. Marine and Army officers, several noncommissioned officers, and a few clerks and drivers. It never totaled more than twelve people and normally averaged a strength of ten.

A second reason driving the small size of the CMOC was an appreciation for the need to remain as nimble, responsive, and nonbureaucratic as possible in order to best meet the needs of the CMOC's customers, that is, the humanitarian organizations. Given the propensity of large organizations (including military organizations) to spend inordinate time and energy looking after their own needs and the unfamiliarity and misgivings of civilian relief organizations in working with the military, a small and efficient CMOC working as a conduit to higher military headquarters was seen as the best alternative. Last, even when increasing CMOC responsibilities led to a requirement for more personnel, additional staff were not readily provided.

The CMOC was supplemented by liaison officers from the various military contingents responsible for the Humanitarian Relief Sectors (HRSs), which had been established throughout the UNITAF area of operations. The liaison officers were not permanent members of the CMOC but would attend the daily information and coordination meeting to brief on activities in their HRS, respond to questions, resolve issues, and be available to do detailed planning with humanitarian organization representatives who were seeking military support.

Four principal missions were defined for the CMOC at the outset of the operation:[7]

- Serve as the UNITAF liaison to the humanitarian community and UNOSOM headquarters.
- Validate and coordinate requests for military support.
- Function as the UNITAF Civil Affairs Office.
- Monitor military support in the regional HOCs.

The CMOC missions evolved over time as the operation matured. Much of the liaison with UNOSOM (except the humanitarian component) eventually became the responsibility of other UNITAF staff sections as disarmament and transition to UNOSOM II issues came to the fore. The civil affairs function was largely handled within each Humanitarian Relief Sector by unit-level representatives, though CMOC continued to perform civil affairs missions and made regular field visits to supervise the U.S. Army Civil Affairs teams. Additional duties were assumed to include chairing the Mogadishu Port Committee, processing identification cards for relief workers, and functioning as an emergency response team.

Interactions Between the Military and Humanitarian Organizations

The mix of organizational cultures was a striking feature of the Restore Hope operation. The military and humanitarian communities had different perceptions, expectations, styles, and agendas, and they had the task of cooperating and settling conflicts in the midst of a major humanitarian emergency. The result of their efforts was, by and large, a remarkably successful and productive relationship. The principal objectives of Operation Restore Hope—securing ports and airfields, opening up lines of communication, and safely escorting relief convoys to their destinations—were achieved quickly and professionally. The arrival of UNITAF not only helped relieve the suffering of the Somali people, it enabled humanitarian organizations to carry out their programs with unprecedented scope and efficiency.

Within this framework of general cooperation and good relations between UNITAF forces and the humanitarian organizations, varying patterns of military-humanitarian relationships emerged. To wit, military-humanitarian relations in Humanitarian Relief Sectors outside Mogadishu were generally good, productive, and without major problems; in Mogadishu, support to humanitarian organizations was maintained, but often in a very contentious atmosphere. The unfortunate outcome was that the extraordinary level of humanitarian support provided by the UNITAF force was often overshadowed by conflicts between the military and the humanitarian community in Mogadishu, which persisted throughout the operation.

Early Stages

The general attitude displayed by the humanitarian community at the beginning of Restore Hope can best be characterized as wary but hopeful. Most of the humanitarian workers had little experience with the military, and some were very vocal in their opposition to the UNITAF intervention, harboring a basic dislike toward the whole concept of military force, particularly in the context of humanitarian assistance. The intervention was occasionally characterized as a public relations exercise that came too late and would not address the long-term needs of Somalia.

Simultaneously, many of the humanitarian organizations had high expectations of UNITAF and what its presence could do for their activities. The initial demand urgently made by the humanitarian community was for an immediate UNITAF presence throughout all of central and southern Somalia and often beyond. UNITAF had planned to take three weeks and more to expand its footprint beyond Mogadishu. This was largely due to the constraints the Mogadishu port and airfield imposed on the force buildup and the desire of UNITAF commanders to achieve force levels capable of meeting any possible threat as they expanded operations. This approach was considered too leisurely by many humanitarian organizations, which argued for near simultaneous troop deployments everywhere. They were concerned that a "bow wave" of lawless elements retreating into the countryside would seize the opportunity for one last looting spree. Ultimately, UNITAF accelerated its deployment schedule and had forces in place in all principal relief sites by December 26, 1992.

The initial UNITAF approach was to take proactive measures to initiate humanitarian support, such as establishing the CMOC and deploying Civil Affairs teams while devoting the bulk of its efforts to force protection, coalition building, and gradual expansion of the area of operations. Extraordinary logistics were required to deploy, establish, and support UNITAF. Available assets would be provided to support humanitarian operations (the first relief convoy was escorted by the Special Purpose Marine Air Ground Task Force on December 12), but primary attention remained focused on force protection and logistics.

Daily coordination meetings with humanitarian organizations were initiated on December 11, 1992. Normally chaired by the humanitarian coordinator, supported by the civilian and military deputies, they became the principal conduit for information, coordination, and liaison. At the initial meeting, the CMOC articulated the UNITAF approach (modeled on those successfully applied in Operation Provide Relief, albeit on a smaller scale) to working with humanitarian organizations.

The military was in Somalia to support humanitarian organizations in carrying out their work, not to take over their responsibilities. Thus the following principles would apply:

• All CMOC meetings would be inclusive, open to all organizations that had a role in humanitarian assistance. Any organization or individual was welcome to make a contribution.

• Information would be shared. All information concerning security conditions and UNITAF and UNITAF support to humanitarian operations would be made public. Humanitarian organizations were encouraged to share their information. The only restriction was on information whose disclosure would compromise military operations.

• UNITAF would respond as quickly as possible to all requests made by humanitarian organizations. If a request could not be met, the organization would be informed as expeditiously as possible.

The UNITAF criteria for supporting humanitarian organization requests were also promulgated:

• The request had to be in concert with the UNITAF mission.
• Sufficient support assets had to be available.
• UNITAF would be as helpful as possible.[8]

The HOC-CMOC meetings rapidly developed into the principal forum for military-humanitarian coordination, information, and problem solving in Somalia. Procedures were put in place for humanitarian organizations to submit support requests that were either answered in the CMOC or forwarded to higher headquarters for response. All outstanding humanitarian support requests were routinely summarized and verified. The security and humanitarian situations throughout Somalia were briefed daily and input solicited from the humanitarian organizations. UNITAF commanders and principal staff officers, visiting senior humanitarian officials from UN agencies and NGOs, and a wide variety of UN and bilateral diplomats and representatives were invited to make presentations on subjects of interest to the humanitarian community. Liaison officers from all contingents controlling a Humanitarian Relief Sector as well as representatives from key facilities of interest to the humanitarian community (port and airfield) were briefed and were available for coordination. UNITAF staff officers from medical, communications and from psychological, legal, and engineering operations provided special briefs on their work and its impact on humanitarian organizations. Questions concerning UNITAF policies (and their application) were addressed. Hundreds of separate meetings to address the needs of individual organizations were organized and conducted.

Due to security and travel concerns of humanitarian organizations located across the "green line" in northern Mogadishu, CMOC representatives went to a separate meeting every other day in order to provide similar briefing and coordination services to northern Mogadishu–based organizations. In sum, the Mogadishu CMOC developed into a humanitarian service center and clearinghouse. Equally important, similar patterns of military-humanitarian coordination and relations developed in interior Humanitarian Relief Sectors within the context of the regional HOCs and their CMOC components.

Stabilization and Development of Humanitarian Support

With the arrival of additional forces and equipment and the lodgment of the UNITAF throughout almost all of central and southern Somalia, UNITAF support to humanitarian organizations increased commensurably. The principal categories of UNITAF direct and indirect support follow.

Convoy escorts. During the period from December 12, 1992, through April 15, 1993, 154 long-haul food convoys (averaging twenty trucks and 600 metric tons per convoy) were escorted from Mogadishu and Kismayu to interior distribution centers;[9] hundreds of additional convoys were organized to move the food on to its ultimate destinations. An estimated 100,000 metric tons of long-haul food was escorted. Additionally, the Mogadishu Food Distribution Scheme delivered a total of 350 tons per day six days per week commencing in February 1993 and continuing through April 30 to thirty-five separate feeding sites in Mogadishu City. Hundreds of security escorts for humanitarian fieldwork or vehicle movement were also conducted (237 organized in Mogadishu alone through April 15, 1993). An Indian naval ship served as a transporter for humanitarian cargoes along the Somalia coast and on to Kenya.

Engineering support. The poor conditions of the roads required a massive engineering effort by over 7,000 UNITAF engineers. They repaired or improved a total of 1,800 kilometers of roads, thus permitting access to all principal relief sites in central and southern Somalia. Additionally, fourteen wells were dug and nine airfields improved to support heavy aircraft such as C-130s or C-141s.[10]

Port and airfield management. UNITAF opened, improved, and operated the ports of Mogadishu and Kismayu, which permitted access for both military and humanitarian cargoes. To avoid conflicts in port priorities in Mogadishu, a shipping committee (chaired by the UNITAF CMOC director) was formed on December 12 with military and humanitarian representatives to ensure that humanitarian organizations had access to the port amidst heavy military usage. Similarly, arrangements and procedures were put in place at Mogadishu airport to ensure humanitarian access.

Technical assistance and support services. A whole array of services was eventually made available to the humanitarian community. These services included provision of fuel to run the UNDP-managed Mogadishu City water project; helicopter reconnaissance and escort flights to locate vulnerable populations, make assessments, and escort returning refugees; medevac services and emergency hospital privileges for humanitarian staff; repair of humanitarian organizational equipment; and permission to fly aboard UNITAF aircraft on a space-available basis. The bulk of these services were coordinated either through the Mogadishu CMOC or a regional HOC.

Planning assistance. A variety of ad hoc planning groups were formed within the CMOC to facilitate relief efforts. These were joint undertakings that included representatives from both UNITAF and humanitarian organizations. A notable example was a planning group that developed a matrix—projected road openings, transport and warehouse capacities and shortfalls, and military escort capabilities—to identify needs for food and coordinate deliveries throughout the UNITAF area of operations.

Areas of Military–Humanitarian Organization Conflict

Amidst all the successful joint efforts conducted by UNITAF and the humanitarian organizations, a series of recurring conflicts surfaced, centered in Mogadishu, that negatively affected the tone and spirit of military-humanitarian relations. These conflicts came about due to frictions created by the overlapping issues of institutional differences, divergent views of security, and application of weapons-control policies.

Institutional Differences

Although the potential for conflict between military and humanitarian institutions is a constant feature of military-civilian humanitarian operations, the two communities in Somalia generally got along well. Over time, teamwork developed and each partner came to appreciate the contributions and strengths of the other. This modus vivendi especially applied in the Humanitarian Relief Sectors outside Mogadishu. Because each unit operated in a relatively sparsely populated area with usually just one military contingent and a limited number of NGOs and UN agencies, problems were more easily identified, addressed, and resolved. Commanders and their HOC-CMOC representatives had the opportunity to work closely with and get to know their humanitarian counterparts. Issues relating to convoys, access to and use of military assets, security for humanitarian facilities, and control of Somali NGO security guards and their weapons were usually worked out in an atmosphere of mutual trust and confidence.

This degree of friendly cooperation was not attained in Mogadishu. It was admittedly a far more challenging situation. Mogadishu's large population (estimated between 700,000 and 1 million people, many of whom were internally displaced); the presence of several clans; the existence of key facilities such as the port and airfield (which attracted more than their share of troublemakers); and the fact that the city was the headquarters and logistics hub of eventually over fifty international humanitarian organizations, UNITAF, UNOSOM I, and the large variety of military contingents all worked to create a complex environment, particularly for the military commanders, who were charged with both maintaining security and supporting humanitarian operations.

Within the Mogadishu environment, the relative differences between the humanitarian community and the military forces tended to stand out. Humanitarian organizations had a large and visible physical presence (approximately 105 office and residence buildings alone), and members enjoyed the relative freedom to move about the city accompanied by armed Somali guards, lived in austere but far better conditions than the military, and even had access to a modest social life. In their dealings with the military, humanitarian organizations were usually supplicants, but this did not prevent some from adopting a confrontational, critical approach that implied a belief that humanitarian workers permanently occupied the moral high ground in all discussions. This behavior was a distinct exception to the generally cordial approach that prevailed, but it tended to reinforce antihumanitarian attitudes held by some military personnel.

The military personnel in Mogadishu were either restricted to their compounds (it was not uncommon for many UNITAF personnel, for either security or transport reasons, to never leave their cantonment) or else patroled the streets in an environment that was dangerous and unpredictable. Among some elements of the military (particularly the U.S. Marines [MARFOR], responsible for the largest portion of Mogadishu), the humanitarian organizations came to be viewed with a combination of suspicion and contempt. This was a minority view, but it was held by sufficient numbers of commanders and staff officers to magnify its impact. The humanitarian organizations were seen as a somewhat undisciplined, disorganized lot whose operations were often counterproductive to achieving the high level of security they demanded that the military establish. For example, they extensively employed suspect Somali guards and lived in personally convenient, comfortable, and dispersed residences but at the same time were quick to call upon the military if danger loomed. A belief frequently expressed was that the humanitarian organizations did not appreciate the magnitude of the military efforts on their behalf or the challenge of maintaining security in Mogadishu. These feelings tended to blend with a latent anti-UN sentiment that increased over time: The food crisis had subsided and UNITAF personnel felt they had accomplished their mission; they blamed their continued presence in Somalia on the slow buildup of UNOSOM. The net effect was an atmosphere characterized by sustained and substantial military support to humanitarian organizations coupled with an often contentious approach that created conflict rather than cooperation.

Security Expectations

Despite the presence of a heavily armed and vigilant UNITAF presence throughout Somalia, security could not be guaranteed. Lawless elements still existed and continued to operate. Newly reestablished local police forces, despite major efforts to facilitate their rebirth, never achieved the ability to carry out much more than minimal traffic control or public presence missions. Military forces, while aiming to establish a "secure environment," did not see themselves as either equipped or tasked to carry out police functions. The military focus was on presence, provision of convoy escorts, force protection, a reduction in level of violence, and transition to the United Nations. This security policy vis-à-vis the humanitarian organizations was interpreted differently among the Humanitarian Relief Sectors in UNITAF. For the most part, the UNITAF security umbrella in interior HRSs was routinely extended to include the relief organizations. This included launching emergency response units if the organizations were threatened or providing UNITAF military guards for their residences and warehouses. For example, in Baidoa, the Australian contingent provided permanent security to ten NGO or UN agency locations; in Kismayu and Jilib the Belgian forces guarded twelve sites.[11]

In Mogadishu, UNITAF was reluctant to respond to requests for site security or emergency assistance.[12] The heavy concentration of humanitarian facilities, particularly in southern Mogadishu, and the extensive patrolling requirements in a large city made provision of troops for humanitarian site security impractical; relief organizations generally understood this and usually requested a permanent UNITAF presence only when they felt directly threatened.

Emergency response was a more difficult issue and was complicated by the presence of armed Somali guards at every humanitarian agency residence, warehouse, or facility. The relief agencies had little choice in the matter. They could not rent a facility (or a vehicle for that matter) without the landlord either providing guards as part of the rental package or insisting the relief organization supply guards in order to protect his investment. In a city with many bandits and no police or phones to summon them if a credible police capacity had existed, relief agencies were well advised to look after their own basic security requirements. The military viewed these guards with disdain. They did not consider them to be reliable and took the view that if the relief agencies were willing to employ the guards, they should look to the guards for their security. An additional complicating factor was that an emergency response, particularly at night, could easily end up in a firefight between "friendlies."

The NGOs in Mogadishu were incredulous at the reluctance of the military to respond when they were in trouble. They saw this as a natural part of the military's mission in Somalia; they failed to see how the establishment of a "secure environment" that didn't include response to relief organizations in trouble could be supportive to humanitarian efforts. This fueled a growing belief among Mogadishu-based NGOs that security was actually deteriorating for humanitarian workers.[13] The working compromise adopted while the security policy was sorted out was the assumption by the CMOC of emergency response duties for humanitarian organizations in southern Mogadishu. Sixteen such missions were carried out without major incident, though the CMOC was neither equipped nor staffed to handle major emergencies. Eventually, in mid-March 1993, military forces began routinely responding to emergencies after a major incident at the CARE USA and World Food Program headquarters, which had been blockaded and threatened by Somalis claiming back wages. This change in policy in Mogadishu came about in the wake of prolonged discussions at the most senior military and civilian levels.

Weapons Control and Humanitarian Identification Cards

Easily the most contentious issue between the military forces and the humanitarian community was the control of weapons used by the relief organizations' Somali guards. This issue was raised soon after UNITAF deployed to Somalia and remained, at least in Mogadishu, a source of conflict and friction for the entire operation.

The initial problem concerned access for humanitarian workers, accompanied by vehicles with Somalia security men, into UNITAF-controlled facilities such as the port and airfield. A system was devised whereby international humanitarian personnel were issued identification cards by the CMOC that permitted access to the port and airfield for them and their security personnel, who left their weapons at the gate. The serialized cards, pink in color, were modeled on an existing UNITAF internal access card but had neither the picture nor name of the holder.

As weapons policies in Mogadishu and elsewhere were changed to emphasize vice control by means of confiscation, the problem for relief organizations increasingly became retention of their weapons in the midst of progressively tightened and rigorously enforced weapons-control programs. Weapons control was focused on removing weapons from the streets in order to reduce the level of violence. The large humanitarian organization armed security presence (an estimated 1,100 vehicle and facility guards in Mogadishu alone) ended up bearing the brunt of the policy; other Somalis quickly learned to keep their weapons out of sight and avoid UNITAF checkpoints. Several abuses of "pink cards" reduced their credibility with military forces.

The weapons-control policies were generally welcomed by Somalis and the humanitarian organizations alike. They had a positive impact on the level of violence as measured by the numbers of Somalis admitted to hospitals with gunshot wounds.[14] However, the humanitarian organizations still needed protection, which the military was often not willing or able to directly provide, and the military viewed the relief organizations' security guards as part of the problem and not part of the solution. This was particularly true for vehicle guards who worked for relief organizations during the day but were left to their own devices at night. Although incidents with relief organization security personnel were rare, those few incidents that did occur fueled military distrust of the security personnel and, by extension, the relief organizations.

Hundreds of weapons were taken from relief organizations throughout December and January, especially in Mogadishu, and often despite the presence of a UNITAF identification card. The relief organizations bitterly complained that the weapons confiscations were seriously affecting their security and ability to work; it was unsafe to move without protection, and their guards and drivers would not normally consider traveling unarmed. Their complaints usually resulted in CMOC personnel retrieving the weapons from the confiscating unit and returning them to the relief organization. This round robin, dysfunctional system often resulted in ironic and almost comical situations: Meetings for the purpose of arranging support for humanitarian programs were dominated by discussions focused on the nuances of UNITAF weapons policies, and relief workers departed burdened with recovered AK-47s and M-16s.

As complaints from the humanitarian community mounted, UNITAF adopted a new identification card[15] that had the bearer's photograph and weapons serial number. Somali security personnel, vouched for by their employers, were issued cards. Although not a foolproof system, it resolved any remaining conflicts in UNITAF's HRSs outside Mogadishu, which in any event had experienced relatively few problems. In Mogadishu, at least in the MARFOR sector, the new cards had little lasting positive effect, partly because the card program was poorly supported by UNITAF (only two clerks were provided to issue several thousand cards, and the film and lamination materials were mostly obtained from NGO sources because of military supply problems) but largely because weapons policies were increasingly subject to a variety of ever stricter interpretations by the units enforcing them. These included confiscating weapons for being "visible." Visible often meant just being seen on the floor of a vehicle when passing a UNITAF checkpoint. Weapons confiscations (and returns)[16] escalated, and the frustrations of the humanitarian organizations rose.

Repeated efforts were made to resolve the problem. There was a series of meetings between senior UNITAF and MARFOR officers with representatives of the humanitarian community. UNITAF belatedly published a brochure in English and Somali that delineated the weapons policies in words and pictures. Briefings for Somali security personnel and security assessments of relief organization compounds were provided upon request. These measures had some positive impact, but as late as the week of March 25 to 31, fifty-four weapons were confiscated from humanitarian organizations for various infractions, real or perceived, of weapons policies.

The net effect of the continuing controversies over weapons was the diversion of much of the military-humanitarian dialogue in Mogadishu from issues of humanitarian assistance and mutual cooperation to weapons policies and differences between the military and relief organizations. The problem, which was resolved only with the departure of the marines from Mogadishu, cast a pall on overall military-humanitarian relations. Given the prolonged nature of the problem, the inability to reach a successful resolution despite numerous efforts at the most senior levels, and the generally compliant nature of the humanitarian organizations, one is led to the conclusion that the sustained confrontation represented more than just the vigorous application of weapons policies and was based on a fundamental antagonism toward humanitarian organizations from some elements within UNITAF.

Reasons for Military-Humanitarian Conflict

A basic question to be answered is why military-humanitarian relations were often difficult in much of Mogadishu as compared to the largely positive relations achieved in other UNITAF Humanitarian Relief Sectors. The humanitarian organizations present in Mogadishu were usually the same organizations that were working effectively with UNITAF elsewhere in Somalia; though not without their own problems, the relief organizations were in the main cooperative and compliant with UNITAF policies. Whereas the environment in Mogadishu was the most challenging, military forces in other urban areas with similar challenges (for example, the Italian forces in northern Mogadishu or the U.S. Army and Belgian forces in Kismayu) managed to achieve a satisfactory relationship with humanitarian organizations that eluded the marines in southern Mogadishu. Nor does the problem appear to have been one experienced solely by U.S. Marines, as marine forces in Bardera had a very positive relationship with relief organizations.

Three factors may explain the reasons for the differences in the quality of military-humanitarian relations in Mogadishu as compared to elsewhere in Somalia and perhaps point to larger lessons for future operations.

Interpretation of the UNITAF Mission

Was the mission of UNITAF solely to escort convoys and create a secure environment or did it envision a more active role in providing security to humanitarian organizations and supporting their assistance efforts? There was a fundamentally different interpretation of the mission among different military contingents within UNITAF and often differences within the same contingent. Most would readily support requests from humanitarian organizations on a fairly automatic basis; some, notably the U.S. Marines in Mogadishu, were often reluctant to take on additional requests. This attitude reflected in part the heavy demands already placed upon marines personnel within Mogadishu. Also, the essential mission was seen by some as the maintenance of a secure environment; this mission, other than the primary responsibility of providing convoy escorts, was not interpreted as automatically including humanitarian agency security.

Military View of Humanitarian Organizations

The various military contingents in UNITAF adopted one of two basic approaches toward the humanitarian organizations. Most took the view that the humanitarian organizations were natural allies whose success would support the success of the military unit. These contingents sought out relief organizations, (even those who were not initially keen on the military presence), mixed well with them, and generally received full cooperation and more from the humanitarian community. In a second approach, the relief organizations were treated as just one more element to contend with and certainly one that did not warrant special treatment. This was often the approach demonstrated in southern Mogadishu, where open hostility toward relief organizations was frequently displayed in a "we versus you" context. This attitude created impressions that sporadic positive overtures to relief organizations could not overcome.

Organizational Arrangements

In Mogadishu, unlike in the other Humanitarian Relief Sectors in Somalia, the contingents responsible for the city (U.S. Marines and Italian forces) did not run the CMOC but relied on UNITAF headquarters staff to do so. The Mogadishu CMOC coordinated on both local and national levels. Thus, the UNITAF contingents in the city were somewhat removed from direct dealings with the relief organizations; perhaps if arrangements similar to those existing in outlying HRSs had been established in Mogadishu, military-humanitarian relations would have improved, if only because the cushion between the two parties would have been removed. It should be noted, however, that this arrangement did not appear to affect the Italian forces in their relations with humanitarian organizations, and both the marines and the Italians maintained a liaison presence in the Mogadishu CMOC with frequent visits from commanders and staff of both contingents.

Lessons Learned and Recommendations for Future Operations

Based on the Restore Hope experience, effective relations between military forces and humanitarian organizations may be achieved if the following measures are adopted.

Mission Clarity

Many of the problems in Operation Restore Hope stemmed from different interpretations of the UNITAF mission. Commanders will always retain the latitude to interpret their mission based on professional judgment, assets available, and the current situation, but a definitive statement on what minimum support humanitarian organizations could expect from the military, conditions permitting, would go a long way toward clarifying relations and adjusting mutual expectations.

Joint Mission Planning

The presence of representatives from the humanitarian community (OFDA, NGOs, UN agencies) at all levels during the planning process, and particularly with the units who will actually perform the mission, would have a positive effect on subsequent military-humanitarian relations. Although each institution has its own unique requirements and missions, sufficient mutual interests exist to create a functioning partnership prior to operations in the field.

Education and Training

Neither humanitarian organizations nor military forces in Somalia knew much about the other prior to Operation Restore Hope. Acquiring this information on the ground in the midst of a crisis, with many other competing priorities, is difficult at best. Incorporation of information on military and humanitarian organization methods, operations, and capacities in each community's respective training programs and exercises will better prepare each component.

Institutionalization of the Civil Military Operations Center Structure

The CMOC structures in UNITAF were created largely on the spot without benefit of a doctrine on missions, procedures, staffing, or equipment. They were effective but would have benefited greatly from a more organized, coherent approach with respect to their establishment and responsibilities. Military forces, in consultation with the humanitarian community, need to develop CMOC doctrine that serves as the basis for specific operational planning. Significant progress is being made in this area. Joint U.S. doctrine on CMOCs is being prepared by the J-7, Operational Plans and Interoperability Directorate, Joint Chiefs of Staff. Within the United Nations, the Department of Humanitarian Affairs (DHA) and the Department of Peacekeeping Operations (DPKO) are developing CMOC doctrine.

Definition of Security Responsibilities

Barring an effective peace-enforcement, Chapter 7–style operation, which assumes all security responsibilities, civilian and military planners need to better delineate the extent of their security responsibilities. A military presence in an environment where the local police force is nonexistent or discredited creates a security vacuum for those outside the military's security umbrella. Whereas security vacuums may impact humanitarian organizations, they are particularly problematic for the local population. It cannot turn to the humanitarian intervention force for security or police services and is simultaneously restrained from providing for its own security due to security policies of the same intervention force. There are no easy solutions, but increased use of military police forces (vice regular infantry), particularly in urban settings, may be an effective approach.

Strengthening of Humanitarian Coordination Capacity

Increasing the capacity and effectiveness of humanitarian coordination mechanisms will lead to the adoption of more coherent humanitarian plans and policies and provide for improved representation of humanitarian views to the military. Recent decisions have been made by the Inter-Agency Standing Committee (which includes the undersecretary-general for humanitarian affairs, the heads of UN humanitarian agencies, NGO and ICRC-IFRC representatives) to define and strengthen the role of the UN humanitarian coordinator in humanitarian emergencies.

Summary

Military-humanitarian relations in Operation Restore Hope were generally effective and helped both the humanitarian organizations and the military accomplish their respective missions. Problems between the two communities did occur, particularly in Mogadishu. Whereas these problems did not diminish overall military support or prevent mission accomplishment by either the military or humanitarian organizations, they persisted throughout the operation.

Most important, many valuable lessons were learned for the long term in this landmark operation and have already benefited both military and humanitarian organizations. For example, the UN Mission in Rwanda (UNAMIR) has established a model support relationship with UN agencies and NGOs. Available military support services have been clearly identified, and little friction between the military and humanitarian communities has developed. Liaison at the working level has been supplemented by regular meetings between the UNAMIR force commander, the UN humanitarian coordinator, and the heads of UN agencies and NGOs.

Similarly, during the U.S. intervention in Haiti there was a marked increase in preoperation joint planning as well as establishment of a CMOC during the very first days of the operation. The preparation and planning for Haiti directly benefited from lessons learned in Somalia, as many of the soldiers (drawn from the 10th Mountain Division) and humanitarian personnel had served together in Somalia.

Notes

1. Humanitarian organizations include nongovernmental organizations (NGOs), UN humanitarian agencies, the International Committee of the Red Cross (ICRC), and the International Federation of the Red Cross (IFRC). Collectively, they are often referred to as humanitarian relief organizations (HROs).

2. It is not at all clear that effective military-humanitarian relations can be maintained when the environment changes from peacekeeping to peacemaking. During UNOSOM II, hostilities in the Mogadishu area diverted military assets and created great strains between the military and humanitarian communities. Simultaneously, in other areas of Somalia where the thrust of military activity remained in the peacekeeping mode, military-humanitarian relations continued to be effective.

3. Joint Task Force Somalia, briefing, Camp Pendleton, California, December 8, 1992.

4. Observations on Somalia relief, I MEF, Camp Pendleton, California, December 8, 1992.

5. Lt. Gen. R. B. Johnston, USMC, verbal orders to Col. K. M. Kennedy, USMC.

6. UNITAF Somalia Humanitarian Operations Center, briefing, Mogadishu, December 20, 1992.

7. Ibid.

8. Ibid.

9. CMOC convoy update, April 16, 1993.

10. UNITAF, briefing for chair, Joint Chiefs of Staff (CJCS), Mogadishu, April 7, 1993.

11. UNITAF and humanitarian relief organizations, briefing, Mogadishu, March 22, 1993.

12. The Italian forces in northern Mogadishu were an exception. They routinely responded to humanitarian agencies in difficulty and provided a permanent presence at several ICRC offices and residences when they were under pressure.

13. Humanitarian personnel often pointed to the killings of three international staff (none in Mogadishu) in the first three months of 1993 as compared to no deaths in 1992.

14. UNITAF, briefing for CJCS, April 7, 1993

15. *UNITAF Identification and Weapon Policy*, February 5, 1993.

16. UNITAF briefing for CJCS, April 7, 1993. Confiscated rifles *nationwide* for the period December 10, 1992, to April 3, 1993, totaled 4,621, of which 710 had been returned to relief organizations. CMOC experience indicates that most of the confiscated weapons returned were in Mogadishu and that the numbers of returned weapons eventually exceeded 1,000.

7

Foreign Military Intervention in Somalia: The Root Cause of the Shift from UN Peacekeeping to Peacemaking and Its Consequences

JOHN DRYSDALE

The idea of having a foreign military presence in Somalia was formulated by the UN secretariat at the turn of the year 1991–1992 in response to events in the city of Mogadishu. The former president of Somalia, Siad Barre, had been ousted twelve months earlier. Since that time, the leaders of opposing factions, Mohamed Farah Aideed and Ali Mahdi Mohamed, had conducted a sometimes peaceful, sometimes violent, power struggle. Currently, gunners from both sides were pounding each other's civilian-occupied areas indiscriminately with heavy artillery and other forms of firepower. The few nongovernment organizations in Mogadishu estimated tens of thousands of casualties sustained by the civilian population.

In this chapter I focus on the consequences of the UN's response to events in Mogadishu in late 1991, which led the UN ten months later to invoke the enforcement provision of the UN Charter. I begin with the interactions between Aideed and Mahdi after Siad Barre's overthrow and up to the time of the UN response to the crisis in Mogadishu. This relationship had not been monitored by the UN secretariat and therefore was not included in its assessment and plan of action.

The Conflict over Succession
Following the Overthrow of Siad Barre

Despite a bitter dispute over political succession to the deposed president, Siad Barre, in January 1991, the hitherto bad relations between Mahdi and Aideed had been put on an even keel following an intervention by the elders of their respective subclans. This truce was a sequel to the failure in May 1991 of the first Italian- and Egyptian-sponsored Somali reconciliation conference in Djibouti.

An agreement signed by Mahdi and Aideed on June 5 removed the political distinctions between factions of the United Somali Congress (USC), to which both leaders belonged, obliging Mahdi to consult with the USC on policy, security, and defense matters and on all senior political and civil service appointments. The USC membership encompassed the huge Hawiye clan, which occupies much of central Somalia, including Mogadishu. Mahdi and Aideed were members of this clan, although of different subclans.

A month later, on July 5, the 700-member USC convened in Mogadishu and overwhelmingly elected Aideed as its chair (he received 72 percent of the vote). In the first week of August, following a second Djibouti conference that, inter alia, accepted the nomination of a USC figure as the two-year interim president of Somalia, the USC Central Committee endorsed the appointment of Mahdi. Aideed recognized Mahdi as the interim president and Mahdi recognized Aideed as chair of the USC. They were virtually on a par with each other, at least insofar as Mogadishu politics were concerned. Two principal conditions arising from the June 5 agreement were given emphatic endorsement, namely that Aideed would form a national army and Mahdi would form an interim government in consultation with the USC.

On October 3, 1991, Aideed withdrew his recognition of Mahdi's interim government, for reasons that will be discussed in the next section, and war broke out between them on November 17 of that year, ten months after Siad Barre had been ousted from power. This phase in the battle for control of Mogadishu, which in its period of greatest intensity lasted six weeks, ended inconclusively save for a contraction of the areas formerly resided in by some of Mahdi's followers and their concentration in northern Mogadishu.[1] Aideed's followers expanded their former areas of occupation in southern Mogadishu up to a point contiguous with positions held by Mahdi's supporters, by now substantially armed.

The UN's Dilemma over Sustaining a Cease-Fire

It was of prime importance that the potential for a renewed political settlement between Aideed and Mahdi (and their elders) be nourished. Both leaders, together with their respective elders, had already demonstrated that each could accept mutually compatible positions of high office. But the restoration of a working relationship between Mahdi and Aideed was not on the UN agenda. As the UN secretariat prepared in late December 1991 to intervene in the dispute—the first UN political contact with Somalia since Siad Barre had been ousted twelve months earlier—it focused exclusively on Mogadishu and the prospect for a cease-fire (to be followed later by the deployment of a peacekeeping force). UN Secretary-General Pérez de Cuéllar dispatched UN Undersecretary-General James Jonah to Mogadishu with that end in mind.

Jonah, before embarking from New York on this dangerous and delicate mission, complained publicly of the paucity of his briefing by the UN secretariat. On arrival in Mogadishu, he was assailed by an obvious dilemma: How was he to treat Mahdi, the interim president of Somalia, and Aideed, the elected chair of the United Somali Congress? Should Jonah, as a representative of the UN secretary-general, recognize Mahdi as an interim head of state and give greater weight to Mahdi's views and thus risk arousing the hostility of Aideed? Or should he politely ignore Mahdi's claim to effective presidential status and deal with both political rivals, together with their respective elders, on the same footing?

In the event, Aideed's perception of Jonah's diplomacy in Mogadishu was that it fell short of evenhandedness, appearing to give unreserved recognition to Mahdi as interim president. This Aideed found unacceptable. In his view Mahdi should no longer have been recognized as the interim leader for several reasons: He had failed to consult the USC Central Committee on the formation of a government—which in any event had collapsed without a parliament ever having been formed; he had exceeded his mandate by unconstitutionally assuming the role of an executive as opposed to a nonexecutive president, thus removing the essence of Somalia's 1960 constitution, which, it had been agreed at Djibouti II, was then in force; and he had nominated as prime minister Omar Arteh, Siad Barre's nomination before he was ousted and a choice Aideed strongly objected to. A majority of delegates at the Djibouti conference had also, for different reasons, specifically ruled out Arteh as a potential nominee for the premiership. By the time of Jonah's visit, Arteh had fled to Saudi Arabia, but he continued to hold office. Thus, in Aideed's view, Mahdi should not have been consulted bilaterally by the UN secretary-general's representative without USC Central Committee participation, especially on an issue affecting Mogadishu exclusively. Mahdi, for his part, claimed that he had acted constitutionally and that he was the legitimate interim president of Somalia for two years, having the authority to make unilateral decisions.

Aideed's suspicion of Jonah's alleged partiality was reinforced when Jonah announced publicly Mahdi's agreement to the deployment of UN military observers to monitor a cease-fire and indicated UN support for Mahdi's unilateral appeal for the deployment of foreign troops in Mogadishu. Thus the suspected formal UN backing for Mahdi as interim president, real or imagined, was enough to ensure that Aideed's further cooperation with the UN would require exceptional diplomatic skills.

Jonah returned to New York convinced that the UN could no longer ignore Somalia and that the first priority was to get a peacekeeping force, together with military observers, into Mogadishu in order to discourage further bloodshed. This was easier said than done. Fighting, mainly artillery duels, continued sporadically as Boutros-Ghali took over in January 1992 as UN secretary-general. He invited the two Mogadishu faction leaders, Mahdi and Aideed, to a conference in New York. They did not speak to each other, but a partial agreement was reach by both sides to order a cease-fire. There was no agreement from Aideed's faction for the deployment of foreign troops. UN diplomacy was needed. Thus the UN concept of a permanent mission to Mogadishu (UNOSOM) was born.

Aideed's Military Victory as UNOSOM Is Formed

Because of Aideed's chagrin with what appeared to him to be a one-sided intervention by the UN, and despite a subsequent personal and impartial attempt by the new UN secretary-general, Boutros Boutros-Ghali, to secure a cease-fire, this was not achieved until March 1992 after a further two months of intermittent warfare. It was a foretaste of things to come.

On April 22 of the same year, Siad Barre tried for the second time to recapture Mogadishu. He and his troops had their base in Baidoa, where they had trained for seven months. Aideed, who had militarily repulsed Siad Barre's first attempt to recapture Mogadishu in April 1991, again prevailed after a six-day war. The former president was forced to flee to Kenya together with the remnants of his regular army.

Two days after Barre had launched his assault from Baidoa, the Security Council passed Resolution 751 establishing the United Nations Operation in Somalia (UNOSOM) under the overall direction of Ambassador Mohamed Sahnoun. The resolution also called for the immediate deployment of fifty UN observers to monitor the cease-fire in Mogadishu and proposed the deployment of a UN security force in consultation with "parties in Mogadishu."

Security Council Resolution Seen by Aideed as Lethal

Sahnoun arrived in Mogadishu on May 4, 1992. Mahdi was in Mogadishu, and Aideed was consolidating his militia in the Kismayu area and in Bardera following Barre's flight to Kenya. Resolution 751 was seemingly innocuous. But from Aideed's point of view the resolution was potentially lethal. He had not given his agreement to the deployment of either contingent. He questioned in particular the purpose of deploying a security force. The forthcoming humanitarian emergency in the interriverine area was not then on the agenda. So what, Aideed asked, was to be the function of a security force other than to assist Mahdi to restore law and order in the capital? Was it to be the thin end of a wedge that would, in Aideed's estimation, inexorably underpin Mahdi's presidency and irrevocably hand him and any government he might form the keys to Somalia's sovereignty? Aideed and his newly formed Somali National Alliance (SNA) claimed the fruits of victory over the former sovereign power of Siad Barre. If Mahdi were supported by a UN security force, would that action not neutralize the SNA both politically and militarily?

Aideed's earlier suspicions that Mahdi's views had prevailed with the UN and that the interim president was bent on securing the maximum advantage of a UN uniformed presence in Mogadishu were now confirmed. Flushed with victory over Barre and his trained soldiers (what remained of them), Aideed was in no mood to yield either to Mahdi or to the United Nations. His dual purpose was to marginalize Mahdi in the eyes of the UN and to ensure that his military (and therefore political) control of all regions in central and southern Somalia—other than Mahdi's enclave in northern Mogadishu—remained outside UN influence. In cahoots with President Abdirahman Ahmed Ali 'Tuur of the breakaway Northwest region (Republic of Somaliland), Aideed also felt confident that his influence could be brought to bear in that region.

Clearly, Sahnoun had in front of him a hard diplomatic furrow to plough. On the one hand, Aideed was seemingly hostile to any form of UN military intervention, and on the other, the Security Council was not prepared during Sahnoun's tenure (May-October 1992) to invoke the enforcement provision of Article 42 of Chapter VII. Sahnoun was thus left with a diplomatic challenge far more exacting than anything his successors had to contend with. He would not, in fact, have had it otherwise. Sahnoun believed in the power of persuasion and not of prescription.

Thus, following the letter of his mandate under the soft option of Article 41, Sahnoun found on his arrival in Mogadishu an acquiescent interim president whose agreement to the mandate had already been assured. But not so among other "parties in Mogadishu," which in essence consisted of Aideed's USC followers. Aideed himself was ensconced at his headquarters in Bardera on the banks of the Jubba River.

Sahnoun and Aideed were soon locked in a battle of wits, to the partial exclusion of processes of political reconciliation, over the deployment of foreign observers (by definition military personnel) and of a security force. Sahnoun's mandate was to consult the "parties," not to seek prior agreement. It was evident to Sahnoun, however, that mere consultation with Aideed would have been an inadequate, even dangerous, response to the required provisions of the mandate, especially now that Aideed's militia presented a more formidable presence, having captured substantial military equipment and ammunition from Barre's fleeing forces. Aideed was clearly a force to be reckoned with, and short of a Security Council mandate invoking unilaterally the enforcement provision, Aideed's prior agreement to foreign military intervention was obviously a prudent measure.

Foreign Criticism of the UN's Relations with Aideed

The necessity, however, for Sahnoun and his successors to have even negotiated with Aideed was questioned by some concerned parties overseas. Academic opinion, and a "significant current of Somali opinion" according to the distinguished social anthropologist I. M. Lewis, advocated that "warlords" be sent by UNOSOM for trial and accused of war crimes. As a substitute for warlords, Lewis observed,[2] it was imperative that local-level leadership "be built upon if viable political structures are to be restored in the south."

This latter observation was, and is, the case in Somaliland (the breakaway northwestern region), and the principle of Lewis's bottom-up approach, as he described it, was the standard by which UNOSOM (and later Security Council Resolution 814 of March 26, 1993) attempted, at the March 1993 Addis Ababa national reconciliation conference, to promote a broadly based system of political representation from grassroots, meaning district, levels. The attempt at reconciliation failed not because UNOSOM "conspicuously lacked insight into the general Somali situation," as Lewis misunderstood the issue, but because a prerequisite to the bottom-up approach, as practiced in Somaliland, was a concordant surrender of power by militia commanders—not something Sahnoun and his successors could possibly have engineered in southern Somalia—let alone a trial for alleged war crimes! Lewis's "best solution" to the Somali crisis, which he claimed was misunderstood by UNOSOM, was an "International trusteeship."

Aideed Successfully Restrains Further Military Intervention

For his part, Aideed, deeply suspicious of the UN secretariat, adopted delaying tactics. The observers, he insisted, would number only seven and they would not be allowed to wear military uniforms. Their deployment was then suspended by Aideed because an Astonov aircraft with UN markings had landed on Mahdi's airstrip and allegedly carried illegal currency and military hardware. Reacting to this unbelievable event, for which there was no credible explanation, Aideed insisted on the suspension of observers until Mahdi had agreed not to circulate his new currency. Aideed needed no further evidence that the UN was fully supporting Mahdi. The seven observers, under the command of a Pakistan officer, Brigadier General Imtiaz Shaheen, eventually reached Mogadishu in mid-July 1992, some three months after Resolution 751 had called for their deployment.

The deployment of a security force of 500 Pakistani soldiers, proposed by the same resolution, presented Sahnoun with even greater negotiating problems with Aideed. Protracted discussions continued until August 12. On that day, Sahnoun, together with Aideed and his three SNA co-chairs, signed the long-negotiated agreement that in the interval had been so emasculated as to raise doubts whether it was worth the paper on which it was written. An additional clause effectively terminated, other than by Aideed's consent, any further increase in the security personnel over the 500 Pakistani soldiers already agreed on.

This postscript, inserted in Sahnoun's own hand, appeared to have been added at Aideed's insistence. Aideed was aware of the July 22 report by Boutros Boutros-Ghali to the Security Council that recommended an increase in the security force, which, the secretary-general maintained, would play an "important deterrent role in the general stabilisation of the situation in Mogadishu." If anything were to undermine Sahnoun's patient negotiating stand, this bolt from the blue was it.

Humanitarian Disaster Coincides with Aideed's Increasing Obduracy

The secretary-general's report, however, was the first official intimation to New York of an unfolding humanitarian disaster coincident with an intransigent Aideed. He had sorely tried the patience of the UN secretariat, now desperate for a green light from Aideed for further military intervention. But the secretary-general's wish to have a security force playing a deterrent role in Mogadishu was guaranteed to convince Aideed not to agree to anything that, in his view, would serve to obstruct his attempted political dominance in Mogadishu while enhancing Mahdi's.

Not surprisingly, therefore, Aideed's agreement with Sahnoun on August 12 enforced a change of title from "Security Force" to "Security Personnel," the word "force" having a negative connotation for Aideed. The "Security Personnel" would have no "peacekeeping responsibilities," he insisted; they could operate only at the Mogadishu port and airport, escorting deliveries of humanitarian supplies to storage and distribution centers in Mogadishu alone. Thus, Aideed had seen to it that UN military intervention in Mogadishu was limited in size and in function (there was no question in his eyes of a deterrent role) and that intervention could not be expanded. Moreover, the intervention was, in effect, debarred from rendering any direct assistance to Mahdi should it have wished to do so.

The 500 "security personnel" from the Pakistani army landed in Mogadishu on September 14, five months after Security Council Resolution 751 had been passed and seven weeks after the UN secretary-general had called for an even larger security force.

Severe Famine: Its Causes and Effects

The secretary-general's urgent request for a higher level of UN military intervention, which inevitably weakened Sahnoun's negotiating position with Aideed, followed reports of a serious famine in the interriverine agricultural areas. The origins of the famine, which eventually gave birth to Operation Restore Hope, were (and still are) misunderstood by the international community and by the world media.

The famine was a combination of drought and a seven-month military occupation of the area by three divisions of Siad Barre's army. The former president had moved his headquarters from the Gedo region to Baidoa on September 15, 1991, to prepare for a military reoccupation of Mogadishu seven months later. Meanwhile, his soldiers plundered grain stores in this agricultural area, destroying pumps and implements in their wake. Farming came to a standstill. Barre's army of occupation did not leave the area until April 22, 1992. On the road to Wanle Weyn it suffered its initial defeat at Aideed's hands before retreating rapidly to the Kenya border. Its seven-month occupation left villages upon villages of destitute farming communities. It took three months for the impact of growing mass starvation to hit the world's television screens.

By August, the Security Council authorized the secretary-general, under Resolution 755 of August 28, 1992, to increase UN peacekeepers in Somalia to prevent the looting by heavily armed gangs of relief supplies arriving at the docks and airports. Two weeks earlier, Sahnoun had concluded his long, drawn-out negotiations with Aideed and the SNA leadership for the deployment of "security personnel," made more problematic by the SNA imposition of a restriction on any further expansion of this Pakistani force of "peacekeepers." Sahnoun now had a huge humanitarian crisis on his hands and a new UN mandate to deploy more peacekeepers to facilitate the flow of relief supplies to the sick and the dying. He had in addition to tackle the problem of political reconciliation, to which, understandably, he could devote only part of his time.

Proposed Deployment of Foreign Troops in Northern Somalia Questioned by Aideed

The cooperative Mahdi, on the whole, presented Sahnoun with no problems on the issue of military intervention, but with Aideed, Sahnoun had to begin all over again, in desperate haste, with a fresh round of talks. This time, though, the purpose of deploying foreign troops, whatever title was given to them, was more readily definable—a humanitarian cause—and Kismayu, not Mogadishu, was the target. Kismayu was a long way from any influence that Mahdi could exert on Aideed's political fortunes.

Sahnoun had made it known, however, that he wished to establish four UNOSOM zone headquarters, in Berbera, Bosasso, Mogadishu, and Kismayu. Sahnoun was able to tell Aideed that the authorities overseeing the ports of Berbera and Bosasso in the Northwest and Northeast, respectively, had already agreed in principle to the deployment of foreign peacekeepers. This news, which was a surprise to Aideed as far as Berbera was concerned, only served to confirm his suspicions of UN intentions. He questioned the necessity of stationing foreign troops in Berbera and Bosasso, where there were practically no humanitarian emergencies. Aideed was convinced that the Security Council's call for yet more peacekeepers was motivated by more than humanitarian concerns. UNOSOM, in Aideed's perception, was growing in ubiquity and mystery, and Sahnoun was perceived as an honest but frustrated broker. Aideed felt more than a little wary.

Sahnoun's hoped-for quid pro quo for having earlier conceded so much to Aideed was a relatively smooth-running negotiation over the deployment of peacekeepers in Kismayu, then under Aideed's SNA control and a significant entry point for relief supplies to the Lower Jubba. Aideed did not see it that way. Nothing was free, certainly not in the way of concessions to the UN. He countered this new demand from Sahnoun by insisting on the employment and training of a Somali police force in Mogadishu by the Pakistani "security personnel," on a one-to-one basis, before he could agree to the deployment of foreign troops in Kismayu.

Aideed Provokes UN to Consider Stronger Measures

Aideed argued that a Somali police force equivalent to the size of a security personnel force in Mogadishu and eventually in Kismayu would be a rational replacement for foreign troops on their departure. Sahnoun accepted the logic of

Aideed's argument, provided the Somali policemen were drawn from all local clans and were under the command of the foreign security personnel. Brigadier Shaheen was also agreeable to the proposal and ordered 500 police uniforms. But Aideed withheld agreement over the Kismayu deployment of 719 extra security personnel, described this time as logistic units, until the Somali police had been recruited and had begun training. There the matter rested.

By late September 1992, the writing was on the wall. If Aideed did not agree to the deployment of peacekeepers in Kismayu, the Security Council would be compelled to take action under Article 42 of Chapter VII—the enforcement provision. Sahnoun advised Aideed accordingly during three separate meetings over nine days at Aideed's Bardera headquarters. But Aideed was unimpressed by threats. By mid-October, Sahnoun felt that the UN secretary-general was adamant about recommending to the Security Council that the enforcement provision of Chapter VII be invoked. Sahnoun resigned, having felt that his old friend Boutros Boutros-Ghali had lost confidence in him. He was replaced as the secretary-general's special representative by Ambassador Ismat Kittani, who took up his post on November 4.

Just before Kittani's arrival in Mogadishu, the Pakistani security personnel, who had been passively encamped on the periphery of the Mogadishu airport, came to a private working arrangement with the militia subclan the Hawadle, who were occupying the airport and collecting various fees from aircraft and passengers alike. This subclan was counted among Aideed's clan supporters and was thus under the jurisdiction of the USC. In practice, the Hawadle leaned rather more toward Mahdi than toward Aideed. The bilateral agreement between the security personnel and the Hawadle militia allowed for the airport to be controlled and guarded by the Pakistanis while the militia continued to collect its fees.

The agreement, which had not been revealed to Aideed, came to a head soon after Kittani's arrival when the BBC Overseas Somali Service, which is beamed to Somalis all over the world, broadcast that the UN had reached agreement with the Hawadle clan (not with the USC) over operations at the Mogadishu airport. Aideed was stunned. To him, this was a deliberate attempt by the UN to undermine his authority. He reacted by threatening to remove both the Pakistanis and UNOSOM from Somalia. Aideed had already successfully declared the head of UNICEF, David Bassiouni, persona non grata (he left under duress).

There was high dudgeon in the Aideed camp. Osman 'Ato, a top adviser to Aideed, was convinced that the UN secretary-general had instructed "Governor Kittani" to take over Somalia with a "divide and rule" policy. Antiaircraft guns, he threatened, would overlook the airport, effectively closing it, and the Hawadle would be punished. The reference to Governor Kittani alluded to a persistent fear of Aideed's that the UN would impose a UN trusteeship over Somalia, which, in Aideed's view, was an unthinkable proposition for a sovereign country.

From Peacekeeping to Peacemaking

The growing tension between Aideed and UNOSOM was overridden by a new turn of events—a change in the Security Council's mandate both in spirit and in the letter: The earlier policy of a hamstrung peacekeeping intervention force was changed, with local consent, to a large-scale humanitarian peacemaking intervention in order to transform southern Somalia into a "secure environment." The UN secretary-general continued to hold that foreign armed deterrence was a prerequisite to stabilization of the situation in Mogadishu and elsewhere in Somalia.

With Kittani's active support, Boutros Boutros-Ghali proposed three options to the Security Council. The first was that UNOSOM troops should undertake a show of force in Mogadishu to "discourage those abusing the relief effort." The second option envisaged a countrywide military operation by a group of UN member states. The third option was a countrywide enforcement action under Chapter VII and carried out under UN command and control. The second and third options were only partly related to the relief effort, which was in large measure an isolated phenomenon in the more sedentary (and thus more economically vulnerable) interriverine areas of southern Somalia. The countrywide application of the enforcement provision had more to do with disarming Somali militias than with the protection of relief supplies. The Security Council chose the second option with an element of the third. In other words, it chose a countrywide military operation (though it did not turn out that way) by a group of member states but without the enforcement provision other than in the famine-stricken areas in southern Somalia.

This change of policy, from peacekeeping to peacemaking, albeit in a restricted area of grave humanitarian concern, was a direct consequence of Aideed's and the SNA militia leaders' opposition to further foreign military intervention. Their opposition was not, however, directed at foreign military intervention per se, even though they were in concert with Somalis in other parts of Somalia that such intervention was an infringement on Somali sovereignty. It was directed at any politico-military intervention that could be seen as advantageous to Mahdi, their political and military rival.

The Advent of Operation Restore Hope

The Security Council's preferred choice merged with an offer by the United States to organize and lead a limited enforcement operation under the authority of the Security Council and limited to the interriverine areas of southern Somalia. Under Resolution 794 of December 3, 1992, the council gave such a mandate, authorizing "all necessary means to establish as soon as possible a secure environment for humanitarian relief operations in Somalia."

The interpretation of this wide mandate fell to the field commander himself, in this case U.S. Marine Lieutenant General Robert Johnston, with diplomatic backing from U.S. ambassador-at-large Robert Oakley. The quality of implementation depended on the commander's strategy, on the uniformity of the training that the peacemakers had received, and on the level of individual and unit discipline maintained. With Operation Restore Hope the units engaged were mainly the U.S. Marine Corps as part of the Unified Task Force (UNITAF) and not an assortment of soldiers with dissimilar training.

When Johnston and Oakley decided to go public in the United States on their interpretation of the Security Council mandate, they must surely have been impressed by the total absence of any limitations on the exercise of their discretionary prerogative. As a consequence, they must have considered the possibility of a hostile political reaction from the man they most wished to appease—Aideed. Johnston, with Oakley's concurrence, defined his own terms of reference before embarking for Mogadishu. He stated publicly that the deployment of his U.S. Marine Corps would be strictly humanitarian and that his soldiers would use only whatever force was necessary to protect themselves and food convoys.

This was a significant policy statement and implied a narrowing of the broadly drafted mandate to establish a secure environment. It satisfied to a large degree the questions the mandate had initially aroused. The statement was a disappointment to the UN secretary-general, who had urged disarmament. Even U.S. Secretary of State Lawrence Eagleburger noted that the aim of the mission would be to "pacify" Somalia.

Disarmament: To Be or Not to Be?

Boutros Boutros-Ghali gave further expression on December 19 to his conviction that UNITAF's self-imposed limitation on the enforcement provision was an opportunity lost. In a letter to the Security Council, he argued that UNITAF should extend its scope of operations to the entire country and defer its decision on a transition from UNITAF to what was to be known as UNOSOM II "until UNITAF had achieved its goal." The goal included securing a cease-fire; carrying out disarmament; removing land mines in Somaliland; and creating a police force. These were laudable but impracticable aims. They were outside the peacekeeping objectives of Resolution 794, if force were contemplated, and beyond any realistic expectation of a time extension for Operation Restore Hope. The creation of a trained and an eventually self-sustainable police force was a very long term commitment, and the clearance of some one million land mines in Somaliland was estimated by experts to be a twenty-year effort.

The secretary-general's concerns were, however, understandable. Clan heterogeneity in the major cities had broken down. That is to say, the natural clan mix among the Somali population of any city, which is possible only in times of inter-clan equilibrium, had reverted to the original clan homogeneity as clan members living in cities other than their own retreated to their homelands for guaranteed security. In these circumstances of clan retraction and consolidation in their respective traditional areas, clan militias were under no political constraints to desist from long-range raiding by gun-mounted vehicles (technicals). These vehicles were a progeny of the lawlessness in vogue during the last years of Siad Barre's tenure. They would seize assets by force from other clans and from vulnerable targets such as foreign relief workers. Looting is a practice common to time-honored pastoral camel raiders.

But as has been demonstrated in Somaliland, the establishment of a secure environment among Somali communities, including disarmament, is not a function of foreign deterrence. It is a function of Somali politics. Where, however, humanitarian circumstances dictate the need for foreign intervention for the specific purpose of saving the lives of innocent people, general disarmament, as the commander of Operation Restore Hope rightly concluded, is a side issue to be negotiated politically after humanitarian objectives have been achieved.

Johnston's military intervention, on his terms, required the formal backing of the peace-enforcement provision only because Aideed and the SNA leadership persistently refused to give Sahnoun their consent to the further deployment of foreign troops in Somalia. Their refusal originated in the fear that UN foreign military intervention (not U.S. intervention) would cause a diminution of their own political power and a corresponding strengthening of Mahdi's political base, not in a fear of intervention itself. Thus, contrary to international media analyses, Aideed reacted favorably to the U.S.-led Operation Restore Hope because he believed the Americans would not change the political balance of power to his detriment.

Aideed's Contrasting Attitudes Toward UNITAF and the UN

A reassurance to Aideed of the political sterility of the U.S.-led operation was the appointment of Oakley, who, unlike Kittani, was a known quantity. He had had a good record as head of the U.S. diplomatic mission to Somalia in the 1970s. Moreover, Aideed's treasurer and top adviser, Osman 'Ato, had close ties with the American oil company Conoco and was not unknown to the U.S. embassy in Nairobi, with which he could liaise. He was instrumental in arranging for the Conoco headquarters building in Mogadishu to house Oakley's diplomatic staff. Unlike Aideed's relations with Kittani, which were shrouded in deep suspicion, his relations with Oakley were cordial—at least to this point.

Aideed's good wishes for Operation Restore Hope before the U.S. Marine Cops landed on the Mogadishu shoreline were welcome news to both Johnston and Oakley, whose priorities above all else were to ensure that UNITAF forces suffered no casualties. The advanced notice of the operation to come, however, gave Somali militia forces ample time to dispatch their heavy military equipment, including technicals, to remoter areas of Somalia and across the border into Ethiopia.

The U.S. Marines landed peacefully along the beaches of Mogadishu on December 9, 1992. Oakley established relations with Mahdi and Aideed independently of UNOSOM, persuading both to sign an agreement and to shake hands at a public ceremony two days later. The agreement lacked substance and had a short life, but it served Oakley's purpose well: an effective UNITAF humanitarian presence with very limited local militia hostility despite the injured pride over Somali sovereignty having been abused. Thus UNITAF forces sustained minimal casualties.

A major criticism of the operation was that a division of infantry and armor was too big an engine for the size of the boat and so unwieldy as to prevent a rapid deployment in the area where a military presence was most urgently needed— Baidoa. Other criticisms included the protection offered by UNITAF to UN agencies and NGOs in Mogadishu, which were ordered to disarm their guards and remove guns from their vehicles. UNITAF soon discovered that despite its numbers and armored vehicles, Somalis were not cowed by impressive hardware and took advantage of unarmed and vulnerable foreign aid workers traveling outside their fortress-like compounds. Only Somalis know how to intimidate Somalis.

An Uncomfortable End to Operation Restore Hope

Oakley and Johnston did eventually fall into bad odor with Aideed. Johnston's marines were scheduled to pull out of Kismayu on February 28, 1993, as part of the general withdrawal of U.S. forces from Somalia when Operation Restore Hope was drawing to a close. In the middle of that month, Aideed got wind of an imminent invasion of Kismayu, then occupied by Aideed's militia, by the Kenya-exiled General Mohamed Said "Morgan," Siad Barre's son-in-law and former minister of defense. Morgan had assembled a militia force from Siad Barre's army that had surrendered to the Kenya government ten months earlier. It was now encamped with its hidden arms in a northeastern province of Kenya just within Kenya's border with Somalia.

Aideed asked Oakley to instruct Johnston to repulse Morgan's militia before it launched an attack on Kismayu. Oakley, according to Aideed, agreed but returned the next day to say that he regretted that he would have to withdraw from this commitment. No reason was given. It would appear that any such action by UNITAF forces would have been in breach of their mandate, which precluded the use of the enforcement provision outside humanitarian relief operations. This was not, however, the end of the story.

With only six days to go before the U.S. Marines were due to pull out of Kismayu, Morgan's militia reoccupied Kismayu after some thirty-five persons were killed in the fighting that ensued between opposing militia. Aideed condemned UNITAF's inaction in Kismayu in a radio broadcast, calling on his supporters to demonstrate peacefully against both UNOSOM and the Americans. Demonstrations were peaceful on the first day, but over the following two days there were unceasing exchanges of heavy machine-gun and rifle fire, rockets and missiles, between militia lodged in tall buildings in Mogadishu and UNITAF forces in their tanks and armored vehicles on the streets below.

There was firm evidence that the outbreak of shooting was not on the agenda of Aideed's militia commanders. Their view was that it was the action of Al-Itihaad (Muslim fundamentalists) and was designed to embarrass Aideed. The demonstrators could also have been part of a large number of demobilized former militia that were no longer receiving rations (in lieu of pay) from their former commanders and were living off the proceeds of theft and extortion.[3]

Oakley, concerned about Aideed's condemnation of UNITAF six days before the U.S. soldiers were due to leave Kismayu on their way home—an event that promised to mar an otherwise overall successful mission—issued an ultimatum giving Morgan forty-eight hours to remove his militia from Kismayu. Aideed was not satisfied with this. He had received a transcript from Kismayu of a radio conversation allegedly between a UNITAF officer in Kismayu and Morgan. The officer was alleged to have said to Morgan that Oakley's ultimatum was unrealistic and that Morgan could leave 60 percent of his militia behind in Kismayu, distributed in private houses. This uncorroborated transcript was believed by Aideed to be authentic, arousing his suspicion that Oakley and Johnston were not as reliable as he had thought. Despite pleadings from Osman 'Ato, Aideed did not speak to either of them again before they left Somalia.

Addis Ababa Conference Holds Out Fresh Hope

In March 1993 a promising reconciliation occurred between Mahdi and Aideed at a conference in Addis Ababa that had been expertly contrived and impartially chaired by Ambassador Lansana Kouyate, the newly arrived secretary-general's deputy special representative to Somalia. Before reconciliation was at hand, Kouyate warned delegates that the Security Council was about to apply the enforcement provision of the UN Charter to the whole country. The implication was that the successor to UNITAF—a UN-led intervention force—would carry out strong measures to disarm the militias and it would be in the interest of political factions to avoid the consequences of direct military intervention by forming a national government. On March 26, 1993, a day before the conference ended in an embrace between Mahdi and Aideed, Resolution 814 was adopted by the Security Council to ensure a seamless transition from the U.S.-led Operation Restore Hope and UNITAF to a UN-led intervention force—UNOSOM II. This resolution widened the scope of peace-enforcement powers from the protection of humanitarian relief supplies to "consolidation, expansion and maintenance of a secure environment throughout Somalia." It went into effect on May 4. With Aideed and Mahdi on cordial terms and plans for the transition to UNOSOM II in place, the scene seemed set for an auspicious aftermath to Operation Restore Hope despite the threatening overtones of an expanded UN intervention force to carry out a disarmament campaign (which UNITAF had studiously avoided, much to Boutros-Ghali's chagrin).

But during May 1993, a nexus of political events arose out of what UNOSOM regarded as a menacing political conference in Mogadishu that had been organized jointly by Aideed and Colonel Abdillahi Yusuf Ahmed of the SSDF (a northeastern political front) to resolve age-old grazing and watering disputes (Aideed's grandfather had been killed because of them) between their respective subclans in the Galkayo area of the central region. The proposed conference gave vent to a severe confrontation between UNOSOM II and Aideed,[4] deepening his conviction that the UN was bent on marginalizing him politically in favor of promoting the interests of Mahdi and his allies.

Major Confrontations Break Out Between
Aideed and UNOSOM II

The month-long heated confrontation in May between UNOSOM and Aideed was mainly over UNOSOM's contention that Aideed was acting counter to UNOSOM's mandate by excluding other faction leaders, such as Mahdi's allies, from his conference. As a side issue, UNOSOM accused Aideed of misusing his radio station for purposes of political incitement.

Mutual antagonism reached a high pitch of intensity by the beginning of June 1993. On June 5, Pakistani forces with UNOSOM conducted an early-morning surveillance of a legal repository of heavy weapons belonging to Aideed's militia. The repository area was shared by Aideed's controversial radio station. While the Pakistanis were conducting their reconnaissance, a crowd of people, some of them armed, had gathered outside the station. When the Pakistani soldiers, under the authority of Resolution 814 of the previous March, entered the radio station, the crowd was incensed. Later that day, militia loyal to Aideed killed twenty-four virtually defenseless Pakistani peacemakers guarding an outside soup kitchen.[5]

Within twenty-four hours of the clash between armed Somalis and the Pakistani peacemaking forces, the Security Council hastily adopted Resolution 837. Acting under the enforcement provision, the council authorized the secretary-general to "take all necessary measures against all those responsible for the armed attacks ... to establish the effective authority of UNOSOM II throughout Somalia, including to secure the investigation of their actions and their arrest and detention for prosecution, trial and punishment." The resolution also urged member states to provide UNOSOM II with the capacity to confront and deter armed attacks, including tanks and attack helicopters.

This resolution, unlike the previous enforcement provisions, was tantamount to a declaration of war against Aideed's militia. The view from Aideed's political and militia headquarters of the unusual scale of this foreign military intervention, including the daily use of helicopter gunships over Mogadishu, was that Aideed, for whom there was a UNOSOM II warrant of arrest, must be protected from capture at all costs. Contrary to the Somali precept of *geeri waanu oggolnahay* (we accept death), Aideed was to be kept alive.

Fierce confrontations in southern Mogadishu between the heavily reinforced UNOSOM II forces and Aideed's militia continued until October 3, when the second major UNOSOM II tragedy occurred. U.S. Rangers and Delta commandos attempted, unsuccessfully, to capture Aideed, and during the fighting, three Black Hawk U.S. helicopters were downed and 18 American and some 200 Somali lives were lost. Michael Durant, a Black Hawk pilot, was wounded and subjected to a humiliating video interview by his Somali captors. Another American pilot, who had been killed, was also seen on video being dragged through the streets to jeering crowds of onlookers. Fighting its way through deadly fire, a relief convoy of UNOSOM forces rescued the beleaguered U.S. Rangers some nine hours after being called. The convoy found sixteen Rangers killed and eighty wounded. Two of the wounded died later.

Peacemaking by UNOSOM II Seriously Questioned

These four months of war between the UN peacemaking forces and a Somali militia commander and his untrained, underequipped guerrilla fighters had no relevance to humanitarian peacemaking, nor to its dubious ancillary–establishing a secure environment. "I want to speak to Oakley," Aideed told me eight months later (October 19) from his hideout in Mogadishu. "I have a bone to pick with him." Oakley had by this time returned to Mogadishu to secure the release of Michael Durant and a Nigerian soldier who had been captured in an earlier engagement some weeks before and to draw Aideed back into the arena of dialogue. Security Council Resolution 878 of November 18, 1993, had effectively made Aideed a free man again, so he could talk to Oakley. Aideed did, and Oakley's mission ended as he had wished.

October 3 was a major UN-U.S. military disaster, but in Somali eyes it was an unprecedented triumph over a perceived tyranny. Whatever had happened to humanitarian peacekeeping? There were powerful lessons to be learned.

Eighteen American and some 200 Somali lives had been lost in the October 3 battle. Humiliating video shots of extreme revulsion brought to a head growing reservations in the United States and among other concerned members of the international community about the acceptability of risks incurred by humanitarian peacemaking. In the United States, serious doubts were expressed about U.S. forces again serving under UN command and whether peacemaking was in the vital national interest of the United States. With the UN and the United States on the defensive, seeking to justify the indefensible (a distorted form of peacemaking), no differentiation was made by the international community between a benign form of peacemaking to carry out urgent humanitarian missions, which was the case with Operation Restore Hope, and the untrammeled exercise of peacemaking with a relentless and all-powerful armed engagement by air and on the ground against local, albeit staunch, Somali militia, which had been the case during the preceding four months.

Afflicted by anguish and consternation, those who rightly questioned the needless loss of life in Mogadishu ordained that October 3, rather than Operation Restore Hope, was the yardstick by which global humanitarian peacemaking operations were now to be judged. This view was illustrated by the myopic shibboleth "the Somalia syndrome."

The needless loss of life on October 3 was uniquely a consequence of the exceptional Security Council Resolution 837, which itself was a reaction to an earlier tragedy—the attack on the Pakistanis on June 5. Only the effect of these two tragedies—much death on the streets of Mogadishu through peacemaking operations—were widely known, giving humanitarian peacemaking a bad name. The evidence that these highly publicized and emotive tragedies bore no relation to humanitarian peacekeeping needs to be emphatically stated.

Conclusions

Operation Restore Hope demonstrated that when humanitarian peacemaking becomes a compelling necessity, interaction between the proposed military command and local militia commanders before physical intervention is a sine qua non; likewise, diplomacy must be carried out with full knowledge of local political, social, and cultural norms.

Operation Restore Hope also conveyed the message that however carefully the strategy for intervention is formulated, individual members of the intervention troops must be prepared to operate in an alien social and cultural environment. In this respect, the issuance to every U.S. Marine of a pocket-sized comprehensive booklet, covering both civil and military aspects of Somalia and including history and social norms, reflected on the professionalism of the UNITAF operation.

In contrast, UNOSOM II forces were inevitably composed of an ill-assorted number of foreign military personnel with disparate training methods and varying degrees of disciplinary control by their respective officers. This is no way to run a humanitarian peacemaking operation. Dr. Boutros Boutros-Ghali was right to advocate an exclusive UN peacekeeping and peacemaking force. But such a force should be a newly recruited multinational force with no previous military experience and trained by officers from the same military genre to ensure common standards of training, equipment, and discipline.

As for Security Council mandates on peacemaking operations, they leave much to be desired. Article 42 of Chapter VII needs redrafting to ensure that first, future enforcement provisions preclude the council from exercising any right to engage in a battle with local forces other than in self-defense and from exercising any right to establish a secure environment other than for the specific purpose of safeguarding UN troops on the ground. Second, foreign forces must operate within specific rules of engagement, a legal and judicial framework, and the UN Charter on Human Rights.

Notes

1. My book *Whatever Happened to Somalia?* (London: Haan Associates, 1994), pp. 27–38, gives a full explanation of the conflict between Aideed and Mahdi and of the military intervention some months later.

2. I. M. Lewis, "Misunderstanding the Somali Crisis," *Anthropology Today* 9, August 1993, p. 4.

3. After the victory over Siad Barre, Aideed's SNA militia forces were no longer regularly employed. Hence looting by armed gangs of relief supplies increased. These gangs could not readily be distinguished from employed militia members.

4. Drysdale, *Whatever Happened to Somalia?* pp. 167–179.

5. This incident is covered in ibid., pp. 180–189.

8

The Experience of European Armies in Operation Restore Hope

GÉRARD PRUNIER

This chapter is somewhat misleadingly titled, since the bulk of this study is devoted to the French forces. But there are several traits common to the French and the various other forces (German, Belgian, and Italian) that were involved in Operation Restore Hope.

I will begin with the motivations for intervention. These were, of course, officially proclaimed to be an independent concern for the well-being of the Somali civilian population, decimated by combat and even more by famine, after three years of steadily escalating civil war. These official declarations should not be taken at face value. In my capacity as East Africa regional specialist for the International Secretariat of the French Socialist Party, I went to see Bruno Delhaye, head of the Africa Unit in the French president's office[1] on December 12, 1992, three days after the U.S. landings in Somalia, that is, at the moment French troops were getting positioned within the UNITAF framework. As I had been extremely critical of the whole Restore Hope concept since it had been announced,[2] I asked Delhaye why the French were involved in the U.S.-led operation. The answer was as follows:[3]

> You see, it is soon going to be Christmas and it would be unthinkable to have the French public eat its Christmas dinner while seeing on TV all those starving kids. It would be politically disastrous. Then I also phoned several of our African friends, such as Presidents Houphouet-Boigny, Diouf, Bongo and Biya. They all agreed: as francophone Heads of State, they would look ridiculous in Africa if the Americans went and we stayed home. But don't worry: as soon as all this stuff blows over and TV cameras are trained in another direction, we will quietly tip-toe out. With luck, it shouldn't last more than three-four months and in the meantime we will try our best not to do anything foolish.

One cannot exactly say that the reasons for the French joining Operation Restore Hope were either deeply thought out or overflowing with the milk of human kindness. France's involvement was simply a diplomatic and political must that had to be complied with whether France liked it or not. And, as we will soon see, the main concern of the French authorities had to do with domestic politics and the fear of any kind of a mishap in the field.

I do not have the same kind of inside knowledge on the decisionmaking process that led several other European countries (and Canada and Australia, for that matter) to climb aboard the rudderless Restore Hope ship, but it seems reasonable to guess that their motivations were somewhat similar. Their participation could be qualified as a sort of NATO-cum-Desert Storm syndrome: Each involved European country had a prudent desire for "solidarity" with the U.S. giant, a need to appear "caring" in the eyes of a domestic public opinion saturated with horrifying TV pictures, a preoccupation—especially following the coalition war against Iraq the year before—with displaying its armed forces in an attractively humanitarian role, and a feeling that its rank as a "power" (even secondary) was linked with membership in the Restore Hope club.[4]

There was a loose public perception in France that intervention European style was not what it pretended to be, as evidenced by this remark of a French journalist :

> We hear everywhere: "We must not go too far; we must not get bogged down." And we hear it would be a good idea to pack up by January 20th or after four months. But in such a short time is it possible to win a war against an army, not against this misery? Then we have to ask ourselves another question: what if we were going to Mogadishu not to help the Somalis, but just to pretend, to give ourselves a feeling of good conscience? Nobody could forgive us for that.[5]

If the "feeling of good conscience" was obviously part of the picture, so were the political considerations linked with the intervention. And they were different for the different national actors involved. We have already seen those of the French. There were others, especially for the Germans and the Italians.

Bonn made the decision to join Restore Hope on December 12, 1995, and it was practically the single-handed decision of *Bundeskantlzer* Helmut Kohl, motivated by three considerations: (1) The German public was moved by the TV coverage of the Somali crisis, and as head of the government, Kohl felt he had to answer that concern. (2) Being head of a conservative party that was slipping in the opinion polls vis-à-vis its socialist opponents, Kohl felt that he should not leave "the monopoly of the heart" to the SPD (Soziale Partei Demokratishe). (3) feeling unhappy about European (especially French) criticism of the German attitude in the Yugoslav civil war,[6] the chancellor wanted to show that Germany's resolution could be exercised in cooperation with its allies and not only in isolation; this participation was also going to be a test of Germany's capacity to extend its military power outside NATO-defined territory. Such military involvement, deemed illegal under the German constitution, was immediately challenged by SPD opposition leader Bjorn Engholm, who threatened to make a case of it in the constitutional court.[7]

The Italians had jumped on the intervention bandwagon from the very beginning, and their troops were assembled and ready to go as early as December 11. Here also the reason was one of domestic political concern. As a former colonial master of Somalia Italiana (1885–1941) and then as a UN-mandated ruler of the same territory (1948–1960), Italy had had a special relationship with the country where intervention was taking place. But the main point was that Italy had not stopped dealing with Somalia when it officially left in 1960. Quite the contrary. It had become involved not only with the democratic regime (1960–1969) but even more with the Siad Barre dictatorship after 1969. And this involvement had not been of a benign nature. Italy had delivered weapons to the dictator, its important economic aid had been a source of patronage to political friends both in Rome and in Mogadishu, the Mafia and the notorious P2 network had become involved, and manipulation of aid money had been used for financing the Italian Socialist Party and for enriching some of its members. Former prime minister Bettino Craxi and his son-in-law Paolo Pilliteri, deputy mayor of Milan, had taken part in these dubious transactions, all of which made Somalia a major (and still contemporary) skeleton in the Italian political cupboard.[8]

But by late 1992 Italy was in the throes of the biggest political change the country had known since the end of World War II, a process popularly known as *mani pulite* (clean hands). Not to intervene would have looked, for a government then trying to remove the stains of years of corruption and *lottizzazione* (sharing out of the spoils), like a refusal to face the ghosts of its own past. But everyone knew that such an intervention was fraught with perils much beyond the obvious danger of military casualties. The operation got off to a very bad start when U.S. presidential envoy Robert Oakley declared on December 9 that it might be better if the Italians waited a little bit before coming "because they had left a pretty bad image." This remark caused such a furor in Italy that the U.S. State Department officially corrected it two days later at the demand of the U.S. embassy in Rome. Even so, the Italian C-130s waiting to take off from Pisa with the troops were not given clearance to land at Mogadishu airport under the pretext that there was "overcrowding." On December 14, Italian minister of defense Salvo Ando had to directly ask his U.S. counterpart, Dick Cheney, to get the necessary authorization.[9] Thus from the very beginning, Italy— a country that had been smarting from real or supposed humiliation since 1918 because of a feeling that, although a major European power, it was not being taken seriously by other members of the great powers club—started its participation in Operation Restore Hope with a chip on its shoulder. As we will see, this feeling was going to persist throughout and cause major problems of political and even military coordination.

As for the Belgians, who had arrived early, they were quickly deployed south toward Kismayu (on December 20). Their participation in Operation Restore Hope was not a major domestic political concern because, contrary to some of Belgium's involvement in former Belgian Central Africa, their forces were going to a country that had no emotional or political connotation for Brussels. Within the field of Belgian domestic politics, the main cause for participation in Operation Restore Hope was a desire for a "unifying" gesture at a time when Flemish-Walloon ethnic politics were taking a turn that could conceivably threaten the country's very future as a national entity. Since the army was one of those institutions that could be called truly "national," any military deployment, especially for a cause so neutral and morally impeccable as helping a starving African population, seemed like a good idea and a modest but effective way of reinforcing national cohesion.

The next step in the various European involvements in Somalia was the problem of these European countries positioning themselves in relationship to the perceived political aims and tactics of both the United States and the United Nations. On this point, I rely more on my evaluation of the French position and deduce that for the Europeans, this was not an easy task. As we have seen, the motivations for joining Operation Restore Hope had little to do with Somalia itself[10] and everything to do with a variety of domestic political and diplomatic concerns. And from that point of view, the picture was far from clear once on the ground. UN Secretary-General Boutros Boutros-Ghali, largely for reasons having to do with his nationality and former position as Egypt's foreign minister,[11] was keen on two points: (1) disarming the militias and, less vocally, (2) recreating a united Somali state.

While negotiating the terms of Resolution 794 with the UN, Washington had insisted that neither of these two goals would be explicitly stated. If the second one remained somewhat theoretical, at least for the time being, it was not so with the first, which had to be either quickly acted upon or definitely neglected. If in some cases the U.S. troop commanders did not seem too sure about how to act in the first few days regarding the matter of militia disarmament, given the overwhelming U.S. hegemony over the whole operation, the matter was even more confusing for European troops. Should they obey the loudly stated but unofficial desire of the UN secretary-general (which was also felt to be a logical one) or should they stick to the strict wording of Resolution 794 and not disarm anybody, as the Americans had clearly decided to do? For the French, things had started on the wrong foot when they shot up a truck at a Mogadishu roadblock on December 10, killing two and wounding seven.[12] Never mind that the truck had tried to run the roadblock at night with its lights off; the men were immediately dubbed "trigger happy" by the U.S. command because of the tough reputation of the French Foreign Legion and because they had come from Djibouti, a place with a kind of beau geste flavor in the U.S. popular imagination. For the French General Staff officers, this was a perfect example of the kind of things they wished to avoid.

Part of the 2,100 French troops deployed within the Restore Hope framework had indeed come from Djibouti. But their history—unknown to the Americans—was somewhat different. Since November 1991, the small French-protected republic had been involved in a low-intensity civil war of its own between the Mamasan Issa-dominated government and the Afar tribesmen, who felt marginalized in the neocolonial system set up by Paris in collaboration with President Hassan Gouled Aptidon since "independence" in 1977. After a number of events, French soldiers had been deployed in the North of the republic to act as an buffer force between government troops and the Front pour la Restoration de la Démocratie (FRUD) insurgents. In the long lulls between short, sharp bouts of fighting, the French forces had had time to get to know the local populace and to realize that its demands were rooted in a grim everyday reality made of poverty, government neglect, and political marginalization. In November 1992, shortly before Operation Restore Hope, President Gouled had come to Paris to ask President Mitterrand to be "understanding" about the "elections" he was about to organize—and about the military offensive he was about to launch against the insurgents' positions in the North. President Mitterrand was indeed "understanding"; the green light was given and the buffer troops, who stood in the way of the proposed offensive, were duly removed. This caused a degree of bitterness among the French soldiers, who knew very well what was coming next.[13] The French military command in Djibouti thought that sending them to Somalia would provide them with a change of atmosphere.

Thus, a proportion of the troops[14] were quite used to the rugged Somali environment and also to being politically manipulated, two types of experience that were to come in handy for their Restore Hope mission.

At first, the French General Staff had thought about an intervention into Somaliland, where French troops would have been by themselves and closer to the Djibouti zone of French influence. An intervention in this area would also have been logistically much cheaper. But the UN refused and Admiral Jacques Lanxade, for lack of anything better, had asked for an area where "nothing was likely to happen."[15] By November 25, the decision to go to Bakool Province had been made, based on French intelligence reports on the internal situation of Somalia. In any case, at the military level, the feeling was that this was an American show and that as long as the French were going to have to watch from the sidelines, they might as well pick safe watching points.

Deployment on the Ground

The French arrived in Hoddur on December 25 and quickly set up their own disarmament and weapons-control policy[16] without bothering too much to check it with the UN. The U.S. command let them know it would look the other way provided they did not boast too much about it. But this policy was feasible only because the French army approached the job in a very different spirit from the overequipped, security conscious, and psychologically tense U.S. forces. From the beginning, General René Delhomme, who commanded the French troops of what had been code-named Opération Oryx by the General Staff, took a very minimal, close-to-the-ground, down-to-earth approach. Most of the heavy equipment was left in Hoddur and the troops fanned out into the bush on foot in small groups of thirty to forty. Carrying their own food and ammunition, they remained in radio contact with Hoddur and were checked periodically from the air.[17] They would walk at night and within forty-eight hours resurface at dawn next to villages and nomad encampments. The surprise effect was strong. The French seemed to be everywhere. Contact was usually a bit tense at first, but later things would relax. Contrary to the U.S. troops, which moved around only in trucks, usually surrounded by a very impressive display of force that in many ways gave out a message of distancing and fear,[18] the French soldiers gave the impression of being at ease in their environment, ready to fight on their enemy's terms if the need arose but friendly enough to be open to verbal contact if fighting could be avoided.

The French troops' manner played a fundamental role in the development of a somewhat improvised disarmament policy. Due to Admiral Lanxade's precaution, the French army was indeed in an area of relative quiet. There were no "technicals" in sight, and the quantity of heavy armament was limited. Such armaments were immediately confiscated and destroyed before the local Ranhanweyn, or even more the marauding Ogadeni nomadic groups, had time to realize that confiscation was not really official UN policy. As for the rifles, they were left with their owners and simply tagged and registered with a serial number. If a man carrying a registered gun was caught doing some mischief, his gun would be "recalled" for a shorter or longer period according to the gravity of the offense. This policy, in spite of the tough approach and dissuasive night infiltrations, would not have worked without a native diplomacy aspect. In fact, this was probably the cornerstone of the whole French philosophy during Oryx.

As soon as they arrived in Hoddur, French forces called for a big *shir* (popular meeting). The local population took it seriously enough to send representatives of all five districts making up Bakool Province.[19] Colonel Michel Touron, chief of humanitarian affairs for Oryx, immediately created a regional committee with a province-wide mandate. He presided over it himself. There were nine other members: the former governor of Bakool, Mohamed Nur Shudduq, who was well respected; the local head of ICRC (a Somali national); the local WFP representative (also a Somali national); two representatives of the NGO Concern (both Irish); the local UNICEF representative (Somali); and three representatives of the French NGO Médecins Sans Frontières (all French, two of them women).

Colonel Touron decided to administratively regroup the Hoddur and Ceel Berde districts for practical reasons. Thus only four district committees were created, all on the same principle: Each one was presided over by a French officer and had three subcommittees on health, security, and administration. Each subcommittee was also presided over by a French officer, but all the other members were Somali. Apart from that, three subcommittees were created at the provincial level,[20] one for security, one for health, and one dubbed "Return to Normal Life," which, as its name indicated, was in charge of any and everything inasmuch as it favored a normalization of life. Its functions could be as diverse as acting as a referral point for puzzled Somali who had to deal with the French administration, gathering intelligence, helping to reorganize civilian transport, or helping to repair a Mosque. The Security Subcommittee was headed by a French major assisted by a French master sergeant. Under them were five Somali NCOs who headed a French-sponsored militia acting as a police force, which proved invaluably helpful in keeping law and order. This militia was paid, mostly in food and with small amounts of cash. It also derived quite a bit of satisfaction from the enhanced social standing of its members.

A quick intervention mechanized force was kept in Hoddur in case things went wrong. But the troops fanned out in the various district locations in groups of about eighty, keeping radio contact with base, where they lived permanently. With a few general purpose machine guns and mortars, their firepower was reckoned to be enough to keep any attacking force at bay long enough for the central force to intervene.[21] This system had the advantage of making the French presence felt throughout, a factor that probably contributed to making the French forces such an effective deterrent.

This system could be criticized for being almost one of recolonization. But it proved extremely effective in preventing violence and restoring some sort of normal life in an area that had been a battlefield for contending clan armies in 1991–1992. In many ways, its authoritarian and yet "nativist" flavor corresponded more to what the Somali population expected from Restore Hope than the mixture of subsidized democratization offered by the UN—which was supported by massive U.S. overkill capacity and involved little human rapport with the natives.

Other European armies did not follow the French model.[22] Why exactly is not clear, for the Belgians at least had the capacity. Of course, French experience in Djibouti proved to be a great asset, especially since fully one-third of the troops involved in Oryx had previously been involved in Operation Iskoutir (the buffer force between Afar insurgents and Somali Issa troops in the northern Randa area of Djibouti). Other forces tended to remain cooped up in towns, the Belgians in Kismayu and the Germans in Belet Weyn. As for the Italians, they shared the apparent limelight and intractable political realities of Mogadishu with the Americans. The concentration of forces in towns and cities was probably a mistake. Any recovery of ground control had to start from the countryside with the intention of slowly pushing the complex and divided towns into a politico-military corner.

Dealing with Somali Politics

Dealing with the political situation in Somalia was everybody's weakest point, especially the UN's. From the point of view of those Europeans who had experience of Somali politics (the French and the Italians), dealing with the warlords from the start as Special Envoy Robert Oakley chose to do, especially without bothering to seriously reduce the amount of weaponry under their control, was a fatal mistake. These men were the symptoms of the political disease that had been gnawing at the very innards of Somali society since the end of the Ogaden War in 1978. Reempowering them by legitimizing their presence surprised everybody in Somalia, reassured them as to the ultimate motives of the intervention, and drove politically conscious Somalis to despair. Then, focusing all attention on the cities, not only on their logistical capacities such as harbors and airfields but on the cities as sociopolitical units, condemned Restore Hope forces to fight sooner or later. In fact, since the clan militias had fought for the control of the cities since 1989, it made those cities even more of a prize in their eyes and put Restore Hope squarely in the field as just another clan militia, the militia of the Gal clan,[23] a militia that was perceived as rich and powerful but dumb. UNITAF–UNOSOM II forces were seen by the warlords and their men as economic resources that should be either befriended or fought against according to the diplomatic possibilities of the day and their perceived sympathies, that is, pro-Ali Mahdi or pro-Aideed. Such calculations were present even before the June 5, 1993, incident and became even more evident during the "UN war" of June to October.

The problem started right away with the fighting between U.S. and Belgian forces on one side and the Somali National Front (SNF) forces of General Mohamed Said Hersi "Morgan" on the other in and around Kismayu on January 25, 1993. Special Envoy Oakley had voiced his distaste of and refusal to talk with Morgan from the beginning, when he was parleying with Ali Mahdi and even Aideed in the capital. After they remained alone in Kismayu, the Belgians could never extricate themselves from being perceived as anti-Harti and pro-Ogaden, something they could very well have done without. Throughout January and February skirmishes went on, which the Belgians, cooped up in their fortified positions in and around the Kismayu harbor and airfield, were not able to control. Worse, on February 22, Morgan eliminated rival warlord Omar Jess, the local Somali Patriotic Movement (SPM) leader linked with Aideed's SNA, right under their noses. As a result, the Belgians were seen as partisan (they had "supported" Jess) and ineffective (they had lost the city to their "enemy"). In Mogadishu, the lesson was not lost for General Aideed: He was furious at the intervention forces, seeing their "loss" of Kismayu as another proof that they supported not only Ali Mahdi but anybody hostile to him; and he also felt that, firepower notwithstanding, it was possible to win against the Gal troops.

Aideed's perceptions were to have disastrous consequences in pushing the Italians to follow their own political line. Foreign Minister Emilio Colombo had gone to New York to tell Secretary-General Boutros-Ghali that a general disarmament was absolutely necessary.[24] He came back from his trip having realized that the UN secretary-general agreed but had no way of forcing the Americans to comply. Then next best for Rome was the attempt at showing the Italian public that at least the present *mani pulite* government had broken with the errors of the past and was following a definitely distinct policy in Somalia. This was a domestic political necessity because the sordid revelations about Italy's past involvement in Somalia kept pouring out. A well-documented article in a Rome weekly[25] detailed how Paolo Pilliteri, assistant mayor of Milan and then president of the Italo-Somali Chamber of Commerce, had received a 900 million lire (U.S.$570,000) kickback on the SOMALFISH aid contract. A few days later, another article revealed that part of the "cattle" deliveries for the agro-zootechnical Italian aid project in Afgoye valued at U.S.$33 million had in fact been weapons.[26] Since former Siad Barre finance minister Mohamed Sheikh Osman had been linked with these deals and since he was by now a key Ali Mahdi man, part of the same post-manifesto group of the United Somali Congress (USC) that the former governments in Rome had supported, the present Italian cabinet had to turn 180 degrees in order to cleanse itself of any possible accusations of following the same path of corruption and dubious political chumminess. The result was that it made new deals, political this time, with General Mohamed Farah Aideed. The problem was to come to a head after the June 5, 1993, incident when, under UN prodding, U.S. forces practically declared war on Aideed's SNA.[27]

UNOSOM's offensive started on June 12, 1993, with an aerial bombardment of SNA weapons sites. U.S. forces wanted European troops to get involved in the U.S.-UN anti-SNA operations, something they were loath to do, thinking the whole scheme was politically inept and militarily unsound. The French and the Italians were involved in the June 17 unsuccessful operation in the Old Town. After analyzing the results,[28] the French command decided to withdraw quietly, which it did after consultation with the U.S. command.[29] But the Italians stayed on. And in the terms of the already quoted UN report, this was going to "bring to a head the controversy which had been simmering for some time between the UNOSOM II Force Command and the Italian Brigade Command."[30]

What the report politely called the "controversy" was a basic difference of approaches in dealing with General Aideed and the SNA. The U.S.-UN forces wanted a clash and a military solution.[31] The Italians felt it was too late and that besides, fighting Aideed would only help Ali Mahdi, something their own past governments had been only too prone to do. The result was that the Italians either dragged their feet or coolly negotiated with Aideed, as on July 9 when they reoccupied Strong Point 42 after talks with the SNA instead of doing it in a blaze of fire as the UNOSOM II Command wanted them to do. This disagreement on strategy launched a major political crisis.

After the UN asked Italy to recall General Bruno Loi, its brigade commander in Somalia, headlines screamed in Rome: "UN Diktat to Italy: You Must Fire General Loi. But Rome Will Not Bend." In the same paper the minister of foreign affairs declared: "There cannot be a 'Loi problem.' The General is the man whom the government has chosen to be at the head of our forces in Somalia. And our government is the only authority which can say who will command our soldiers. And that is all there is to say about that."[32]

This matter posed very openly the question of the legitimate chain of command for the European troops involved in the whole UNOSOM II adventure. When faced with a political and military policy it found completely unpalatable because of its domestic political constraints, Italy had decided that its troops were its own and that the U.S.-UN command had no business ordering it about.

France made a declaration to try to bring together the two violently opposed points of view but at the same time to show where its basic sympathies lay: "France hopes for a friendly solution to the conflict between Italy and the UN. But it shares the Italian concern about better information and a better coordination on the ground."[33] For "information" and "coordination on the ground," translate in plain English: "The Americans keep us in the dark, push us around and take for granted that we will go along with whatever they want us to do." This was indeed the common feeling among the French officers, and they sympathized with the plight of the Italians.[34]

This state of affairs even had some repercussions on the somewhat calmer German position. On July 16, Volker Ruhe, member of the Christian Democratic Union (CDU) and German defense minister, had to publicly defend the UN record in Somalia, which he qualified as being "globally positive" following a declaration by his foreign affairs colleague Klaus Kinkel (Liberal) who had said two days before that Germany might withdraw its forces if the conflict between the UN and Aideed got worse.

The whole UNOSOM II image, including the image of its European participants, was not much improved by revelations of gross violations of human rights by the Belgian troops stationed in Kismayu. Belgian paratroopers, ashamed of what they had seen, bore witness anonymously on Belgian Radio, saying that "official kill figures should be multiplied by four or five."[35] It soon became obvious that most of the statistics in those "kill figures" were in fact unarmed civilians.[36]

Looking for a Quick Way Out

The so-called Olympic Hotel battle on October 3 in which eighteen U.S. Rangers were killed and seventy-eight wounded with two helicopters shot down marked the beginning of the end. Among the Europeans, there had been a widespread feeling that if the Americans did not know what they were doing, this was not a reason to keep following them. In Germany, Defense Minister Volker Ruhe, who had to cover for his party's decision to have committed Bundeswehr troops to Somalia, had suddenly decided that the whole crisis should have "a political solution and not a military one," in other words that it was time to negotiate with General Aideed. By late October, he was insisting that in no way would the Germans remain after the Americans left.

In Italy, the political director of the Ministry of Foreign Affairs, Ferdinando Salleo, had declared that "it would be ridiculous to quarrel with Washington in order to keep our flag flying over the ruins of Mogadishu."[37] In due course General Loi was called back; so was the Italian ambassador in Somalia, Enrico Angelli, who was strongly disliked by the UNOSOM II command. In Brussels, Defense Minister Léo Delcroix had to face strong parliamentary attacks from the Flemish extreme right party Vlaams Blok, which accused him of having sent the troops on "a useless mission."[38] By late October–early November, troop withdrawals began. They were staggered until mid-March 1994 and on March 21 the last European soldiers—a few Italians—were gone.

Conclusion

The European presence in Operation Restore Hope was a rather mixed bag. It was motivated by a variety of different domestic political considerations and remained dominated by them throughout. In terms of tactics, the French were the only ones to try something different. Whether their experience could have been generalized remains to be seen, since they operated in a rather "easy" environment. But what is sure is that France had no intention of accepting the UN political leadership the way the Americans did, a somewhat paradoxical phenomenon because the United States was popularly seen as the driving force behind both UNITAF and UNO-SOM II. My impression is that it was, but only at the military level. In fact, they were politically blind to Somali political reality because, just like the Europeans, their motivation for coming was also linked with domestic political considerations. The UN secretary-general was the only one who had a clear view of what he was doing, and his view was basically flawed by his past acquaintance with Siad Barre's Somalia. As a result, the United States put its military muscle behind the secretary-general's erroneous political schemes, something that was to cause it considerable problems, not least a growing sense of disengagement and disenchantment with the UN on the part of a large segment of the U.S. public.

European governments that had been followers rather than initiators in the whole process then became even more disenchanted, feeling that an intervention under U.S. leadership was a case of the blind leading the blind. If for the French the lesson seems to be a simple "never again," for some of the Europeans—the Belgians and the Germans most definitely—the lesson seems to be more one of "if we do it again, let's do it alone and our way." Opération Turquoise in Rwanda some three months later, in spite of all its ambiguities, was a perfect example of French thinking on the matter of armed humanitarian interventions for the future.

Notes

1. Given the "special relationship" between France and Africa, there is a special Africa Unit in the president's office in Paris. Taking its orders directly from the president, it is not part of any ministry and is not accountable to anybody except the head of state. Its role has often been criticized, and Lionel Jospin, the unsuccessful Socialist candidate in the previous presidential election (April-May 1995), had advocated its disbanding.

2. See Gérard Prunier, "La politique bafouée," *Le Monde des Débats,* January 1993. This article, which faulted the UNITAF concept for its lack of background information, clear political plans, and attention paid to local Somali conditions, had been written during the first week of the intervention.

3. Bruno Delhaye, interview with the author, Paris, December 12, 1992.

4. This was particularly clear in the case of some countries, such as Norway and Greece, that sent very small, symbolic contingents.

5. Guy Sitbon, "Le sauvetage ou la honte," *Le Nouvel Observateur,* December 10–16, 1992.

6. Paris felt (and let it be known in Bonn) that the German decision to quickly recognize the independence of Croatia and Slovenia had been a major factor in the violent breakup of the Yugoslav Federation and in the subsequent civil war.

7. Henri de Bresson, "Le Chancelier Kohl veut engager la Bundeswehr dans des opérations de maintien de la paix de l'ONU," *Le Monde,* December 19, 1992.

8. For a documented study of the questionable aspects of Italy's involvement in Somali politics, see Angelo Del Boca, *Italia e Somalia: Una sconfitta dell'intelligenza* (Rome: Laterza, 1993).

9. See "Les Américains font la moue pour accueillir les troupes de l'ancienne puissance coloniale," *Le Monde*, December 18, 1992.

10. This was true even in the case of Italy. What was crucial in Italian terms was not what was going on in Somalia but how the Somalia events could or would reverberate on Italian domestic politics through the linkage with past Italian involvement there. This is why (and that point was largely missed by the Americans) the Italian cabinet had to follow, or at least be seen by its public as following, a "Somali policy" radically different from the one followed by past Italian governments. As I will show, this translated very clearly in terms of Italy's relationship both with interim president Ali Mahdi and with General Mohamed Farah Aideed.

11. As a Christian Arab, furthermore married to a Jew, Boutros-Ghali had always had an ambiguous position in the Egyptian political establishment. Although he actually ran Egypt's diplomacy, he was never officially a full minister but only an assistant minister, and he was not allowed to represent Egypt at Arab League meetings, to which the official (and in fact rather theoretical) Muslim minister would be sent. In his capacity as leader of Egyptian diplomacy, he had dealt for years with the Siad Barre regime and taken care of the substantial financial and military aid given by Cairo to the Somali dictatorship. He had been a major player (together with the Italians) in the last-minute negotiations in November-December 1990, which were aimed officially at a smooth transition out of the dictatorship but which were also designed to preserve the interests of some of its supporters. As a result, he was never seen by the Somalis as a neutral player but rather as somebody who still had the same political agenda, using the UN's rather than Cairo's resources. This resulted in the UN intervention being from the start supported by the Ali Mahdi group and considered as hostile by the Aideed coalition, a view not altogether without grounds and something that was generally missed by U.S. diplomacy.

12. *Libération,* December 11, 1992.

13. Next came the expected offensive during which the insurgents were crushed with great loss of civilian life. The elections were also duly "organized" and gave a massive victory for President Gouled's party.

14. Others came from the Central African Republic and from metropolitan France.

15. Interview with a French superior officer, Paris, April 7, 1995.

16. Eight hundred to 1,000 kilograms of weapons and ordinance were destroyed every day in late December 1992 and most of January 1993. See Catherine Simon, "Les multiples tâches des soldats français à Hoddur," *Libération,* January 5, 1993.

17. The Oryx force had been supplied with twenty-two helicopters, roughly 1 per 100 men.

18. They both inspired fear and were perceived as being fearful; they wanted always to be in flak jackets, with helmets, protected by helicopters, and so on. French soldiers never wore their helmets, never wore flak jackets except when on operations where fighting was a strong probability, and when off duty often wore the native *futah* (skirt), a garment well adapted to Somalia's hot climate. Among themselves, the Somalis often joked about the

Americans' physical appearance, calling them "human tanks." Without the Americans realizing it, this was a constant irritant and a definite factor in the Somali aggressiveness toward them during Summer 1993.

19. Ceel Berde, Rab Duure, Tiyeglow, Waajdit, and Xuddur. (This last spelling is the proper Somali spelling of "Hoddur." But since the town and surrounding district were spelled Hoddur on maps and in press articles, this spelling has been kept in the text.)

20. See Appendix E for the organizational chart of the French administration in Bakool Province.

21. In fact, it never became necessary to use this security precaution; the few firefights that had occurred had always been controllable by the local forces.

22. But the Australians in Bay Province operated pretty much in the same way, and with equal success. When they left, the French spread south and took over the administration of their area without any major problem.

23. *Gal* (meaning "infidel") is the name given by the Somali to all Westerners.

24. AFP dispatch, March 9, 1993.

25. *L'Espresso*, February 28, 1993.

26. *L'Europeo*, March 3, 1993.

27. The June 5, 1993, incident during which twenty-four Pakistani Blue Helmets were killed and fifty-seven others wounded is far from clear. Presented at the time (and to a large extent still today) as a deliberate attack by SNA forces on the UN, it seems in fact to have been a UN attempt, both belated and ill designed, to hit at the heart of Aideed's strength in Mogadishu by confiscating his heavy weaponry and shutting down his radio station. For a very cautious appraisal of the incident, see the confidential UN report of a committee chaired by Matthew Ngulube: *Report of the Commission of Inquiry Established Pursuant to Security Council Resolution 885 (1993) to Investigate Armed Attacks on UNOSOM 2 Personnel Which Led to Casualties Among Them* (New York: UN, February 24, 1994) (Henceforth *UN War Report*).

28. In five minutes of intense fighting in the almost blind narrow alleys of the Old Town, the Moroccans who had been put in the vanguard of the operation had lost five men killed, including their commander, and forty wounded (see *UN War Report*, sec. 146). The purpose of the operation had been to confiscate some SNA weaponry.

29. This led to an interesting political comment. Upon returning to Hoddur, the French forces feared complications with the local SDM-SNA leadership. But Mohamed Nur Adiyow, the local SDM chief, told the French officers: "No problem. We know that in Mogadiscio you had to obey the Americans. Here, it is different." (Interview with a French officer, Paris, April 7, 1995).

30. *UN War Report*, sec. 147.

31. On June 23, 1993, Admiral Howe had decided to put up a $25,000 reward for Aideed's head with a wanted poster in the purest Tombstone–OK Corral tradition. As for Secretary-General Boutros-Ghali, he had declared that General Aideed's "physical elimination" would help the situation (*La República*, July 15, 1993).

32. *La República,* July 15, 1993.

33. Communiqué of French Foreign Affairs Ministry, AFP dispatch, July 16, 1993.

34. Interviews with several French officers between April 1994 and April 1995.

35. *Indian Ocean Newsletter*, September 4, 1993.

36. See African Rights, *Somalia: Human Rights Abuses by the United Nations Forces* (London: African Rights, July 1993).

37. *Indian Ocean Newsletter,* October 2, 1993.

38. *Indian Ocean Newsletter,* October 9, 1993.

PART 4

Decisionmaking During Intervention

9

U.S. Government Decisionmaking Processes During Humanitarian Operations in Somalia

James L. Woods

The development of the Somalia humanitarian crisis in 1991–1992 found the United States poorly positioned to follow events and to plan and implement an appropriate response. The embassy had been evacuated and looted in January 1991, when the civil war came to Mogadishu and forced President Siad Barre to flee to his tribal base in southwestern Somalia. The U.S. diplomatic presence in Somalia was nonexistent (indeed, only the Egyptian embassy remained open), and only the barest of local intelligence assets were still available. In Washington, the substantial strategic interest in Somalia that had characterized the 1980s had given way to a new attitude approaching indifference. With the Russians and Cubans gone home from East Africa and the Red Sea littoral, the Cold War won, and the Mengistu regime in Ethiopia on the ropes, there was little need or value seen in retaining any positive involvement in Somalia. Somalia was accordingly assigned only a modest priority at the policy, operational, and intelligence desks in the interagency community.

Nevertheless, the disintegration of Somalia political and economic structures— especially after the fall of Mogadishu to the forces of General Aideed in January 1991—had led to the progressive development of an ominous disaster situation. The Department of State and the Agency for International Development's Office of Foreign Disaster Assistance were following this trend as closely as possible given the lack of official presence and hard information.

Initial Humanitarian Involvement
(February 1991–April 1992)

Based primarily on reports from neighboring posts and the ever more involved PVO (private voluntary organization)-NGO community at work in Somalia, the State Department had moved as early as February 1991 to begin extending extraordinary assistance to Somalia, and on March 25 Assistant Secretary Herman Cohen made a formal declaration that a state of disaster, originating in civil strife, existed in Somalia.

Over the next year and a half, the State Department and AID would undertake an ever-lengthening list of emergency response measures in an attempt to contain and correct the Somalia disaster, with money and food flowing to Save the Children Fund (U.S.-UK), Médecins Sans Frontières (Holland), CARE, UNICEF, the World Food Program, the International Medical Corps, World Concern, the UN high commissioner for refugees, the UN Children's Fund, the ICRC, Catholic Relief Services, and Action International Contre la Faim.

Formal involvement by the UN and its specialized agencies was, however, slow in developing. Despite deteriorating political, security, and economic conditions throughout 1991 and the emergence in late summer and fall of reliable reports of a developing famine, the world declined to give much priority to Somalia. Then, in November 1991 and continuing for four months, heavy and very destructive fighting broke out in Mogadishu between the forces of General Aideed and those of Interim President Ali Mahdi. Thousands of Somalis died and at last the international community was obliged to pay attention. Following Boutros-Ghali's installation as the new secretary-general on January 1, 1992, one of his first acts was to receive the report of Undersecretary James Jonah, just returned from a fact-finding mission to Somalia. Jonah had met with both Aideed and Ali Mahdi, but—apparently because of objections from Aideed—did not recommend that the UN involve itself in trying to arrange a cease-fire. Indeed, in subsequent remarks to journalists, Jonah declared the situation to be one of "total anarchy."[1]

Boutros-Ghali, however, reacted to Jonah's report by urging a more proactive UN policy. He faced substantial resistance in the Security Council, especially from the United States and Russia. As summarized by Herman Cohen, writing after his retirement from the State Department,

> Among the council's permanent members, the United States and Russia were the least enthusiastic about UN involvement in Somalia beyond that of humanitarian relief. A dozen UN peacekeeping operations had been authorized in the previous twenty-four months, and costs were mounting at extraordinary rates. The Cambodia operation alone was budgeted for $2 billion. . . . Both the United States and Russia were running considerable arrears in their peacekeeping accounts even before Somalia's crisis appeared on the council's agenda. Hence, both governments insisted that UN involvement in Somalia in early 1992 be limited to humanitarian operations, which are financed within the regular UN budget.[2]

Up to this point, there was no widespread press or public clamor in the United States for official action; some interest had developed in the Congress, but the only direct calls for action had come (in early January) from two proactive members of the Senate Africa Subcommittee: Senators Paul Simon and Nancy Kassebaum. Although State, AID, and the U.S. mission at the UN were devoting substantial time to the crisis, it was still a third-tier issue in the Washington scheme of things, and there existed a hope at intermediate and high policy levels that the United States could avoid the costs and complications of a deeper involvement.

On January 23, 1992, the UN Security Council unanimously passed Resolution 733; the council urged an increase in humanitarian aid to Somalia and recommended appointment of a "special coordinator" to oversee delivery. It also urged the secretary-general and concerned organizations to work with the warring factions to facilitate the delivery of food. The UN, with tepid support from the Security Council, had opted for limited involvement with emphasis at this point only on expanded humanitarian and diplomatic efforts. The United States had gone along without enthusiasm given the lack of priority accorded Somalia, other pressing problems (for example, Bosnia), and domestic and UN funding problems. Nor at this point had the U.S. official community begun to organize itself for extraordinary or emergency actions on Somalia. All of this was to change over the next six months.

Initially, the UN's diplomatic efforts, strongly encouraged by the United States, seemed to be bearing fruit. Aideed and Ali Mahdi sent assurances to New York that they would organize a cease-fire. After intensive negotiations in Mogadishu—with substantial international presence—the two sides signed a cease-fire agreement on March 3. The UN-led joint delegation also achieved an agreement among several of the factions to organize a national reconciliation conference and undertook measures to increase food deliveries to the main ports. But in fact conditions inside Mogadishu remained tense, and outside the capital armed bands roamed freely, often preying on food convoys and distribution points. In a further report to the Security Council in mid-March, the secretary-general painted a generally gloomy picture and argued that UN military monitoring would be essential to ward off famine.

The Security Council responded with a further resolution, UNSCR 746 of March 17, 1992. Its main emphasis was an appeal to all Somali factions to cooperate in honoring the cease-fire of March 3. Within the U.S. government, increasing emphasis was now being placed on the growing crisis in Somalia, but it was still only looking to enhance diplomatic and humanitarian efforts. In March, the United States signed an agreement with the ICRC to provide 24,270 metric tons of food aid to Somalia; in April, the United States announced a pledge of 20,000 metric tons of sorghum to the World Food Program for Somalia. Despite its reservations on expanding the UN's involvement in Somalia, the United States had become and would remain by far the largest donor of humanitarian assistance to Somalia.

Deepening Involvement: UNOSOM I and Operation Provide Relief (April 1992–December 1992)

Despite active UN diplomacy (appointment of David Bassiouni as the UN's coordinator for humanitarian assistance to Somalia and dispatch of a technical team to Mogadishu to discuss cease-fire implementation), the situation continued to deteriorate. Serious security problems continued at the Mogadishu docks; a World Food Program ship was shelled in the harbor in early March and departed without unloading. Food deliveries in the outlying areas were disrupted by banditry and racketeering. In effect, the relief effort had begun to generate its own pernicious dynamic; food had become the main item of commerce, to be commandeered at the point of a gun without regard to the effects on the general populace. Aid workers were harassed and in some cases killed as security deteriorated. And even more ominous reports were coming in from Somalia's richest agricultural area, to the south between the Jubba and Shabelle Rivers. If these estimates of a general crop failure (80 percent drop in 1991, even worse predicted for 1992 due to pilferage and lack of planting) were accurate, a potentially catastrophic famine would come later in the year and carry into 1993.

Against this backdrop, the UN technical team in Mogadishu negotiated, after considerable difficulty with the Aideed faction, an agreement that the UN would be allowed to deploy up to fifty unarmed military observers along the "green line" dividing Mogadishu between Aideed and Ali Mahdi. This recommendation was subsequently endorsed in UNSCR 751, passed unanimously by the Security Council on April 24. The resolution established the UN Operation in Somalia (UNOSOM, or as it later was sometimes called, UNOSOM I) and called for the introduction of a 500-person armed security force in addition to the cease-fire monitors—a proposal not endorsed by Aideed. Mohamed Sahnoun, an experienced UN diplomat who had recently been in Somalia on a fact-finding mission for the secretary-general, was named head of UNOSOM.

But again the actual effective engagement of the UN faltered; the limited progress made by UNOSOM lagged behind the acceleration of the humanitarian crisis in the countryside. Deployment of the fifty monitors authorized by UNSCR 751 took three months (from April 24 to July 23; an advance party of four observers had arrived on July 5). Although the cease-fire was generally holding in the cities—in no small measure owing to the personal diplomacy of Sahnoun—banditry in the countryside remained rampant. And overall food deliveries and any other form of practical international assistance were slow to materialize. Various study and technical missions and local reports had established a clear and pressing need for urgent and massive action, but even by June there had been very little follow-through, and concern was mounting among both the international community representatives in the country and those monitoring the situation from their national capitals or in New York. On June 25, Sahnoun sent a lengthy and bleak report to the secretary-general, describing the massive problems facing him in Somalia and urging the UN to accelerate its assistance.

In response, the secretary-general recommended sending yet another technical assessment team to Somalia. The Security Council, on July 27, endorsed the recommendation in UNSCR 767, directing two tasks for the team: (1) determine how UN "security guards" could be used to protect relief workers, and (2) convene a conference to work for political reconciliation. The resolution also asked the secretary-general to mount an airlift of food supplies—an action especially necessary to reach remote areas where food supplies were unavailable owing to the lack of security at the ports and along the distribution routes. Four days later the United States authorized an additional emergency food commitment of almost 24,000 tons to the World Food Program.

Indeed, in the United States, pressure for a more proactive stance toward the Somalia crisis was steadily growing. Staff-level activities had intensified; although the technical planning and operations were still focused at AID-OFDA, there was growing interest and involvement by State, DOD (OSD and Joint Staff), National Security Council (NSC) staff, and intelligence community officers. Interest on the Hill had also evolved, and a stream of hearings had gradually moved the crisis near the front burner. Over the January-June period, State officials had been called six times to give formal testimony before House and Senate committees. In addition, there were numerous informal meetings and briefings with Hill principals and staff.

This growing congressional interest, and the ever-rising flood of reports that the UN mission was so far utterly failing to meet the needs of Somalia, had also begun to have an impact on the White House. It was made known that President Bush had taken a personal interest and was following events with growing concern. Within DOD, a Somalia task force was established by order of the assistant secretary of defense for international security affairs. The issuance of UNSCR 767 on July 27 gave the United States a set of more specific proposals to rally behind. On the same day the Department of State made a public statement in favor of dispatching armed UN security elements to Somalia; as Herman Cohen later noted, this was "the first US 'pro-security' statement since the crisis began."[3] A briefing by OFDA's Jim Kunder the following week reemphasized the gravity of the situation, with an estimated 1,500,000 Somalis—one-quarter of the population—at risk of starvation, one-fourth of all children under the age of five already dead, and 800,000 Somalis displaced or refugees.

At this point, there was extensive U.S. interagency discussion of how best to deal with the crisis. On August 13, the president, having sorted through the options and arguments presented, announced several forward-leaning decisions that would propel the United States substantially deeper into direct engagement:

- The United States would offer to transport UN security forces to Somalia (the 500-man Pakistani contingent).
- DOD was ordered to begin an immediate emergency food airlift to Somalia and to refugee camps in Kenya.
- The UN would be asked to convene a donors' conference.
- An additional 145,000 tons of food would be made available.

And on August 16, the president designated Andrew Natsios (AID assistant administrator) as his special coordinator for Somali relief.

On August 18, U.S. Central Command (CENTCOM) announced the formation in Mombasa of Joint Task Force Operation Provide Relief to implement the airlift ordered by the president. For better or worse, the United States was clearly moving into the lead on Somalia. The airlift was in fact quickly established, consisting both of DOD assets and OFDA civil charter aircraft and coordinated by a U.S. Air Force team on site in Kenya. From its inception in late August until it was terminated the following February, Provide Relief aircraft flew some 2,500 missions, carrying 28,000 tons of relief supplies to airfields in some of Somalia's hardest-hit areas (Baidoa, Bardera, Belet Weyn, Oddur).

On August 28, the Security Council, responding to a further recommendation from the secretary-general, passed UNSCR 775 authorizing the expansion of the UN's protective force in Somalia from 500 to 3,500. This action, however, caused a serious backlash from General Aideed (and indeed from Mohamed Sahnoun toward his own UN leadership), who had not been informed of the proposal and apparently felt he had been deceived in negotiating a just-concluded agreement with Sahnoun for deployment of the 500-man Pakistani contingent. This incident was to poison Aideed's future relationship with UNOSOM, keep the Pakistani battalion penned up at the airport, and contribute to Sahnoun's own resignation in October.

Meanwhile, the overall situation in Somalia continued to deteriorate. Humanitarian and logistics planners realized that to effectively address the general problem of starvation there would have to be substantial movement of food through the ports and along major highways; dependency on the airlift alone could never do the job, and in the meantime the death rates in the interior were still rising. But lack of security at the ports and along the roads either made movement impossible or created opportunities for bandits or factions to seize shipments in transit. As noted, the 500-man Pakistani battalion (delivered by the U.S. Air Force in November) was unable to obtain the cooperation of General Aideed and never got beyond its camp at Mogadishu airport. Clearly, more would need to be done. But what, and by whom?

Throughout fall 1992, interagency efforts to devise a more effective strategy were substantial. The problems of Somalia were subject to extensive analysis in the various concerned agencies, and a network of planning and coordination groups was built up that would be used even more intensively in the UNITAF and UNOSOM II phases to follow. As the responsible command, CENTCOM (and its army, navy, air force, and marine components) worked intensively to draft concepts and courses of action and possible operations plans. The Joint Staff (especially J-3/Operations and J-5/Plans and Policy—but with substantial inputs from the J-4 logisticians and other specialized staffs) interfaced with the field commands but also with the interagency policy mechanisms in Washington. At the top level, although formal National Security Council (NSC) meetings were very rare, the secretaries of state and defense, the national security adviser, and the chairman of the Joint Chiefs of Staff (JCS) conferred frequently and at length on Somali courses of action and apparently had full access to the president when needed.

This does not mean that there was agreement on all major points. Generally, there was not full agreement even within particular agencies given the magnitude and complexity of the problems—substantive, bureaucratic, political, and fiscal. But after several months of intensive consideration in the August–mid-November time frame, several conclusions had essentially been arrived at in "the interagency":

1. The expanded humanitarian effort was failing. Interference from the warlords at Mogadishu port and on the highways was preventing food from getting through in quantities adequate to turn the corner. The airlift, even with DOD planes flying ten or twelve missions a day, would never in itself be able to bring starvation under control.

2. The UN emergency intervention had essentially failed. The Pakistani battalion remained at the airport, endless debate continued in New York about augmentation forces, Mohamed Sahnoun had resigned in disgust, and it was obvious that—whatever the longer-term possibilities—the UN offered no immediate solutions to Somalia's crisis.

3. An effective short-term solution, one that would bring dramatic improvement in a matter of weeks, could be mounted only by the United States, alone or leading a coalition (the success of Desert Storm being very much in mind). But this would heavily involve the U.S. military and in general give the United States a broad overall responsibility; and many in the executive branch and in Congress remained very uncomfortable with this approach.

4. If the United States were nevertheless to leap into the fray, the operation would perforce be a very "heavy" one, probably a "2-division plus" force, heavily armed and inevitably with huge logistics support requirements. This meant that the locus of the main effort would be Mogadishu, and the operation would necessarily be heavily involved in getting the ports open and working, as well as the road network into the countryside. Alternative scenarios that would have avoided or minimized the use of Mogadishu were discarded by military planners in these weeks. In particular, the ideas of Fred Cuny[4] to introduce a much smaller and more flexible force operating outside of Mogadishu through the small ports and augmented by over-the-beach and some airborne-heliborne deliveries were decided to be inadequate for the type of intervention required. Although this concept, or variants, had generated considerable interest in Washington—and in DOD, particularly among the Special Operations community—by November it was essentially dead as a U.S. planning option. In summary, it died because it failed to meet the U.S. military's new insistence on the application of massive, overwhelming force and also because of the military's determination that only a heavy logistical operation based through Mogadishu could work.

With these considerations in mind, the NSC Deputies Committee fashioned a presentation of options for the president in Thanksgiving week 1992. According to press reports at the time, the options were basically to (1) proceed with the augmentation of UNOSOM to 3,500 in the hope that this could force cooperation from the warlords; (2) sponsor a very substantial UN force augmentation with a mandate to use force to carry out the mission and with U.S. quick-reaction forces in armed support; or (3) have the United States lead an immediate, large-scale intervention to aggressively fix the problem. The president's decision was made the day before Thanksgiving: The United States would ask the UN to authorize a large-scale coalition effort, led by the United States, to relieve the humanitarian crisis in Somalia. On Thanksgiving Day itself, Deputy Secretary of State Eagleburger went to New York and obtained Boutros-Ghali's agreement to the undertaking, confirmed by UNSCR 794 on December 3.

The authoritative explanation for this U.S. decision to lead a major humanitarian intervention into a failed state where the United States had no important political or strategic interests will probably have to await the publication of George Bush's memoirs or release of his papers. What seems clear is that it was truly his personal decision, based in large measure on his growing feelings of concern as the humanitarian disaster continued to unfold relentlessly despite the half-measures being undertaken by the international community. Presumably, growing criticism from the numerous involved NGOs, from the Hill, and from the Clinton camp was a contributing factor. Objectively, the interagency analysis (mentioned previously) that only a major U.S. intervention could quickly turn things around provided a planning rationale and ruled out other approaches. A coalition approach presumably was appealing in principle and also because of the warm afterglow of Desert Storm.

But probably the clinching factor was the contribution of the Joint Staff, which finally, in November, gave the interagency a course of action that it felt could work if the president decided to intervene. As Bob Oakley and John Hirsch report in their recent monograph, "On November 21, [interagency deputies] committee vice chairman Admiral David Jeremiah, Powell's representative, startled the group by saying, 'If you think U.S. forces are needed, we can do the job.'"[5] He then outlined a two-division coalition force concept developed by Central Command, and this concept provided the basis for the "heavy option" in a three-options paper sent to the president after that meeting. Again, however, the decision was the president's, especially since no recommendations accompanied the options paper. The interagency, without much enthusiasm, had given the president the opportunity to make a definitive choice, and to the surprise of some he quickly chose the maximalist course of action with the United States boldly in the lead.

On November 27, the full-time Somalia Working Group was formally established at State, with Ambassador Brandon Grove as director and Ambassador David Shinn as deputy director. On December 4, the president announced to the nation his decision to send in U.S. armed forces, a decision generally popular with the public and with the majority in Congress—and also one immediately endorsed by President-elect Clinton. The same day, the president announced the appointment of former (retired) ambassador Bob Oakley to replace Ambassador Pete de Vos as U.S. special envoy for Somalia. Oakley left immediately for Somalia, arriving and plunging into his diplomatic work a day ahead of the arrival of the first marines on December 8. The stage was now set for speedy and spectacular success in ending the humanitarian crisis, to be followed by almost equally speedy and spectacular disappointment and failure in finding a lasting solution to Somalia's continuing political crisis.

The U.S.-Led Coalition: UNITAF
(December 1992–May 1993)

The U.S.-led coalition was anchored by marines from Camp Pendleton and army troops from Fort Drum. The force, under the command of Lt. Gen. Bob Johnston, was designated UNITAF: Unified Task Force. From the approved "concept of operations," its goals were clear and limited: Seize Mogadishu port, airfield, and environs and prepare them for a major logistical throughput; seize airfields and place coalition security elements at a number of regional hubs in the hunger zone; open the roads for truck transport; and provide adequate security throughout the operational area for the safe conduct of humanitarian operations, including the transport of humanitarian supplies.

UNITAF was not committed to rebuilding infrastructure, although it did considerable work in repairing roads and bridges; it was not committed to enforce any kind of general disarmament, although it did require that heavy weapons and technicals be stored or removed from the operational area and did confiscate several thousand small arms and automatic weapons found in prohibited areas; it had no mandate to organize or revive local security forces, although it did recruit a substantial number of personnel, including former police, to perform local security functions that directly supported the command's operations. And it had no mandate whatsoever to intervene in Somalia's politics, public administration, or justice system. There was no imposition of martial law, no establishment of a UNITAF political command structure. The entire UNITAF operation was to be short term and highly focused only on accomplishment of the humanitarian mission; it was, in addition, to make essential preparations for relief by and turnover to follow-on UN peacekeeping forces.

In fact, UNITAF succeeded in its assigned tasks quickly and well and with minimal casualties. Notwithstanding the predominant U.S. role, intensive diplomatic and parallel military-to-military talks produced a wide-ranging set of credible coalition partners, especially tough French and Belgian units. A separate fund was established under the UN to help defray some of the costs, with an immediate contribution of $100 million from Japan—to prove, alas, also the only substantial contribution, although Saudi Arabia did subsequently provide $10 million.

When challenged by the warlords, the UNITAF forces showed no hesitation in using measured force to destroy technicals and illegal weapons caches. Within a few weeks of the initial landing, the port was open, major highways were opening, several of the major regional cities were occupied and at peace, a truce was in place between Ali Mahdi and Aideed, and in general the UNITAF operation was well on its way to accomplishing its mission. Indeed, in accordance with President Bush's initial announcement of a very short term operation, 1,500 U.S. troops were actually withdrawn before January 20, 1993—President Clinton's inauguration day.

Once U.S. forces were committed, lead responsibility for implementation of the agreed strategy passed to the military chain of command, from General Johnston on the ground through CINCCENT General Joe Hoar to the Joint Staff and especially the chairman, Gen. Colin Powell, and thence through the secretary of defense to the president. A half-dozen specialized working groups and task forces were active, and their work continued to come together at the NSC Deputies Committee. Throughout the planning and conduct of the Somalia intervention, the Deputies Committee would be the single most important mechanism for the fashioning and fine-tuning of U.S. policy and tactics in all aspects to include—selectively—some military matters as well.

It is not my purpose here to review in depth the activities and accomplishments of UNITAF, and of Ambassador Oakley's parallel diplomatic efforts. Suffice it to say that within ninety days UNITAF had accomplished its mandate and was ready to withdraw. Within that time, the famine in Somalia had been brought under control, a measure of tranquillity restored, and some important first steps taken to start the process of reconciliation. However, although it was not yet glaringly evident, other decisions had been made, other things had not been done, that would doom the follow-on UN-led operation to failure.

Turnover to the UN: UNOSOM II and the Hunt for Aideed (May 1993–October 1993)

It had been the firm intent and expectation of the U.S. forces to turn over the operation in Somalia to an expanded UN force within a few months. No one had expected the U.S. force, or substantial elements of it, to be out of Somalia by January 20 (although, as noted previously, a token withdrawal was achieved, probably in part for political effect). But a turnover within four to six months was considered achievable and reasonable. As events transpired on the ground, a turnover date of April 1 would have been warranted had the UN been willing and, more important, organized to assume responsibility. But already two tendencies had become manifest that were to portend the failure of the UNOSOM II operation to follow:

- UNITAF's refusal to take on expanded tasks, despite the urgings of the secretary general, to make UNOSOM's follow-on job more manageable.
- UN slowness, verging on foot-dragging, in mounting that operation and critical associated activities in the civil, police, and justice sectors.

Both problems were fundamental to the ultimate failure of the UN mission. But one must observe a critical distinction. With respect to UNITAF's refusal to take on expanded responsibilities on behalf of the UN (expand the areas of operation to include even the North; engage in general disarmament; destroy or seize weapons caches known to exist in the remote countryside), the U.S. refusal was firmly based in the restrictions of the formal mission and also in continuing political guidance from the National Command Authorities. As noted, the UNITAF mission was not to deliver humanitarian services, not to engage in activities designed to affect the political power structures in Somalia, not to disarm except as essential to accomplishing the assigned mission; that mission was to establish, only in designated geographic areas, a situation of general security in which the UN, NGOs, and other agencies could accomplish their work in peace. It is true that on its own volition, UNITAF did go far enough in some collateral areas that U.S. command echelons and policy circles did worry, from early on, about functional or geographic "mission creep," and a considerable effort was exerted to fend off or contain such tendencies.

From Washington's perspective, this constant reaffirmation of the limited nature of UNITAF responsibilities was also necessary to fend off continuous efforts by the UN to get UNITAF to do what Washington felt should properly be left to the follow-on UN forces themselves. There was also concern that substantial involvement in such activities could delay the departure of U.S. units and give the UN further opportunities for delay in bringing in its own peacekeepers. Although an argument might have been made (indeed, the secretary-general repeatedly attempted to make it) that the UNITAF forces, with their much greater firepower and general capabilities, should do more to ensure the subsequent success of smaller and weaker and less well organized UN forces, U.S. authorities were quick to reject this approach wherever it reared its head.

So UNITAF came, accomplished its assigned mandate quickly and well, and then waited, with considerable impatience, to be withdrawn. It would leave the UN—in a transfer that was supposed to be "seamless" but fell well short of that standard—in a country that was economically prostrate and still awash in weapons and with the warlords unbroken and recalcitrant.

What of the new, expanded, and improved UNOSOM force (UNOSOM II), authorized by the UN on March 26? To get on top of its responsibilities, two requirements were basic. The first was to persuade or force the warlords—especially General Aideed—to accommodate to a process of reconciliation and shared power. The second would be to get UN structures and processes to perform adequately and in some reasonable time frame. It is hard to calculate in which aspect the UN failed more miserably.

At the policy level, there was little disagreement between the United States and the UN on what would be required, including the force needed to carry out the expanded UN mandate. UNSCR 824 of March 26 had provided for a large (28,000) force with a robust Chapter VII mandate. The entire operation would be under the watchful gaze of an American, retired admiral (and, more important, former deputy national security adviser) Jon Howe, who had in March replaced Ismat Kittani as the secretary-general's special representative. The Turkish general in command of UNOSOM II, Cevik Bir, had been selected with the approval of the United States. And after exhaustive military planning and diplomatic discussion, the United States had committed a very substantial follow-on troop effort to UNOSOM II, including critical supporting logistical elements and also a potent quick-reaction force with armed helicopters and on-call C-130 gunships. There was a keen recognition that the job would be difficult and an expectation that the warlords, or at least General Aideed, would present the UN with an early challenge.

This probability existed notwithstanding notable political progress among Somali factions starting in March to include steps toward comprehensive disarmament and the restoration of Somali political and administrative capabilities at national, regional, and local levels. There were high hopes that UNOSOM II could build on this progress but also apprehension that the path would soon be blocked in a challenge from, most probably, General Aideed.

This was not long in developing. Aideed had not been pleased with the UN intervention from the beginning. He had reacted badly to the UN decision to augment its original force above the 500-man level negotiated by Sahnoun. His forces had been manhandled on several occasions by UNITAF (technicals destroyed, arms caches seized or destroyed). In the South, UNITAF had not prevented General Morgan from making inroads into territory controlled by Aideed's ally, Colonel Jess. And in general, Aideed seemed to feel the United States and especially the UN were biased in favor of his arch rival, Ali Mahdi. He also was growing nervous and suspicious of UNOSOM activities, which seemed to be showing undue interest in his command and radio facilities.

On June 5, 1993, fierce fighting broke out between Aideed's militia and supporters and the Pakistanis, triggered by an earlier Pakistani search of an Aideed weapons site colocated with his radio station. By the end of the fighting, twenty-four Pakistani soldiers were dead. The UN reacted with UNSCR 837 on June 6, condemning the attack and asking the secretary-general, under Chapter VII, to take "all necessary measures" against those responsible, to include arrest, detention, trial, and punishment.

On June 12, UNOSOM forces, including U.S. AC-130 gunships and helicopters, attacked Aideed weapons-storage sites in Mogadishu. On June 17, in another firefight, Aideed's forces killed one Pakistani and four Moroccan soldiers, including the Moroccan force commander. On June 27–28, two more Pakistanis were killed; on July 3, three Italian soldiers; on July 7, six Somali UN employees. On July 12, UNOSOM struck back, this time harder. Attacking Aideed's main command and control site violently and without warning, UNOSOM killed over twenty of Aideed's followers; Aideed claimed a higher number of deaths among civilians caught in the raid. In effect, and regrettably for the operation and for Somalia, UNOSOM and Aideed were now at war.

Also regrettably, the new focus on armed confrontation with Aideed took the impetus out of other promising initiatives that were getting under way, often after months of agonizingly slow UN activity. Especially significant were agreements (at the national reconciliation conference held in Addis Ababa in late March) to reconstitute political and administrative authority, an agreement (in March, prior to Ambassador Oakley's departure, and thereafter strangely neglected) for a general plan of disarmament to implement agreements reached in Addis Ababa on January 15, and the beginning of efforts to reconstitute Somali police forces and a court system. These undertakings, promising in March-May, were on hold from June on and in most instances failed to progress substantially for the balance of the UN intervention. They too had fallen victim, more by neglect than design, to the preoccupation with the armed struggle with Aideed and its debilitating consequences, as well as to initial hesitancy followed by demonstrable inadequacy on the part of the UN's civil components.[6]

These developments had been followed with increasing concern by the new Clinton administration Somalia team (the Deputies Committee was now being chaired by Sandy Berger; other agency principals usually included Frank Wisner from Defense, Peter Tarnoff from State, and Admiral Dave Jeremiah representing the Joint Staff). In its deliberations and in the myriad details of its work in these months, the U.S. community was almost schizophrenic in its pursuit of two very different courses of action. On the one hand, vast energy was expended in trying to persuade, cajole, and assist the UN to energetically fulfill the broad mandate of UNOSOM II, including effective actions to fill important posts in Somalia, get a police assistance operation in place, and accelerate activities to empower local and regional structures. There were arguments and sharp disagreements on many matters, not all issues of detail (for example, as to whether a top-down or a bottom-up approach should be the basis of political revitalization efforts, surely a critical issue). But there was a broad consensus that if Somalia were to be rebuilt, all of these elements would need to be put in place quickly; there was a growing realization that this was not happening.

At the same time, and contrary to later assertions from critics of the operation, the United States was deeply and—in a technical sense at least—enthusiastically engaged in the military confrontation with Aideed. Partly this reflected the animosity created by the provocative actions of Aideed, animosity fanned by the increasingly frustrated communiqués of Admiral Howe; partly it reflected the frustrations of the UNOSOM military command as it saw its patrols and facilities mocked, harassed, and ambushed with no relief in sight; and formally it reflected the perceived obligation to do what was required to support the UN politically, especially after passage of UNSCR 837 on June 6. In spring, suggestions had been made that the United States should bring in special elements, later described generally as Rangers, to hunt down and capture Aideed. This recommendation had more support in the field than in Washington and from the beginning was resisted by the U.S. military leadership, which viewed this as yet another, and very long, step down the slippery slope—and as an operation with high risk and very modest chances of success. There was particular concern when Admiral Howe issued, on June 17, an arrest warrant for Aideed and posted a $25,000 reward for his capture. Many U.S. analysts and policymakers felt the policy train was off track and threatening to carry the United States no one knew where in an increasingly militant and personalized vendetta against Somalia's premier master of urban warfare. But as pressures grew and Aideed emerged as a mocking and elusive media personality, visibly twisting the UN and U.S. tails on the world's stage, the decision was reluctantly approved in August; and the Rangers were sent in.

Interestingly, there was a concurrent effort to wrench the policy train back onto a more constructive track. Having concluded that U.S. as well as UN policy was drifting without apparent cohesion, and cognizant of growing congressional and public apprehension, Secretary of Defense Aspin had directed his staff, working with the Joint Staff, to come up with a public presentation setting out an integrated strategy to salvage a deteriorating situation. In an August 27 major policy address, speaking on behalf of the Clinton administration, Aspin called on the UN to pull together urgently a cohesive and better-focused program of action, to include attention to the need for police, and a coordinated economic-political-security approach. He urged revitalization of the peace process and emphasized the necessity of bringing all the parties to the table

Had there been time and a U.S. commitment to vigorously assist the UN to pursue the broad Aspin agenda, the unfavorable drift of events might yet have been reversed. The Aspin plan was broad and demanding and in most respects constituted a belated acknowledgment that the UN operation was failing to unfold in all of the key sectors, in many cases because the essential initial planning had yet to be completed. The following are extracts of Aspin's prescriptions, constituting in a sense a remarkable indictment of the lethargy of the collective effort up to that point:

First, we should bring UN combined troop strength up to planned levels. The United States has recently added 400 more combat troops to its Quick Reaction Force. UN-OSOM II, however, is approximately 5,000 troops short of its planned complement of 28,000. We fully expect others to do their share, as they have promised.

Second, additional efforts to set up a police force should begin immediately . . . Third, we should continue removing heavy weapons from the militias and begin planning for implementation—in conjunction with Somali police—of a consistent weapons control policy. . . . Fourth, the United Nations must develop a detailed plan with concrete steps that will put together its economic, political, and security activities into an overall strategy. And it must provide adequate staff and budget to make progress on its political and economic objectives in Somalia. Fifth, the United Nations should draw on the experience of its success in Cambodia to form a core group of nations to support and speed its work in Somalia. . . . Sixth, the United Nations and the Organization of African Unity should act now to bring the parties back together on the peace track. They might use the promising model of two previous conferences on Somali national reconciliation held in Addis Ababa.[7]

But even as efforts to implement this agenda proceeded, the orders to the Rangers stood; the hunt for Aideed was being intensified, and the possibility of having time to pursue the Aspin strategy was about to be extinguished.

Catastrophe and Retreat
(October 1993–March 1994)

For all practical purposes, the U.S.-UN effort to impose any external vision of reconciliation and nation building on Somalia ended on October 3, 1993. Shocked by the death of eighteen U.S. Rangers (seventy-eight more were wounded) and hundreds of Somalis in a bitter fight with Aideed's followers in southern

Mogadishu and inundated with public and congressional criticism, the Clinton administration immediately abandoned the ongoing policy and adopted a policy looking to minimize any further casualties while seeking a formula for early U.S. withdrawal under circumstances other than humiliation. Orders went out at once to the troops to desist in the hunt for Aideed or any further attacks on his infrastructure and to "bunker down" to enhance security. In statements and briefings running from October 6 to 13, the administration announced that it would bolster the security of the forces in Somalia by dispatching heavy armor and other combat elements (which it had earlier refused to send in the hope of avoiding a further militarization of the situation). The brunt of the ensuing congressional and public criticism for the failure to send armor fell on and was accepted by Secretary Aspin, and that decision came to be symbolic of perceived drift, weakness, and confusion in the administration's Somalia policy, as well as contributing directly to the Ranger debacle. I find the general criticism warranted but see little direct connection to the fate of the Rangers. Even if the additional tanks had been sent, they would not have headed off the shootdown of the two helicopters and the ensuing firefight, which entailed substantial loss of life. Indeed, even if Aspin had approved sending the tanks, it is unlikely that they would have been on the scene by October 3. The fact of the matter is that neither the Congress nor the public, and perhaps not the higher levels of the White House, adequately understood that the Somalia operation had been for several months a volatile and high-risk military endeavor. The loss of the eighteen Rangers was truly an accident of war waiting to happen; equally plausible and probably more substantial loss of American life could have occurred on any day if Somali gunners had been able to bag an American transport plane or if one of Aideed's mobile 160mm mortar shells had actually detonated inside the UNOSOM compound, where several had landed. The inherent and continuous great risks of ongoing operations were neither highlighted to nor at all understood by the home front.

The administration defended its policy of engagement in Somalia but acknowledged that "personalizing" the quarrel with Aideed and neglecting the possibilities for a political solution had gotten the policy off track. To give the UN a reasonable chance to salvage the operation, the president said U.S. forces would remain until March 31. After that, the UNOSOM contingents would remain but without the presence of the U.S. military.

These announcements, essentially unilateral, seemed to threaten the entire operation with unraveling. But the prompt dispatch of the promised reinforcements, congressional acquiescence (after emotions had cooled somewhat) to the March withdrawal deadline, and a stabilization of the political situation in Mogadishu engineered by again-dispatched presidential emissary Oakley gave the operation time to recover. Attempts were once again launched to bolster the political reconciliation process, to expand and accelerate the humanitarian assistance program, and to build up the skeletal Somali police elements. It was, of course, too late. Although gratified by the new U.S.-UN approach and publicly pledging cooperation, General Aideed made it clear by his actions that he had no intention of allowing any activities that would reduce his power or displace him. Violence returned gradually to the countryside, significant progress on the UN's ambitious agenda failed to materialize, and when U.S. forces in fact departed Somalia in late March, the prospects for a peaceful evolution were minimal.

Failure and Withdrawal
(March 1994–March 1995)

And so it was. Despite some reinforcements and the arrival of heavier combat equipment for force protection, the will of the UNOSOM II leadership to actively pursue its mission had been broken by the U.S. abandonment. The effort was to continue, pro forma, for another year, but at ever-decreasing force levels. In July 1994 the UN announced a major, phased reduction of UNOSOM forces; in August the United States announced closure of the U.S. liaison office in Mogadishu together with its fifty-eight–man marine FAST (Fleet Anti-Terrorism Support Team) security force. Emboldened by the progressive enfeeblement of UNOSOM, Somalis increased their attacks against both peacekeepers and the NGO community, leading to a dynamic of ever-diminishing presence and capabilities to fulfill any of the plans laid out only a few months earlier by the UN. Thanks to prudent military management and the return of heavily armed U.S. forces to guard the final phase of the UNOSOM withdrawal, no major catastrophe befell the final UNOSOM elements, even as Somali looters closed in on the heels of the evacuees, carrying off the abandoned debris of the once-ambitious operation. The humiliation was complete.

Did We Accomplish Anything?
Did We Learn Anything?

As Bob Oakley and John Hirsch have reminded us, at least the UNITAF phase of Somalia operations succeeded—within its mandate—exceedingly well, enabling humanitarian operations to resume to end the famine within a few weeks, thereby saving hundreds of thousands of lives; in brief, the UNITAF phase constituted an incredible achievement. One can also argue, and U.S. authorities have, that the operation gave the Somalis new opportunities to find peace among themselves and put in place some structures and agreements—local, regional, and national—among the Somali parties that still offer hope for the future. I consider this argument also quite valid as far as it goes.

Beyond these achievements, the first substantial, the second less so and as yet unfulfilled, the argument has been made that all concerned have learned a great deal from the Somalia operation. This dictum, however, cuts in two directions. On the positive side, certainly the UN learned (if it did not already know) just how feeble are its organizational staffing and procedures to deal with this type of massive operation. The United States—and other contributing nations—learned how to help the UN improve and apply these capabilities in a myriad of practical ways, and some of these technical lessons learned have subsequently been applied (the careful and successful planning for Haiti is probably the best example). Everyone involved was also reminded sharply, as crises repeatedly overtook the process, of the need for effective programs of political consultation, of dialogue with national legislatures, and of a forthcoming and proactive public affairs posture. The Somali operation was poorly understood in large part because it was very poorly explained, whether to the public or the U.S. Congress or the German parliament.

But these truths, simple and powerful, should not have had to be relearned in Somalia. The new, and much more important, truths revealed in the Somalia operation (and to be repeated thereafter in Rwanda, Bosnia, perhaps yet in Haiti, perhaps yet in Burundi, perhaps yet in a dozen other places) are more somber: The UN is not up to such tasks and needs to be vastly improved and much more adequately financed if it is going to take on problems such as failed/failing states, genocide, and civil war or anarchy. This is not merely a matter of improving its military or peacekeeping and peacemaking capacities; it is a matter of improving performance—especially timely response—of all involved agencies, across the board, by several orders of magnitude. Regrettably, however, the United States, and probably other important international actors and donors, are not in the near term going to give the UN the kind of charter, assistance, and funding needed to raise it to such standards. Although the United States (possibly alone in the world) has the capabilities and resources to undertake such missions with good prospects for success, it has at least temporarily lost the will and therefore the capacity to lead internationally. In part this arises because there is no longer even the semblance of consensus among the public and between the Congress and the administration as to what its broad international interests and responsibilities are in the post–Cold War period. This confusion did not occur because of Somalia but was revealed by the stress that the Somalia operation put on the U.S. system. More specifically, the international community, and certainly the U.S. leadership, knows how to deal with armed and violent oppositionists but generally now lacks the will or motivation to do so; this will apparently not soon change, particularly where poor and backward lands are involved. This was actually first revealed starkly not in Somalia but in the collapse and destruction of Liberia starting two years earlier.[8]

Thus we will probably have more, not fewer, Somalias until the international community matures in its sense of responsibilities or until U.S. leadership finds its true bearings on international issues again. Those in the United States who oppose such interventions in the first instance will continue to find much comfort and advantage in raising the banner of nationalist sentiment with such slogans as "No U.S. troops under UN command," as though this had actually occurred in Somalia or as if some of the more disastrous events had been committed by other than U.S. troops, under U.S. command, following U.S. policy.

Reflections on U.S. Government Decisionmaking Processes

The preceding narrative has unfolded along a time line and with limited attention to the details of U.S. government decisionmaking processes. In my view, in the

Somalia case there was little of great interest or importance in the mechanics of those processes. They were, in a word, adequate. The effort focused on Somalia was massive, dedicated, and well organized. The interagency perhaps got off to a bit of a slow start (outside of AID-OFDA and some of the State desks) and suffered throughout from inadequate hard information from the field, but there is little doubt that it developed reasonably accurate estimates of the situation, proposed reasonable courses of action, and in myriad ways coped with the tasks of coordination with hundreds of diplomats and bureaucrats around the world involved in various aspects of the Somalia operation.

The key players in the interagency structure, and those sent to lead the U.S. and UN efforts in the field, were almost without exception among our best and brightest. Talented staffs worked nights and weekends to feed the appetites of interlocking circles of agency and interagency study groups, working groups, and task forces, capped by the very active—and I would add on the basis of attending numerous sessions, very thoughtful—Deputies Committee. Some commentators have found a significant weakness in the process of transfer of responsibility from the Bush to the Clinton administrations, characterizing the former as experienced, focused, and generally on top of the operation and the latter as—to put it charitably—markedly less so. I find little merit in this argument. After all, the staffs remained essentially the same; the same key military players, all the way to the chairman of the JCS, stayed in place; and the previous key NSC player—Jon Howe—was repositioned in an equally critical position as the UN's (and for that matter, the U.S.'s) leader in the field. And on the face of it, the policies stayed the same. So in fact there was a great deal of continuity—of personalities, of process, of structure, of policy.

The important differences were twofold: (1) the nature of the challenge as the humanitarian mission gave way to the agreed follow-on mission of reconstituting Somalia (what came to be sneeringly identified as "nation building") and (2) the fact that now the UN and not the United States was in the lead. It is my conclusion, looking backward, that there was no way the operation could have succeeded in any case because it was built on false premises, premises that became policy dictates in shaping and circumscribing both the U.S. and UN interventions. Those premises were that the operation could be politically neutral, that the major Somali political actors and warlords could be persuaded or forced into a process of reconciliation, and that a UN-led international operation could restore the basic structures of Somali society in a time frame adequate to capture and sustain the momentum of the initial UNITAF phase and then to consolidate those gains to prevent backsliding into renewed strife and anarchy.

These assumptions were highly dubious, and some skeptics had noted this from the first days of the operation. Most notorious was the acerbic observation of Ambassador Smith Hempstone, whose (promptly leaked) message from Nairobi warned Washington that the operation was ill fated, that "if you liked Beirut, you'll love Mogadishu," and that the United States should "think once, twice and three times before you embrace the Somali tarbaby."[9] Washington told Hempstone, not nicely, to shut up; as it turned out, Hempstone was very much on target. The sharpness of the Washington response, I believe, had only a little to do with the Hempstone challenge to the wisdom of the decision and more to do with the nagging doubt that not only was he possibly right but, in particular, he should not be raising problems that could be, should be, left to the incoming administration and to the UN. The silencing of Hempstone, and other doubters, at this early point in the drama was mainly a decision, by reflex, to kick these basic concerns downstream to those who would later be responsible. Coupled with the narrow focus placed on the UNITAF operation, this reaction would also complete the formula for near-certain failure. In essence, and contrary to hopeful premises, the Somalis would not be tractable and the UN would not be capable. But this was not known at the time and would ultimately and reluctantly be accepted only after energetic attempts to prove the opposite.

The main Somali warlord, to the surprise of some and the frustrated nonsurprise of others more familiar with Somalia, would not be co-opted, would not yield on his key demands, and would struggle bitterly to hold on to the gains he and his followers had won in Mogadishu in the final death struggle with Siad Barre. But whereas General Aideed had tested UNITAF and, meeting quick and forceful responses, thereafter acted with professional restraint, he calculated correctly that UNOSOM II could be confronted with less risk and—as he was reported as telling his followers—with sufficient casualties could be driven into the ocean. When this violence brought the U.S. Rangers in search of him, he continued to fight bitterly, accepting heavy losses but ultimately breaking the will of U.S. authorities to persevere in the face of mounting American casualties and public and congressional outrage. From Aideed's perspective, the UN had invaded Somalia, had sought by innumerable actions to diminish his stature and power, and in June had declared war on him; another battle to the death followed, and the UN—with the United States finally sounding retreat—lost the war. From October 3 on, there was no "UN solution" realistically available for Somalia.

Those who argue that the Somalia operation under guidance from the Bush team was sound and successful, whereas the operation under the Clinton team was unsound and disastrous, seem to me unwilling to confront the main point: The policy stream was continuous, and the complete seeds of disaster were put in place by decisions and guiding principles and assumptions carrying over from the beginning of the operation. The fruit was bad because the seed was bad. The fundamental flaws in the policy seed were several: (1) we were there only to restore security, not to decide a political outcome (later recast into the catchy not-our-problem-after-all phrase, "African solutions for African problems"); (2) we had no obligation to and would not defang the warlords and gangs; and (3) it was up to the UN to put quickly in place the broad institutional capabilities and resources needed to revitalize at least the minimal elements of a functioning Somali society and government. As to the final point, and confirming suspicions that had been widely shared in interagency planning sessions from the earliest months, the UN would prove utterly incapable of doing this, a fact that in and of itself was probably enough also to doom the operation in the midterm had the failure not already been complete in the short term.

It should be observed that the United States, when confronted with the undeniable evidence that the UN was neither organized nor staffed to actually fulfill the mandate it had given itself in Somalia, chose not to rally round with new heroic measures of support. There was a tremendous amount of diplomatic effort and technical staff work expended, but the emphasis was on somehow forcing the UN to perform without substantially raising the level of U.S. effort within the UN system. For example, there was a readily apparent need for U.S. civil affairs officers, in large numbers, to strengthen the UN's field operations. There was a desperate need for public safety advisers and technicians to actually help implement the sensible plans to restore the police and court systems that had been worked out with the Somalis. The United States did not offer to fill these and other critical voids, partly for reasons of cost, partly for reasons of concern with personnel security, partly because neither the Department of Defense nor the White House wanted to increase the number of military personnel in Somalia, in whatever status. But mainly, the United States refrained from offering to do more because of the fear of blurring the handoff of responsibilities to the UN. UNITAF had been a U.S. responsibility, but UNOSOM and the parallel UN civil operations were not; and the United States did not want to do anything that would tarnish the purity of the transfer of responsibility, especially with an increasingly hostile Congress nipping at the policymakers' heels. In terms of the UN's existing institutional capabilities and available personnel resources, the effect was on a par with turning over the helm of a ship in boiling waters to a five-year-old with an admonishment to sail safely. The ensuing shipwreck was both inevitable and predictable. But at least the United States could identify it as a UN failure.

The UN failure in Somalia was not a failure of policy, of process, of personalities, or of tactics. It was in part a failure of strategy, in part a failure of capabilities, and mainly a failure of collective will and leadership. Those most astutely aware of the limitations of international collective action, and of the shallow support such actions enjoy with the public and with national legislative bodies, had cautiously stayed on the sidelines two years earlier as Liberia self-destructed, finally finding small comfort in assisting the efforts (also futile) of the Economic Community of West African States (ECOWAS) to find a West African solution to a West African debacle. After failure in Somalia, the international community would again sit by as Rwanda imploded with a minimum of a half-million persons slaughtered in an orgy of genocide. Today, a similar delicate unwillingness to be excessively involved continues to drive Western policy on the catastrophe in Bosnia and the impending ethnic slaughter in Burundi.

Thus the Somalia operation was for a time a potential important exception to normal practice, perhaps even a precedent—an actual attempt to leap into and resolve a vicious internal situation verging on or perhaps gone beyond civil war. But even as the operation went through its gargantuan labors, it narrowed down its

objectives and responsibilities in a way that made the event into an exercise in ir-
relevancy, or perhaps irreality.

Any operation like the UNITAF-UNOSOM intervention in Somalia is by nature political and will involve the intervening powers intimately in all the dynamics of the situation. If the base cause of conditions requiring intervention is political and it is therefore deemed essential to correct it, then the will to frankly
identify the problem and to follow through with strong corrective action needs to
be in place from the beginning. The public and the legislatures concerned need to
be brought into the game plan and their understanding and support put on a solid
basis. There must be a willingness to be frank about the facts of the situation and
about the costs that will probably come, including substantial loss of life. And
whereas there is need for skillful and active diplomacy and political consultation
on the ground, there must also be a willingness and capability to deal with great
force, when necessary, with those who stand forcibly in the way of implementation of the international mandate, whatever its flaws. These factors were never
firmly in place for UNOSOM II, although there was much huffing and puffing
about them, thereby encouraging U.S. officials to delude themselves about the
depth and seriousness of the national commitment—but apparently never fool-
ing General Aideed.

If the formidable energies and talents of the Somalis can be focused and har-
nessed, through their own volition, on reconciliation and reconstruction, a vi-
brant Somalia could quickly rise from the present ruins. If the focus remains on
confrontation and violent quarrels over diminishing scraps of piratical opportunity, it is all too likely that the miserable conditions of 1991 will return, then con-
founding the international community with yet another massive crisis that it
will, understandably, hesitate to address. Perhaps the Somali leadership fully appreciates this and will accordingly redouble its efforts toward reconciliation.
Perhaps.

Notes

1. Keith Richards, "Envoy Finds Somalia in Dissolution," *Washington Post*, January 7,
1992, p. A1.

2. Herman Cohen, "Intervention in Somalia," in Allan E. Goodman, ed., *The Diplomatic
Record, 1992–1993* (Boulder: Westview Press, 1994), p. 54.

3. Ibid., p. 60.

4. Cuny was well known for his active involvement and expertise in humanitarian operations as president of the NGO Intertect Relief and Reconstruction.

5. John Hirsch and Robert Oakley, *Somalia and Operation Restore Hope* (Washington,
DC: U.S. Institute of Peace Press, 1995), p. 43.

6. Ibid., chaps. 5, 6.

7. Les Aspin, "Remarks Prepared for Delivery by Secretary of Defense Les Aspin at the
Center for Strategic and International Studies, Washington, D.C., August 27, 1993," Office
of the Assistant Secretary of Defense (Public Affairs), news release no. 398-93.

8. There is little doubt that the U.S. naval-marine task force dispatched to Liberia could have intervened decisively to bring an early end to the Liberian civil war precipitated by Charles Taylor. Instead, the Bush administration denied responsibility for resolving the crisis and limited the task force's functions to emergency evacuations and protection of the U.S. embassy compound. The task force remained offshore for months, "sailing and sailing," as one Liberian put it, while doing nothing to stop the slaughter or to end the conflict that would over the next several years destroy the country.

9. See *U.S. News and World Report*, December 14, 1992. Hempstone's document deserves now to be given the serious attention denied to it at the time.

10

Relations Between the United States and United Nations in Dealing with Somalia

JONATHAN T. HOWE

Of all the relationships between member countries and the organizations they create, the one between the United States and the UN is perhaps the most unique, complex, and important. Both the United States and the UN will be critical actors in defining any future role the world organization may play in dealing with massive humanitarian catastrophes resulting from ethnic cleansing, genocide, or man-made starvation. Therefore, it is important to examine U.S.-UN relations during these entities' demanding and unprecedented joint effort to help the failed state of Somalia from 1992 to 1995.

The UN and the United States approach problems from different perspectives. The interests, obligations, and capabilities of the organization of nations are not the same as those of an individual member country. A nation's first loyalties, for example, are to its own constituency. A democracy must satisfy the requirements of its citizens. If a nation experiences severe internal criticism, its government may not be able to sustain an institutional commitment even if the leadership is willing to do so. The UN answers to member nations—not to an electorate. When blame is spread among the 180 member nations of this institution, it is more easily diffused. Conversely, since the UN has no domestic constituency, it may become a convenient scapegoat for nations that do.

Those who work for the UN understandably put priority on protecting the institution and meeting the wishes of a broad consensus of nations. They must respond to pressures from many different directions. For example, the UN may look at a particular crisis in the context of a global balancing act in trying to meet worldwide demands. A single success or failure among a dozen tests does not necessarily look the same to the UN as to the principal nations involved in a particular mission. The UN may be willing to trade a nation's assistance in one crisis situation for its help in filling a larger gap somewhere else. Preventing further starvation and helping a country such as Somalia to recover may be just one among many humanitarian "world interests." UN missions in the field, however, have a more narrow perspective. They concentrate on how they can meet the mandates of the Security Council and what is in the best interests of the people they have come to help.

For most Americans, tolerance of sacrifice is related to perceptions of national interests. Vital security interests should be protected, even at high cost. But Somalia never met this description. In the aftermath of the Cold War, Somalia was no longer a U.S. national security interest. U.S. intervention in Somalia was motivated primarily by a humanitarian desire to help prevent further death from starvation and disease. By way of contrast, in leading a military coalition in response to the Iraqi invasion of Kuwait, the United States was meeting external aggression and a threat to a declared vital interest of the Western world.

The workings of the UN and the relationship of that institution to its member states are not widely understood. The UN does not have organizational independence but rather is a creature of its nations. It is dependent on them for direction and resources. In dealing with peacekeeping operations, the fifteen members of the Security Council are equivalent to a board of directors for the UN. Council members establish guidance and broad policy. When the secretary-general is confronted with tough policy choices he presents a range of options to the Security Council for its decision. The nations are an integral part of the UN. When they criticize the UN for various actions, they often are, in effect, engaging in self-criticism. This is especially true of a country as influential as the United States.

In undertaking a complex and dangerous peace-enforcement mission, the UN has little equipment and no troops of its own. Resources flow from a very deliberate bureaucratic budget process involving many nations. Members are assessed annually for the funding of certain requirements of the peacekeeping budget, but other needs associated with humanitarian peace enforcement such as relief and development assistance and restoration of police, justice, and penal systems depend on voluntary contributions over and above annual assessments.

Individual nations must volunteer to answer the call for UN troops if there are going to be peacekeepers in the field. This is not an obligatory requirement of membership. Requests of the secretary-general and resolutions of the Security Council do not automatically produce volunteers for tough assignments. Whereas an individual country finding itself in difficulty overseas can simply dispatch more of its troops or armaments, the UN has no such reserve. It must make reports to the Security Council, justify additional numbers, float competitive bids for equipment, and obtain budgetary authority. The UN cannot force countries to extend their units beyond agreed time frames; and it must even rely on persuasion to ensure compliance with existing commitments.

As the UN faced the challenges of peace enforcement in Somalia, it already was in overload, drained by Cambodia, Bosnia, and other competing priorities. The world's most difficult problems were being dumped in the UN's lap without the accompanying restructuring necessary to cope with them effectively. As an organization of some 180 nations, the UN is not geared for rapid staffing and decisionmaking. It certainly is not yet optimally organized to manage a complex peace-enforcement operation. The UN's huge bureaucracy is not streamlined for crisis management and long-range planning. It has neither the responsive infrastructure nor the discretionary funding authority necessary to support the field adequately. For example, the peacekeeping staff did not have the organizational authority to expeditiously meet emergent requirements in Somalia.

In presenting options to the Security Council on November 29, 1992, prior to acceptance of the U.S. offer to lead UNITAF, the secretary-general reported that "the United Nations Secretariat did not currently have the capability to command and control an enforcement operation of the size required."[1] Accepting the U.S. offer was tacit recognition of the lack of UN readiness to manage a Chapter VII operation.

In this chapter I examine different U.S. and UN perspectives in dealing with the various challenges of Somalia and their consequences. I then briefly explore some of the awkward U.S.-UN arrangements that accompanied the changing U.S. military contribution at various phases of the mission. Finally, a few lessons are enumerated for strengthening U.S.-UN relations and establishing a better relationship for undertaking future peace-enforcement challenges.

Different Perspectives and Their Consequences

After exhausting traditional methods of trying to deal with the humanitarian disaster in Somalia and faced with the prospect of thousands more deaths due to disease and starvation, the Security Council accepted on December 3, 1992, a U.S. offer to lead a military coalition to Somalia and provide the bulk of the force. This agreement took the already close U.S.-UN relationship on Somalia to a new level.

UN leaders expected that with significant U.S. help the tangled problems of Somalia finally could be solved. The United States, however, had a more limited interim role in mind. From the beginning of its exploration with the UN about the possibility of greater involvement in Somalia, the United States was clear that its active participation would be restricted in both scope and duration. The United States offered only to help restore the flow of humanitarian relief in the area of greatest starvation. It expected the coalition to be relieved of that task in a short time by a conventional UN peacekeeping force. Fearing further entanglement in Somalia, the United States resisted suggestions that sounded like "mission creep."

The UN, however, hoped that the United States would help establish conditions for a more enduring solution for Somalia. For example, it wanted the U.S.-led coalition to disarm the Somali militias at the outset of its operation. From a UN perspective, this was the precise psychological moment when the foundation could have been laid for disarmament. In his report to the Security Council of December 19, 1992, the secretary-general suggested that a decision on transition from UNITAF to normal UN peacekeeping functions "should await the establishment of a cease-fire, the control of heavy weapons, the disarming of lawless gangs and the creation of a new police force."[2]

But the United States was not willing to take on such a complex task except when arms interfered directly with conduct of the relief mission. Given the number of weapons that existed, the insecurity of various clans and factions, and the need to rehabilitate youths and militia members, even limiting the effort to large weapons would be a challenging and lengthy undertaking. The United States was not in for the long haul.

The UN also wanted the UNITAF coalition to strengthen stability throughout Somalia. But such an expansion to areas not requiring immediate emergency assistance exceeded the U.S. interpretation of its limited obligation to "establish as soon as possible a secure environment for humanitarian relief operations."[3]

With the approaching transition to a new administration, President Bush hoped U.S. forces would be out of Somalia so that a new president would not be immediately confronted with an overseas involvement. It was clear, however, before the UNITAF operation commenced in December 1992 that the turnover to the UN could not be accomplished even in the best of circumstances until several months after the presidential inauguration of January 20, 1993.

Nonetheless, the United States approached the task with a very short military involvement in mind. It had other security responsibilities in the world and did not want to be bogged down in a remote area that did not involve vital interests. Humanitarian support in Somalia, once reestablished, did not appear to require the full capabilities of U.S. forces. The U.S. military did not want to be tied down in long-term policing or to pay the costs of participation from eroding service budgets.

The UN viewed the mission with a much longer time frame in mind. The subsequent twists and turns in U.S. policy were difficult for the UN to absorb.

In March 1993 the United States championed a resolution in the Security Council[4] designed to support the Somali people in getting back on their feet with a representative government, the ability to control law and order, and a functioning economy. The United States, however, did not change its goal of eliminating its direct military support as soon as feasible. Residual U.S. military participation would consist of only a token quick-reaction force. This small unit would act as a reserve on land in the early period after UNITAF's departure, then move offshore and ultimately depart the region. U.S. logistics units would support the UN directly but eventually would be replaced by military contingents of other countries and civilian contractors. In sizing its residual contribution, the United States, and to some extent the UN, appeared to underestimate the enormity of the task ahead and to overestimate the capabilities of a fragile UN structure to deal with the challenges it would face.

When the UN was viciously attacked on June 5, 1993, the United States only partially helped meet urgent UN requests for beefing up military capabilities in order to accomplish its mandate and the requirements of Resolution 837, passed on June 6. In responding to this emergency, the United States seemed to try to have it both ways—wanting to be helpful but at the same time to avoid becoming reengaged in Somalia. For the UN, it was the beginning of an unending story of too little too late.

Even though the United States had carefully limited its commitments and had begun to express the need for a change in policy, there was a sense of betrayal in the UN when the United States decided in early October 1993 to withdraw by March 31, 1994, in reaction to the tragic losses suffered by the units sent to help arrest General Aideed. Other UN contingents were ready to wrap up their missions as well and depart under the cover of U.S. forces.

In the following paragraphs I examine in more detail four critical junctures in the U.S.-UN relationship during 1993. I explore the fault lines rather than the strengths of the relationship, as follows: (1) the early needs of an ambitious mandate, (2) the turnover of military responsibilities from U.S. to UN leadership, (3) the U.S. response to hostilities encountered by the UN, and (4) the U.S. reaction to adversity.

Filling Mission Needs

The UN was dependent on the United States for military backing but also needed its support early in its mission to fulfill the broad requirements for beginning the recovery of the country. In addressing the expanded requirements of Resolution 814, UNOSOM needed a rapid infusion of talent, resources, and support in a wide range of other areas from internal media to representatives throughout the country. The United States was willing in principle to help in a wide range of activities, but bureaucratic responses and a seemingly business-as-usual approach meant that the UN mission did not receive the full and timely support it needed to exploit opportunities for progress. The UN bureaucracy itself was a significant impediment to obtaining assistance from nations. The UN needed determined help and pushing by the United States to solve the many problems it faced in Somalia.

There were many examples of instances in which a rapid infusion of assistance could have energized a program with synergistic impact. One dysfunctional Somali institution, for example, that had potential for rapid revival in many areas around the country was the Somali police force. It was essential to reestablishing law and order. Under the long-term strategy it was also the eventual ticket home for UN forces. The police force would not be able to deal with well-armed militias, but if properly trained and supported it could apprehend the bandit and criminal element and give protection to ordinary citizens.

There was no lack of declaratory support from nations for this idea, and the fledgling police forces desperately needed training, uniforms, buildings, and equipment. The United States and other UNITAF members did some things ad hoc to foster a revival of the police in areas where units were present, but the opportunity was lost to initiate a full-blown program. Critical months went by before the UN could provide tangible support other than paying some salaries or providing food for work. Countless survey missions were conducted and review meetings held in New York. But it was more than seven months later, after the U.S. decision to withdraw, that strong U.S. leadership and significant direct contributions began to give the understaffed and underresourced UN the means to initiate a viable program.

The police program is just one example among many of the UN's needs for nations to help it establish programs early in its mission. It also reflects the problem of making such a vital program dependent on the independent decisions of nations to make voluntary contributions. When the UN undertakes a major mission it needs to be front-loaded for success. The lesson of Somalia, repeated in many different areas, was that timely action by the UN will require a strong hand from a well-resourced country such as the United States. UN processes are simply too slow.

Military Responsibilities

Passage of Security Council Resolution 814 and the Addis Ababa accords, an agreement among Somali leaders[5] within several days in late March,[6] marked the official beginning of UNOSOM II and the commencement of a "prompt, smooth and phased transition from UNITAF to UNOSOM II" military command.[7]

The different perspectives of the two organizations, however, complicated the relief. While U.S. forces resolutely executed their withdrawal plan, UNOSOM worried that capabilities the UN would need—such as engineers and seabees; radio and newspaper personnel and production equipment; and lift, scout, and attack helicopters—were disappearing without replacement. UNITAF appeared to measure its success by the timeliness of its withdrawal; UNOSOM worried about maintaining continuity in the near term and the much broader two year commitment ahead.

UNITAF adopted May 1 as the target date for departure. This widely publicized date had been arbitrarily selected in New York as the time for an accounting transition when the UN would begin paying the differential rate to countries for troop costs.[8] The departing U.S. troops, however, assumed they would be going home no later than May 1.

Once such a date sticks it has major psychological ramifications and a significant influence on decisions such as whether to undertake military operations or whether to complete restoration projects. For example, an old proposal was resurfaced within UNITAF that a force occupy a strategic area in central Somalia. This suggestion was welcomed by the UN, but UNITAF considered, inter alia, that it would be too difficult logistically due to the distances involved. Nothing happened.

UNOSOM, noting the heavy wear on the road network and worried about the approaching rainy season, pleaded to no avail for more U.S. heavy engineer units to stay. The only U.S. engineers that remained were those specifically assigned to support the U.S. Quick Reaction Force (QRF).

With regard to intelligence on worst-case scenarios, UNITAF could not anticipate anything more ominous than the violent demonstrations it had already faced. But the UN was going to be a weaker force in a much more demanding situation. The two groups seemed to have had a classic half-full, half-empty perspective on the situation ahead.

It is no easy feat to get a force extracted and out in good order, and the process has to begin much earlier than one might expect. Nonetheless, a priority for UNITAF needed to be how it could ensure that those who stayed would be successful. Departing on time with minimum risk could have high costs in the future. In retrospect, a policy decision in Washington was probably needed to alter departure priorities in the field. Under the circumstances, such a shift would have been more consistent with championing the so-called nation-building resolution (Resolution 814), which substantially broadened the challenge for the relieving force. Although the United States had done far more than any other nation, this was precisely the reason it had more of a stake in what happened to those left behind.

The UN refused to speculate on the turnover date, explaining that it would be determined by the progress of the relief, the situation on the ground, and the secretary-general's ultimate approval. As the arbitrary May 1 date approached, the UN was worried about a number of things: relief forces for the very capable forces that were leaving, the slow buildup of UN military and civilian staff, and the lack of resources to do the job. While articulating publicly the mutual goal of a "seamless transition," the UN was very concerned that there would be a perceptible drop in its ability to do even the limited job at hand of continuing humanitarian relief in southern Somalia.

UNOSOM anticipated a drop to as low as 16,000 military personnel before the numbers eventually climbed back to the authorized strength of 28,000. The Indians, who had been expected in April with a full brigade force, were delayed politically and had not yet committed to a firm arrival date. They eventually came in September 1993 with a well-equipped and trained force. Two of the most capable units, the Australians and the Canadians, were scheduled to leave in mid-May and June with no relief forces in sight. Australian vehicles had already come in from the countryside and were being cleaned in the port for shipment home. The French and Italian commanders, who were asked if their units could stretch to cover the Australian and Canadian areas of responsibility (AORs), initially said they could not. Ultimately, under heavy pressure they acquiesced when Zimbabwean and Nigerian units were pulled out of Mogadishu to assist them in filling the gaps. To help replace U.S. units, the relatively small but very effective Botswanan unit also was withdrawn from the city, further weakening the grip of UN forces there.

The biggest relief task had fallen to the Pakistanis, who would assume responsibilities from the U.S. Marines for security in southern Mogadishu. They had been given the formidable task of maintaining stability in the toughest of neighborhoods. Besides not being as numerous or well-equipped as the U.S. Marines, the Pakistanis were just starting to arrive by air in the last weeks of April. Much of their equipment had not yet come. Many of their vehicles, for example, were still on the high seas. Most of these new troops arrived without flak jackets, standard protection in Mogadishu.

The UN command was anxious to get on with the job as soon as possible. Operating with two command structures with different objectives generated frictions. There was a big job ahead, and very little seemed to be happening during this period of transitional limbo. The overriding factor, however, was that UNOSOM was not yet ready for these responsibilities.

On hearing the pros and cons of readiness for a relief on May 4, as had just been proposed by the commanders, the secretary-general asked the United States to delay the turnover for one month. Presumably believing that the U.S. Quick Reaction Force provided enough insurance and determined to uncouple from Somalia, the United States turned down this request.

American goals seemed mixed. On the one hand the United States wanted the UN to succeed and was willing to give it considerable help (for example, logistics forces and the QRF). On the other hand, it was unwilling to accept that a changed mandate might require a new approach, one that would include more U.S. involvement for a longer period of time. Having engaged so visibly in Somalia, the United States was finding it difficult to disengage.

One U.S. argument for not further delaying the change of command was that almost all U.S. forces had been shipped home. Heavy equipment had been loaded. What force remained would not make an appreciable difference. By then UNITAF and UNOSOM were practically just relieving headquarters staffs. But there was an important distinction. A force commanded by a responsible superpower and backed by the military reserves of the United States is not the same as a grouping of small national units under a multinational UN headquarters. On May 4, there was a transfer of military responsibilities from a superpower to a much weaker UN command.

Whether June 5, 1993, would have been a different day in UN and Somali history if the United States had maintained command until June 4 is a matter of speculation. The UN at least would have been better prepared. In retrospect, the United States, in its desire to conclude what already seemed like a never ending obligation, appeared to have simply overestimated UN capabilities to cope with the situation ahead. The United States should have comprehended that the UN was weak and should have accepted that it had a genuine need for substantial assistance. It is not clear whether the United States saw the request to delay the turnover as a scheme to drag it further into Somalia unnecessarily, saw it as an overly conservative UN estimate of the situation, or simply was willing to accept greater risks in order to get the next phase started.

Response to Hostilities

Reactions to the military difficulties faced by the UN were also illustrative of different U.S. and UN perspectives. When confronted with an unexpected attack against UN peacekeepers in Mogadishu on June 5, 1993, the Security Council responded immediately with a very strong resolution.[9] Among Resolution 837's provisions was a call for the "arrest, and detention for prosecution, trial and punishment" of "those responsible for the armed attacks . . . , including those responsible for publicly inciting such attacks."[10] Another provision urged "member States to contribute, on an emergency basis, military support and transportation, including armoured personnel carriers, tanks and attack helicopters, to provide UNOSOM II the capability appropriately to confront and deter armed attacks directed against it in the accomplishment of its mandate."[11]

The UNOSOM mission was faced with a critical situation, and the Security Council had decided to respond with strength to the premeditated attacks against UN peacekeepers. In spite of this strong expression of outrage by member nations, the UN had difficulty assembling in a timely manner the military capabilities necessary to deal with this emergency. The United States was again key. Two examples are illustrative. First, there was the problem of obtaining a specially trained force to facilitate the capture of individuals considered responsible for the attacks of June 5. Second, the UN could not obtain tanks for the Pakistanis.

Among the specific UN requests within several days of the June 5 incident was that the United States send a specially trained force for hostage rescue and for tracking and detention of individuals. UNOSOM was concerned that a reaction to its more forceful actions might be the kidnapping of UN personnel. Hostage taking was a favorite tactic of some Somali groups, and civilians were especially vulnerable. The UN also needed the capability to locate and arrest individuals responsible for the June 5 attack without significant numbers of casualties to Somalis or to those troops executing any capture operation. There were only a few nations in the world with this type of highly specialized unit, and the United States had a reputation of being second to none.

Timing was critical. Opportunities for surprising and successfully detaining those responsible for the June 5 attacks were greater in the confusing immediate aftermath. There was no guarantee that such an operation would be successful, but improving intelligence and capabilities to make arrests increased the odds. Although serious consideration reportedly was given by the United States to a positive response, the request ultimately was refused. The UN then turned to other countries but found no takers.

As guerrilla attacks against the UN increased and there still appeared to be no way to gain peaceful compliance by General Aideed with the provisions of Resolution 837, the UN continued to press for some help in this area. Shortly after Americans suffered their first losses of UNOSOM II on August 8, 1993, when a jeep carrying four military police was destroyed by a remote-control device, the UN received the good news that the United States would be sending a special force to Somalia after all. Arriving in late August, that force captured some close Aideed confidants, but its operations were abruptly terminated with the tragic loss of eighteen men on October 3, 1993. The story might have been different if these special units had arrived in mid-June.

The Security Council's "emergency" request for tanks was also illustrative of the difficulties in responding expeditiously to a new situation. Within several days of the June 5 attack, the UN had also asked the United States for help in obtaining at least one of the two companies of tanks the Pakistanis felt they needed in order to continue operations in Somalia. As UNOSOM prepared to deal with much heavier weaponry than it had anticipated, these tanks were as important for their psychological as for their military impact.

There were numerous complications associated with UN procurement of military equipment. Various U.S. congressional restrictions were associated with aid to Pakistan because of concerns about nuclear proliferation. The Pakistanis were trained to operate only certain types of tanks. Nonetheless, frustrating weeks went by before eight old U.S.-manufactured tanks were released by Turkey and shipped to Somalia.

When these tanks, which had been in storage in Turkey for nearly a decade, finally arrived in mid-July they had a number of defects, including breech blocks that would not close properly. A few tanks were put in operation, but many needed frequent repairs.

The tanks eventually were invaluable. On September 9, U.S. engineers, under Pakistani escort, were trapped by a large SNA ambush as they tried to remove a roadblock on a principal artery in Mogadishu. One of the tanks was lost to heavy weapons fire during this attack, but the engineers were rescued with the combined help of a Pakistani tank and QRF helicopter fire. On October 3, when the U.S. Rangers were pinned down near helicopter wreckage and the lightly armored QRF could not break through to extract them, it was these same Pakistani tanks, along with Malaysian APCs, that participated in the dangerous but successful nighttime rescue.

The difficulties in filling the need for special forces and tanks appeared to be symptomatic of a larger problem. In responding to emergent requirements throughout the period of hostilities, the United States still did not appear to appreciate the inadequacy of the UN or the criticality of a timely response to its requests for assistance. For the United States, steady UN progress was also important. There is only a narrow time frame of political and public patience. This is particularly true in a purely humanitarian operation not involving national security interests. One can only conjecture as to what might have happened if a force of the capability of the U.S. task force that ultimately came to Somalia after the October 3 tragedy had been dispatched in mid-June. But such a dramatic response did not seem politically feasible at the time.

Throughout the period of organized hostilities against UN forces, U.S. policy appeared to reflect conflicting goals. The United States wanted the UN to succeed, but it did not want to increase its involvement. Such a conflicted mind-set was also seemingly reflected in unilateral decisions on operations. Augmenting forces were provided, then often restricted in what they could do and fairly rapidly withdrawn. This was true in the case of marine amphibious task groups, AC-130 gunships, and some operations proposed for the QRF.

The United States, in effect, seemed unintentionally to manage UN requests on the margins, providing enough to keep operations going but not enough to ensure success. The same ambivalence seemed to be reflected in the widely publicized and subsequently controversial decision to reject direct requests by the U.S. commander in Somalia in August 1993 for Abrams tanks, Bradley fighting vehicles, and mine-removal equipment as car bombs, mines, and other devices were employed against U.S. forces.

Confronting Adversity

The most stressful time for the U.S.-UN relationship was in the immediate aftermath of the tragic U.S. losses during the raid of October 3, 1993. As fingers of blame pointed wildly in all directions, the United States came under heavy domestic pressure to justify a nation-building agenda in general and the hunt for Aideed in particular. The president's decision, after consultations with Congress, to beef up forces in Somalia with a heavily armed U.S. force was welcomed by the UN, but setting a fixed deadline for withdrawal of all U.S. forces by March 31, 1994, was not.

However reasonable this decision may have been in U.S. terms of dealing with what had become an unpopular policy domestically, the UN felt a sense of betrayal and was confronted with practical policy dilemmas regarding continuation of the Somali mission. Given its close relationship with the United States in crafting Somalia policy, the UN took exception to finding itself in the role of convenient scapegoat. It was even more difficult for the UN to fathom how the nation that had championed a more enduring solution to Somalia was now seemingly abandoning that concept.

It also was hard to accept that the world's only superpower, after suffering losses at the hands of the same group, was giving up on bringing into a legal process the alleged perpetrators of the crimes against the UN forces of June 5. It was difficult for the UN to explain internationally why the United States would no longer put its soldiers at risk when the Pakistanis had suffered similar losses and persevered. Having dealt with a pervasive atmosphere of distrust as various nations appeared to be promoting individual agendas, it was a blow for the UN that its most stalwart backer had also seemingly become unreliable.

The UN was faced with a potential stampede of other troop-contributing countries rushing to exit before the United States. Why should its people continue to face dangers the United States was no longer willing to accept? What kind of reliable backup would there be with no U.S. QRF or logistics units? The mission was on the verge of losing its entire force. For some in the UN, these realities meant it was time to wrap up the effort. Lack of success could be blamed on the U.S. decision to withdraw.

Although the U.S. decision to send reinforcements for six months would help shore up the situation and could provide more negotiating leverage, this was a time of deep disappointment and shattered expectations for the UN. The return of U.S. forces a year later, in March 1995, to assist in the departure of the last elements of the UN force was a very reassuring step for U.S.-UN relations

In sum, because of strong U.S. leadership in the early stages, the UN seemed to become overly dependent on the United States to solve the Somalia problem.

Having made a tacit obligation to long-term success, the United States found it difficult to make a clean break. A premature turnover of responsibilities to an unready UN appeared counterproductive in the long run.

The four previously covered divisive situations illustrate that different U.S. and UN perceptions of scope, timing, and need had adverse consequences and indicate several important approaches for future relations:

- A UN mission must have adequate means to carry out its assigned mandate. If the Security Council broadens the mission, there must be a concomitant strengthening of commitment by member nations, including providing necessary resources expeditiously.
- If a UN mission is challenged militarily and new needs are identified, there must be a strong and immediate response by sponsoring nations.
- The UN and the principal contributors need to have the same degree of commitment. The United States, other participating nations, and the UN must strive to stay on the same course during the inevitable ups and downs. This is not easy to accomplish when the United States and UN begin with a different sense of mission, when sacrifice is required to achieve a nonvital U.S. interest, and when U.S. domestic support is uncertain.

Awkward Arrangements

The U.S.-UN relationship was also complicated by crossing lines of authority. The strong American role in Somalia at times created an awkward and uncomfortable situation for the UN and the United States. It also caused some confusion for the Somalis and opportunities for mischief makers. The military arrangements changed a number of times during the sixteen months of American presence.

With the landing of U.S. forces in December 1992, the major military force was no longer under the direct control of the UN mission. UNOSOM directed only the blue-helmeted Pakistani battalion, still operating under traditional Chapter VI peacekeeping rules. The UNITAF commander reported through his U.S. chain of command. The United States also was politically active on the ground. But in UN eyes, UNOSOM I "remained fully responsible for the political aspects and for humanitarian assistance."[12] The coexistence of the U.S.-led coalition and the UNOSOM I mission made for an awkward relationship.

The UN representatives, who were trying to promote political reconciliation and coordinate humanitarian activities, did not have control of the power on the ground. To some extent the UN role seemed to be marginalized. Nonetheless, political and humanitarian conferences were held in Addis Ababa during early 1993. Adding to UN sensitivities and creating some confusion was U.S. criticism of many aspects of the UN-managed Addis Ababa political reconciliation conference involving Somali leaders.

In late March 1993 with passage of Resolution 814 establishing UNOSOM II, the UN assumed overall responsibility in the field for a demanding new mandate. Direction of the forces, however, remained with UNITAF, operating under its original guidelines and focusing primarily on transition, turnover, and departure. Problems were minimized by close liaison, but the two organizations were clearly on different tracks.

Even on May 4 with the official turnover of military forces by the United States to the UN, an awkward command relationship persisted because the U.S. QRF remained under U.S. control. Potential problems were mitigated by the fact that the QRF commander reported to a U.S. general who also wore the hat of the deputy UN commander.[13] Nonetheless, UN-proposed QRF operations often had to be approved in the United States. Some operations were briefed publicly by Washington before being announced by the UN, increasing the impression of U.S. ownership.

When the Rangers arrived in late August, they came with their own commanding general, who reported to two higher commands in the United States while keeping the same dual-hatted U.S.-UN general informed. UNOSOM did not control these Ranger operations but assumed it had broad authority to suspend them altogether if the political situation warranted. The possibility was discussed several times as progress was anticipated in the dialogue with the SNA.

In the wake of the tragic October 3 incident, the U.S.-introduced joint task force came with its own commanding general, who also reported to the Central Command (CENTCOM) in the United States. This commander also served, however, under the overall direction of the same senior U.S. military commander who was deputy UN commander.

Organizationally, these augmenting forces were under total U.S. control. With the return to Somalia of a high-level U.S. emissary with instructions, for example, to implement U.S. policy priorities, the picture became fuzzy at times. In addition, an Ethiopian-Eritrean mission was attempting to promote SNA reconciliation with the UN. Although the UN was kept closely apprised of these missions, suspicions that they might have independent diplomatic agendas added to an unsettled atmosphere.

There was a major effort by all concerned to make the awkward U.S.-UN relationships work. Nonetheless, all parties contributed to a sense of unease at times about who was doing what to whom.

It is unfair, however, to use Somalia as an example of the negative consequences of U.S. forces being placed under UN (foreign) command. The QRF and the Rangers were fully under U.S. control. The only U.S. forces directly under UN command were the logistics, engineer, communications, and other support units. These support forces were commanded by a U.S. general who reported to a foreign UN commander[14] whose deputy was an American. No American unit commander was asked by the UN to do anything he felt was inappropriate. There were, however, times when recommendations of U.S. unit commanders in the field were denied by higher U.S. authority. Somalia is a good example of the difficulties of peace enforcement, but it is a poor example of the dangers to U.S. forces of working under the UN. Perhaps the only added vulnerability of working alongside the UN in Somalia was that sufficient resources would more likely have been provided in a timely manner if the entire operation had been a U.S. responsibility.

Lessons for Future U.S.-UN Partnership in Peacekeeping

The difficult experience in Somalia provides many important lessons for the U.S.-UN relationship in future undertakings.

Recognize That the UN Is Weak

Even with substantial strengthening and reform, the UN peacekeeping apparatus is inherently weak. The UN will never be the equivalent of a large nation-state such as the United States in terms of efficiency, available resources, and political cohesion. Institutional loyalties are not likely to equate with allegiance to nation. In assigning tough peace-enforcement missions to the UN, nations must recognize success will depend on their own willingness to make contributions. For any assignment given to the UN, the requirements of the mandate should not exceed the means nations are willing to provide the UN in a timely manner. It also must be acknowledged that many missions will be beyond the capacity of the UN.

If the United States had fully understood the inadequacy of the UN mechanism in Somalia and its dependence on the United States, it might have taken much stronger and more timely measures to shore up the UN or looked for other approaches to solving the problem of Somalia. In any near-term UN operation involving the United States, Americans should expect to bear a significant portion of the load and to help lead other contributing nations.

Strengthen UN Capability

The UN needs radical improvement of its peacekeeping mechanism if it is to become effective in the post–Cold War period. In some ways efforts in Somalia represented an attempt to carry out a Chapter VII operation with a Chapter VI organization. Such radical reform will not occur unless the United States pushes hard for it. If it does not, it should not expect the UN to become a viable alternative for dealing with extremely demanding situations, certainly not those requiring Chapter VII authority.

The UN, for example, needs to strengthen its cadre of experienced people to carry out missions in a timely manner; it needs to have resources available to facilitate solutions to political, humanitarian, and judicial problems from the beginning of its involvement; and it needs new approaches to solving the problems of providing a politically and militarily cohesive force. The support mechanism in New York needs significant upgrading, including streamlined procedures, more responsive resource support, and adequate staffing in the Peacekeeping Operations (PKO) Department.

The UN is currently not ready for missions other than those that are benign in nature and have the prior consent of disputing parties. Given its inherent organizational limitations, it is unlikely to acquire an effective capability to deal directly with situations such as Iraq's invasion of Kuwait other than by sanctioning the actions of well-integrated national forces, as occurred with Desert Storm. Nonetheless, with major reform and adoption of concepts such as a crisis-response headquarters integrated with well-trained and dedicated national units or a small all-volunteer UN cadre, the UN could develop the capability to deal effectively with some of the complex problems that fall between a Chapter VI and VII situation. For example, a well-organized and immediately available force in Rwanda might have saved many lives. However, even these limited capabilities would require major reform and the whole-hearted support of key member nations such as the United States.

Concur on Policy and Persevere

Nations that undertake missions such as Somalia as troop contributors to the UN need to agree in advance on policy and determine to persevere in good times and in bad. They should meet frequently enough with the UN to ensure they are satisfied with the policies being implemented. Where feasible, they need to agree in advance to enter and leave the field together. Fortitude and political cohesion are especially important in the case of major countries such as the United States. The UN, in turn, must be receptive to frequent and candid reviews of policy. It may be advisable to establish a standing policy task force within the UN of principal troop contributors to work alongside and augment the UN staff.

Recognize That Force May Be Necessary

As tough and challenging as it is, peace enforcement should not be written off as a potential mission for the UN without finding other alternatives for the use of force in humanitarian catastrophes. Ignoring circumstances such as genocide, ethnic cleansing, or mass starvation is not consistent with U.S. values as a society or with the founding principles of the UN. Anarchy, with resulting humanitarian chaos, is likely to be prevalent in the next two decades, and effective mechanisms for dealing with it are needed.

Ensure Adequate Means

Both the civilian and the military sides of a UN operation must be adequately trained and equipped. This must be implicit in a commitment to a complex operation. Dramatic steps must be taken immediately to correct newly identified shortcomings and to provide a mission with sufficient capabilities to do the job assigned.

If the UN is the only available institution for coping with such situations, it must have a strong enough force to deter, to the extent possible, attacks against it and to respond effectively if challenged. It cannot have just marginal support; it must be able to obtain sufficient capability rapidly enough to succeed. Force will remain the essential underpinning of successful negotiation and peaceful resolution of these contentious situations.

The Ideal Relationship

Ideally, U.S. and UN interests in any future undertaking would coincide, but it is unlikely that the perspectives of any single nation and a large organization of nations such as the UN will be the same on all important issues. The UN, nonetheless, must try to find a consensus among principal contributing nations. If a mission is to succeed, the United States and UN need to be nearly of one mind in their commitment and in their policy objectives. The same is true of the UN and other key nations.

In Somalia, there was considerable effort by both parties to ensure that U.S. and UN policies stayed on track. There was regular contact between the UN and the U.S. mission, delegations came frequently from Washington to New York, and U.S. staff assistance was given directly to the UN in certain areas. Close liaison in the field was facilitated by the presence of an active U.S. mission and an American as SRSG for a year. The liaison mechanism in New York and the field, nonetheless, did not produce the full range of timely support the UN felt it needed. There were differences of opinion on policy and nervousness on the part of some in the UN that Washington's influence was too great.

This perception that liaison was too close was complicated by the fact that the United States, in addition to being the dominant military force in UNITAF, was the major donor of humanitarian aid and active politically in Somalia and throughout the region. A pervading paranoia in New York, for example, made it difficult to fill UN personnel gaps in the field when Americans were ready to help temporarily. Ideally, the principal troop-supporting states should be well represented on the civilian side of the mission. This, in fact, may be a good way to rapidly augment the civilian staff, since there is added incentive for troop-contributing nations to strengthen the mission. Nonetheless, there will likely be an underlying concern by longtime UN employees about inadvertently surrendering broad institutional integrity to the expediency of the task at hand.

The active diplomatic support of the United States was essential throughout. For example, a coalition was rapidly assembled only because of active lobbying by the U.S. president. The U.S. QRF performed in an extraordinary manner and did far more than called for in the terms of its special understanding with the United Nations. U.S. diplomatic assistance was essential in helping convince nations to remain after U.S. departure. In spite of this assistance, both the United States and the UN underestimated what it would take to ensure success at this embryo stage of development of UN peacemaking capabilities.

Whether the United States should have provided the SRSG for the period of transition between UNITAF and UNOSOM II is open to question. There were advantages to having close communication between U.S. and UN camps during the turnover period, the United States had logistics forces and the QRF in Somalia, and many Somalis respected the United States as fair minded and perceived the presence of a high official as a hopeful indication of continued American support for its recovery. On the other hand, with the United States trying to uncouple itself from this obligation and to decrease its visibility in the country, another nationality as SRSG made sense.

The UN is not yet ready for large, complex, and dangerous peace-enforcement missions. If such operations are required, it may be necessary to have a coalition arrangement, depend on a NATO-type regional organization if it is willing to undertake such a task, or rely on heavy involvement by a few large nations. The Haiti model may prove to be a good example of what is required in a more benign situation. It will be very difficult, however, for the United States to play such a prominent role in situations that do not involve its vital security interests.

Since catastrophic humanitarian situations involving the potential requirement to use force are more likely to be interests that are universal, the UN is a logical political choice for dealing with such situations. Such an option will be possible, in the long-term, however, only if there is a sustained effort to build a viable UN peace-enforcement capability.

As difficult as U.S. and UN experiences were in Somalia, they should not be used to rule out the idea of peace enforcement as an approach in appropriate circumstances. Hard lessons were learned about the inadequacies of readiness for peace enforcement, but these problems should not obscure what may be possible in the future with a dedicated effort to develop an adequate capability. They should also not lead to disparaging the noble efforts that were made by the UN, the United States, and other participating nations in the first attempt by the UN to cope with a failed nation. At a minimum, thousands of lives were saved and considerable time was bought for Somalis to try to work out their differences. Although the jigsaw puzzle of Somalia is still in pieces, the world went the extra mile to give Somalis an opportunity to put their nation back together.

It is hoped that experiences in Somalia will lead to a stronger relationship between the United States and the UN in tackling difficult peacekeeping problems. A healthy relationship will, however, depend first on a decision by Americans that helping with man-made humanitarian catastrophes is part of the responsibilities they are willing to share with others in the post–Cold War period. This will require a significant evolution in current American thinking about the obligations to the UN and to other peoples of the world.

Notes

1. Boutros Boutros-Ghali, letter to UN Security Council, November 29, 1992, reference paper of May 1, 1994, "The United Nations and Situation in Somalia," UN Department of Public Information, p. 6.

2. Ibid., p. 7

3. Security Council Resolution 794 of December 3, 1992, para. 10.

4. This would become UN Resolution 814 of March 26, 1993.

5. The accords were signed by leaders of the fifteen political parties participating in the conference on March 27 and subsequently approved by acclamation in a plenary meeting of the First Conference on National Reconciliation on March 28, 1993. The faction leaders made a supplementary agreement on March 30, 1993, at consultations held in Addis Ababa following the conference.

6. Resolution 814 was passed by the Security Council on March 26, 1993, and the Addis Ababa accords were signed on March 27, 1993.

7. Security Council Resolution 814 (1993), para. 14.

8. The UN paid countries a differential cost for each soldier of close to $1,000 per month.

9. Security Council Resolution 837 of June 6, 1993.

10. Ibid., para. 5.

11. Ibid., para. 8.

12. Boutros-Ghali, letter to UN Security Council, November 29, 1992, reference paper, p. 7.

13. Maj. Gen. Thomas Montgomery served as commander of U.S. forces in Somalia and as deputy UN commander for UNOSOM II.

14. Lt. Gen. Cevik Bir of the Turkish army was force commander of UNOSOM II. He was relieved by Lt. Gen. Aboo Samah Bin Aboo Bakar of Malaysia on January 18, 1994.

11

Congress and the Somalia Crisis

H A R R Y   J O H N S T O N
A N D
T E D   D A G N E

The 102nd (1991–1992) Congress played a crucial role in getting the United States to act to save starving Somalis; the Democratic-controlled 103rd Congress (1993–1994) forced the withdrawal of U.S. troops, a step that resulted in subsequent UN withdrawal. Many mistakes and unfortunate events occurred during the Somalia mission that led to the withdrawal of UN troops from that Horn of Africa country: the lack of clarity in the mission; the policy reversal on disarmament; the anti-Aideed policy; the killing of the Pakistani soldiers in June 1993; the October 1993 firefights and the death of U.S. troops; the mounting cost of the UN mission in the face of limited progress; and most important, the inability and unwillingness of the Somali leadership to reach a compromise.

The Somalia debacle had serious ramifications for the foreign policy agenda of the Clinton administration. Its delayed action in mid-1994 at the United Nations Security Council, which sought U.S. logistical support to deploy an African-led UN peacekeeping force to Rwanda, contributed to the unnecessary deaths of many Rwandans. The stalling at the United Nations, no doubt, was to appease the administration's critics in Congress and to demonstrate that the administration could be tough on the United Nations. Rwanda, therefore, became the first victim of the administration's Presidential Decision Directive 25 (PDD 25). The directive restricted U.S. participation in UN peacekeeping missions by requiring stringent conditions for U.S. involvement. This ill-conceived measure would later propel the Republican-controlled Congress to legislate additional restrictions under the National Security Revitalization Act of 1995 (House Resolution [H.R.] 7).

The debate in Congress did not suggest the evolution of a new foreign policy doctrine but reflected uncertainty among policymakers about the U.S. role in the post–Cold War world. The opposition was certainly concerned about the mounting cost and safety of U.S. troops in Somalia and was largely led by members of the Republican Party. Deteriorating conditions on the ground and critical media reports were important contributing factors that led many members of Congress to join the opposition. Another contributing factor was domestic politics. Some in the opposition clearly intended to score political points by embarrassing President Clinton in what was for him a no-win situation.

The Republican-led opposition seized the opportunity to attack the president's policy but was ill prepared to offer an alternative. The Clinton administration sought to respond to the isolationist mood sweeping the corridors of Congress by offering the "National Security Strategy for Engagement and Enlargement" in July 1994. The administration's post–Cold War strategy called for continued U.S. engagement in world affairs, and the document stated that "American leadership in the world has never been more important." In this chapter we examine the role of the U.S. Congress during the Somali crisis and review the legislative process during that period.

Early Congressional Engagement

The dominant Africa issue in the latter part of the second session of the 102nd (1992) Congress was the anarchy and famine that developed in Somalia, a nation of about 6.5 million people. Congress had taken an interest in Somali affairs over many years, and some felt a special responsibility to come to the aid of the Somali people in their hour of need. Because of concerns over regional arms races and the lack of democracy in Somalia, Congress had long exercised close oversight with respect to the U.S. military assistance program there.[1] On July 14, 1988, the House Subcommittee on Africa held a hearing after government troops reportedly killed several thousand civilians in northern Somalia.[2] In 1989, the Bush administration reversed an earlier decision to continue aid to the Barre government, largely because of congressional pressure. Consequently, U.S. aid funds originally intended for Somalia were diverted to other purposes and U.S. military aid was terminated.

The Siad Barre government fell in early January 1991 amid chaotic violence in the capital. With widening instability in Somalia, Congress began to express concern in late April 1991 in a Senate resolution introduced by Senator Nancy Kassebaum (R-Kans.). At a time when the international community's attention was focused on the Persian Gulf, Senate Resolution (S.R.) 115 called on the president of the United States to "lead a world-wide humanitarian effort in Somalia to relieve the suffering and for the United Nations to make the humanitarian crisis in Somalia an item of high priority."[3]

In March 1992, the Senate Subcommittee on Africa requested that the Congressional Research Service (CRS) organize a seminar on the Horn of Africa, and in conjunction with the seminar, the subcommittee held its own hearing on all the Horn countries. At the hearing, during a period of questioning the assistant secretary of state for Africa, Herman J. Cohen, Senator Kassebaum argued for a more activist role for the United States and criticized the Bush administration for having "watered down"[4] the language of a UN Security Council resolution calling for the deployment of UN peacekeeping troops to Somalia. The senator also pushed for a special envoy for Somalia instead of the technical team the United Nations was planning to send. Shortly after the Kassebaum proposal, the UN secretary-general appointed an Algerian diplomat, Mohamed Sahnoun, as special envoy for Somalia. He was later replaced by a U.S.-educated Iraqi diplomat, Ismat Kittani.

Congressional Push to Engage Mounts

By the end of the second session (December 1992), a total of seven hearings had been held on Somalia—two in the Select Committee on Hunger, three in the House Subcommittee on Africa, and two in the Senate Subcommittee on Africa. Over a dozen letters were sent out by members to key players, including Secretary of State James Baker, President George Bush, UN Secretary-General Boutros Boutros-Ghali, Somali faction leaders, and several international organizations, urging stronger efforts to provide a secure environment for humanitarian assistance and peace talks to bring an end to the civil war. Beginning in late 1991, several congressional delegations visited Somalia, and the Hunger Committee sponsored a week-long fact-finding tour of northern Somalia, Eritrea, Ethiopia, Sudan, and Djibouti. Senator Kassebaum was the first member of Congress to visit the famine-stricken and war-torn region of southern Somalia.

Congressional activities were influential in publicizing the Somalia crisis, pressuring the UN and the executive branch toward action, and articulating the basis of a policy of intervention for the United States. As the crisis deepened, hearings attracted widespread media attention. The Hunger Committee hearing on Somalia on July 22, 1992, focused media attention on alleged U.S. reluctance to support a UN peacekeeping force there. Senator Kassebaum, who had just returned from Somalia, testified and presented the committee with a firsthand account of the Somalia tragedy. She affirmed that "the situation has reached the point where the United Nations should go forward with the security force with or without General Aideed or Ali Mahdi's consent."[5] Chairman Tony Hall (D-Ohio) criticized the administration for "holding back" on Somalia.

The July 22 hearing, initiated to clarify the administration's policy concerning the U.S. commitment to peacekeeping in Somalia, showed growing congressional interest in forceful intervention in Somalia for humanitarian purposes. Congressional efforts to assess administration views on this issue and to determine whether there were divisions within the State Department on intervention were frustrated when the administration refused to send the assistant secretary for African affairs to a hearing at which the assistant secretary for international organization affairs would also be testifying. Many observers believed that the Africa Bureau was sympathetic to deploying a peacekeeping force to Somalia and that the International Organization Bureau was opposed. Representative Alan Wheat (D–Mo.), in opening the hearing, expressed his "disappointment" at the State Department's decision.[6]

At the center of congressional concern was the Bush administration's role in the United Nations. Some members of Congress were of the opinion that the administration was not doing enough to lead the world body in responding to the Somali crisis, although they supported the administration's humanitarian assistance program and its commitment of Department of Defense aircraft for the delivery of food supplies. A particular issue was the apparent reluctance of the United Nations to move ahead on Somalia even when action had been authorized by the Security Council. The council had approved a military and humanitarian mission in April, but the fifty observers authorized at that time did not arrive until July.

In late August, the Security Council approved 3,000 peacekeepers, to be led by a smaller group of security guards from Pakistan, but the first contingent of Pakistanis did not arrive until the end of September. General Mohammed Aideed, one of the major warlords in Mogadishu, stalled the deployment of UN peacekeepers for months, reportedly because of a concern that their presence would downgrade his political status. Congress expressed its view on this issue in a concurrent resolution that "the United Nations Security Council [should] deploy these security guards immediately, with or without the consent of the Somalia factions."[7]

On October 1, 1992, in the face of worsening famine and civil strife in Somalia, the Senate Subcommittee on African Affairs called a hearing on UN peacekeeping in Western Sahara and Somalia. Although the Pakistani guard force had begun to deploy to the Somali capital, it had not moved out of the area of the airport, and relief efforts around the country continued to be disrupted by Somali factions and gangs. UN efforts to send additional peacekeepers, as voted by the Security Council, were stalled because of Aideed's refusal and hesitation at the United Nations. At the hearing, Senator Paul Simon (D–Ill.) announced that he and other senators were proposing a measure that would allow the Defense Department rather than the State Department to pay U.S. expenses for UN peacekeeping. Simon's proposal was that the "Secretary of Defense [should be] authorized to spend up to $300 million for any U.N. peacekeeping efforts not covered by the State Department."[8] This initiative was designed to facilitate U.S. involvement in UN peacekeeping missions during a period of budgetary constraints.

Senator Simon also revealed that in a joint effort with other members he had explored the possibility of using "up to 2,000 volunteers" from the armed forces of the United States, upon the approval of the president, as a humanitarian interventionist force. The idea of using U.S. troops was initially suggested by Senator Kassebaum several months earlier, although it was considered then by some observers as unlikely to win support either in Congress or in the executive branch. A number of members visited Somalia again late in the second session, and Representative John Lewis (D–Ga.) led a particularly large delegation. The visits were followed by a number of high-level consultations with executive branch officials. Many observers believe that these talks played an important role in the president's decision to send U.S. troops to Somalia in early December 1992.

The Role of the Congressional Black Caucus

The Congressional Black Caucus was highly active as the crisis worsened. In April 1992, the caucus sent a letter to Secretary of State James Baker asking the United States to take "the initiative in the United Nations in forcefully advocating a high-level U.N. presence in Somalia." In October, a member of the caucus, Representative Lewis, introduced a resolution calling for a U.S. role in a possible humanitarian intervention in Somalia. The resolution asked the president to "express to the United Nations Security Council the desire and the willingness of the United States to participate, consistent with applicable United States legal requirements, in the deployment of armed United Nations guards, as authorized by the Security Council, in order to secure emergency relief activities and enable greater numbers of international and Somali organizations and people to provide relief and rehabilitation assistance."[9] In addition, outside interest groups and a fairly large Somali community in the United States played an important role in urging U.S. action.

The Decision to Move

On December 4, 1992, one month after the Republican president had been defeated and after Congress had adjourned, President Bush announced that the United States would deploy a substantial military force to Somalia in order to create a secure environment for the delivery of humanitarian relief. This announcement came one day after the UN Security Council had enacted Resolution 794, authorizing the use of "all necessary means to establish as soon as possible a secure environment for humanitarian relief operations in Somalia." This resolution stated that the "magnitude of the human tragedy in Somalia constituted a threat to international peace and security"—a determination that permitted the use of force under Chapter VII of the UN Charter.[10]

Congressional concern about the Somalia situation, expressed through hearings, trips, resolutions, letters, and informal contacts, had clearly helped to lay the groundwork for this large-scale humanitarian deployment. Indeed, in a December 10 letter reporting the deployment to congressional leaders, President Bush specifically stated that he had taken congressional views on the urgent need for action into account in deciding to take action. On December 4, the president briefed a number of members at the White House and secured broad support for the action. House Speaker Thomas Foley said that the "President [had] acted wisely, and in circumstances where he had very little choice without grave humanitarian consequences resulting."[11]

Equally important in the Somalia debate was the role of the media. The media played a crucial role in the decisionmaking process to engage and subsequently to disengage. Television scenes of starving Somali children significantly contributed to the cause of intervention and to increased interest and attention in Congress.

By the same token, the media was instrumental in forcing change in U.S. policy. The gruesome television footage of dead American soldiers being dragged in the streets of Mogadishu by Somali militia forced even those who had supported the U.S. engagement in Somalia to call for disengagement.

The U.S. deployment, named Operation Restore Hope, began on December 9, and in January 1993, it peaked at about 25,800 U.S. troops joined by thousands of troops from other countries. Somalia continued to experience many grave problems, but the operation swiftly achieved its objective of allowing the resumption of humanitarian relief to stricken towns and villages. Feeding programs for children and adults were resumed, and widespread starvation came to an end. It could be argued that the mission could have been expanded to include disarmament without compromising the mission and alienating public support in the United States. General Aideed and Ali Mahdi were both weakened after months of intense fighting and were positioning themselves for political roles rather than military confrontation. Moreover, the large U.S. military presence had intimidated the militias and would have posed no serious threat. The opportunity to pursue an expanded mission was lost early because of confusion over rules of engagement.

Caution in Congress

Although supporting the operation, many members pressed the executive branch to define its objectives clearly and to terminate the operation when those objectives were achieved. Representative Lee Hamilton (D–Ind.) urged that when the troops "accomplish what they are supposed to do, they come out."[12] A few members expressed serious reservations about the decision to deploy. Some worried that it would set a precedent for costly deployments in humanitarian crises in Bosnia, Liberia, and too many other suffering countries or that humanitarian operations would divert funds and other resources needed by the military to protect national security interests.

Many of these concerns were aired at a December 17 House Foreign Affairs Committee hearing on the Somalia deployment. At this hearing, Representative Hamilton asked whether Somalia's humanitarian crisis could indeed be resolved if U.S. forces refrained, as they had done from the outset, from disarming the warring Somali factions. This issue continued to be debated in the first months of the 103rd Congress. The new Congress also had to deal with another issue raised by the president's postadjournment deployment—whether Operation Restore Hope was consistent with the 1973 War Powers Resolution and might require specific congressional authorization under that resolution, the UN Participation Act, or the general war powers of Congress.[13]

The Somalia operation did not have broad-based support in Congress even though key members of the House and Senate had pushed for U.S. engagement beginning in early 1991. The decision to engage was made by President Bush, and Congress's role was not a decisive factor. In fact, many in Congress were caught by surprise, and those who called for the U.S. engagement did not expect or ask for a large-scale involvement. With conditions deteriorating rapidly and the cost of the U.S. mission mounting, the limited support that existed in Congress began to erode rapidly.

The 103rd Congress: The Call to Disengage

The 103rd Congress (1993) began with some members of Congress in both houses raising concerns about continued U.S. engagement in Somalia. Some of these concerns were raised by a handful of members during the deployment of U.S. troops. The primary concerns of members were the objectives of the mission, the role of the United States in a UN-led mission, congressional authorization of continued U.S. engagement in Somalia, and the amount of money being spent for the military operation.

Beginning February 1993 through November, over a dozen hearings and numerous briefings involving multiple committees were conducted in both the Senate and the House, ranging in focus from the role of U.S. troops to the War Powers Resolution as it related to the Somalia mission. An estimated fifteen bills and resolutions were also introduced. Most called for the withdrawal of U.S. troops from Somalia, although many of these resolutions died in committees or during floor debates.

With the situation in Somalia deteriorating, dissent against the Somalia mission began to mount. Interestingly, opposition to the Somalia mission was not partisan at the beginning of the debate, although it appeared a move to embarrass the democratic president. The Clinton administration did not take the concerns of some members seriously and made a series of mistakes in dealing with Congress as a whole.[14] These omissions would eventually force the administration to shift policy.

The Debate Over Congressional Authorization and Costs

During the first session of the 103rd Congress, dissent against the Somalia policy began when the powerful Senate Appropriations Committee chair, Senator Robert Byrd (D–W.V.), raised several issues with respect to the U.S. mission on the floor of the Senate in July 1993, before many in Congress questioned the role of the United States in Somalia. Senator Byrd argued that the cost of the U.S. share in the UN peacekeeping efforts was too large for U.S. taxpayers to shoulder. He charged that "the operation in Somalia has been estimated to cost $1.5 billion for one year. The peacekeeping, reconciliation, and rebuilding effort in Cambodia, which at least enjoys the partial security of a negotiated settlement, is estimated to cost $1.9 billion for a single year." He questioned "how many such efforts like this the United States or any other country can afford to support."[15]

Senator Byrd's opposition was not limited to costs. He also stated that the Senate did not authorize sending troops to Somalia and that he did not "remember voting to grant the U.S. military the authority to chase down competing African warlords and conduct house-to-house searches in Mogadishu to confiscate weapons." Apparently, the Clinton administration did not take Byrd's concerns seriously. Some senators attempted to alter the opinion of the senator from West Virginia but to no avail. Senator Simon, for example, promptly offered a rebuttal and a defense for the mission the next day on the Senate floor. He argued that "it would be unfair to the 22-nations for us to pull our troops out. We are needed, among other things, for technical reasons."[16]

The Passage of Senate Joint Resolution 45

Earlier in February 1993, the Senate passed Resolution 45, which authorized the use of U.S. armed forces in Somalia pursuant to UN Security Council Resolution 794. The resolution, though not opposed or supported by the administration, set out a narrow definition of the mission reflecting the position outlined by President Bush when he deployed U.S. troops in December 1992. The passage of Senate Joint Resolution 45 was pro forma according to Senate majority leader George Mitchell (D–Maine), since U.S. troops were already on the ground. The consideration and the passage of the bill, however, signified the importance of the War Powers Resolution for many members of Congress.

It took several months of heated debate for the House of Representatives to consider Resolution 45 and pass it, in part because of the expanded objective of the U.S. mission. The House version of the resolution was significantly altered from the original Senate version, which led to stiff Republican and Democratic opposition in the House Foreign Affairs Committee. The Subcommittee on Africa passed the resolution along party lines. At the full committee level, the resolution was passed by a one-vote margin and only after Speaker Tom Foley pressured wavering Democrats. Representative Benjamin Gilman (R–N.Y.), the ranking minority on the Foreign Affairs Committee, currently chair, utilized a rarely used House rule forcing a vote on his amended version of the resolution.[17]

The House version of Resolution 45 was different than that of the Senate in many respects. It retained the Senate objective of providing "a secure environment for famine relief efforts" but also indicated its support to "help restore peace, stability and order through reconciliation, rehabilitation and reconstruction of Somali society and to help the people of Somalia create and maintain democratic institutions for their own governance." In the views of some critics of the Somalia mission, this statement amounted to "nation-building." The resolution also asserted its authority and mandate to declare pursuant to the War Powers Resolution. It stated that "consistent with section 8(a)(1) of the War Powers Resolution, the Congress declares that subsection (a) is intended to constitute specific statutory authorization."[18]

The House version of Resolution 45 was strongly opposed by Republican members of the House Foreign Affairs Committee. Congressman Gilman argued that "the Hamilton resolution [Resolution 45] strongly implies that the authorization will be extended as long as the United Nations wants."[19] By contrast, Gilman's substitute resolution would have required the president to seek authorization if U.S. forces were exposed to hostilities as stated in the War Powers Resolution. Most important, Gilman's substitute would withdraw U.S. troops from Somalia within six months. The Senate agreed to a twelve-month withdrawal deadline. The Clinton administration, however, was opposed altogether to setting a deadline. Representative Gilman's substitute was defeated 179 to 248. An amendment submitted by Representative Toby Roth (R–Wis.), which called for an immediate withdrawal of U.S. troops, was also defeated, by a 127 to 299 vote. On May 25, 1993, after a series of amendments and votes, the House version of Senate Joint Resolution 45 was passed by the House by 243 to 179. This version of the resolution was not taken up by the Senate because Senate majority leader Mitchell would not allow debate.

Some members of Congress continued to complain about the role of U.S. troops in Somalia even in the face of a decreased U.S. role in the UN-led UNO-SOM II operation and after the passage of Resolution 45. The killing of Pakistani troops by Aideed forces in June and a U.S.-led helicopter attack on Aideed's headquarters in which sixteen senior members of the Somali National Alliance were killed sparked intense military confrontation between Aideed forces and those of the United Nations. This situation was exacerbated by the decision of the UN Security Council to capture those responsible for the killing of the Pakistani troops and subsequently by the posting of a bounty on General Aideed by the UN special envoy, retired navy admiral Jonathan Howe.

Renewed Congressional Opposition: August to October

Once again deteriorating security conditions renewed congressional opposition and led to a call for the withdrawal of U.S. troops from Somalia. UNOSOM's assertive and at times aggressive behavior in Somalia became a source of distress for many in Congress who had initially supported the UN mission. Some members and staff who visited Somalia at this critical time felt, despite misgivings, that the policy was a correct one. The go-after-Aideed policy, they felt, would resolve the problem faced by the UN peacekeepers and would facilitate the political reconciliation process. In retrospect, this was a major mistake on the part of the United Nations and the United States. For reasons that some in Congress still do not understand, this new policy was described as one that could be carried out without serious repercussions. Congress was led to believe that Aideed's militia numbered somewhere around 400 and that he did not have the support of the people. This was a major intelligence failure that had severe policy implications.

In early September, shortly after the summer recess, the debate over the role of U.S. troops in Somalia formally resumed. Senator Byrd renewed his opposition to the U.S. role in the newly expanded UN-mandated mission in Somalia. He argued that "the United Nations mandate to disarm the warlords and rebuild a civil society in Somalia, approved by the UN Security Council, was never addressed, never debated, or never approved by this [Senate] body, even though it sought to establish a new era for UN peacekeeping."[20] Indeed, the Senate never debated this issue; it had passed Senate Joint Resolution 45 in early February, several months before the UN Security Council expanded the UN mission in Somalia.

The House, however, debated and included in its version of the resolution the new mandate for UNOSOM II, and the two resolutions never made it to conference in order to reconcile the differences between the two chambers. This situation would later become a major source of frustration for leaders of both parties. Senator Byrd sought to restrict U.S. participation in the UN mission by eliminating funding for the Somalia mission unless authorized by the Congress. On September 8–9, he introduced an amendment to the Department of Defense Authorization Act of 1994 to cut off funding by the end of October. The debate, although focused on authorization by Congress for the new Somalia mission, was about the role of the United States in the post–Cold War world, setting off a new, though temporary, realignment in Congress between isolationists and internationalists.

On September 9 a compromise was reached in which both Senator Byrd and the Senate leadership agreed on a substitute to Byrd's amendment. The substitute called on the president to "report to the Congress by October 15 of 1993 a description of the mission, command arrangement, sites, function, location, and anticipated duration in Somalia of American forces. Additionally, it expresses [the sense of Congress] that the President thereafter should, by November 15, 1993, seek and receive Congressional authorization in order for the deployment of United States forces in Somalia to continue."[21] The substitute amendment, which had the support of the leaders of both parties and that of Senator Byrd, passed by a vote of 90–7. On September 28 the House also passed an identical amendment to its version of the Defense Authorization Bill (H.R. 2401) by a vote of 406–26.

The October Clash and the Shift in Policy

In the wake of the October 3 armed clash between the U.S. forces and General Aideed's militia in which eighteen U.S. Rangers were killed, once again senators and representatives took to the floor of Congress to condemn the Somalia mission. Senator Byrd launched his attack by saying, "Americans by the dozens are paying with their lives and limbs for a misplaced policy on the altar of some fuzzy multilateralism." Pressure mounted in both houses for the president to send his report to Congress sooner than the October 15 deadline. One by one, members of Congress demanded the immediate withdrawal of U.S. troops from Somalia, even members who had voted in support of the House version of Senate Joint Resolution 45, which provided the necessary authorization to the president. With Somalis dragging dead U.S. soldiers in the streets of Mogadishu and congressional offices receiving about 300 calls a day from angry constituents, no one was willing to support the UN mission.

On October 7, 1993, President Clinton addressed the nation and offered four policy objectives for the Somalia mission. He articulated a clear mission for the U.S. military in his report to Congress and said U.S. forces would have four tasks:[22] (1) protect U.S. troops in Somalia and their logistic bases; (2) keep open and secure the key roads and lines of communication that are essential for the United Nations and relief workers to keep the flow of food, supplies, and people moving freely throughout the country in order to stave off a return to starvation and anarchy; (3) keep the pressure on those who originally cut off relief supplies and attacked U.S. troops; and (4) through that pressure and the presence of U.S. forces, help make it reasonably possible for the Somali people, working with others, to reach agreements among themselves so that they could solve their own problems and survive after the withdrawal of U.S. forces. Most important, the president stated that U.S. forces would pull out of Somalia by March 31, 1994.

With the new policy from the White House, the debate in Congress shifted from congressional authorization to how soon American troops should withdraw from Somalia. Rank-and-file Democrats as well as Republicans favored an immediate withdrawal, ranging from within a few weeks to no later than January 31, 1994. The leadership in both parties favored the March 31 deadline set by the White House. Another issue was the scope of the mission as articulated by President Clinton, which in the view of some members still supported "nation building." The Republican leader in the Senate opposed setting a deadline because it would only "embarrass the President and place Congress in the position of 'micromanaging' foreign policy."[23] The opposition, led by Senator Byrd, sought to force the president to pull out U.S. troops by January 31.

After tense debate and maneuvering by both sides, a compromise was reached between the Senate leadership and Senator Byrd. The compromise amendment kept the president's March 31 deadline but limited the scope of the U.S. mission to humanitarian support. The administration agreed to drop its plans to continue to pressure Aideed militarily and its plans for "nation building." With Senator Byrd now in support of the compromise, conservative Republicans launched their own attack on President Clinton's new policy and against the Senate leadership plan. After five hours of debate, the Senate finally agreed to the compromise language offered by Senator George Mitchell and Senator Robert Dole (R–Kans.) in a 76–23 vote. Despite this victory in the Senate, the president was seriously bruised, and many felt his policy toward Haiti and Bosnia would face stiff opposition in Congress.

Confused Signals from the House of Representatives

Unlike the Senate, the House sent a confused signal on Somalia when it voted twice on the same issue. In the wake of mounting pressure from constituents and lack of support for the Somalia mission, House members voted 224–203 on November 9 in favor of a measure that called for the withdrawal of U.S. troops from Somalia by January 31, 1994. But an hour later the House reversed itself when it voted 226–201 in favor of a measure supporting Clinton's March 31 deadline. Consistent with the procedures set by the Rules Committee, the latter amendment prevailed. Interestingly, fifty-five Democrats voted with Republicans in support of the January 31 Republican-sponsored amendment; twenty-four of these Democrats would later support the March 31 deadline after an hour of debate and intense pressure from the White House and the Democratic leadership. Although the resolution was nonbinding, the effort by the opposition was to embarrass the president and score political points.

A New Assertiveness in Congress

The legislative branch has become increasingly intrusive in the making of foreign policy since the Vietnam War. The 102nd Congress can claim some credit for the deployment of U.S. troops to Somalia in December 1992 to save lives, and the 103rd Congress presided over the dismantling of the U.S. involvement in the Somalia mission.

The clash between U.S. soldiers and General Aideed's militia on October 3–4, 1993, left eighteen U.S. soldiers dead, seventy-eight wounded, and over 1,000 Somalis dead. In almost eighteen months in Somalia, an estimated thirty Americans were killed, but the U.S. saved as many as 300,000 Somalis from starving to death. In Grenada, nineteen Americans were killed within a few days, and in Panama twenty-three Americans were killed in an attempt to arrest military strongman and drug lord General Noriega. The death of any human being is regrettable, but we must never forget how many lives we saved as a result of our intervention in December 1992.

The withdrawal of U.S. troops marked the beginning of a shift toward isolationism in the U.S. Congress that was demonstrated by greater wariness over subsequent deployments to Haiti and Rwanda. Whereas the extent of this trend is still unclear, the Somalia episode fundamentally changed the course of U.S. foreign policy, as evidenced in the Republican-controlled 104th Congress. There appears to be limited support among the American public for active U.S. participation in the international scene. With the U.S. presidential election scheduled for 1996, the focus of politicians will increasingly be on domestic issues. Whether the new isolationism proves temporary or permanent will depend on how Americans come to view their role in the post–Cold War world.

Notes

1. In August 1980, for example, the House Foreign Affairs Subcommittee on Africa rejected the Carter administration's request for military aid to Somalia, although limited

military assistance was eventually allowed. The executive branch tended to favor military aid during the Cold War because of Somalia's strategic location and neighboring Ethiopia's alliance with the Eastern bloc.

2. House Committee on Foreign Affairs, Subcommittee on Africa, *Reported Massacres and Indiscriminate Killings in Somalia*, hearing, 100th Cong., 2nd sess., July 14, 1988.

3. S.R. 115. Introduced April 25, 1991; referred to Senate Committee on Foreign Relations April 25, 1991; reported to Senate by Senate Committee on Foreign Relations June 27, 1991; agreed to in Senate without amendment and with a preamble by voice vote June 28, 1991.

4. Senate Committee on Foreign Relations, Subcommittee on African Affairs, *The Horn of Africa: Changing Realities and the U.S. Response*, hearing, 102nd Cong., 2nd sess., March 19, 1992, p. 20.

5. House Select Committee on Hunger, *Somalia: The Case for Action*, hearing, 102nd Cong., 2nd sess., July 22, 1992, p. 6.

6. Ibid., p. 3.

7. Senate Concurrent Resolution 132. Introduced July 31, 1992; passed the Senate by voice vote on July 31, 1992; referred to House Committee on Foreign Affairs August 4, 1992; agreed to in House by voice vote August 10, 1992.

8. Senate Committee on Foreign Relations, Subcommittee on Africa, *U.N. Peacekeeping in Africa: The Western Sahara and Somalia*, hearing, 102nd Cong., 2nd sess., October 1, 1992, p. 1.

9. House Concurrent Resolution 370. Introduced October 2, 1992; referred to House Committee on Foreign Affairs October 2, 1992; agreed to in the House by voice vote October 2, 1992; received in Senate October 3, 1992; referred to Senate Committee on Foreign Relations October 3, 1992; passed Senate by voice vote on October 8, 1992.

10. Raymond W. Copson and Theodros S. Dagne, "Somalia: Operation Restore Hope," CRS Issue Brief 92131, continuously updated.

11. Pat Towell, "Somalia: Suffering Spurs Unprecedented Step As U.N. Approves Deployment," *Congressional Quarterly*, December 5, 1992, p. 3759.

12. Ibid., p. 3761.

13. Ellen C. Collier, "War Powers Resolution: Presidential Compliance," CRS Issue Brief 81050, continuously updated.

14. Thomas Ricks, "Secretary Aspin Draws Heaviest Fire As Criticism Mounts over U.S. Role in Somalia," *Wall Street Journal*, October 8, 1993, p. A16.

15. *Congressional Record*, 103rd Cong., S8793–95, July 15, 1993.

16. *Congressional Record, S8856*, July 16, 1993.

17. According to Representative Hamilton, former chair of the House Foreign Affairs Committee, the committee was compelled to approve the Gilman resolution on the grounds that "section 5(c) of the War Powers Resolution states that any time U.S. armed forces are engaged in hostilities abroad without specific statutory authorization, such forces must be removed by the President if the Congress so directs by concurrent resolution. Under section 7 of the War Powers Resolution, concurrent resolutions introduced under section 5(c) are referred to the House Foreign Affairs Committee and one such resolution must be reported out with recommendations by the committee within 15 calendar days. In practical terms, the committee must consider such a concurrent resolution today." Congressman Hamilton made the above statement on November 3, 1993, at a committee markup of H.R. 170.

18. *Congressional Record*, 103rd Cong., H2745, May 25, 1993.

19. *Congressional Record*, 103rd Cong., H2748, May 25, 1993.

20. *Foreign Policy Bulletin*, November-December 1993, p. 20.

21. *Congressional Record, 103rd Cong.,* Senate, September 9, 1993.

22. President Clinton, "Report to the Congress on US Policy in Somalia," October 13, 1993.

23. *Washington Times*, October 13, 1993, p. A15.

PART 5
Conclusions

12

Rekindling Hope in UN Humanitarian Intervention

Thomas G. Weiss

Policymakers, pundits, and the public are not required to have long historical perspectives. But their recollections of humanitarian intervention appear particularly shortsighted and confused. Three brief years separated the vigorous military intervention overriding sovereignty and supporting humane values in northern Iraq in April 1991 from the passive response to the Rwandan bloodbath in April 1994. Observers usually point to Somalia as the turning point—when Pollyannaish notions about intervening militarily to guarantee access to civilian victims of violence were replaced by realistic assessments about the limits of such actions.

The apparent failures of agonizing U.S. and UN efforts in this hapless country have led to the "Somalia syndrome." Multilateral interventions to thwart starvation, the forced movement of peoples, massive violations of fundamental rights, or even genocide are no longer thought to be either politically or operationally feasible. Reflection could, however, lead elsewhere, to the need for a new doctrine by which UN decisions would trigger humanitarian intervention subcontracted to coalitions led by major powers or deployed entirely by them. The UN would ensure accountability for such undertakings but continue traditional peacekeeping and humanitarian actions after them. This is the real lesson of recent UN experience, both successes and failures.

I first discuss some of the so-called lessons and then the dominant views against humanitarian intervention as a basis to examine the conceptual and operational voids that emerge from the experiences in Somalia and elsewhere. Eight propositions follow that suggest elements of a new doctrine as well as the need to create a new UN institutional capacity.

Avoiding the Wrong Conclusions

Somalia cast an ominous shadow on Washington, where the Clinton team and the commander in chief in May 1994 issued Presidential Decision Directive 25 (PDD

25). Supposedly the remaining superpower had "wisely retreated from the overly sanguine expectations held by the administration when it began its term."[1] The first real test of the policy was Rwanda. As one senior State Department official close to human rights policy quipped during an off-the-record discussion, "It was almost as if the Hutus had read it." The new restrictive guidelines made it possible for the United States not only to remain on the sidelines but also to prevent others from getting involved while genocide proceeded apace.

This volume details numerous military, political, and humanitarian shortcomings in Somalia; they should not be examined in isolation but rather contextualized in light of other efforts in northern Iraq, Bosnia, Haiti, and Rwanda. And although the international community's efforts in Somalia clarify limitations of the United Nations, this experience does not demonstrate the futility of humanitarian intervention.[2]

Viewing Somalia out of context and drawing the wrong conclusions has fanned the smoldering ashes of policy nihilism in Washington and has led to ignoring international norms against war crimes and genocide in Bosnia and Rwanda. The residue from Somalia continues to foster isolationism. Military and diplomatic authorities now tend to emphasize the reasons to forgo effective participation in humanitarian interventions rather than those that point toward engagement where it would make a difference. The House's National Security Revitalization Act (H.R. 7) and the Senate's Peace Powers Act of 1995 (S. 5) are the most recent manifestations of such isolationist views.

Starting with Operation Provide Comfort in northern Iraq and in spite of thorny problems, Western powers have demonstrated the ability to intervene effectively if they so choose. However, efforts of this sort fly in the face of the military doctrines articulated by former secretary of defense Caspar Weinberger and subsequently embroidered by former chair of the Joint Chiefs of Staff General Colin Powell and others. According to post-Vietnam logic, the United States should not intervene unless it is committed to total victory with full support from the public and Congress in situations where massive firepower can ensure attainable objectives, minimal U.S. casualties, and a clear exit timetable. These are hardly characteristics of the civil wars that represent a dominant security challenge of our turbulent times, when the unpredictable interplay of fragmentation and cheap weapons makes chaos commonplace.[3]

I have argued that there is a "collective amnesia" regarding northern Iraq[4] that even such a thoughtful skeptic as UN High Commissioner for Refugees Sadako Ogata deems "a rare example of successful humanitarian intervention."[5] In that instance, superior military force was subcontracted to the allied coalition that secured direct access to civilians; but afterward the operation was turned over to civilian humanitarian organizations with NATO firepower in reserve in Turkey. At the same time, too little international attention has been paid to the significant humanitarian benefits of the U.S. invasion of Haiti and to the contribution of elite French troops during Opération Turquoise to help stabilize Rwanda and forestall another Goma—the overnight conversion of a sleepy provincial capital in Zaire into a Detroit-sized refugee city with cholera.

The use of military force should be a last resort. But my aim should be specified from the outset—identifying the ingredients for effective and increased, not decreased, humanitarian intervention when massive civilian suffering cannot be stopped by other means. The goal is to enhance humanitarian efforts in active war zones while insulating both the secretary-general and the UN system from enforcement operations within which they operate with great difficulty and about which they are ambivalent or outright hostile.

Arguments Against Humanitarian Intervention

Talk-show hosts, academic conference-goers, politicians, and the proverbial woman in the street are preoccupied with what the editor of *Foreign Affairs* described, prematurely, as the "springtime for interventionism."[6] They are hesitating at a fork in the road about whether to use military force in support of humanitarian objectives. One route leads back toward traditional peacekeeping and the other toward the measured application of superior military force in support of more ambitious international decisions including the enforcement of humane values.[7]

The balance of opinion at present definitely favors the former, and Somalia is critical in this weighting. Reticence from the armed forces about humanitarian intervention in an era of no-risk and no-casualty foreign policy ironically joins the objections of critics who see U.S. dominance in multilateral military efforts as a continuation of American hegemony.[8]

Two unlikely apologists for outside military forces, Alex de Waal and Rakiya Omaar, have observed: "Humanitarian intervention demands a different set of military skills. It is akin to counterinsurgency."[9] This realization will not be comforting to the Pentagon and others still recovering from the "Vietnam syndrome."[10] The United Kingdom's efforts in Malaysia undoubtedly are more relevant for failed states than those from Operation Desert Storm.

Dissenters from humanitarian intervention include many developing countries clinging to the notion that state sovereignty does not permit outside intervention, a stance that serves to protect them against major-power bullying.[11] They also argue, and perhaps rightfully, that intervention is messy and it is easier to get in than get out. And the Security Council's definition of what constitutes "threats" to international peace and security is both expanding to cover virtually any subject and remaining selective in application.

These developing countries essentially are trying to put on blinders in order to avoid an emerging reality of the post–Cold War era. Sovereignty should be exercised within the limits of human rights norms or be voided. "Use it responsibly or risk losing it" summarizes the framework that has characterized world politics since the early 1900s. State sovereignty remains the basis for everyday international relations, but it can be overruled when mass suffering or genocide occurs and the international community is prepared to act. The acceptable degree of outside interference in the domestic affairs of rogue states and of insurgents is considerably more intrusive than in the past.

Sovereignty is viewed differently by international lawyers, for whom there normally are not degrees of sovereignty—it either exists or it does not—and political scientists. For the latter, sovereignty and human rights can coexist, and it is possible to be more or less sovereign. Third World countries are understandably concerned that lines not be drawn such that even greater infringements on their feeble sovereignty occur. However, mass civilian suffering in northern Iraq, Somalia, Rwanda, and Bosnia clearly qualify these countries for intervention, and in fact the vast majority of developing countries have supported interventions in these countries.[12]

Other critics of vigorous intervention are civilian humanitarians working in the trenches. For them, "humanitarian war" and "military humanitarianism" are oxymorons.[13] There are of course pacifists like the Quakers and Mennonites. However, they are not the only dissenters from more robust action. A fair number of other practitioners argue that humanitarian initiatives are strictly consensual and are premised on impartiality and neutrality. Protected by the international law of armed conflicts, of which the International Committee of the Red Cross (ICRC) is the custodian, political authorities in armed conflicts should be persuaded, according to this argument, to meet their commitments for access to and respect of civilians.

A thornier position for which historical interpretations are controversial regards the futility of intervention because the failure of some states represents a natural process that should be allowed to run its course.[14] The vast majority of state-formation attempts in Europe, for example, failed or involved considerable bloodshed over several centuries. There is no reason to believe that states created in the wake of colonization and decolonization will do better. Somalia may be a particularly obvious case in point because it is such an obviously artificial construction.[15]

Yet with 1 in every 115 people on earth forced into flight from war, humanitarian intervention may sometimes be the only way to halt massive abuses of human rights, starvation, and genocide.[16] Thus, partisans of the other route at the fork in the road, of which I am one, are open to the option of outside military forces to assist civilians trapped in wars. When consent cannot be extracted, economic and military coercion can be justified in operational and ethical terms. When there is sufficient political will, an effective humanitarian response may include military backup that goes far beyond the minimalist use of force in self-defense by traditional UN peacekeepers. Rather than suspending relief and withdrawing, the international community can use enough force to guarantee access to civilians, protect aid workers, and keep thugs at bay.

Humanitarian intervention is not an end in itself but a last-ditch effort to create breathing room for the reemergence of a modicum of local stability and order, which ultimately are prerequisites for the conduct of negotiations that can lead to consent—about humanitarian space and eventually about lasting peace as well. The Commission on Global Governance has proposed "an appropriate Charter amendment permitting such intervention but restricting it to cases that constitute a violation of the security of people so gross and extreme that it requires an international response on humanitarian grounds."[17] In the aftermath of the UN's fiftieth anniversary, it is worth recalling that this world organization was supposed to be different from its defunct predecessor, the League of Nations. The provisions for coercion in the UN Charter were designed to back up international decisions to stop atrocities in such places as Somalia, Bosnia, Rwanda, northern Iraq, and Haiti.

Avoiding Conceptual Shortcomings

UN activities in the post–Cold War period have spawned a veritable cottage industry of analyses,[18] especially since the 1992 publication of Boutros Boutros-Ghali's *An Agenda for Peace*. However, many discussions in UN circles are still characterized by a remarkable confusion between traditional peacekeeping and enforcement and by the gray areas of the "second generation."[19] One of the values of the present volume is that too many other analyses of Somalia fail to distinguish among the very different mandates of and problems encountered by UNOSOM I, UNITAF, and UNOSOM II—especially the clumsy shift from Chapter VI to VII. As one senior UN official responsible for Somalia quipped during the discussion of drafts for this volume: "Somalia was a laboratory for all types of peacekeeping."

"Wandering in the void"[20] describes not only the literal position of UN troops but also the more figurative stumbling of many analysts, diplomats, and UN staff. Some are merely confused; but even experts employ "peacekeeping" as an omnibus term to encompass all UN security efforts, including those where consent is absent or problematic and where military capacity rather than moral authority is foremost. Some militaries attach misleading adjectives—for example, "extended" peacekeeping in Whitehall or "aggravated" peacekeeping in the Pentagon. The confusion is even greater when an operation shifts from Chapter VI to VII (Somalia and Rwanda) or combines the two (the former Yugoslavia).

Although Dag Hammarskjöld dubbed the mandate for peacekeeping operations "chapter six-and-a-half," it is really extrapolated from Chapter VI rather than from a would-be Chapter VII. On the one hand, a number of both management and financial reforms could undoubtedly improve the UN's peacekeeping efforts—each operation still is put together from scratch in an ad hoc manner on the basis of best-case scenarios with inadequate resources. On the other hand, the UN is quite incapable of handling Chapter VII. We should have known before Somalia, but now it is perfectly clear. According to Chester Crocker, "The United Nations' attempt at a militarily challenging 'peace enforcement' operation shows that it cannot manage complex political-military operations."[21] Boutros Boutros-Ghali agrees. The secretary-general's *Supplement to An Agenda for Peace* is fundamentally a plea for scaled-down expectations and missions: "Neither the Security

Council nor the Secretary-General at present has the capacity to deploy, direct, command and control operations for this purpose."[22] The world organization's diplomatic and bureaucratic structures are simply inimical to putting together and overseeing military efforts while serious fighting rages and coercion rather than consent is the norm.

Part of the problem is that the United Nations has extrapolated from past operations when stumbling into post–Cold War crises rather than clearly delineating their distinct new characteristics. Boutros-Ghali contributed to the confusion in 1992 when he defined peacekeeping as "the deployment of a United Nations presence in the field, *hitherto* with the consent of the parties concerned, normally involving United Nations military and/or police personnel and frequently civilians as well."[23] However, peacekeeping is not a panacea for the chaos of ethnonationalism but rather a discrete tool for conflict management under consensual circumstances. The secretary-general retreated from his earlier stance and recognized the UN's limitations when he wrote that peacekeeping and enforcement "should be seen as alternative techniques and not as adjacent points on a continuum."[24]

Nonetheless, the argument is not against the use of coercion under UN auspices. During the Cold War, peacekeeping was a substitute for big-power enforcement, but it should now be seen as a supplement. The Security Council can and should continue to make decisions about the use of force for humanitarian intervention or to counteract blatant interstate aggression. It is impossible to imagine in the foreseeable future how many of the raging or potential conflicts—be they in the former Third or Second Worlds—can be controlled or resolved without outside military force. That is, of course, unless the international community chooses to permit the virtual subjugation or the actual annihilation of certain belligerents and ethnic groups.

Coercion should, however, be routinely subcontracted to a coalition of states or a military alliance with Security Council oversight but well insulated from the office of the secretary-general. There has been a significant development in world politics regarding the need for international sanctioning of actions by major powers in the post–Cold War era. This can usefully be seen as a third analytical phase for outside military intervention. During the age of empires, imperial masters openly intervened when and where they wished. Then, as a result of decolonization, major powers increasingly opted for less noticeable economic and political arm-twisting to foster their interests rather than for more obvious military force. But when they made use of their armed forces, there was no requirement to seek and no advantage to seeking international approval. Since the early 1990s, however, the desirability of securing an international imprimatur for military intervention by major powers represents a crucial change in international relations.

The conduct of such operations should be kept under close scrutiny by the international community. Accountability to a larger group authorizing such interventions would represent healthy progress in global order. Although major powers inevitably flex their muscles when their geopolitical interests are at stake, they do not inevitably subject themselves to international oversight and norms.

Moreover, the strength of the office of the secretary-general is derived from the lack of vested interests. Former UN assistant secretary-general Giandomenico Picco has argued that "transforming the institution of the Secretary General into a pale imitation of a state" in order "to manage the use of force may well be a suicidal embrace."[25] When the security situation has somewhat stabilized, the secretary-general must be prepared to facilitate the administration of collapsed states after warring parties are exhausted or repulsed from a territory or after a humanitarian intervention has taken place. This capacity should be separated from a military intervention that should aim to break a cycle of violence and create a respite and the preconditions for a return of an interim authority.

The failure to distinguish between military operations that the UN secretariat can manage (impartial peacekeeping) and those that it cannot and should not (partial enforcement) has led to an unfortunate situation. The decision to deploy peacekeepers both in UNOSOM II and in Bosnia rather than coalition forces, which could have managed a more effective humanitarian intervention, has called into question UN credibility. As one analyst has noted, "By shying away from enforcement actions and ceasing to use peacekeepers as symbols, the Security Council can do much to solidify the United Nations' legitimacy and therefore its ability to compel states to abide by its decisions."[26]

Avoiding Operational Shortcomings

The conceptual weaknesses in examining Somalia and other humanitarian interventions are supplemented by institutional shortcomings. Many of the errors in Operation Restore Hope were made in Washington, but the UN's own handling of military efforts before, during, and after form a sad pattern. The UN secretariat has not kept pace with dramatically increased demands. The professional capacity of the UN secretariat to plan, support, and command peacekeeping, let alone enforcement, is scarcely greater now than during the Cold War. Or in one analyst's view, "The U.N. itself can no more conduct military operations on a large-scale on its own than a trade association of hospitals can conduct heart surgery."[27]

After stable levels of about 10,000 UN peacekeepers in the early post–Cold War period, their numbers increased rapidly. In 1994–1995, UN forces averaged some 70,000 to 80,000 blue-helmeted soldiers. They were authorized by the UN's $4 billion annualized "military" (peacekeeping) budget. These statistics only hint at the magnitude of overstretch and related problems. Unpaid assessments for the regular budget and peacekeeping operations in mid-1994 approached some $3.5 billion (that is, about three times the annual regular budget of the world organization). Both the numbers of soldiers and the budget dropped dramatically in 1996, by two-thirds. Overextension was clearly a major problem.

Modest progress in establishing a situation room in New York and some consolidation in UN administrative services are hardly sufficient to make the militaries of major or middle powers feel at ease about placing the United Nations in charge of combat missions.[28] The United Nations and its member states are increasingly bogged down in multidimensional operations in civil wars hardly imagined as a possible task by the framers of the UN Charter, and certainly not where the UN has had success. There are increasing political, economic, and military pressures in Washington and other Western capitals to avoid engagement.

The "assertive multilateralism" trumpeted at the outset of this administration was perhaps only a political ploy, but it had become totally untenable as a result of Somalia. Alain Destexhe, the former secretary-general of Médecins Sans Frontières, linked the American reaction directly to the international community's unwillingness to react to genocide in Rwanda: "The intervention fiasco in Somalia and the deaths of more than 30 professional soldiers so shocked the American public that the Clinton administration had to rethink its foreign policies."[29]

Toward Filling the Doctrinal Void

What lessons emerge from the comparative contextualization of Somalia and other efforts at humanitarian intervention? What would constitute a better doctrine and infrastructure? Eight propositions suggest elements of a new doctrine for UN involvement in humanitarian intervention, which in turn leads to the need for a new institutional capacity.

Intervene in a Timely and Robust Fashion or Not at All

In the rush to avoid another Somalia, there has been a remarkable effort to overlook accomplishments in northern Iraq. Efforts there were sufficient to maintain access; the will to stay the course was, and still is, present.

Unlike other humanitarian interventions, symbols did not dwarf effective military measures. The initial deployment of crack troops from the United States, Britain, France, and the Netherlands was backed by NATO air cover. As the soldiers withdrew, humanitarian efforts were turned over to civilians. But aircraft based in Turkey remained an effective deterrent for Saddam Hussein because bombing sorties were used along with other punitive measures. Iraqi Kurds have fared better than their Somali, Bosnian, Rwandan, and, for about three years, their Haitian counterparts. The ineptness of UNOSOM I was followed by the narrowness of the mandate for UNITAF. Because of the unwillingness to remove heavy arms from warring factions and to remain in place until a semblance of order was present, UNOSOM II was then doomed to failure. The initial U.S.-led intervention was not long enough or ambitious enough to ensure the preconditions for a successful UN takeover.

For Bosnia-Herzegovina, governments switched to Chapter VII rhetoric for the UN Protection Force in the former Yugoslavia (UNPROFOR) but without an accompanying military commitment to implement the mandate. "All measures necessary" was quintessential UN double-speak. UN troops in Bosnia have never fought a single battle with the numerous factions who routinely disrupt convoys; and other than an occasional pinprick, air power has been an empty threat.

Governments watched Rwanda's massive tragedy unfold until France's Opération Turquoise at the end of June 1994. Although lasting only two months, this effort was a welcome reversal of the international community's do-nothingness. Simultaneously, Security Council Resolution 940 in July 1994 authorized Chapter VII action to restore the elected government of Jean-Bertrand Aristide and reversed the astonishing retreat of the U.S.S. *Harlan County* from the harbor of Port-au-Prince in September 1993. In September 1994 the U.S. troops in Operation Uphold Democracy mounted a large police action after three years of unnecessary civilian suffering.

The most recent French and American efforts indicate that military efforts in favor of humanitarian values are still possible, although neither tested the will of these governments to sustain casualties or stay the course in the face of public disenchantment. One analyst has aptly noted the constraints of a no-risk and no-casualty foreign policy: "An intervention that can be stopped in its tracks by a few dozen casualties, like the U.S. operation in Somalia was, is one that should never have begun."[30] International military intervention in support of humanitarian objectives should be timely and robust or shunned altogether.

Communicate Clearly About Essential Goals

Increasingly the United Nations deploys multifunctional operations that combine the military, civil administration (including election and human rights monitoring and police support), and humanitarian expertise with an overlay of political negotiations and mediation.[31] How do we measure success?

The requirement for clearer mandates has been a preoccupation for peacekeepers for some time, and the multiplicity of tasks in more recent and complex operations cries out for still more exactitude. If policymakers are not more specific about the time frame used to determine the durability of results, there will be a fundamental ambiguity about "success" and "failure." Were short-term efforts in Somalia successful because death rates dropped dramatically in 1993 and some quarter of a million lives were saved, or were they a long-term failure because billions were expended to stop the clock temporarily only to witness the country revert to banditry and chaos in 1994–1995?

The overwhelmingly negative impressions of the Somali experiences, in whatever phase, should be contrasted with the generally more positive ones in Cambodia and Mozambique. Narrowness in approach, particularly during Operation Restore Hope, was exemplified by Washington's unwillingness to remove heavy arms and to stay the course. The more comprehensive efforts in Cambodia of the UN Transitional Assistance Commission (UNTAC)—which encompassed a variety of military, civilian, and humanitarian elements—meant that when one aspect of the operation was in trouble, others could compensate. The value of having eggs in separate baskets contributed to what observers see as a success in spite of the generally accepted failures in five of the seven baskets.[32] The UN Operation in Mozambique (UNOMOZ) also represents a comprehensive peace implementation scheme under UN auspices after more than a decade of grisly civil war in Mozambique. Although the implementation went more slowly than anticipated, there is nonetheless progress on a wide range of humanitarian and political tasks as well as a transition government following relatively free and fair elections.[33]

Neither Cambodia nor Mozambique was a humanitarian intervention, but the ambitiousness of intervention in those countries suggests lessons for coercive operations. With the number of multifunctional operations clearly on the rise, there should be greater efforts to clarify purpose.

Emphasize Prevention

It is always easier with hindsight to demonstrate that an earlier investment in prevention would have been worthwhile than to anticipate events when experts first warn of impending disaster. The dilemma has been that prevention is cost effective in the long run but cost intensive in the short run. In Somalia, Haiti, and the former Yugoslavia, the "long run" has been a few years, whereas in Rwanda it was reduced to a matter of weeks. The notion that an earlier and more sustained use of military force could have been more economical and ultimately could have led to less civilian suffering than the tardy or inadequate efforts in Somalia, Haiti, and the former Yugoslavia runs into a theoretical problem: the inability of governments to look very far into the future. Consequently they magnify the benefits of avoiding immediate expenditures and discount the disadvantages of incurring future ones. A brief look at U.S. efforts in Somalia is illustrative. The cost of Operation Restore Hope itself was five to six times greater than total U.S. development assistance to Somalia for three decades and more than assistance in 1994–1995 to all of sub-Saharan Africa.

In Rwanda, the time-frame was condensed. The costs of deaths, displacement, and a ruined economy were borne immediately by the same donor governments—the United States and the European Union—who refused to respond militarily only a few weeks earlier. Donor assistance to the Rwandan emergency alone amounted to at least $1 billion in 1994 (and almost $2 billion according to some estimates), corresponding to about 2 percent of total overseas development assistance and 20 percent of emergency assistance in the same year by member states in the Organization for Economic Cooperation and Development (OECD). Commenting on the illogic, two observers noted that "the Administration felt able to hold up a minor contribution to a UN force intended to stop mass murder, but was compelled to spend far greater sums on emergency aid."[34]

Except for the military's ability to plan for worst-case contingencies to defend *raisons d'état*, governments and politicians rarely make anything except myopic calculations. Nonetheless, prevention has entered the policy debate—at this stage, "an idea in search of a strategy."[35] Perhaps the most essential element of a workable doctrine would be the early movement of troops with an advance decision to respond should they be challenged.

Deal Straightforwardly with Human Rights

In virtually all operations, UN staff could have been utilized better for human rights monitoring, what Human Rights Watch has called "the lost agenda." The reluctance to be more active has "led to the squandering of the U.N.'s unique capacity on the global stage to articulate fundamental human rights values and legitimize their enforcement."[36] Member states and, less justifiably, the senior staff within international secretariats have been timid about publicly confronting the perpetrators of human rights abuses and war crimes. The need to reinforce the UN's neutrality provides the most sanguine explanation for such behavior, but the world organization's leadership wishes to sidestep confrontations with states, move ahead with negotiations, and be seen as an impartial partner once ceasefires go into effect. Human rights fall victim to misplaced evenhandedness even in the face of genocide in Rwanda, where the UN's "obsession with 'neutrality' actively impeded any attempts to address the crisis."[37] The continuation of negotiations with the Bosnian Serb leaders in spite of their forthcoming indictment as war criminals is another illustration.

As the executive head of an intergovernmental organization, Boutros-Ghali ultimately reaffirms a fairly conventional interpretation of sovereignty when it clashes with other international norms.[38] If humanitarian intervention were the exclusive domain of military forces authorized by the Security Council but not commanded or controlled by the secretary-general, UN officials would be better positioned to use the bully pulpit as part of a new doctrine.

Make Better Use of Humanitarians

The globe's safety mechanism for civilians in times of war lacks specialization. The failure to ascertain who does what best is frequently rationalized as inevitable, but it also hides structural weaknesses and fund-raising imperatives.

International responses require a clearer and better division of labor among humanitarians. "Coordination" is probably the most overused and least understood term in international parlance. Everyone is for it, but no one wishes to be coordinated. It would be unfair to denigrate the courage and dedication of individuals or agencies. Yet humanitarian action is marred by unnecessary duplication and competition among the bevy of outside helpers—bilateral, intergovernmental, nongovernmental, ICRC—who normally flock to the scene of disasters. A mid-summer 1994 census in Kigali, Rwanda, for instance, already registered over 100 international NGOs, prima facie evidence that economies of scale and critical mass were absent from calculations. No institution could have been absent from

Goma in June 1994; resource mobilization for Rwandan and other operations would have suffered.

In December 1991 the General Assembly authorized the UN secretary-general to appoint a humanitarian coordinator. The creation of the UN's Department of Humanitarian Affairs (DHA) was supposed to rectify the numerous operational problems criticized by donors during the international response to the crises in the Persian Gulf.[39] DHA has made little difference to leadership or performance, although information sharing is better and NGOs have begun to be included in consultations and assessments. The structural weaknesses are obvious and include a coordinator without budgetary authority who does not outrank the heads of subordinate units. Erskine Childers and Brian Urquhart have argued that the inability to establish a division of labor within the UN system and between it and nongovernmental organizations "remains seriously neglected in the continued jockeying and jostling of UN-system organizations vis-à-vis each other and the intrinsically weak new DHA 'Coordinator.'"[40] A better international division of labor and a more centralized structure that takes advantage of the resources and energies of all humanitarians should form part of a new doctrine.

Do Not Be Driven by the Media's Priorities

While Western citizens, legislatures, and governments seek to avoid commitments, poignant media coverage sometimes elicits halfway measures when massive and egregious human rights abuses as well as widespread violence and starvation become particularly unpalatable. The media's influence on humanitarian responses to civil wars is not new, but technology seems to have altered media influence in post–Cold War crises.

Although precise causal links are far from certain, the media can provoke action; but they also can encourage wishful thinking, underestimate long-term realities, and overlook crises where journalists do not find convincing copy or footage for their editors. The media's capacity to inject uncertainty into the policy process is magnified with the formless agenda of the post–Cold War era.[41] Without a well-articulated rationale, governments frequently react randomly. Instead of shaping public opinion or standing firm on the basis of a policy, they can be buffeted about by successive shifts in public opinion.

Whatever one's views about Somalia, supporters and critics alike agree that it was more poignant images—first of starvation and later of indignities suffered by dead marines—than analyses that drove U.S. policy. As well as dramatizing needs, stimulating action, and generating resources, the media can distort the kinds of assistance provided, skew the allocation of resources and personnel among geographical areas, ignore the role of local humanitarians, and focus attention on perceived bungling.

Some commentators see the media as shameless manipulators bound to convey shallow and misinformed conclusions. Others view them as helpless victims of circumstances beyond their control, particularly the harsh economics of the industry itself. A more basic understanding is required of their exact impact on both policy formulation and action.[42] One element of a new doctrine is clear, however: Humanitarian interventions should be driven by analyses, feasibility, and legitimate demands rather than by media supply.

Do Not Overestimate Regional Organizations, but Use Them When Possible

Advocates for regional institutions find them an attractive alternative to an overextended United Nations.[43] Because member states of these institutions suffer most from the destabilizing consequences of war in their locales, they have the greatest stake in the management and resolution of regional conflicts. Regional actors also understand the dynamics of strife and cultures more intimately than outsiders, and thus they are in a better position to mediate. Issues relating to local conflict are also more likely to be given full and urgent consideration in regional forums than in global ones, where there are broader agendas, competing priorities, and distractions.

This theory contrasts starkly with efforts by the Arab League, the Organization of African Unity (OAU), and the Islamic Conference, which were so ineffective that only cognoscenti of the Somali crisis are vaguely aware of their involvement. In general, advantages of regional organizations exist more in theory than in practice for humanitarian intervention. Most such existing institutions have virtually no military experience or resources. They normally also contain hegemons whose presence colors regional decisions with illegitimacy.

At the same time, three Security Council decisions between late June and late July 1994 indicated the growing relevance of military intervention by major powers in regions of their traditional interests: a Russian scheme to deploy its troops in Georgia to end the three-year-old civil war, the French intervention in Rwanda to help stave off genocidal conflict, and the U.S. plan to spearhead a military invasion to reverse the military coup in Haiti. One analyst commented that the growing sense that peacekeeping is so ineffective a tool for resolving crises like Somalia or Bosnia leads to the conclusion that "it might well be better to scrap it altogether and leave the policing of the world's trouble-spots to great powers or regional hegemons."[44] The secretary-general himself seemed to agree in his first press conference of 1995, when stating that "the United Nations does not have the capacity to carry out huge peace endorsement operations, and that when the Security Council decides on a peace enforcement operation, our advice is that the Security Council mandate a group of Member States, (those which) have the capability."[45]

The decision in Budapest in December 1994 by the Conference (now Organization) on Security and Cooperation in Europe (OSCE) to authorize 3,000 troops to keep the peace after a cease-fire in Ngorno-Karabakh is another illustration. These experiments indicate that the evident gap between international capacities and increasing demands for help could be filled in the immediate future by regional powers or even hegemons operating under the scrutiny of a wider community of states that would hold the interveners accountable for their actions.[46]

Bill Maynes's "benign realpolitik" straightforwardly recognizes this reality, which amounts to a revival of spheres of influence with UN oversight.[47] The Security Council is experimenting with a type of great-power politics that the United Nations was originally founded to end. But this capacity is increasingly pertinent and should form part of a feasible doctrine for humanitarian intervention because of the inherent difficulties of multilateral mobilization and management of military force.[48] As Boutros-Ghali has noted, "They may herald a new division of labour between the United Nations and regional organizations, under which the regional organization carries the main burden but a small United Nations operation supports it and verifies that it is functioning in a manner consistent with positions adopted by the Security Council."[49]

Be Prepared for Painful Decisions

The morally wrenching process of triage is a reality. Not only are financial pressures in Western parliaments clashing with burgeoning requests for outside help but a world organization with a universal mandate and membership as well as a global operational network means that there is virtually no crisis *not* on the UN's agenda. Consequently, as does the surgeon on the battlefield, the international community must increasingly confront stark choices: who needs no help, who cannot be helped, and who can and must be helped.

Even though much remains to be done to get more from existing humanitarian resources and machinery, policymakers and citizens cannot avoid painful choices. Humanitarian practitioners estimate that ten to twenty times more can be done with the same limited resources to attack what UNICEF has called poverty's "silent" emergencies—as opposed to the "loud" ones resulting from wars.[50] Both governments and individuals are more likely to respond to appeals on behalf of the victims of war than to those on behalf of the victims of poverty. But what are the claims of the 35,000 to 40,000 children worldwide who perish daily from poverty and preventable diseases? Should they not have some claim on resources that donors prefer to commit to soldiers and costly logistics in more visible war zones?

Avoiding the term "triage" does not mean that decisions are not already being made about who gets help and who gets ignored. For example, in 1992–1993, when Operation Restore Hope was mounted to the tune of $1.5–$2 billion, the situation in neighboring Sudan was comparable and in Angola, worse. Resources were not available for reconstruction and land redistribution in El Salvador, where a tenuous peace process "could be on a collision course" with structural adjustment.[51] Cost-benefit calculations should be an explicit part of a new doctrine rather than an implicit part of decision-making.

A New Institutional Capacity

These eight propositions suggest a new doctrine according to which UN decisions would trigger humanitarian intervention subcontracted to coalitions led by major powers or even staffed entirely by them. This means that the UN should continue with traditional peacekeeping and with humanitarian action after a humanitarian intervention—for example, in Haiti or in Rwanda at present or in Somalia had UNITAF stayed the course.

But what about the delivery of emergency relief during such interventions? The military itself has an important logistic capacity in the most dire of circumstances. Over and above any military assistance to a civil authority, civilian succor would continue to be required.[52] Governments are loathe to consider new organizational entities, but one should be created to deliver emergency aid in those active war zones with Chapter VII economic or military sanctions. This specialized cadre would be a truly "international" ICRC. These volunteers should not be part of the common UN staff system because they would have to be appropriately insured and compensated. In many ways, these persons could well be more in harm's way than soldiers. In December 1994, the General Assembly recognized the vulnerability of soldiers and civilians in humanitarian operations and approved the text of a treaty for ratification by states. It requires signatories to protect UN personnel and to arrest those responsible for crimes against them.

The effective protection of the new category of humanitarian workers would be enhanced by the implementation of an international decision to treat attacks against humanitarian personnel as an international crime. This procedure would build upon the logic of earlier precedents in that the effective prosecution of terrorists and airplane hijackers is no longer subject to the vagaries of national legislation or the extraditional whims of host countries.

Resources and capable relief specialists could also be siphoned from existing humanitarian agencies with distinguished records in armed conflicts—like UNHCR, UNICEF, and the World Food Program (WFP). But under this arrangement, the UN's humanitarian agencies themselves would be absent when Chapter VII is in effect. If a peacekeeping operation changed to enforcement, they would withdraw.

This argument would have been anathema to UN humanitarian practitioners only a few years ago, when there was an unquestioned imperative to respond to life-threatening suffering wherever it was found. The politicization of humanitarian action in Bosnia and Somalia—or the perception of its politicization, which has the same impact—is changing the conventional wisdom. London's International Institute for Strategic Studies has suggested possible new principles that are based on an internal UN memorandum concerning humanitarian action when outside military forces are involved. Although controversial, to say the least, the new bottom line was the recommendation that civilian humanitarians "should not embark on humanitarian operations where, over time, impartiality and neutrality are certain to be compromised" and that "if impartiality and neutrality are compromised, an ongoing humanitarian operation should be reconsidered, scaled down or terminated."[53]

Along with the military forces deployed for a humanitarian intervention, this new civilian delivery unit should form an integral part of a unified command that would report directly to the Security Council and not to the secretary-general. The non-UN troops authorized by the council and staff from the new humanitarian unit would together constitute a core of soldiers and civilians in possession of expertise and military wherewithal—a "HUMPROFOR," or Humanitarian Protection Force.

The new UN humanitarian entity should also have ground rules for mounting and suspending deliveries. An essential element, for example, would be the explicit agreement by troop contributors that the UN-blessed interventionary forces would be bound by the Geneva Conventions and Additional Protocols. Instead of using customary international law and its incorporation into national military law, they should submit themselves to an international prosecution mechanism devised for the purpose.

This new unit's civilian humanitarians would no doubt be more comfortable than the staffs of most UN organizations with "tough-love"—imposing either economic or military sanctions with inevitable consequences for vulnerable groups. Although their assistance would go to refugees and internally displaced persons without regard to juridical status, it would undoubtedly be unfairly distributed by favoring those within the areas under international coercive control. The new unit might well be dominated by retired military personnel who would not reject out of hand the necessity to subordinate themselves and work side by side with military protection forces within a hierarchical and disciplined structure. It should in any case be experienced in working with military forces and able to bridge the military-civilian cultural divide that has impeded effectiveness in many war zones. Moreover, a single instead of a decentralized UN structure would make buck-passing, a standard clause in job descriptions, more difficult.

Attaching this unit to the Security Council would insulate the office of the UN's chief executive from Chapter VII's partiality. The UN secretary-general should be kept available for more impartial tasks, and an especially important one will be administering what has entered the public policy lexicon as "collapsed" or "failed" states.[54] Proposals calling for recolonizing those countries that "are just not fit to govern themselves" are implausible.[55] But the UN no doubt will be called upon selectively to assume temporary trusteeship or governorship in some instances. The fact that Somalia, as well as Iraq and Rwanda, were trusteeships earlier in this century should also indicate that this is no cure-all but rather a provocative idea whose implementation will necessitate much experimentation.[56]

This new unit attached to the Security Council would be a humanitarian adaptation of the precedent set for Rolf Ekeus. As executive chairman of the Special Commission on Disarmament and Arms Control in Iraq, he was appointed by and reports to the council rather than to the secretary-general. As part of the

Chapter VII enforcement governing the terms of the cease-fire after the Gulf War, Ekeus is the Security Council's emissary. Boutros-Ghali remains a potential interlocutor for even a pariah regime or its successor.

Conclusion

In spite of the present disarray, there is simply no substitute for leadership from Washington, or in Thomas Friedman's summary of recent UN efforts, "There is no multilateralism without unilateralism."[57] Would that Somalia were an aberration. But continued vacillations in the former Yugoslavia, inaction in Rwanda until it was too late, retreat in Haiti, and subsequent negotiations mixed with an intervention-cum-collaboration have failed to attain the previous high-water mark of humanitarian intervention in northern Iraq. There is even the impression that vigorous action is somehow undesirable and impractical. With direct pertinence for the conclusion to this chapter and volume are the words of Chester Crocker: "The question is whether Americans will learn from Somalia or recoil from the experience—and from peace operations generally."[58]

The administration abandoned its pro-UN stance well before the congressional sea change in November 1994. After a year of fierce interagency feuding, ill-fated military operations in Somalia and Haiti, dithering about the former Yugoslavia, and burying its collective head in the sand, the administration issued PDD 25 in May 1994. It rationalized a policy about-face after what one analyst labeled "test marketing" of a new policy "given the universal allergic reaction toward peacekeeping within the executive branch in the aftermath of Somalia."[59]

The so-called policy—no fewer than seventeen conditions to be met prior to committing U.S. forces to a UN-approved operation that might see combat—reflects the extent to which Washington has abandoned the mantle of leadership. Having approved new ground rules, the Clinton administration then found itself fending off congressional efforts to delimit the scope and duration of U.S. activities in Haiti as specified in the new policy. The administration helped set in motion the momentum for the National Security Revitalization Act (H.R. 7) and the Peace Powers Act of 1995 (S. 5), which it subsequently was obliged to resist.

A White House so seemingly inconsistent in its conduct of foreign policy has placed thugs at ease and exacerbated civilian suffering. As one critic has written, "Effective multilateralism is not an alternative to U.S. leadership; it will be a consequence. The question is whether the world's only superpower will choose to behave like one."[60]

The moral of U.S. actions in Somalia—as well as in the former Yugoslavia and Rwanda and in Haiti until September 1994—contrasts with those in northern Iraq and those of the French in Rwanda. Half-steps, symbolic actions, and misplaced evenhandedness are not necessarily better than no action at all. There is no need to minimize the serious difficulties of intervening in ethnonational armed conflicts generally or of working around the perennial obstacles to UN action more particularly. There is also no reason to take issue with the unquestionably valuable services of traditional peacekeepers where consent is present or to have illusions about the world organization as "utopia lost."[61]

Earlier and more robust humanitarian intervention—approved and monitored by the Security Council under Chapter VII but handed over to a coalition or to a major power rather than under the command and control of the secretary-general—should be pursued or situations left to the warring parties to settle themselves. Limited and supposedly impartial interventions are likely to be counterproductive, to prevent peace rather than facilitate it. Even in the face of genocide in Rwanda, the UN's "obsession with 'neutrality' actively impeded any attempts to address the crisis."[62] Impartial intervention is a delusion. Would-be interveners should, as a minimum, "do no harm."[63]

However, if an intervention occurs, military force should be subcontracted to major powers or coalitions and UN humanitarian assistance should come from a special new unit attached to the Security Council rather than from UNHCR, UNICEF, and WFP. In such cases, the military forces should carve out defensible areas within which they can take command without constant friction with combatants or local factions. The model is Operation Provide Comfort and Opération Turquoise rather than UNITAF, UNOSOM, or UNPROFOR.

The new humanitarian unit obviously could not have compensated for the unwillingness of states to commit substantial ground troops to Bosnia until the Dayton agreements, but even there it would have made humanitarian efforts more effective. Moreover, such a unit would be considerably quicker off the mark and more efficacious in working in tandem with soldiers during operations when superior military force is applied (for example, in the Gulf and in Somalia) or when only modest military force is necessary but insecurity is widespread (for example, in Rwanda). In effect, this tough-love humanitarian unit would be ready to be committed by the Security Council from the outset of a Chapter VI or VII operation and also be prepared to work with military units and to take over any responsibilities that might be required as the result of the departure of relief groups should a traditional Chapter VI undertaking be changed into a coercive one.

During Chapter VII military operations, the ICRC should maintain its independent presence to protect prisoners of war and to keep lines of communication open among belligerents. There is no more committed group of humanitarians than the ICRC, and it will no doubt remain active in such war zones.

But other nongovernmental organizations should keep their distance until security is reestablished, which in fact was the case for most man-made crises during the Cold War. No one commands the nongovernmental relief community, but its increasing reliance upon governments for large-scale financing of emergency operations means that governments could decide to limit their presence under Chapter VII operations.[64]

The international community's inconsistency has produced the worst of many worlds: enormous expenditures; unspeakable suffering by civilians in war zones; tattered U.S., NATO, and UN credibility; compromised UN humanitarian agencies; the legitimization of ethnonationalism; and a diminishing public support for multilateralism. But the tensile strength of the military and civilian safety net under war victims can and should be increased. It is time to mount Operation Rediscover Hope, not only for the victims of armed conflicts but also for ourselves.

Notes

1. David C. Hendrickson, "The Recovery of Internationalism," *Foreign Affairs* 73(5), September-October 1994, p. 38.

2. For the most complete and balanced evaluation to date, see John G. Sommer, *Hope Restored? Humanitarian Aid in Somalia 1990–1994* (Washington, DC: Refugee Policy Group, 1994).

3. See Michael E. Brown, ed., *Ethnic Conflict and International Security* (Princeton: Princeton University Press, 1993); and Ted Robert Gurr and Barbara Harff, *Ethnic Conflict in World Politics* (Boulder: Westview Press, 1994). As the leading student of media coverage of post–Cold War crises has concluded: "The new generation of conflicts can never be of the short, sharp, overwhelming kind that politicians and military planners now believe is vital to sustain a public consensus for involvement." See Nik Gowing, *Real-Time Television Coverage of Armed Conflicts and Diplomatic Crises: Does It Pressure or Distort Foreign Policy Decision?* (Cambridge: Harvard University Press, 1994), p. 86.

4. See Thomas G. Weiss, "Triage: Humanitarian Interventions in a New Era," *World Policy Journal* 11(1), Spring 1994, pp. 1–10; "Humanitarian Interventions, 1991–1993: On the Brink of a New Era?" in Don Daniel, ed., *Beyond Traditional Peacekeeping* (London: Macmillan, 1995); and "UN Responses in the Former Yugoslavia: Moral and Operational Choices," *Ethics and International Affairs* 8, 1994, pp. 1–22.

5. Sadako Ogata, "Role of Humanitarian Action in Peacekeeping Operations," keynote address, Vienna, July 5, 1994, p. 4. See also Lawrence Freedman and David Boren, "'Safe Havens' for Kurds in Post-War Iraq," in Nigel Rodney, ed., *To Loose the Bonds of Wickedness: International Intervention in Defence of Human Rights* (London: Brassey's, 1992), pp. 43–92.

6. James F. Hoge Jr., "Editor's Note," *Foreign Affairs* 73(6), November-December 1994, p. v. For a wide-ranging collection of essays, see Paul A. Winters, ed., *Interventionism: Current Controversies* (San Diego: Greenhaven Press, 1995), and Gene M. Lyons and Michael Mastanduno, eds., *Beyond Westphalia? State Sovereignty and International Intervention* (Baltimore: Johns Hopkins University Press, 1995).

7. See Adam Roberts, "The Crisis in Peacekeeping," *Survival* 36(3), Autumn 1994, pp. 93–120; and Thomas G. Weiss, "Intervention: Whither the United Nations?" *Washington Quarterly* 17(1), Winter 1994, pp. 109–128.

8. For example, see articles "On Intervention" by Noam Chomsky, Christopher Hitchens, Richard Falk, Carl Coretta, Charles Knight, and Robert Leavitt in *Boston Review* 18, December-January 1993–1994, pp. 3–16.

9. Alex de Waal and Rakiya Omaar, "Can Military Intervention Be 'Humanitarian'?" *Middle East Report* nos. 187–188, March-April/May-June 1994, p. 7.

10. See Richard A. Melanson, *Reconstructing Consensus: American Foreign Policy Since the Vietnam War* (New York: St. Martin's Press, 1991).

11. For a reasoned presentation of some negative arguments, see Ernst B. Haas, "Beware the Slippery Slope: Notes Toward the Definition of Justifiable Intervention," in Laura W. Reed and Carl Kaysen, eds., *Emerging Norms of Justified Intervention* (Cambridge: American Academy of Arts and Sciences, 1993), pp. 63–87. See also Marianne Heiberg, ed., *Subduing Sovereignty: Sovereignty and the Right to Intervene* (London: Pinter, 1994).

12. See Jarat Chopra and Thomas G. Weiss, "Sovereignty Is No Longer Sacrosanct: Codifying Humanitarian Intervention," *Ethics and International Affairs* 6, 1992, pp. 95–117.

13. Adam Roberts, "Humanitarian War: Military Intervention and Human Rights," *International Affairs* 69, 1993, pp. 429–449; and Thomas G. Weiss and Kurt M. Campbell, "Military Humanitarianism," *Survival* 33(5), September-October 1991, pp. 451–465.

14. See Mohammed Ayoob, *The Third World Security Predicament: State Making, Regional Conflict, and the International System* (Boulder: Lynn\e Rienner, 1994).

15. See Ali A. Mazrui, "The Blood of Experience: The Failed State and Political Collapse in Africa," *World Policy Journal* 12(1), Spring 1995, pp. 28–34.

16. For these and other gruesome statistics, see Sadako Ogata, *The State of the World's Refugees 1995: The Challenge of Solutions* (Oxford: Oxford University Press, 1995).

17. Commission on Global Governance, *Our Global Neighbourhood* (Oxford: Oxford University Press, 1995), p. 90.

18. The best examples of the growing analytical literature are William J. Durch, ed., *The Evolution of UN Peacekeeping: Case Studies and Comparative Analysis* (New York: St. Martin's Press, 1993); Paul Diehl, *International Peacekeeping* (Baltimore: Johns Hopkins University Press, 1993); Mats R. Berdal, *Whither UN Peacekeeping? Adelphi Paper 281* (London: International Institute for Strategic Studies, 1993); John Mackinlay, "Improving Multifunctional Forces," *Survival* 36(3), Autumn 1994, pp. 149–173; and Steven R. Ratner, *The New UN Peacekeeping: Building Peace in Lands of War After the Cold War* (New York: St. Martin's Press, 1995).

19. See John Mackinlay and Jarat Chopra, "Second Generation Multinational Operations," *Washington Quarterly* 15(2) Spring 1992, pp. 113–131; and *A Draft Concept of Second Generation Multinational Operations 1993* (Providence: Watson Institute, 1993). See also John Mackinlay, ed., *A Guide to Peace Support Operations* (Providence: Watson Institute, 1996).

20. John Gerard Ruggie, "Wandering in the Void," *Foreign Affairs* 72, November-December 1993, pp. 26–31.

21. Chester A. Crocker, "The Lessons of Somalia: Not Everything Went Wrong," *Foreign Affairs* 74(3), May-June 1995, p. 5.

22. Boutros Boutros-Ghali, *Supplement to An Agenda for Peace: Position Paper of the Secretary-General on the Occasion of the Fiftieth Anniversary of the United Nations*, January 3, 1995, document A/50/60, S/1995/1, para. 77.

23. Boutros Boutros-Ghali, *An Agenda for Peace* (New York: United Nations, 1992), para. 20, emphasis added.

24. Boutros-Ghali, *Supplement*, para. 36.

25. Giandomenico Picco, "The U.N. and the Use of Force," *Foreign Affairs* 73(5), September-October 1994, p. 15.

26. Michael Barnett, "The United Nations and Global Security: The Norm Is Mightier Than the Sword," *Ethics and International Affairs* 9, 1955, p. 53.

27. Michael Mandelbaum, "The Reluctance to Intervene," *Foreign Policy* 95, Summer 1994, p. 11.

28. For a review of these concerns, see Frank M. Snyder, *Command and Control: The Literature and Commentaries* (Washington, DC: National Defense University, 1993); *U.N. Peacekeeping: Lessons Learned in Recent Missions* (Washington, DC: General Accounting Office, December 1993), document GAO/NSIAD–94–9; and *Humanitarian Intervention: Effectiveness of U.N. Operations in Bosnia* (Washington, DC: General Accounting Office, April 1994), document GAO/NSIAD–94–156BR.

29. Alain Destexhe, "Confronting the Genocide in Rwanda," *Foreign Policy* 97, Winter 1994–1995, p. 10. See also his *Rwanda: Essai sur le génocide* (Brussels: Editions Complexe, 1994).

30. Richard K. Betts, "The Delusion of Impartial Intervention," *Foreign Affairs* 73(6), November-December 1994, p. 31.

31. See Thomas G. Weiss, ed., *The United Nations and Civil Wars* (Boulder: Lynne Rienner, 1995).

32. See Jarat Chopra, "UN Transition Authority in Cambodia," occasional paper no. 15, Watson Institute, Providence, Rhode Island, 1994; and Janet E. Neininger, *Peacekeeping in Transition: The United Nations in Cambodia* (New York: Twentieth Century Fund, 1994).

33. See Cameron Hume, *Ending Mozambique's War: The Role of Mediation and Good Offices* (Washington, DC: U.S. Institute of Peace Press, 1994).

34. Rakiya Omaar and Alex de Waal, *Rwanda: Death, Despair and Defiance* (London: African Rights, 1994), p. 712.

35. Michael Lund, *Preventive Diplomacy and American Foreign Policy* (Washington, DC: U.S. Institute of Peace, 1994), p. 27. See also his *Preventing Violent Conflicts: A Strategy for Preventive Diplomacy* (Washington, DC: U.S. Institute of Peace, 1996).

36. See Human Rights Watch, *The Lost Agenda: Human Rights and U.N. Field Operations* (New York: Human Rights Watch, 1993); and *Human Rights Watch World Report 1995* (New York: Human Rights Watch, 1994), quote at p. xiv.

37. Omaar and de Waal, *Rwanda*, p. 682.

38. See Boutros Boutros-Ghali, "Empowering the United Nations," *Foreign Affairs* 71, Winter 1992–1993, pp. 89–102. For a critique, see Thomas G. Weiss, "New Challenges for UN Military Operations: Implementing an Agenda for Peace," *Washington Quarterly* 16(1), Winter 1993, pp. 51–66.

39. See Larry Minear and Thomas G. Weiss, "Groping and Coping in the Gulf Crisis: Discerning the Shape of a New Humanitarian Order," *World Policy Journal* 9, Fall-Winter 1992–1993, pp. 755–788.

40. Erskine Childers with Brian Urquhart, *Renewing the United Nations System* (Uppsala: Dag Hammarskjöld Foundation, 1994), p. 114.

41. See James F. Hoge Jr., "Media Pervasiveness," *Foreign Affairs* 73, July-August 1994, pp. 136–144.

42. See Jonathan Benthall, *Disasters, Relief and the Media* (London: Tauris, 1993). See also Robert I. Rotberg and Thomas G. Weiss, eds., *From Massacres to Genocide: The Media, Public Policy, and Humanitarian Crises* (Washington, DC: Brookings Institution, 1996); and Larry Minear, Colin Scott, and Thomas G. Weiss, *The News Media, Civil War, and Humanitarian Action* (Boulder: Lynne Rienner, 1996).

43. See S. Neil MacFarlane and Thomas G. Weiss, "Regional Organizations and Regional Security," *Security Studies* 2, Fall-Winter 1992–1993, pp. 6–37; and "The United Nations, Regional Organizations, and Human Security," Third *World Quarterly* 15(2), April 1994, pp. 277–295.

44. David Rieff, "The Illusions of Peacekeeping," *World Policy Journal* 6(3), Fall 1994, p. 3.

45. Boutros Boutros-Ghali, "Transcript of Press Conference," press release SG/SM/5518, January 5, 1995, p. 5.

46. For an extended discussion, see Jarat Chopra and Thomas G. Weiss, "Prospects for Containing Conflict in the Former Second World," *Security Studies* 4(3), Spring 1995, pp. 552–583.

47. Charles William Maynes, "A Workable Clinton Doctrine," *Foreign Policy* 93, Winter 1993–1994, pp. 3–20.

48. See John Mearsheimer, "The False Promise of International Institutions," *International Security* 19(3), Winter 1994–1995, pp. 5–49; and Adam Roberts, "The Crises in Peacekeeping," *Survival* 36(3), Autumn 1994, pp. 93–120.

49. Boutros-Ghali, *Supplement*, para. 86.

50. See James P. Grant, *The State of the World's Children 1994* (New York: Oxford University Press, 1993).

51. See Alvaro de Soto and Graciana del Castillo, "Obstacles to Peacebuilding," *Foreign Policy* 94, Spring 1994, p. 70.

52. This is a major theme in Larry Minear and Thomas G. Weiss, *Mercy Under Fire: War and the Global Humanitarian Community* (Boulder: Westview Press, 1995); and *Humanitarian Politics* (New York: Foreign Policy Association, 1995).

53. International Institute for Strategic Studies, "Military Support for Humanitarian Operations," *Strategic Comments* no. 2, February 22, 1995. The ICRC is increasingly preoccupied by this subject. See Umesh Palwankar, ed., *Symposium on Humanitarian Action and Peace-Keeping Operations: Report* (Geneva: ICRC, 1994).

54. See Gerald B. Helman and Steven R. Ratner, "Saving Failed States," *Foreign Policy* 89, Winter 1992–1993, pp. 3–20; and I. William Zartman, ed., *Collapsed States: The Disintegration and Restoration of Legitimate Authority* (Boulder: Lynne Rienner, 1995).

55. Paul Johnson, "Colonialism's Back—and Not a Moment Too Soon," *New York Times Magazine*, April 18, 1993. See also William Pfaff, "A New Colonialism? Europe Must Go Back into Africa," *Foreign Affairs* 74(1), January-February 1995, pp. 2–6; and Peter Lyon, "The Rise and Fall and Possible Revival of International Trusteeship," *Journal of Commonwealth and Comparative Politics* no. 31, March 1993, pp. 96–110.

56. See Adam Roberts, "A More Humane World?" draft study for the Commonwealth Secretariat dated December 1994.

57. Thomas L. Friedman, "Round and Round," *New York Times*, April 2, 1995, p. E5.

58. Crocker, "The Lessons of Somalia," p. 8.

59. Holly J. Burkhalter, "The Question of Genocide: The Clinton Administration and Rwanda," *World Policy Journal* 11(4), Winter 1994–1995, pp. 48, 53.

60. Richard N. Haass, "Military Force: A User's Guide," *Foreign Policy* 96, Fall 1994, p. 37. See also "Paradigm Lost," *Foreign Affairs* 74(1), January-February 1995, pp. 43–58.

61. Rosemary Righter, *Utopia Lost: The United Nations and World Order* (New York: Twentieth Century Fund, 1995).

62. Omaar and de Waal, *Rwanda,* p. 682.

63. Richard K. Betts, "The Delusion of Impartial Intervention," *Foreign Affairs* 73(6), November-December 1994, pp. 20–33.

64. See Thomas G. Weiss, "Humanitarian Action by Nongovernmental Organizations," in Michael E. Brown, ed., *International Implications of Internal Conflicts* (Cambridge: MIT Press, 1996), pp. 435–459.

13

The Lessons of Somalia for the Future of U.S. Foreign Policy

ROBERT I. ROTBERG

Whether the United States can, or should, flex its undeniable muscle for the betterment of less fortunate peoples across the globe depends on defining the national self-interest in a manner that would support the existing imperatives of liberal internationalism against the powerful, easily allied forces of entropy, disdain, isolationism, and national narcissism. That is the new challenge for U.S. foreign policy and the makers of U.S. foreign policy, wounded as it and they have been by the mistakes made during and as a result of the U.S. intervention in Somalia.

The United States has long pursued its legitimate national interests by intervening forcefully in the affairs of other countries. The methods of intervention have varied from classical gun boat diplomacy to the sponsorship of proxy wars and outright occupation. Yet isolationism—a fear of being entangled in the messy imbroglios of foreigners—has always been second nature to Americans; assertive adventures overseas have thus had to appeal for justification and consensual approval to overriding national interests, not just to the needs of sensible foreign policy.

Most instances of intervention have consequently occasioned controversy, with criticism coming in some generations from the domestic left, in some generations from the domestic right. Nonentanglement and isolationism have been the lodestars of principle, but, in practice, jingoism has often prevailed. There has been a strain of noblesse oblige, too, but it has rarely been dominant.

One generation's justifications and acceptances have been anathema to the next. Today, when the military might of the United States is unquestioned and theoretically decisive in world affairs, the impulse for the United States to be active overseas in the cause of humanitarianism comes largely from the domestic left (which opposed the anti-Communistic interventions of the 1960s and 1970s) and is opposed by the domestic right and by a new doctrine of military insularity.

Anthony Lake, the Clinton administration's national security adviser, asserted that the (new) American "policy of engagement in world affairs [was] under siege, and American leadership [in the world was] in peril." He attacked the nation's rising wave of isolationism, arguing that "back-door isolationists" were attempting to undo a post–World War II international balance of power that had been predicated on American military might, ample foreign assistance, and moral leadership.

For Lake, the back-door isolationists and "unilateralists" had cast themselves as the true guardians of U.S. power. But they could well become the agents of a U.S. retreat and the unwitting but real accomplices of Iraqi aggression, Sudanese terrorism, and similar disturbances to the world's political equilibrium in the late 1990s.

"Persistent engagement and hands-on policies," some of which could lead to peacemaking and humanitarian interventions overseas, was the antidote to this new, actually renewed, wave of isolationism.[1] Indeed, in the new transnational world, still half unfree despite the death of Soviet communism, the role of a dominant superpower like the United States can hardly be any less critical in encouraging freedom throughout the globe than it was during the depths of the Cold War.[2]

The history of U.S. intervention overseas is instructive; a few of its more powerful lessons might have guided us profitably in Somalia, and in deciding when to go in and when to leave. Those lessons are also relevant when we argue for a new humanitarian impulse and against a resurgence of isolationism.

Throughout the nineteenth and twentieth centuries, the isolationist tendency has been expressed more easily and viscerally than that of liberal internationalism, despite shifting ideological support, sometimes from the left and sometimes from the right. Thus the surface lesson of the U.S. intervention in Somalia (1992–1995) is that any activity overseas that has indistinct or only partially articulated humanitarian political goals (and is not simply a relief effort) is immediately hostage to the loss of American lives. But given the long history of U.S. involvement on foreign shores, the lessons of the Somali intervention for the future of U.S. foreign policy in the late 1990s are much more nuanced and much more critical to global order.

When the United States was a young nation it was remarkably self-centered. As a nation it was also insecure; enhancing its security seemed to so many of its leaders to mean the avoidance of involvements beyond its shores that would arouse the antagonism of world powers or engage its energies wastefully. The United States was expanding intracontinentally; focusing on objectives elsewhere demanded explanation.

Yet it did intervene overseas when its interests were threatened. It chased Barbary pirates. It enunciated a Monroe doctrine and frequently reinterpreted it and expanded upon its meaning. It shook a succession of big sticks. The Civil War brought the United States allies and enemies and taught both sides the importance of diplomacy. But the United States still sought to avoid deep involvements and entanglements while simultaneously (and paradoxically) practicing dollar diplomacy and creating a sphere of influence in the Caribbean basin.

The United States continued shaking big sticks. It captured Puerto Rico, liberated Cuba, and annexed the Philippines. In Cuba, remember, Congress and President McKinley resolved that Cuba "by right ought to be free and independent." Yet for three years the United States exercised a trusteeship function, and the Platt Amendment subsequently allowed it to return at will to Cuba, which it did, to protect "life, property, and individual liberty."[3] The United States supported a coup and moved into Hawaii. It annexed Midway and took Guam from Spain. It fostered the creation of Panama and dug a canal. It occupied Haiti, the Dominican Republic, and Nicaragua and stayed for decades in those dominions without encountering more than episodic protests at home.

Yet the same leaders and the same publics that had led the United States into and acquiesced in the occupation of those territories only reluctantly joined the allied democracies of Europe when they fought the first war to end all wars against Germany. Later, too, a weakened President Wilson lost an important battle to take the United States into the League of Nations. As a result, the United States forfeited influence over the outcome of the Italian invasion of Ethiopia, over German rearmament, over Sudetenland, and over much else. It paid an enormous and lasting price for indulging in another bout of isolationism.

When it seemed important enough, however, the United States intervened to foster shifting definitions of the American national interest and then justified its shows of force on shaky, if not positively dubious, premises. Having exerted its influence in Haiti nineteen times from 1857 to 1914, it finally occupied that Caribbean nation in 1915 as a humanitarian response to the total collapse of indigenous abilities to maintain law and order. In the seven years before the intervention, seven presidents had entered and left office in Haiti, the last having been pulled literally from limb to limb by a wildly angry mob and the others having been ousted by one or more of the twenty insurrections that enveloped the country in those difficult years.[4]

In that instance, President Wilson was concerned about Haiti's inability to govern itself and about the possibility that Germany would occupy Haiti if the United States did not and then threaten U.S. shipping and the Panama Canal. But the United States intervened for a third reason: President Wilson wanted to help the First National City Bank of New York (now Citibank) collect its debts, a difficult undertaking amid Haitian chaos.

In the Haitian and other cases, U.S. leaders articulated an American national interest—a national responsibility to the citizens of the United States and to less fortunate peoples—that predisposed the United States to intervene. It invaded and occupied because of manifest destiny, to save indigenous peoples from their own corrupt and misguided ruling classes, to protect free (that is, American) trade, to spread democracy, and—much later in the twentieth century—to deter the spread of the Communist evil empire. (Iran, Guatemala, the Dominican Republic, Lebanon, Grenada, and Angola [1975] are the cases that quickly come to mind.)

U.S. leaders justified and explained these adventures overseas with relative aplomb. They even managed successfully to throw a mantle of honor over the lives of Americans who were forfeited during these various escapades. Most of the actions abroad had critics: The *Nation* thundered and a few maverick members of the House and Senate voiced displeasure, but U.S. leaders invariably managed deftly to evoke resonant chords of national self-interest. President F. D. Roosevelt even prepared the country for a war that many responsible Americans did not want, and then Japanese miscalculations at Pearl Harbor and Hitler's errors suddenly made it easy for the United States to enter that war and become the unquestioned leader of the free world.

The hard-won peace was succeeded, sooner than anyone wanted, by the Cold War and by a battle for Korea. The lessons of the Korean war are often misunderstood. There, by 1950, the United States had withdrawn its peace-prevention troops from the South, studiously ignored the growing buildup of threatening forces in the North, and accepted a high-level doctrine of noninterference promulgated by the Joint Chiefs of Staff and applied to Korea and Taiwan. The United States thus helped to make it both logical and important for the Soviet Union and China to encourage the North Koreans to attack the South.

Undoing those early Cold War errors proved very costly. President Truman, however, understood the need to act decisively despite the Joint Chiefs doctrine and despite the fact that the U.S. public had not been warned about events in Korea or involved in the decisionmaking. He also understood the importance of cooperating with the United Nations. President Truman led us decisively into a war that everyone now accepts was critical for the freedom of the world, for the containment of communism, and for the strengthening of U.S. credibility in a nuclear world.[5]

North Vietnam's attacks on South Vietnam soon reminded the United States of Korea. The situation there appeared to present another Korean-like challenge to the freedom of the world. Again, the United States intervened in order to contain communism. Indeed, in lurching into the morass of Vietnam, U.S. policy and U.S. policymakers were strongly influenced by what they thought had been the several crucial lapses in U.S. pre–Korean War policies.

But the United States failed in Vietnam because it was not another Korea. It was not a dagger pointed at Japan. It was not an early Rubicon in the prosecution of the Cold War against the Soviet Union and China. The United States had fewer strategic interests. It had already stopped the dominoes from tumbling. Most of all, without a UN cloak to throw over its efforts, it could never have achieved a decisive victory in that war without invading the North. The war against North Vietnam was a flawed cause, and U.S. leaders consequently failed to mobilize American public opinion behind their assaults. South Vietnam was perceived as more corrupt than North Vietnam. So, hobbled by its ambiguous past and commendable national ethos, the United States refused to be an all-out aggressor; but it was, and out of that confusion of ethics and military ambiguity, its efforts were doomed, especially when the bombs began to fall massively on Hanoi and Cambodia. Moreover, U.S. leaders did not know how and when to lose (as had President Charles de Gaulle so graciously in Algeria).

Korea; Vietnam; Operations Desert Storm, Restore Hope, Restore Democracy (the Haitian adventure); and other late-twentieth-century U.S. interventions all provide lessons, negative and positive, for the role of the United States in the troubled, anxious post–Cold War world. So do recent U.S. failures to intervene in Bosnia, Rwanda, Burundi, Sierra Leone, and Liberia.

We live in a world where civil wars in far-off places are the norm—where thirty wars erupt annually, where there are twenty complex humanitarian crises every year, where 50 million persons are now displaced (ten years ago only 5 million were so displaced), and where millions of people were killed during 1991–1995 in one corner of Africa alone.

Three propositions flow from a reading of the meanings of distant and recent U.S. adventures overseas:

- Obviously the United States cannot take on every cause. It cannot alone counter every threat to the peace of the globe. It is not and cannot be the tribune of the world. It cannot intervene militarily where victory is unlikely or where the price of victory cannot be rationalized or explained even by the most thoughtful and articulate of leaders.
- The United States ought to intervene only in those cases where its leaders can express the reasons for actions clearly and persuasively and where their explanations can be linked to closely held American core values.
- The United States ought to refuse any commitments to refrain from any particular action, preclude no honorable actions, and prepare for a decade of troubled uncertainty punctuated more by crises than by stability.

A number of other lessons follow and are important to the future of all peoples in the post–Cold War era and to the formulation of a responsible role for the United States beyond the end of the present century.

No intervention can succeed without decisive leadership. The American people will instinctively reject engagements abroad unless their leaders can overcome the public's visceral isolationism with cogent appeals to a larger, worldly wise self-interest, and to a greater morality. President Bush, having lost an election, was still able to engage Americans in Operation Restore Hope. Americans cared nothing for Kuwait and worried little beforehand about protecting supplies of petroleum, but President Bush was able to persuade them to recognize an overriding national self-interest in the struggle against an Arab despot.

A strong United Nations is essential if the peace of the world is to be maintained. Even if the UN and regional multilateral organizations will never be able to substitute effectively for what a wise and well-led United States single-handedly can do for peace, the United States often needs the UN as its proxy, as its collaborator, and as its mantle of legitimacy. As peacekeeper and as peace beneficiary, the United States cannot itself function well without a revitalized and well-supported

UN. The United States thus needs to take the lead in strengthening, not eviscerating, the peace-maintaining and peacebuilding, as well as the peacemaking, heart of the UN. The National Security Revitalization Act and similar legislation in the House of Representatives are wrongheaded and counterproductive, like so much else that reflects the destructive spirit of the 104th Congress.

The United States can act more responsibly and more effectively for peace, taking on only the most important tasks, if the UN can play a supportive and a cooperative role, especially in the crucial arena of preventive diplomacy. But this superpower needs to find ways to fund its rightful proportion of UN expenses, including peacekeeping costs. Nothing is more important for global aggression reduction. The United States must also provide funding up front for its own peacekeeping and peacemaking interventions. "There is no excuse for underfunding and undermanning missions that warrant U.S. support," writes Chester Crocker.[6]

A standing military rapid-response mechanism is essential. The formation of a rapid-response team for timely intervention in a zone of incipient hostility, like Rwanda on April 6, 1994, Burundi in July 1995 (and before), and Bosnia, Liberia, and Sierra Leone on innumerable occasions, would be ideal. But it is unlikely that the UN can effectively organize such a team under its own financially and administratively weakened auspices. Weiss has suggested that the UN contract out its military rapid responses in humanitarian and other emergencies to the big powers (mostly to the United States) or to regional and subregional actors (like South Africa in Africa).[7] But that prospect is unlikely, too. The bickerings over Bosnia and the dallyings over Rwanda and Burundi offer little confidence in such a contract mechanism. The failure of ECOMOG (the ECOWAS Monitoring Group) in calming Liberia is also instructive.

Other alternative forces are available for hire, however. The UN could, on a standing basis, contract with an existing mercenary force like the French Foreign Legion (which played a salutary role in Somalia) or British-trained Gurkhas to contain crises whenever ordered to do so by the Security Council. The Legion, the Gurkhas, or a similar force would have the advantage of its own equipment, its own esprit de corps, its own officers, and its own traditions. Unlike a cobbled together collection of UN peacekeepers, it would have a distinct chain of command and suffer from no inconsistencies of training or firepower. Obviously, payment mechanisms would have to be in place beforehand; the United States would have to help provide for such a mercenary force. There is every likelihood that the employment of such a standing mercenary force would prove less expensive than current methods of peacekeeping. A common awareness of rapid Foreign Legion or Gurkha deployment could also prove a deterrent. If the United States wants to prevent future genocides in distant corners of the globe, the availability of such well-organized, tightly disciplined mercenary forces could help it intervene effectively, if by proxy. Had the Legion, say, moved into Somalia or Rwanda early, perhaps many fewer local inhabitants would have lost their lives.

Prevention is more effective and less expensive than relief and rehabilitation. This lesson is obvious, but it will apparently have to be relearned over and over. Missing the magic moment to intervene early is dangerous and costly. For example, General Romeo Dallaire, in Kigali at the time of the first massacres, claims credibly that he could have averted or slowed down the Rwandan genocide had the UN authorized the timely movement of his 400 troops. There is every likelihood that a similarly forceful hand in Burundi could have calmed the Tutsi militias in 1995 and mid-1996. The United States should have gone in very much earlier in Somalia. It should have supported Mohamed Sahnoun's efforts there more thoroughly. As he wrote, the world wasted a year while the Somali situation "descended into hell." [8] The United States should have disarmed the Somalis immediately after it invaded, and the UN should have had the will to do so even earlier.

Disarmament and demobilization are critical in situations like those that prevailed in Somalia in 1993. Disarming militias and warlord forces has a symbolic as well as an actual function. But both disarmament and demobilization help create an atmosphere of security. In anomic crises like those in Somalia, the United States must create disincentives for insecurity.

It is important to provide positive, not negative, reinforcement. But for the competing warlords the United States did the reverse: Having failed to disarm the competing factions in Somalia, U.S. forces compounded the error by telegraphing their departure and creating a dozen other reinforcements for negative behavior. Making peace was thus not in the self-interest of the competing clans and subclans. Security was absent, and without security, attempts at reconciliation were premature and unproductive.

Leaving a job half done greatly diminishes the relevance and the overriding lessons of a successful effort, as in Desert Storm, Restore Hope, and Haiti. We should not talk tough without meaning it. Admittedly, our leaders must fully comprehend the core goals of their actions.

As anachronistic as it may seem, we need to consider finding ways to recommit countries (like Somalia) to the good offices of the UN Trusteeship Council. The term "tutelage" might be employed to describe temporary custodial care by the UN of states that have either in fact or in effect given up their nationhood and sovereignty. Somalis themselves might, at the appropriate moment, have welcomed such temporary recommitment to the UN. There was a time when such a commitment was appropriate for Rwanda, too. Training or retraining in the arts of civil administration, re-creating justice systems and national police forces, and much more could occur effectively under Trusteeship Council control.

The United States must reconceptualize its national self-interest. The peace of the world, the reduction of ethnic and religious hostilities, and the effectiveness of the

UN in contributing to a diminution of global combat depend in large measure upon whether U.S. leaders are capable of articulating a new definition of the national self-interest that emphasizes humanitarian core values and elevates the freedom of peoples around the globe to the same heights that containing communism once reached. The political values, moral stature, and domestic tranquillity of the lone global superpower are genuinely threatened by strife and killing fields wherever they occur—even well beyond the usual geographical spheres of U.S. concern. Intrastate conflicts, massacres, and episodes of genocide will continue unabated and will ultimately compel U.S. engagement, as they have done in the recent past.

Given the Know-Nothingism of the 104th Congress and the domestic climate of opinion that congressional leadership has aroused and to some extent represents, redefining the national interest in this manner will prove difficult, if not improbable. The missteps, indecision, and confusion of U.S. foreign policy in recent years has hardly prepared Washington or the American people for such a redefinition, no matter how necessary and timely.

It is now much harder than it was a few years ago for Washington to recognize, let alone uphold, its responsibilities to the peoples of the world and thus to its own citizens. In an earlier era, those responsibilities would have been considered on their merits, and debated. Now, whether it is the fault of back-door isolationists or vacillating leaders, the United States seems much more prepared to abdicate than to assume the arbitrating authority of a mature superpower.

The U.S. national interest has been defined as preserving the American way of life as a nation. If that concept is extended, it can easily encompass a concern for humanitarian values—for helping others help themselves to achieve better standards of living, human rights, basic liberties, and perhaps even participatory government. The United States should be a nation that "promotes democratic values."[9]

Some argue forcefully that there is no generic national interest that includes the promotion of fundamental human rights elsewhere. They say that the "well being of the United States is not affected by such occurrences as human rights violations and deaths in Rwanda." They go on to assert that liberty in the United States is not threatened by, say, the fall of a democracy like Peru, but that it would be jeopardized by the collapse of a European democracy.[10]

Congress exhibits a similar tunnel vision; its efforts to limit U.S. contributions to the UN, to dismantle and diminish foreign assistance, especially to the world's poorest countries, and to gut international professional and student exchanges such as the Fulbright program all reflect the proposition that the United States no longer needs to play a leading role in world affairs. Such arguments are reminiscent of the attacks on President Wilson and the League of Nations.

The United States no longer has the luxury of retreating from the world or choosing an involvement in Russia, Israel, or India over involvements elsewhere. The global village has become a reality, just as planetary warming and cross-national pollution affect us irrespective of our geographical locations. Communications are indeed instantaneous. Mass killings anywhere hit much closer to home. Genocide in Burundi does impinge upon Americans' enjoyment of their freedoms just as the abridgment of human rights in Burma threatens their assertion of the universality of core moral values. Both the morality and the stability of the United States as a nation are less than fully assured when vast numbers of people around the globe are malnourished, dying from AIDS and malaria, poorly educated, and unfree.

Just as we have a national interest in reducing the cascade of conventional as well as nuclear arms, so do we have a national interest in developing poorer countries. Indeed, higher economic growth in developing countries positively benefits the residents of today's rich countries as well as enhances the spread of democratic tendencies throughout the world.[11] It makes sense, said Brian Atwood, USAID head, "to invest in development and treat the root causes of instability before a situation becomes chaotic."[12] Chaos and anarchy abroad encourage chaos and anarchy at home.

Giving priority to such seemingly soft interests alongside our more easily conceptualized, more traditional, national interests may well seem naive. The destruction of nuclear weapons and the prevention of nuclear proliferation; the integrity of Europe, Japan, and Israel; the growth and progress of the transitional states; free trade; and an improved environment all should be appreciated as significant national interests. In today's world reducing conflict beyond U.S. borders and enhancing the peace of the planet has become no less a fundamental national interest. "Just as it cannot be U.S. policy to protect oil supplies but ignore genocide, it cannot be U.S. policy to protect Kurds but ignore Tutsis."[13]

Improving the world has never before been so important. Heeding such imperatives will not be easy in the current U.S. domestic climate. Indeed, doing so will be impossible without dedicated and extraordinary leadership.

The world will become more governable, and the United States more secure, only when its response to severe strife and mass instability in at least the developing world is perceived to be swift and certain. Among the key reasons for the interventions in Kuwait, Haiti, and Somalia was that intervention would prevent threats to democratic stirrings elsewhere. The complete failure to pacify Iraq and to disarm and reunite Somalia and the muddled hesitancy over Haiti have cost the United States more in terms of global disruptions and economic turmoil than would have the demonstration effect of completed missions. In those operations, especially in Somalia, the United States also lost considerable moral stature.

Ethnically and religiously inspired turmoil will not vanish. We may even find ourselves back in Somalia. Burundi's problems are becoming more desperate by the hour. Sierra Leone and Liberia remain chaotic. Nigeria, with more than 100 million people, and Zaire, long ago eroded from within, may both soon explode. What then? Can the world's only superpower afford to do nothing? Should the United States not prepare itself by accepting its role as the world's last barrier to the spread of anomie and chaos?

If U.S. policymakers refuse to take to heart the true lessons of Somalia and of recurring ethnic, religious, and intercommunal conflicts, the world (and the UN) will remain the poorer for their failures. If the United States leads hesitantly or refuses to lead at all, the peoples of the world will continue to suffer, and so will the compelling American national interest in a peaceful and stable global order. It is not in the U.S. self-interest to have democratic movements submerged, peoples imprisoned by their own leaders, minorities and majorities oppressed, and freedom imperiled. Ultimately, each crisis ignored leads to crises that affect the United States or its partners more directly.

The major lessons of Operation Restore Hope are active rather than passive. Acting responsibly, decisively, and early—and completing the mission—should be the watchwords of our restored policies for the later 1990s and beyond.

Notes

1. Anthony Lake, quoted in *New York Times*, April 28, 1995.

2. Stanley Hoffmann, "The Crisis of Liberal Internationalism," *Foreign Policy* 98, 1995, p. 173.

3. Quoted in Wayne S. Cole, *An Interpretive History of American Foreign Relations* (Homewood, IL: 1974), p. 254.

4. See Robert I. Rotberg, *Haiti: The Politics of Squalor* (Boston: Houghton Mifflin, 1971), pp. 105–116.

5. Ernest May, "The Nature of Foreign Policy: The Calculated Versus the Axiomatic," *Daedalus* 91(4), 1962, pp. 653–667.

6. Chester A. Crocker, "The Lessons of Somalia: Not Everything Went Wrong," *Foreign Affairs* 74, May-June 1995, p. 6.

7. Thomas Weiss, "Overcoming the Somalia Syndrome—'Operation Rekindle Hope'?" *Global Governance* 1, 1995, pp. 172, 179–181.

8. Mohamed Sahnoun, *Somalia: The Missed Opportunities* (Washington, DC: U.S. Institute of Peace, 1994), pp. 5–10, 28–37. See also Crocker, "Lessons of Somalia," p. 6.

9. Philip Zelikow, "Traditional Geostrategic Interests," session 2 of the Council on Foreign Relations Boston National Interest Study Group meeting, April 15, 1995.

10. Richard H. Ullmann, "National Interest and Human Rights: Democratic Enlargement and Humanitarian Assistance," summary of the Council on Foreign Relations New York City National Interest Working Group meeting, March 2, 1995.

11. This is the conclusion of a sophisticated paper by Richard N. Cooper, "Is Growth in Developing Countries Beneficial to Developed Countries?" in Michael Bruno and Boris Pleskovic, eds., *Annual World Bank Conference on Development Economics, 1995* (Washington, DC: World Bank, 1996), pp. 249–283.

12. Brian Atwood, quoted in *Financial Gazette* (Harare), July 13, 1995.

13. Crocker, "Lessons of Somalia," p. 8.

14

Somalia and the Future of Humanitarian Intervention

WALTER CLARKE
AND
JEFFREY HERBST

The U.S.-led operation in Somalia that began when U.S. Marines hit the Mogadishu beaches in December 1992 continues to have a profound effect on the debate over the future of humanitarian intervention. The Clinton administration's refusal to respond to genocide in Rwanda, beginning in April 1994, was due in part to its retreat from Somalia, announced after the deaths of eighteen U.S. Rangers on October 3, 1993.

Even more important, the Somalia operations have had a profound effect on the doctrine of both the United States and the United Nations. Presidential Decision Directive 25, issued in April 1994 shortly after the United States left Somalia, sharply curtails the possibility of future armed humanitarian interventions and marks a retreat from the early Clinton administration's rhetoric on assertive multilateralism. The current efforts in Congress, notably bills to sharply restrict U.S. contributions to UN peacekeeping efforts, are also a direct response to the perceived failures in Somalia. Finally, the 1995 (second) edition of *An Agenda for Peace*, the fundamental document on UN peacekeeping written by Secretary-General Boutros Boutros-Ghali, is less optimistic about the possibilities for intervention than the 1992 (first) edition of the same document, in large part because of the UN's searing experience in Somalia.[1]

Whereas the Somalia case should be of considerable importance in setting precedent for interventions in the post–Cold War world, it is not clear that the right lessons have been learned. Much of the received wisdom on Somalia is based on patently incorrect information that was hurriedly transmitted during the press of events. There has also been a substantial effort on the part of some individuals and governments to reinterpret the Somalia interventions in order to protect their own interests.

The Nature of the Mission

The most commonly heard charge about the Somalia intervention is that the mission changed. The general argument is that the extremely limited U.S.-led intervention (known as UNITAF—the United Task Force) initiated to feed people by President Bush in December 1992 was a success. However, it is said, the operation floundered when the UN took over in May 1993, initiated what became known as UNOSOM II (the second UN Operation Somalia), and greatly expanded the mission to include rebuilding basic state institutions and "nation-building." For instance, former assistant secretary of state Chester Crocker argues that a major discontinuity between the U.S. and UN missions in Somalia was the adoption of a "sweepingly ambitious new 'nation-building' resolution by the Security Council (Resolution 814, March 1993)."[2] Similarly, John Hirsch and Robert Oakley argue in their book that the mission changed between UNITAF and UNOSOM II but the United Nations had neither the assets nor the doctrine to execute a more "prescriptive, broader set of policies."[3] The *New York Times* spoke for many editorial pages when it lamented that "the nature of the mission changed dramatically in June [1993], right after Washington turned control over to the UN."[4]

In good part because of the perception that the mission had changed, that the United Nations had tried to take on more than it could control, many commentators have argued for a strict division between humanitarian intervention to feed people and nation building. For instance, Richard Hass distinguishes between humanitarian intervention ("providing protection and other basic needs"), nation building ("recasting the institutions of the society"), and peacemaking and argues that humanitarian intervention is much less complex than nation building. He suggests that in Somalia the mission changed from humanitarian intervention to nation building because "policymakers got ambitious."[5]

The reasons for the emphasis on the shift in the nature of the mission are complex. Certainly, the images of U.S. troops pursuing General Aideed while fighting hostile Somalis in August 1993 were jarring to an American public that had, a few months before, seen pictures of American soldiers providing food to grateful, emaciated people. The disastrous firefight on October 3–4, 1993, prompted many, particularly in the Clinton administration, to try to distance themselves from the deaths of American soldiers by blaming the UN. For instance, President Clinton, when meeting with families of the dead Rangers, tried to separate the US from the UN mission by saying that he was surprised that the United Nations was still pursuing General Aideed.[6] Working from President Clinton's statements, some members of Congress have tried to blame the entire October 3 debacle on the UN, saying it was the result of U.S. troops being under foreign command. For instance, Senator Mitch McConnell, now chair of the Foreign Operations Subcommittee of the Senate Appropriations Committee, wrote an op-ed article soon after the

October 1993 battle, arguing that American lives were lost because "we surrendered our interests and leadership to the United Nations." Senator McConnell further noted that President Clinton, after the October battle, "re-established US command over US soldiers."[7]

More generally, many commentators who recognize the enormous positive results of the Somalia intervention, most notably the fact that perhaps 100,000 people were saved from starvation, have tended to stress the problem of the mission changing as a way to salvage some good from what is now popularly seen as a disastrous foray into a foreign country. Finally, bureaucratic and turf fights have heightened the desire on the part of some to claim that there was a fundamental change from the successful UNITAF intervention to the disastrous UN operation. For instance, the U.S. Marines were largely associated with the UNITAF operation; the U.S. Army supplied most of the assets to the UN operation.

The truth about the nature of the Somalia mission, and how much it did change, is much more complicated. At the factual level, it is simply false, as some have charged and President Clinton has implied, that U.S. troops, including the Rangers involved in the October 3 firefight, were under UN command. Those troops were formally outside the UN command structure. They were commanded by Major General William Garrison, a U.S. Special Forces officer temporarily stationed in Mogadishu who in turn reported directly to Central Command in Florida. The various operations in search of General Aideed, including the operation that led to the eighteen Ranger deaths on October 3, were individually approved by the national command authorities of the United States.

Also, although the United States did hand over formal control of the operation in May 1993, it still determined the nature of the operation. At a personal level, Admiral Jonathan Howe, who had been deputy national security adviser in the Bush administration, was named the secretary-general's special representative to Somalia and therefore took charge of the operation. At the doctrinal level, it is simply not true that the UN greatly broadened the mission that the United States had decided to limit. In fact, all of the major Security Council resolutions on Somalia, including Resolution 814, the "nation-building" resolution, were written by the United States, mainly in the Pentagon, and handed to the UN as a fait accompli. It was only after the October 3 firefight that the United States tried to wash its hands of an operation that it had initiated and then directed almost in its entirety. As one international civil servant noted to us, the UN had been seduced and then abandoned by the United States.

Finally, the distinction between humanitarian intervention and nation building that is critical to so much of the critique of the Somalia operation, and of intervention in general, is extremely problematic. The implication of those who support only humanitarian intervention—in Somalia or elsewhere—is that somehow people were starving because of an act of nature. In fact, the famine that gripped Somalia in 1992 was fundamentally the result of how the country's political economy had evolved. As Andrew Natsios, the former deputy director of the U.S. Agency for International Development during the Somalia relief operations, has noted, "Food imported through the relief effort became an enormously attractive objective of plunder by merchants, by common working people without a source of income, by organized gangs of young men, and by militia leaders in need of the wealth represented by food aid which they would use to purchase more weapons and keep the loyalty of their followers."[8] Indeed, Natsios notes, "Merchants would actually request the local militia or bands of thieves to steal more food as their stocks diminished each day."[9] Basically, the entire country revolved around the plunder of food.

When U.S. troops intervened in December 1992 to stop the theft of food, they immediately disrupted the entire political economy of Somalia. Therefore, the United States immediately stepped deeply into the muck of Somali politics because the most fundamental institution in any country is order. By supplying some aspects of order, the United States inevitably became involved in providing the basic framework for future Somali politics and was therefore doing . . . nation building. Although analytically attractive, the distinction between the different types of intervention, at the heart of so much of the current debate, is not particularly helpful. Indeed, at a practical level, it is hard to see how anyone could believe that landing 30,000 troops in a country was anything but a gross interference in major aspects of a country's politics.

Much of what went wrong in the Somalia operations can be traced to the Bush and early Clinton administrations' schizophrenia when confronted with the fact that any intervention would deeply involve the United States in Somali politics. At one level, the Bush administration did recognize just how profoundly it was going to intervene in Somalia. For those who claim that the UN later changed the mission, it is useful to remember President Bush's words when he announced the American intervention (December 4, 1992): "Our mission is humanitarian, but we will not tolerate armed gangs ripping off their own people, condemning them to death by starvation. General [William] Hoar and his troops have the authority to take whatever military action is necessary to safeguard the lives of our troops and the lives of Somalia's people."[10] President Bush then stated, "The outlaw elements in Somalia must understand this is serious business." However, the Bush administration refused to acknowledge the extent of its intervention for several reasons. First, President Bush wanted to get the troops out quickly, perhaps by the time Bill Clinton was inaugurated on January 20. Second, General Colin Powell and his doctrine of overwhelming force for limited missions so dominated both administrations that it was impossible for a different vision of the U.S. mission to be enunciated.

It was not the case that the United States intervened smartly in a limited humanitarian mission while the UN bumbled because it chose to do nation building. Rather, the two missions differed fundamentally because U.S. leadership simply ducked the problems that logically followed from the decision to intervene and then get out of Somalia as quickly as possible. The UN was then left to confront the problems raised by the American intervention and inevitably found the going to be quite rough. The UN had to explicitly address the issue of the ordering of Somali society because no one, including the United States, would have been happy if the status quo that existed before the marines landed was quickly allowed to reappear. Thus, an understanding of what the problem actually was in Somalia leads to an immediate appreciation that simply stopping the warlords from stealing food for a few weeks was hardly an adequate solution.

Nowhere were the problems caused by the U.S. refusal to face up to the implications of its decision to intervene greater than in the area of disarmament. The United States had the greatest amount of military assets on the ground when the roughly 30,000 troops landed in December 1992 and therefore the greatest capability to disarm the belligerent forces. However, the United States said to the warlords that they could keep their weapons as long as they were moved out of the city limits or placed in special cantonment areas controlled by warlord troops. Although Ambassador Robert Oakley is correct that Mogadishu could no more be disarmed than areas in Western countries,[11] it is also true that heavy weapons mounted on vehicles (the much-feared "technicals") do not patrol the streets of U.S. cities; nor do people in even gun-saturated America openly parade around with light-caliber machine guns. A concentrated effort to remove and destroy the heavy arms present would have been possible and would have sent a very strong message at the beginning of the operation that the United States and the UN were serious about restoring order. Indeed, in the March 1993 Addis Ababa accords, all of the Somali factions had agreed to disarm. Thus, the United States could have argued that as an impartial force, it was only helping enforce what the Somali's themselves had decided upon. Indeed, many Somalis fully expected to be disarmed and were surprised at the lack of action on the part of the U.S.-led forces.[12]

Failure to confront the warlords immediately meant that the massive U.S. force, assisted by elite troops including the French Foreign Legion, Belgian Para Commandos, and Italian paratroopers, did little to change the military situation on the ground. For instance, the Belgian force commander in Kismayu, following his extremely limited mandate, allowed ten technical vehicles to disappear into the bush despite the fact that he had them in his sights for five days.[13] The warlords, always acutely sensitive to the correlation of forces, quickly understood that their fundamental power was not being challenged. They therefore could wait until the United States and allied units left and then challenge a UN force that would inevitably be less well armed and with a more complicated command-and-control structure. Indeed, one of the fundamental mistakes in attributing success to the United States and failure to the UN is that the American forces made it so clear that they would not challenge the warlords and that they would be in Somalia for such a short period of time that it was in the interests of the warlords not to hinder the Americans and to speed their departure.

Indeed, the U.S. did quickly draw down its forces, to be replaced by far less well trained and well armed soldiers from a multitude of countries, and the UN was left to confront warlords who were better armed than some of its soldiers. For instance, in May 1993, as the UN was taking over, the Australians and the Canadians, two of the most capable forces, were scheduled to leave with no relief in sight. Indeed, Australian vehicles had already come in from the countryside and were being cleaned for shipment back home. At the same time, the Pakistanis, who were supposed to assume the policing of southern Mogadishu from the U.S. Marines were just starting to arrive as the Americans departed. Most of their vehicles were still on the high seas and, somewhat pathetically, they did not even have the flak jackets that had become standard fashion in the neighborhood they were supposed to stabilize.[14]

However, at the same time that the force was being decreased, there was an increasing appreciation for the need for disarmament in Washington. In a speech given by Secretary of Defense Les Aspin on August 27, 1993, the United States formally acknowledged that significant disarmament of the clans was necessary.[15] However, at that point the 30,000-troop expeditionary force was gone, and only the 1,200-member quick-response force, composed of certain units of the U.S. Army's elite 10th Mountain Division, remained in Somalia. This lightly armed and highly specialized force was not appropriate for the task of disarmament. However, continuing the inability to the United States to match means with ends, Secretary Aspin also denied U.S. force commander Major General Thomas Montgomery's request for tanks that might have helped the forces on the ground better confront the warlords. The administration feared a sharp congressional reaction to the increased U.S. firepower. Indeed, the central irony of the operations in Somalia is that as the military assets were being decreased, the UN was faced with ever more demanding tasks in implementing the U.S.-planned operation.

The asymmetry between U.S. forces and operational goals became complete after October 3 when President Clinton finally sent the military assets (notably gunships and tanks) that the military commanders had previously requested but had been refused. However, the U.S. forces then adopted a purely defensive force-protection mode, unilaterally ended the hunt for Aideed, and bunkered down until just before the March 31, 1994, deadline that President Clinton placed on U.S. involvement in Somalia. The UN was left high and dry to pursue sharply limited aspects of the nation-building program the U.S. government had designed for it fifteen months earlier.

There were many other examples of where the United States, once it had committed itself to deeply intervening in the domestic politics of Somalia in December 1992, did not allocate the correct resources so that it could implement a sensible policy. For instance, the initial plans for Operation Restore Hope included the activation of eight to ten reserve civil affairs units (about 250–300 personnel) to help restore the government, especially to perform the critical tasks of rebuilding the police and judiciary. However, activation of these units was opposed by the Joints Chiefs of Staff because the operation was supposed to last only six weeks.[16] In addition, the marines, who had lead responsibility during the early months of the intervention, have extremely weak civil affairs capacity in comparison to the U.S. Army, and there was great reluctance in Central Command, led at that time by Marine Corps General Hoar, to risk any political action in Somalia. In the end, only three dozen civil affairs specialists were sent to Somalia. In contrast,

1,000 civil affairs specialists were committed to Kuwait City *after* the Iraqis had been expelled and that city was at peace. Money and attention was devoted by the United States to rebuilding the Somali police force only after the October 3 battle, but by then it was too late.

Similarly, there was essentially no development aid or expertise available during the Somalia operations beyond that which went to feeding hungry people. The failure to fund significant development or infrastructure programs led one senior disaster relief specialist to conclude that there was no connection between relief and development in Somalia.[17] For instance, disaster relief specialists were forced to write an economic recovery program for Somalia—a task well outside of their expertise—because there was no one else available. As a result, one of the few direct economic effects of UNITAF was to increase the already large demand for armed guards. Given that so much of the economy revolved around the plunder of food, the failure to develop plans that would move the economy back to a more normal situation was a particularly grievous error and emblematic of the failure of the mission to address anything other than short-term exigencies.

It is interesting that, in contrast to the conventional wisdom that humanitarian intervention with no nation-building component is more appropriate, the Haiti intervention actually demonstrates that some lessons were learned in Somalia. In contrast to Somalia (and also to Rwanda), the Clinton administration managed to find $500 million for development assistance that, among other things, employed thousands of Haitians cleaning the streets. Also, a significant number of civil affairs officers were sent to Haiti, and attention was given to rebuilding the police and justice systems.

The illusion that where people are dying in large numbers because of civilian conflict there can be a type of intervention that does not immediately interfere with the domestic politics of a country and include a "nation-building" component should be discarded. Where famine is man-made, stopping the famine means rebuilding political institutions to create order. Successful operations will recognize that no intervention in a situation such as Somalia can succeed in a few weeks and that substantial attention must be devoted to the rebuilding of institutions whose collapse led to the disaster in the first place. A critical lesson many in the Pentagon learned in Vietnam was that overwhelming resources must be marshaled when addressing a problem. Perhaps there is an analog for the much more important civilian side: Unless development aid and assistance are marshaled in a manner that recognizes the long-term political and economic implications of intervention, the mission has little chance of success. Also, as the military has come to understand, the entire nature of the operation must be spelled out in advance in order to generate and retain public support. One of the reasons that the public and congressional reaction was so quick and virulent after the October battle was that the Clinton administration appears not to have focused on the deteriorating situation on the ground in Somalia after it took office in January 1993 and attached no importance to explaining the nature of the continuing mission in Somalia.

The understanding that humanitarian intervention almost inevitably means interference in domestic politics and institution building is not only important analytically but also has implications for force structures. For instance, in the U.S. military, only 3 percent of current civil affairs soldiers are on active duty; the remainder are in the reserves.[18] It is very difficult for military authorities to call up these units because they tend to be composed of lawyers, small-town mayors, police officers, and others who cannot be repeatedly activated without disruption. A force with the capability to intervene for humanitarian purposes would be helped by a larger active-duty civil affairs contingent.

Promoting Reconciliation and Relations with "Warlords"

A critical issue in any intervention in a strife-torn area is how to promote reconciliation and relate to those who have the arms. This issue is particularly difficult because promoting long-term reconciliation may mean empowering those who are not armed, whereas short-term exigencies will inevitably require coming to some kind of modus operandi with the warlords. This problem has, somewhat simplistically, been cast in terms of promoting reconciliation from the bottom up or from the top down. In fact, actual reconciliation is always a much more complex process involving not only local dispute settlements, which may boil up to the national level, but also the agreement on the part of the major combatants that the civil strife they have perpetuated should finally be stopped.

In Somalia, there was no explicit vision of how reconciliation should proceed. The United States formally envisioned its mission as being short and limited to opening supply lines so that it would not have to become involved in Somali politics. Nor did the UN have a clear roadmap as to how reconciliation was to occur. However, there was the desire on the part of both the United States and the UN to stay neutral in the midst of the combatants. The U.S. experience in Lebanon, where the U.S. role evolved quickly from mediator to fighter with ultimately disastrous results, obviously was an important influence, especially for the marines, who commanded the operation. For the UN, the precept of neutrality had been a hallmark of peacekeeping activities that had been a central function of the world organization for decades. Indeed, a central aspect of the critique of the Somali operations was that the UN lost its neutrality when it began to pursue General Aideed after his forces had killed twenty-four Pakistani soldiers on June 5, 1993.

However, although formally neutral by acts of both commission and omission, the United States and the UN ended up not successfully promoting reconciliation but, instead, enhancing the roles and status of the warlords. Most important, the failure to disarm the major combatants meant that, quite literally, those with the most weapons still had the most power. Symbolically, the failure to disarm signaled the entire population that neither the United States nor the UN was willing to change the balance of power in Somalia. As Keith Richburg, the former East Africa correspondent for the *Washington Post* noted, "The non-confrontational, diplomatic track accorded the warlords a certain legitimacy, making them responsible for controlling their factions and feeding into their own egotistical view that they represented a kind of de facto 'government' in the areas they controlled. That may have served well the goal of avoiding American casualties during the US-led phase of the intervention, but that strategy later made it far more difficult for the United Nations to try (as it did, with U.S. backing) to 'squeeze' the warlords, marginalize their influence, or cut them out of Somalia's future political equation."[19] Richburg goes on to note that Admiral Howe and U.S. Ambassador Robert Gosende tried to reduce the warlords' influence but that their credibility was largely undercut by the good relations their predecessors had established with General Aideed in particular. Of course, when U.S. Ambassador Robert Oakley returned to Somalia after the October battle to secure the release of a captured Ranger, he again made peace with General Aideed and went so far as to provide the warlord with air transport to a conference. At that point, it was reaffirmed to everyone in Somalia that the warlords would be rewarded, rather than punished, for continuing their old ways.

More generally, the short time frame associated with U.S. involvement meant that it was very difficult for the United States to take many credible steps to promote reconciliation. After years of fighting a civil war, the combatants were somehow expected to resolve their differences in a few months. It was more or less inevitable that in this short period of time groups who were not prominent because they did not control large stocks of weaponry could not come to power. It clearly would have taken a much different time frame to cultivate precisely those elements of Somali society who had to disappear during the long years of warfare. The emphasis on neutrality also served as an important obstacle in any effort to promote the kind of wholesale restructuring of Somali society required if the warlords were to become less powerful.

Also, there was a failure to understand who the victims were in Somalia. Collapsed states like Somalia are often pictured as reverting to a Hobbesian state of nature where there is a battle of all versus all. The reality is more complicated. Certainly, part of the problem in Somalia was the failure of any one clan to win out in the military struggle following the ouster of President Siad Barre in 1991. However, mortality was most concentrated among the Bantu and Benadir peoples, sedentary coastal groups who traditionally live an uneasy coexistence with neighboring ethnic Somali groups, and among the Ranhanweyn clan, who work the rich agricultural land in the Jubba and Shabelle river valleys in the South and who were the weakest from a military perspective. Indeed, much of what appears to be incomprehensible warfare in Somalia is a struggle for land between the clan-based nomadic groups in the North, who are better armed, and the African farmers in the South.[20]

The illusion of neutrality was finally swept aside when General Aideed's forces ambushed the Pakistani soldiers on June 5, 1993. The battle between General Aideed's forces and the UN quickly ratcheted up. Soon there was a price on Aideed's head, the secretary-general was talking approvingly of his "physical elimination," and the U.S. soldiers (whose presence was designed as a backup to UN forces in the event they fell afoul of the warlord militias) undertook the increasingly violent operations to catch Aideed and incapacitate his movement that would end in the October 3 firefight. In retrospect, it is easy to claim that the hunt for Aideed was a mistake. However, what should have been the UN response to the massacre of Pakistani troops is a complicated issue. The issue at hand was how an attack on international forces themselves as opposed to continued attacks among Somalis (which, despite President Bush's rhetoric, were not interfered with) should be met. The precept of neutrality and noninterference in internal affairs—developed for peacekeeping operations where the UN usually arrived after the fighting was over and where no one had any real incentive to target the "blue helmets"— was of little use. In addition, there was the very practical consideration that around the world there were thousands of peacekeepers who were in potentially vulnerable situations. Failure to act against a direct attack in Somalia, the Clinton administration felt, would put these other forces in jeopardy. Further, there was the understanding that, especially given Somali culture, such a direct attack had to be met with some kind of response. Indeed, the experience of the UN in Bosnia, where the Serbs have attacked peacekeepers with impunity, shows the dangers of allowing peacemaking forces to lose their credibility among the local populations because they are unwilling to fight.

Certainly, the hunt for Aideed was a mistake if the United States and the UN believed that Somali society could more or less instantly reconstruct itself. The policy was simply too contradictory. It made little sense to hunt down Aideed if the international force was unwilling to confront the nature of the warlords. Indeed, without a long-term policy of confronting the entire power structure of the warlords, even capturing Aideed may not have contributed significantly toward solving the problem. Here U.S. and UN officials in Mogadishu were not guilty of expanding the initial mission but of not understanding that the mission had been so sharply curtailed in the initial months of implementation that any action to significantly alter the power balances in Somali society was not viable.

A policy stance that would have allowed forces other than the warlords to emerge and that would have fundamentally changed the power balances in Somali society would have begun with a much longer time frame. Somalia reached its nadir through a process that took years, and it therefore does not seem unreasonable that it might take years for it to undergo a fundamental reconstruction. In a comprehensive survey of the reconciliation attempts, Professor Ken Menkhaus found that regional reconciliation efforts generally worked better than the efforts at national reconciliation. However, these efforts took months and succeeded only when substantial efforts were made over a long period of time to implement the initial accords.[21] If peace had broken out in Somalia by region, the process would had to have been husbanded for a significant period of time.

Unfortunately, the international community currently lacks the tools to address such a long-term problem of political reconstruction in a country that does not have a government. Indeed, the UN since 1945 has basically been a decolonization machine: Its primary purpose has been to proclaim as quickly as possible that every country is able to rule itself. The idea that Somalia was not able to rule itself and could not for a long period of time went so much against the organizational grain of the UN that a conceptual approach that would have allowed for long-term reconstruction was never considered. For instance, although it was obvious when U.S. troops hit the beaches that the country was essentially being taken over, no one seriously considered trusteeship or any other legal concept other than continuing the fiction that Somalia was still a sovereign state. Instead, the United States and the UN needed to pretend that Somalia could begin to govern itself quickly, and that pretense almost automatically led it to cooperate explicitly and implicitly with the warlords. For instance, Omar Arteh, a former Somali prime minister now residing in Saudi Arabia, actually proposed the resolution on intervention to the Security Council so that the UN could pretend that the Somali state was asking for the intervention. When some steps were taken later in the operation, mainly by the UN, to try to develop a broader process of reconciliation, it was simply too late.

Much was made of the fact that when the Somalia operation began, it was the UN's first attempt at peacemaking or peace enforcement. However, the posture of the force and the initial policy decisions were curiously at odds with the mission of making peace. Indeed, surprisingly little energy seems to have been devoted to the concepts actually needed to make peace or the processes that would lead to the end of armed violence. Instead, the United States and the UN seem to have been left with the hope that the warlords would somehow become peacelords. It was never explained why the warlords would perceive that it was in their interest to do so, and given that their power resided in their control of private armies that would necessarily be dismantled by any viable state, it was hard to believe that peace was going to be gained by dealing with the hard men with guns.

The U.S.-UN Relationship

It is patently clear that the UN did not have the resources or the ability to do the job that was drawn up by the United States. Indeed, UN officials desperately pleaded with the United States to stay, given that its large and well-trained force was likely to be replaced by a less capable force. However, the United States was exceptionally eager to leave. Indeed, U.S. officials announced that they were ready to leave as early as January 1993 despite the fact that little, if anything, had changed on the ground other than that the warlords had temporarily lost control of the main channels of communication in southern Somalia. Eventually, the United States agreed to stay until May, although even the transition at that time was purely cosmetic. The UNITAF command had steadily but assuredly diminished its force presence throughout March and April, and by May 4, the remaining UNITAF force was able to ride to the airport in the back of one army truck.

The particular errors that the UN made have already been chronicled at some length. It was slow in making appointments; it did not appoint very qualified people;

its bureaucracy was cumbersome when making most decisions, especially compared to the decisive U.S. Marines; and it sometimes made extremely poor decisions, as when it delayed in helping to recreate the Somali police force because it preferred to have a government in place first. Some of these errors may be correctable within current UN structures, and attention should quickly be given to better procedures. Certainly, it is the case that few can go wrong by arguing that the UN should improve its procedures.

However, realistically the UN simply is not designed to take over a task as big as Somalia. As noted previously, it is a decolonization machine, not a peacemaking outfit, and it is therefore unclear that even maximum efficiency and perfect policymaking would have enabled it to carry out successful reconciliation in Somalia. Of course, with the United States, the organization's largest single contributor, threatening to reduce its fees on a number of fronts, it is unclear that the UN can build its capabilities to successfully intervene in the near future.

There was a widespread appreciation that the end of the Cold War would finally, after decades of gridlock induced by superpower vetoes, enable the United Nations to move forward. Somalia is the most obvious case to date of the world organization taking on new duties in order to build the new world order. However, most noticeable in retrospect is how little the UN's capabilities have actually changed in response to these new challenges. Much of the blame can be lodged with the UN bureaucracy itself, which simply must be reformed. However, the UN's major donors must also take responsibility for providing neither the financial nor intellectual leadership necessary to allow the UN to move, as an organization, toward accomplishing these new tasks.

It may not be, especially given the current climate in the U.S. Congress, that the world's powers are willing to have a revitalized UN available to facilitate the new world order that President Bush envisioned a few years ago. That would be an unfortunate decision but one that would at least allow for rational policy planning. Certainly, what happened in Somalia is unacceptable: A weak UN was assigned an enormous task and then forced to take full control of the operation before it was even minimally ready.

The implications of not creating a stronger UN must be made clear. There will undoubtedly be more Somalias as the fiction that all the countries that were so recently under colonial rule can quickly establish durable institutions becomes ever more apparent. By not building up the UN, world leaders and the United States in particular will be making the explicit decision that the pictures of suffering and starvation that so moved the American people and President Bush in November 1992 will, in the future, be tolerated. To not admit that the alternative to building stronger and more appropriate international institutions is starvation and suffering of millions of people would be dishonest. Indeed, a preview of the future toleration of disorder occurred in Rwanda in April 1994 when, still paralyzed by the outcome of Somalia, the world did nothing as the Hutu government slaughtered upward of 500,000 Tutsis.

The Future of Intervention

Given the isolationist currents within the U.S. Congress, it may seem strange now to speculate about the future of intervention. However, the pendulum is bound to swing back, especially because the American public and its leaders show little appetite for a future where large numbers of tragedies, publicly televised, occur while the world does nothing. Indeed, opinion polls consistently suggest that there is more support for peacekeeping operations than is commonly acknowledged in Congress.[22] Also, other countries may intervene from time to time in order to promote humanitarian objectives (as France did in Rwanda). Finally, the UN may not always be hobbled by the legacy of Somalia and may some day again aspire to play the kind of role in the new world order that it began to sketch out in the early 1990's.

Three major lessons can be drawn from this discussion of the Somalia experience. First, there must be a much clearer understanding of what is implied by humanitarian intervention. As noted previously, a fundamental problem with the Somalia operations was that although the United States knew that the warlords were fundamentally responsible for the widespread diversion of food, it did not acknowledge that its intervention would immediately thrust it deep into Somali politics. Future policymakers must understand that there is no such thing as a humanitarian surgical strike. Accordingly, the time frames for interventions must be adjusted. The American idea that Somalia would be "fixed" in a few weeks was so at odds with even President Bush's description of the problem that it was obvious from the beginning that there was not the will to see the solution through. Future operations must be grounded in the understanding that there will be no quick answers.

The second area that needs considerable development is in the conceptual understanding of a failed state. The UN, being a collection of governments, went through a fictional process in order to pretend that Somalia still existed as a state. The imperative to relate to a government inevitably drove the United States and the UN into the hands of the warlords because they were the closest thing to organized power centers in the country. The awkwardness of intervening in a country still formerly viewed as sovereign also contributed to the undue urgency so many parties felt in wanting to leave Somalia quickly, even though it was obvious that the operation required a long time horizon.

Understandably, there is a considerable reluctance to term nations trusteeships—about the only option that the United Nations has—given that term's close association with colonialism. Some new concept will have to be developed that expresses the idea that a state's fundamental institutions have so deteriorated that it needs external long-term help, predicated not to institutionalize foreign control but to create stronger domestic institutions. The development of an international political equivalent to U.S. bankruptcy law is not merely an arcane task for international lawyers. Rather, the development of a clear roadmap as to what happens to a

failed state and the relationship of that state to the international community is absolutely essential if the mistakes of Somalia are not to be repeated.

Third, the proper forces must be developed in order to intervene. There has
been much talk, although little action, of a UN army that could potentially intervene in troubled areas. The long-term prospects for such a force are still very unclear. Peacemaking operations call for commanders who are skilled in handling
the highly complex task of wedding political imperatives with solid war-fighting
skills. The Somalia experience suggests that any force—either a single country or
a multinational unit—must have units highly trained in executing political-
military operations. Civil affairs officers could have played an important role in
Mogadishu, as Australian units did in parts of western Somalia. They did important work in Kuwait City and Port-au-Prince. Such a force would also have to include significant units devoted to psychological operations and intelligence. Few
militaries other than the American have such units. In the U.S. military, the civil
affairs component is largely consigned to the reserves, making it very difficult to
quickly deploy a force that can constructively interact with the local population
and promote reconciliation.

Conclusion

As is now increasingly being recognized, Somalia was not an abject failure. The
United States initiated an operation that saved approximately 100,000 lives. That
is an accomplishment that stands out starkly amidst the general apathy with
which the world has addressed the major humanitarian crises of the 1990s.
However, the operations, in the end, did not come close to what anyone would
have seen as a desirable outcome. At the same time, there was the tragic loss of
troops from the U.S. and other militaries that had gone to Somalia with the best
of intentions to help save fellow human beings. Accomplishing anything positive
would have been exceptionally difficult in Somalia. However, we have argued that
the mission was doomed because the United States essentially set the UN up for
failure by refusing to confront the important tasks that could be accomplished
only by a highly trained force. Faced with a difficult mission, all of the UN's
problems were clearly on display, and it was unable to recover from its difficult
start after the precipitous U.S. withdrawal. To do better, Americans and others
must have a much clearer idea of what intervention entails and how they are realistically going to accomplish their mission. It will be extremely difficult to develop new concepts and more appropriate force structures to allow humanitarian intervention to succeed, but the payoff could mean saving an enormous
number of lives.

Notes

1. Boutros Boutros-Ghali, *An Agenda for Peace*, 2nd ed. (New York: UN Department of
Public Information, 1995).

2. Chester Crocker, "The Lessons of Somalia: Not Everything Went Wrong," *Foreign Affairs* 74, May-June 1995, p. 5.

3. John L. Hirsch and Robert B. Oakley, *Somalia and Operation Restore Hope: Reflections on Peacemaking and Peacekeeping* (Washington, DC: U.S. Institute of Peace, 1995), p. 157.

4. "Spell It Out to the United Nations on Somalia," *New York Times,* October 6, 1993, p. 20.

5. Richard Hass, "Military Force: A Users Guide," *Foreign Policy* 96, Fall 1994, pp. 26–27.

6. "Ill-Fated Raid Surprised, Angered Clinton," *Buffalo News,* May 13, 1994, p. 6.

7. Mitch McConnell, "Multilateralism's Obituary Was Written in Mogadishu," *Christian Science Monitor,* October 27, 1993, p. 19.

8. Andrew Natsios, "Humanitarian Relief Interventions in Somalia: The Economics of Chaos," Chapter 5 in this volume.

9. Ibid.

10. George Bush, "Humanitarian Mission to Somalia: Address to the Nation, Washington DC, December 4, 1992," *US Department of State Dispatch* 3(49), December 7, 1992.

11. Hirsch and Oakley, *Somalia and Operation Restore Hope,* p. 105.

12. We are grateful to Martin R. Ganzglass for this point.

13. Charles Petrie, "The Price of Failure," paper presented at the conference "Learning from Operation Restore Hope: Somalia Revisited," Princeton University, April 21–22, 1995, pp. 4–5.

14. Jonathan Howe, "Relations Between the United States and the United Nations in Dealing with Somalia," Chapter 10 in this volume.

15. Les Aspin, "Remarks Prepared for Delivery by Secretary of Defense Les Aspin at the Center for Strategic and International Studies, Washington, DC, August 27, 1993," news release, Washington, D.C., Office of Assistant Secretary of Defense (Public Affairs), p. 5.

16. Martin R. Ganzglass, "The Restoration of the Somali Justice System," Chapter 2 in this volume.

17. Petrie, "The Price of Failure," p. 10.

18. Stanley John Whidden, "United States Civil Affairs Support to United Nations Operations Somalia During 1993–1994," paper presented at the conference "Learning from Operation Restore Hope: Somalia Revisited," Princeton University, April 21–22, 1995, p. 13.

19. Keith Richburg, "Relations with the Warlords and Disarmament," paper presented at the conference "Learning from Operation Restore Hope: Somalia Revisited," Princeton University, April 21–22, 1995, pp. 5–6.

20. Lee V. Cassanelli, "Somali Land Resource Issues in Historical Perspective," Chapter 4 of this volume; and Natsios, "Humanitarian Relief Interventions in Somalia," Chapter 5 in this volume.

21. Ken Menkhaus, "International Peacebuilding and the Dynamics of Local and National Reconciliation in Somalia," Chapter 3 in this volume.

22. See, for instance, Jon Stewart, "Public Opinion and UN Peacekeeping," *San Francisco Chronicle*, March 28, 1995, p. 6.

Appendixes

Appendix A   United Nations Security Council Resolutions and Secretary-General Reports on Somalia (1992–1996)

Resolution (Date)	New Element	Notes & Secretary-General Reports
UNSCR 733 (January 23, 1992)	Calls for an arms embargo (Under Chapter VII), urgent UN humanitarian assistance, and cease-fire.	Absence of UN presence in Somalia for over a year. Nonprocedural Somali request for assistance in report S/23445.
UNSCR 746 (March 17, 1992)	Secretary-general to send technical team to Mogadishu. Clans requested to follow cease-fire provisions.	March 3, 1992, cease-fire sparks some optimism (see S/23693, 3/11/92).
UNSCR 751 (April 24, 1992)	Establishes UNOSOM, with an immediate deployment of 50 UN observers. Calls for secretary-general to continue consultations with the parties in Mogadishu.	Secretary-general names special representative (see secretary-general's report S/23829, 4/21/92).
UNSCR 767 (July 27, 1992)	Grudging agreement from Aideed for deployment of 50 observers.	See S/24243, 7/22/92.
UNSCR 775 (August 28, 1992)	Calls for the establishment of four UN zone offices and an increase in UNOSOM observer strength. Urges establishment of airlift.	See S/24480, 8/24/92.
UNSCR 794 (December 3, 1992)	Declares situation in Somalia "intolerable" and authorizes the deployment of a military force led by a "member state" to "create a secure environment."	See S/24859, 11/24/92, and S/24868, 11/29/92. UNSCR 794 drafted in Pentagon to satisfy CENTCOM force-protection concerns.

Appendix A   continued

Resolution (Date)	New Element	Notes & Secretary-General Reports
UNSCR 814 (March 26, 1993)	Authorizes the establishment of UNOSOM II under Chapter VII. The "mother of all resolutions" includes the "nation-building" tasks that CENTCOM didn't want.	Need to establish replacement force to U.S.-led UNITAF. Drafted by the same Pentagon team that wrote UNSCR 794. See S/25354, 3/3/93.
UNSCR 837 (June 6, 1993)	Reaffirms right to take all necessary measures against those responsible for armed attacks against UN personnel.	Ambush of Pakistani peacekeepers by Aideed militia. Security Council calls for apprehension of the responsible parties. See S/26022, 7/1/93.
UNSCR 885 (September 22, 1993)	Calls for a detailed plan setting out a concerted humanitarian, political, and security strategy.	Growing frustration in U.S. and world community about search for Aideed. See S/26317, 8/17/93.
UNSCR 878 (October 29, 1993)	Extends UNOSOM II mandate to November 18, 1993.	U.S. announces intention to quit UNOSOM after bloody 3–4 October firefight. See S/26738, 11/23/93.
UNSCR 885 (November 16, 1993)	Establishes Commission of Inquiry to Investigate attacks on UN personnel.	Results of first commission of inquiry into 5 June ambush politically incorrect, not made available to public. Second inquiry results published in S/1994/653, 6/1/94 (no one responsible).
UNSCR 886 (November 18, 1993)	Renews mandate until May 31, 1994. Calls again for cease-fire and creation of police, penal and judiciary systems.	See S/1994/12, 1/6/94. Reports the rush to develop district councils, as U.S. pushes to close down the operation.

Appendix A   continued

Resolution (Date)	New Element	Notes & Secretary-General Reports
UNSCR 897 (February 4, 1994)	In face of inability to maintain military levels after departure of U.S. forces, authorizes reduction in UN force to 20,000.	See S/1994/614, 5/24/94. Includes (hollow) 3/24/94 Nairobi declaration by Somali political leaders as annex 1.
UNSCR 923 (May 31, 1994)	Extends UNOSOM II mandate to September 30, 1994. Again calls for support to reestablishment of Somali police.	See S/1994/839, 7/16/94. A rosy interim report is published S/1994/977, 8/17/94. Further progress reported in S/1994/1068, 9/17/94.
UNSCR 946 (September 30, 1994)	Extends UNISOM II mandate for one month.	U.S. pressing to close down the operation. See S/1994/1166, 10/14/94. Special Security Council Mission to Somalia, October 26–27, 1994, reports S/1994/1245, 11/3/94.
UNSCR 953 (October 31, 1994)	Extends UNISOM II mandate for four days, until November 4, 1994, while debate on final date decided.	Purely procedural resolution while secretary-general fights to save operation.
UNSCR 954 (November 4, 1994)	Extends UNISOM II mandate to final closure date of March 31, 1995.	See S/1995/231, 3/28/95.
Security council requests written report on secretary-general's efforts in Somalia (December 14, 1995).	Follows non-U.S. criticism of apparent UN neglect of Somalia; announces that UN office will be maintained in Nairobi.	See S/1996/42, 1/19/96. Covers full period since previous 3/25/95 report. Does this indicate an annual UN report on the Somali disaster?
According to UNSC President Tono Eitel (Germany) the Security Council urges Somali factions to implement a cease-fire and negotiations (August 13, 1996).	Following death of SNA leader Mohamed Farah Aideed in combat in Mogadishu, the Security Council calls for another conference of Somali warlords outside the country.	A flat learning curve prevails here. The UN Security Council has obviously learned little about Somalia in the past four years. This resolution is promptly rejected by Hussein Aideed as "foreign interference in internal affairs."

Appendix B   Humanitarian Operations Center (HOC)

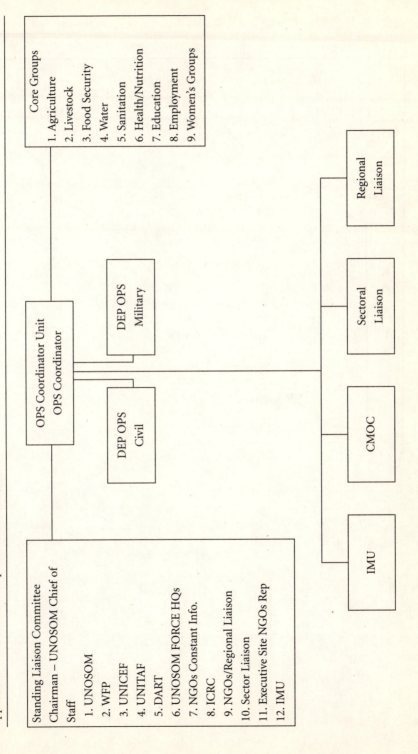

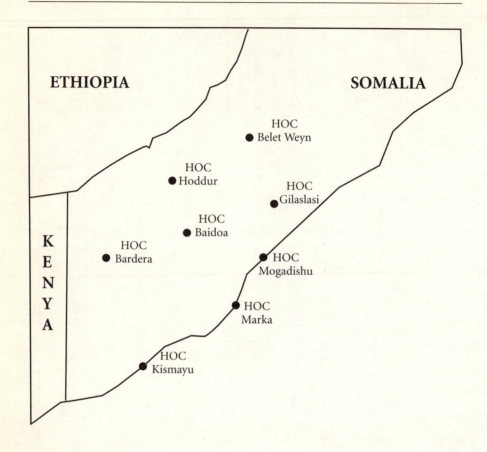

Appendix D   CMOC Mogadishu Organization

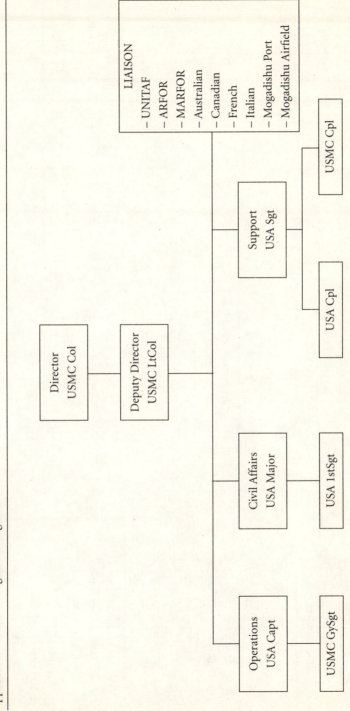

Appendix E   The French Administration in Bakool Province

Health
Subcommittee

Security Subcommittee
(Militia Forces)

Regional Executive
Committee

Provincial Level
(in Hoddur)

"Return to Normal Life"
Subcommittee

District
Level

Subcommittee for
Rab Duure District
(same)

Subcommittee for
Waajdit District
(same subunits)

Subcommittee for
Tiyeglow District
(same subunits)

Subcommittee for
Hoddur–Gel Berde
Districts

1. Executive
2. Security
3. "Normal life"
4. Administration
5. Health

About the Book and Editors

The United States–led intervention in Somalia that began in December 1992 is the most significant instance to date of "peacemaking" by the international community. The heady promise of Operation Restore Hope and the subsequent disappointments have had a resounding impact on the policies of Western governments and the UN as they have tried to cope with humanitarian emergencies in Rwanda, Bosnia, and elsewhere. However, it is questionable how correct the lessons so quickly derived from the Somalia experience actually were. At the same time, many important organizational and operational innovations during the Somalia exercise have not received sufficient attention. Learning from Somalia is therefore critical if the international community is to respond better to tragedies that threaten millions of human lives.

Contributors to this book, many of whom are policymakers who were either in Mogadishu or Washington during the relief missions, examine the intervention in Somalia and draw lessons for future peacekeeping operations. They analyze many aspects of peacemaking that are not well understood, including efforts to rebuild the police, the dynamics of the economy, the relationship between the military and nongovernmental organizations, and the performance of European armies. The authors also discuss international politics surrounding the crisis, especially the relationship between the United States and the UN and the legal justifications for intervention. In the concluding chapters, the authors discuss the prospects for intervention efforts in light of the Somalia experience.

Walter Clarke is adjunct professor of peace operations at the U.S. Army's Peacekeeping Institute. A retired senior foreign service officer with extensive experience in diplomatic, military, and academic circles, he was Deputy Chief of Mission at the U.S. Embassy in Mogadishu in 1993.

Jeffrey Herbst is associate professor of politics and international affairs at Princeton University's Woodrow Wilson School.

About the Contributors

Lee V. Cassanelli is a professor in the Department of History at the University of Pennsylvania.

Ted Dagne is a foreign affairs analyst at the Congressional Research Service, Foreign Affairs and National Defense Division. He served as a Professional Staff member at the Subcommittee for Africa under the chairmanship of Representative Harry Johnston (1993–1994).

John Drysdale is an independent adviser to the president of Somaliland. He was formerly political adviser to UNOSOM I and II.

Martin R. Ganzglass is an attorney, a former Peace Corps volunteer, and a former legal adviser to the Somali National Police Force. He was in Somalia during Operation Restore Hope as special adviser to the State Department.

Jonathan T. Howe is president of the Arthur Vining Davis Foundations. He was formerly special representative of the secretary-general in Somalia.

Harry Johnston (D–Fla.) was a senior member of the House International Relations Committee and the former chair of the Subcommittee on Africa (1993–1994).

Kevin M. Kennedy is senior humanitarian affairs officer, UN Department of Humanitarian Affairs. He was formerly the commander of the Civil Military Operations Center in Somalia.

Ken Menkhaus is an associate professor of political science at Davidson College in Davidson, North Carolina. For nine months in 1993–1994 he served as special political adviser in UNOSOM in Somalia, and in 1994–1995 he was a visiting professor at the U.S. Army Peacekeeping Institute. He is the author of numerous articles on Somalia.

Andrew S. Natsios is vice-president, Worldvision Relief and Development. He was the assistant administrator of USAID during Somalia relief operations. He was also director of the Office of Foreign Disaster Relief Assistance.

Gérard Prunier is a professor at the National Center for Scientific Research, Paris.

Robert I. Rotberg is president of the World Peace Foundation.

Thomas G. Weiss is associate director of Brown University's Thomas J. Watson Jr. Institute for International Studies and executive director of the Academic Council on the United Nations System.

James L. "Jim" Woods served as deputy assistant secretary of defense for African affairs from December 1986 to April 1994. In that position, he served as chair of the OSD Somalia Task Force and as a member of various interagency groups organized to deal with the Somalia crisis. He is presently active as a private consultant, as a senior associate in the African Studies program of the Center for Strategic and International Studies, and as vice-president of an international consulting firm, Cohen and Woods International, Inc.

Index